BOOKS BY LOUISE HALL THARP

ADVENTUROUS ALLIANCE
The Story of the Agassiz Family of Boston

CHAMPLAIN
Northwest Voyager

COMPANY OF ADVENTURERS

LOUIS AGASSIZ
Adventurous Scientist

MRS. JACK
A Biography of Isabella Stewart Gardner

THE PEABODY SISTERS OF SALEM

SAINT-GAUDENS & THE GILDED ERA

THREE SAINTS & A SINNER

THE APPLETONS OF BEACON HILL

THE APPLETONS
OF BEACON HILL

Boston Common and Beacon Hill, 1804–1811. (From The
Memorial History of Boston, *edited by Justin Winsor, 1883.)*

THE
APPLETONS
OF
BEACON HILL

by LOUISE HALL THARP

LITTLE, BROWN AND COMPANY — BOSTON–TORONTO

FIRST EDITION

T 11/73

Library of Congress Cataloging in Publication Data

Tharp, Louise (Hall), 1898–
    The Appeltons of Beacon Hill.

    Includes bibliographical references.
    1. Appleton family. I. Title.
CS71.A65 1973   917.4'03'30922 [B]   73-10207
ISBN 0-316-83918-3

Published simultaneously in Canada
by Little, Brown & Company (Canada) Limited

PRINTED IN THE UNITED STATES OF AMERICA

To my family

To fill up the hollow night
with interest, tales were told . . .
TOM APPLETON

CONTENTS

ILLUSTRATIONS

PRINCIPAL CHARACTERS

Early Appletons

FIRST SAMUEL, 1586–1670

Born Little Waldingfield, England; emigrated to America with his second wife and six children, 1636. Granted land in Ipswich, Mass. Acreage still in Appleton family.

SECOND SAMUEL, 1625–1696

Fifth child of First Samuel; major, militia. Born Little Waldingfield, England; came to Ipswich, Mass., 1636. Officer King Philip's War; jailed for sedition by royal governor; early patriot — escorted royal governor to jail. Eleven children.

Isaac Appletons

FIRST ISAAC, 1664–1747

Second son of Second Samuel. Born Ipswich, Mass. Married Priscilla Baker of Topsfield, Mass. One son and six daughters survived infancy.

SECOND ISAAC, 1704–1794

Fourth child of First Isaac. Born Ipswich, Mass. Married Elizabeth Sawyer of Wells, Me. Ten children, including Rev. Joseph, father of William Appleton of Beacon Hill.

Appletons of New Ipswich, N. H.

THIRD ISAAC, 1731–1806

Oldest son of Second Isaac. Born Ipswich, Mass. First New Ipswich, N.H., Appleton settler. Married in 1760 Mary Adams (1742–1827) of Concord, Mass. Twelve children:

1. Isaac, 1762–1853, married Sarah Twichell of Dublin, N.H.
2. Joseph, 1764–1791. Graduated Dartmouth; unmarried.
3. Samuel, 1766–1853. Married Mary Lekain Gore (Aunt Sam), 1818. First Beacon Hill Appleton to arrive in Boston.
4. Aaron, 1768–1852. Married, first, Eunice Adams of New Ipswich, N.H.; second, Keziah Bixby of Keene, N.H.
5. Dorothy, 1770–1859 (Aunt Everett). Married David Everett who died in Marietta, Ohio, 1813. She returned to New Ipswich.
6. Moses, 1773–1849. M.D. Married Ann Clark of Waterville, Me., 1801.
7. Mary, 1775–1853 (Aunt Barrett). Married Joseph Barrett of New Ipswich, N.H.
8. Ebenezer, 1777–1780
9. Nathan, 1779–1861. First Appleton to live on Beacon Hill. Married, first, Maria Theresa Gold of Pittsfield, Mass. (1786–1833); five children. Married, second, 1839, Harriet Coffin Sumner (1804–1867); three children.
10. Emily, 1781–1809. Married Moses Jewett of Burlington, Vt. Children: Harriet, 1805–1806; Isaac Appleton, known as Jewett, 1809–1847.
11. Eben, 1784–1833. Married Sarah Patterson of England. Eben was also of Boston, but not of Beacon Hill. He had four children; one son, Samuel Appleton Appleton married Julia Webster, daughter of Daniel Webster. Eben's granddaughter, Caroline Le Roy, widow of Newbold Edgar, married Jerome Napoleon Bonaparte of Baltimore (1871).
12. Emma, 1787–1791

Beacon Hill Appletons

SAMUEL, 1766–1853

Third son of Third Isaac. Went to Boston as a young man; gave his two younger brothers and his first cousin William a chance to become merchants. Married, at the age of 52, Mrs. Mary Lekain Gore, known as Aunt Sam, a widow, age 30 (1788–1870). No children. Sam took a special interest in Isaac Appleton Jewett, only child of sister Emily, and in Samuel Appleton Appleton, his namesake and brother Eben's oldest son.

NATHAN, 1779–1861

Ninth child of Third Isaac. Married, first, Maria Theresa Gold, 1806. She died in 1833. They had five children, all born in Boston:

1. Thomas Gold, 1812–1884. Unmarried. Painter, writer, gourmet, famous Boston wit, much quoted, sometimes pirated.
2. Mary, 1813–1889. Married, in 1839, Robert James Mackintosh, 1806–1864, of London and Scotland, governor-general, British Leeward Islands. They had three surviving children, Ronald, Eva, Angus.
3. Charles Sedgwick, 1815–1835. Entered his father's business, died of tuberculosis.
4. Frances Elizabeth (Fanny), 1817–1861. Married Henry Wadsworth Longfellow in 1843. Children:
   Charles Appleton, 1844–1893
   Ernest, 1845–1921
   Fanny, 1847–1848
   Alice Mary, 1850–1928
   Edith, 1853–1915
   Annie Allegra, 1855–1934
5. George William, 1826–1827

Nathan married, second, Harriet Coffin Sumner in 1839. Children:

1. William Sumner (Willie), 1840–1903
2. Harriot, 1841–1923. Married Major Greeley Stevenson Curtis, Nov. 17, 1863.
3. Nathan (Natey), 1843–1906

WILLIAM, 1786–1862

Son of Rev. Joseph Appleton; grandson of Second Isaac; first cousin of Samuel, Nathan, and Eben, who were children of Third Isaac. Born in Brookfield, Mass. Assisted by Samuel and Nathan Appleton to become established in Boston. Married, in 1815, Mary Ann Cutler (1794–1860), known as Aunt William. Children:

1. William Sullivan, 1815–1836
2. James Amory, 1818–1843. Married Mary Ellen Lyman, 1840.

3. Mary Ann (Marianne), 1820–1852. She married John Singleton Copley Greene, 1844.

4. Sarah Elizabeth, 1822–1891. Married Amos Adams Lawrence in 1842. They had seven children. Their son William (1850–1941) became bishop of Massachusetts. William's two sons, William and Frederic, both became bishops in the Protestant Episcopal Church.

5. Francis Henry, 1823–1854. Married Georgianna Silsbee, 1846.

6. William (formerly Warren) born in 1825, married Emily Warren.

7. Edward, 1827–1827

8. Harriet Cutler, 1828–1857. Married F. Gordon Dexter. One son, born 1857. The Amos A. Lawrences took him into their family upon his mother's death.

9. Mehitable Sullivan, "Hetty," born in 1831. Married T. Jefferson Coolidge in 1852.

10. Charles Hook, 1833–1874. Married Isabella Mason in 1856.

THE APPLETONS
OF BEACON HILL

ONE

THE DELECTABLE PART OF TOWN

"AT THIS SEASON OF THE YEAR, this part of town is truly delectable," Nathan Appleton said in a letter to his older brother, Samuel, who was in London. The part of town was Beacon Hill, Boston, Massachusetts, the season was mid-June, and the year, 1809. Nathan was the seventh son of a New Ipswich, New Hampshire, farmer, twenty-nine years old and a home-owner for the first time in his life. He was in a mood to boast.[1]

To his younger brother, Eben, also abroad, Nathan wrote that the house he had bought the previous November was all he had expected "in pleasantness." Better still, "it is universally allowed to be the cheapest house which has been sold in this town this long time. I could take it to three thousand advance any day." For one of a pair of twin town houses, Nathan Appleton had paid James Colburn $13,500. Number 54 Beacon Street would be the scene of Appleton family hospitality, anxieties and successes, for years to come.

"Our neighbors are very stylish," Nathan wrote, "but have not annoyed us by their civilities. Mrs. C. [Mrs. Colburn] has not yet called on us in a neighborly way." As early as 1808, Beacon Hill had established a reputation for being exclusive.

James Colburn built twin houses in 1806 — the same year that Asher Benjamin, architect, author and founder of an architectural school in Boston, built a house for himself just down Beacon Hill, toward Charles Street. Asher Benjamin, although less well known than Charles Bulfinch, was an artist, as his New England churches, with their pillared porticoes and delicate spires, still prove. His own house at 58 Beacon Street was burned but 54 and 55 are still standing. With their white columns, wrought-iron balconies, classic detail and their location, these houses may be by Benjamin.[2]

In 1806, Nathan Appleton had married Maria Theresa Gold of Pittsfield. Two months after the wedding he contracted with Gilbert Stuart to paint her portrait — proving beyond a doubt that his twenty-year-old bride was beautiful.

Maria Theresa was dark. Her hair, parted in front and brought forward in curls to touch the outer edges of her eyebrows, was then combed back at the crown into ringlets which cascaded along the nape of her neck. Her gown, in the painting, with its high waist, was cut very low.

Perhaps it was Gilbert Stuart who reminded young Mr. Appleton that a pair of portraits would be better than one. The Stuart portrait of Nathan showed a remarkably handsome man, blue-eyed with light reddish brown hair curling like a cockscomb over the top of his head, a curl or two over his forehead. He had sideburns, a sensitive mouth and very pink cheeks. According to a passport, Nathan was five feet nine inches tall, and had a "rosey" complexion — so Gilbert Stuart was right. He had a "middling nose," said the passport, but Stuart saw the Roman nose so often the heritage of Yankee traders of British descent.

Of course Maria did not go alone to "Gilbert Stuart's Painting Room." Her school friend, Eloise Payne, older than she, went with her and described the scene, June 20, 1806. Eloise "never passed three hours more pleasantly." She found Stuart "a very anecdotal man and he exerted himself today to be agreeable. He is a vain man and a great egoist, so that we had an opportunity of paying him many fine compliments without offending his delicacy. We availed ourselves of this opportunity and put him in a wonderful good humor."

These portraits must have looked handsome in the parlors at 54 Beacon Street, but in 1806 Maria was not there to admire them. Nathan explained to his brother Samuel, "Her debility during the winter was such that every exposure to the atmosphere was sure to give her a cold and a spring of uncommon dampness has compelled her almost constantly to keep home, but her health in other respects is perfectly good and from the effect of the late fine weather, I have sanguine hopes of her perfect restoration in health and strength." The "other respects," referred to Maria's hope of having a child. She had gone to Pittsfield to spend the summer with her parents, since Berkshire air always seemed

Nathan Appleton, by Gilbert Stuart.
(Courtesy of the Longfellow House Trustees.)

Maria Theresa Gold Appleton, by Gilbert Stuart.
(Courtesy of the Longfellow House Trustees.)

to do her good. But she left Boston reluctantly, having made a long list of items she would like to have for her new house.

Although engaged in buying textiles for his brother to sell in Boston, Samuel Appleton was most willing to search out and buy all sorts of furnishings for 54 Beacon Street. Everything was still in a London warehouse, crated or baled but not sent. It seemed unwise while the port of Boston was under embargo to risk shipment. The Jefferson Embargo brought about the forced sale of number 54 Beacon Street however — since Colburn was a merchant who had suffered reverses. But the Appletons were among the few Boston merchants to whom this ill wind brought good.

"The embargo has dished democracy in this state for this year, so now Jeffersonian Gloom is acquiring a good deal of popularity," Nathan wrote.[3] But "Now for business — the non-importation law being repealed, no impediment remains to the execution of Maria's order.

"We want a pair of Grecian Lamps — rather elegant than showy and some handsome chimney ornaments — novel and elegant — a pair of stylish bell ropes for the drawing rooms — something tasty, prevailing colors orange and light green with some wood color or pearl color — but you know the paper and will judge for yourself." All this was in addition to Maria's first list and her husband could think of more — "perhaps a couple of pair of side lamps that will burn well and spill no oil." He looked around his parlors on the second floor. "Yes, we shall want 'em," he added. And after signing himself "Your Affectionate Brother, N. Appleton," there was a postscript. Why didn't Samuel send "some English cheese — and what is cheese without Porter — freight is cheap now."

If the proud owner of number 54 Beacon Street had stepped out of the bow-front parlor windows onto his balcony and looked to his right, he would have seen the waters of the Charles River lapping the wood pilings on Charles Street. There was as yet no Public Garden to make this view "delectable" but there were rope-walks; long, low, barn-like buildings where ropes for Boston's sailing-ships were spun by hand, a boy slowly turning a huge spinning wheel and a "walker" skillfully feeding carded hemp to fast-whirling spindles. Wheels and spindles had been stilled by the embargo, rope-walks closed and people out of work, but as soon as rope-walking picked up again, Nathan Appleton would prefer these factories to the sight of rose gardens.

Directly across from 54 Beacon Street was the Boston Common and the center of town was so near the docks that the Common might still seem to be a pasture for sheep and cattle as it was once. To the left of Nathan Appleton's balcony was the Bulfinch State House, opened in January, 1798, and forever to be called "new" — in deference to the Old State House, still standing in State Street. The new building had been built in Bulfinch's pasture. Just down Beacon Street from the State House was the Governor Hancock country house surrounded by orchards and gardens which had also been built by Bulfinch. Next to this, Bulfinch had designed another country house, painted yellow, for Dr. John Joy.

Then there was open land with three small houses opposite the Common just below Joy Street. This was a tract bought parcel by parcel over the years, beginning in 1769. It had belonged to John Singleton Copley. The painter was now in England, his great career drawing to a close, his once large fortune dwindling. Dr. Joy, heading a real-estate syndicate, had acquired the Copley land, plus a good deal of litigation which came with it. Nathan Appleton could see, in his mind's eye, where some handsome town houses could be built, once the title was clear. The view higher up the hill might be even more "delectable."

Writing in a half serious, half humorous vein, Nathan prophesied that he would one day sell number 54 to Samuel and build himself a bigger, more impressive house on land he did not as yet own.

This prophecy turned out to be remarkably accurate. In 1819, Nathan Appleton, with Daniel P. Parker, bought the upper Copley house, tore it down and in that same year built a pair of houses; numbers 39 and 40 Beacon Street.[4] Alexander Parris was the architect of these handsome houses with massive rather than delicate columns framing the front doors. There were bow-fronts and balconies but no colonnade. Parris had been a carpenter's apprentice, and a schoolteacher. Unlike Asher Benjamin, he actually signed his name to his work by having it cut on a stone in the basement of the Parker side of the houses. Nathan Appleton kept number 39 for himself. The parlors were to be the scene of the romantic marriages of each of his three daughters.

Samuel Appleton was ahead of Nathan by one year when it came to building on the sunny, open slope of Beacon Hill, facing the Common.[5] A bachelor until he was fifty-three, Samuel bought his Beacon Street property in 1818. In November, 1819, he married Mary Lekain Gore, widow of John Gore, a former business associate. "Aunt Sam," as Nathan Appleton's children called her, was a delightful lady, ready to plan elaborate dinners and dancing parties — or to become a sympathetic listener to young people's problems. The Beacon Street mansion that Samuel Appleton built for her covered "the full frontage of a lot" later numbered 37 and 37½. The house was spectacular with an interior colonnade under which stood white marble nymphs in scanty attire. Here the Samuel Appletons sat for their portrait, Aunt Sam in satin with voluminous sleeves — lace cap and diamond brooch, the gift of her husband. Beside her stood Samuel, five feet ten inches according to a passport but dwarfed by the high fluted columns. He was bald-headed and looked a little dismayed, perhaps because of what the portrait painter was doing.

It was William Appleton who bought number 54 Beacon Street from his first cousin, Nathan. Although known as "Uncle William" to the Appleton children (his wife, the former Mary Ann Cutler, as "Aunt William") he was the son of Nathan and Samuel's uncle, originally of Ipswich and then of New Ipswich. Nathan sold his house to cousin William for $14,000 plus "1,000" for "glasses" — those huge floor to ceiling mirrors essential to front and back parlors, carpets — and perhaps the Grecian lamps and side lamps. Born in 1786, William was twenty years younger than Samuel and seven years younger than Nathan. His father, the Reverend Joseph Appleton of North Brookfield, Massachusetts, died at the age of forty-four — leaving "two sons and three daughters and a property worth about four Thousand five hundred dollars . . ." in William's own words.[6] His mother sold his father's "effects" and moved to "Hawke, Kingston, her native place near Exeter, New Hampshire," where she had an estate inherited from her father "worth about Three Thousand dollars." Two years later, in 1798, she married Major Daniel Gould of Lyndborough, New Hampshire, and moved there with her three youngest children. The oldest son Phineas "soon went into a store" while William was sent to New Ipswich Academy and later to other schools.

When William was "about nineteen to twenty years Old" he went into business in a town called Temple, a few miles from New Ipswich. William had inherited "about seven hundred dollars" and he had two hundred dollars he "drew in a Lottery." At the end of the year, "I sold my stock, having made about eight hundred dollars. Soon after, I came to Boston . . . about 1807," he wrote.

Samuel and Nathan Appleton regarded themselves as established Boston merchants by the time William arrived. They were inclined to think of him as their protégé and were ready to show him the ropes. But William had an instinct for business and the Midas touch, as his diary, begun in 1832, most clearly shows.

By 1819, the three Appletons of Beacon Street were all assembled and here they, or their children, lived for most of the rest of their lives. Samuel, the eldest, seemed to worry least as he amassed his handsome fortune. He enjoyed spending it and giving private, unobtrusive help to friends — eventually handing over to his executors (after taking care of his wife, relatives, and friends) two hundred thousand dollars, to be spent on such public organizations as they considered worthy. Perhaps his best-known gift was Appleton Chapel at Harvard.

Nathan Appleton was the most creative. His children sometimes teased him by calling him "the Great Manufacturer," the way the newspapers did. But he was that and more, his writings and speeches in Congress showing a remarkable insight into the problems of banking and currency as well as those of the emerging Industrial Age. He believed in the young nation for which his ancestors fought and he was outspoken against those who he felt were doing harm to his country. Life in the newly built factories of which he was proud was far easier than the life of the men and women he had grown up with, and he saw himself as a benefactor, his paid employment bringing comfort to many a family in the New England hinterland. He was generous with his money when he thought a cause was good — but he hated organized begging. Such groups were forever airing their complaints against him in the papers.

William, youngest and last to come to Beacon Street, was the only one who frankly and honestly admitted that he loved to make money. But he was very religious and his conscience troubled him. In his diary, he wrote, "My mind is much, quite too much, engrossed in business, not so much for the love of money as an unaccountable desire for business success. I fear it will be my ruin. I try to devote some time every day to the all important subject, my future existence, but when I get into a vortex of business I find my mind so much engrossed that I can hardly free it when I return to my family or even on the Sabbath!"

On Beacon Street today, Samuel Appleton's mansion has succumbed to the wreckers' battering ram and bulldozer; the fountain that tossed golden balls in the air is gone; Victorian brownstone usurps the place. But the "little bird-cage of a house" his widow built still stands, a charming tower-like place, all bow-window. Nathan Appleton's number 39 Beacon Street is beautifully preserved, along with the original twin neighbor, Daniel Parker's house. They are the headquarters of the Women's City Club, where various Appleton family heirlooms receive great care. Number 54, home of both Nathan and William Appleton, still stands — altered very little and now protected by an awakened public appreciation for houses as works of art where people have lived whose lives seem today like chapters from a novel, or scenes in a play. Theirs was a world in which many letters were written, and journals kept and preserved for generations so that these Appletons speak for themselves.

Samuel began the tale by recalling a scene in New Ipswich, New Hampshire, when he was about thirteen years old.[7] "A man with a drove of cattle passed my father's house . . . on his way to a pasture for them in the town of Hancock. Being in want of assistance to drive his cattle, and seeing a flaxen-haired boy at the door, he bargained with my father that I should assist him on his way as far as the mills in Peterboro, distance ten miles; for this service to be performed by me, my father received ninepence lawful money. . . . We arrived at the mills, a rickety saw and grist mill . . . about five o'clock. The man of cattle then offered me half as much as he had paid my father and a night's lodging if I would go with him through the woods to Taylor's Tavern." There was "only one house between the mills and the tavern. All the rest of the way was dreary wilderness." But Samuel Appleton "readily consented to go." He "pocketed the cash" — and walked back home next day. It was a new sensation — this pocketing four and a half pence of his own.

Nathan Appleton wrote of his "first public appearance."[8] It was "at a very early age," he said, at the town school, high on a hill about a mile from his father's farm. "I recited 'Aurora, now fair daughter of the dawn,' to the great admiration of several old women who particularly praised me in the lines

> *I fix the chain to great Olympus' height*
> *And the vast world hangs trembling on my sight.*

"This was the first occasion of my appearing in jacket and trousers." The costume "consisted of red Calamanco." This handsome wool material, usually made of camel's hair, had checks woven in the warp so that they showed on only one side. Later Nathan often mentioned calamanco to his brother Samuel who shipped it to him from England. Beginning with this day when he first appeared in jacket and trousers, the future Honorable Nathan Appleton made impressive public appearances.

In 1780, Samuel Appleton, future "merchant of Boston," had the first real adventure of his life. He had been visiting his mother's father in

Concord, Massachusetts, when his uncle, Deacon Joseph Chandler of Concord, invited him to go to Boston.

"Two horses were got ready for the journey and loaded with provisions of the farm, Butter, Cheese, Geese, Turkeys, Fowles and two legs of mutton. We set out about twelve o'clock at night and arrived at five o'clock in the morning at a tavern in Cambridge where the road separated, one leading to Charlestown — the other to the Colleges. One room in the tavern, with a scanty fire, was kept open for the accommodation of Marketers that passed that way.

"Cold and fatigued, I very much enjoyed an hour's rest by the fire. We then proceeded to Charlestown and were conveyed over the ferry to Boston, where we soon disposed of our variety of provisions. For my part in this business, I had given me a pair of chickens, which I sold for twenty-five cents." This time, Samuel did not put the money in his pocket for long. His first mercantile transaction in Boston, after selling his two chickens, was to buy himself "a large pair of brass sleeve buttons."

There were eight sons in all, born in New Ipswich to their father, Deacon Isaac Appleton, and their mother, the former Mary Adams of Concord. The youngest was Eben, and with the help of Nathan and Samuel, he too left the farm to go to Boston. He never lived on Beacon Hill but spent most of his time in Liverpool, England, or in Lowell when the mills were being built. He wrote poetry which was published in local newspapers and periodicals when he was a young man. Some of his friends said he gave up a promising literary career to become a merchant, and in comparison with the others, his was not a great financial career, but he had the leisure and the curiosity to look up the English Appletons.

When Samuel came to spend much of his time in London, and when Nathan arrived in England, it was Eben who led them to Little Waldingfield, Suffolk County, to look at the tombs of the Appletons, their coat of arms in the parish church, a chest of ancient documents on a shelf above the family tomb and over it an ancient iron helmet. Samuel later bought the helmet, and in 1818 Nathan wrote: "As old helmets are of no value in England, I think I may claim from you to sell this relic to me. I have made a niche purposely for it in my new house." But it seems that the helmet was not for sale, and the niche in the wall of the spiral staircase would have to be filled with an urn full of artificial flowers or a marble statue.

Samuel, when he retired from active business after building his

Beacon Street mansion, took a tremendous interest in the preparation of an Appleton genealogy. William seems to have been too busy making money and worrying about heaven and his health to bother much about ancestry, but he too visited Little Waldingfield. Following Eben's lead, the second generation of Beacon Street Appletons combined to resurrect Samuel Appleton of Ipswich, their first American immigrant ancestor.

TWO

FIRST SAMUEL

THE NAMES in the Appleton genealogy sound like a recitation of the Books of the Bible and their lives in the colonies had an Old Testament flavor.[1] The first American immigrant was Samuel, born in Little Waldingfield, Suffolk County, England, in 1586. Next in direct line was another Samuel, a second son, also born in England, in 1625. So it was "First and Second Samuel" — taking their Colonial grants under "First and Second Kings," their "First and Second Chronicles," those of Ipswich and New Ipswich. But the given names were not Ezra, Nehemiah and David but Isaac, Isaac and Isaac — three of them in succession!

The first Samuel negotiated in England with the Winthrop Company to adventure money in New England, each "Adventurer" being entitled to two hundred acres for every fifty pounds invested.[2] The first Appleton grant amounted to 468 acres, approximately, and he and his family embarked on the *Elizabeth* out of Ipswich, England. This first Samuel took the Freeman's Oath in May, 1636. Out of sixty-two men admitted freemen at this time, only three others were entitled to be called "Mister." His wife and daughters were called "Mrs." according to early records, although the girls, Martha, Sara and Judith, were just children. They could be called "Spinster" before they were married — provided they learned to spin.

The date of entry on the books for the first Samuel's grant was December 20, 1638. This was the year when the Agawam Indian chief sold "his fee in the soil of Ipswich" to John Winthrop, Jr., for twenty pounds, sterling. South of the town was an Indian "plantation" where a family or two of Agawams still lived. They communicated with the settlers through an interpreter, and trade with the settlers had made them wealthy enough to attract the envy of less fortunate Indians. About a hundred marauders in three canoes attacked the Ipswich Agawams. Sturgeon nets, biscuits and several women were carried off, a ransom in wampum and beaver skins demanded for the women. The settlers helped their Ipswich Agawams and gave them rifles, a privilege of which the Indians were proud.

There were incidents of assault and robbery to be sure. As a punishment, arms were withdrawn but restored upon promises of good behavior. Indians also paid fines in beaver skins. Ipswich had been on good terms with their Indians in the south part of town. But when Samuel Appleton arrived times were beginning to change.

In 1637, the General Court in Boston ruled that "each town is to be supplied with a watch house before the last of July." Ipswich was already provided with "its share of muskets, bandoliers and rests . . ." The town had "the use of two sakers and a drake" for which they had to provide carriages. The village carpenter, wheelwright and smith set to work, and the following year town records proudly announced the arrival of "eight swords."

As a part of his grant, Samuel Appleton was given eight acres in town. The General Court had ruled that "no dwelling house shall be built above a half mile from the meeting-house in any new plantation, except mills and farm houses of such as have their dwellings in town." Only men could be left alone in farmhouses at night. Women must come into town at nightfall, "each town to provide a retreat for their wives and children."

Samuel Appleton, almost immediately upon his arrival at Ipswich, was made deputy to the General Court and assistant with Daniel Dennison "at the particular court" of the town. For some time to come, after 1637, laws and ordinances were partly of his making. There was a law that "every householder whose estate is rated at £500 and upward shall keep a sufficient hound or mastive [sic] dog . . ." People with one hundred to five hundred pounds sterling as their estate valuation had to "provide a sufficient hound or beagle . . . for the better destroying or defraying wolves from the town." The Appletons must have had a mastiff.

Wolves, although not yet desperate for lack of deer to kill, had developed a taste for lamb and mutton. Almost a hundred years later, records tell that "wolves were so abundant and so near the meeting house that parents would not suffer their children to go and come from worship without some grown person." The mastiffs, sufficient hounds and beagles had not "defrayed" the wolves to speak of and in 1756 "it was a common thing to hear the wolves commence their howl after sun-set, when it was very dangerous to go near the woods."

A cryptic notice in Winthrop's diary reads, "For Mr. Appleton, take no money of him. He can have no cows; there came not on shore one half of them." Before long the first Samuel had herds of cows and flocks of sheep but they would have to graze on cow-common land, each settler being entitled to cow-common rights in proportion to the extent of his grant. Ipswich had 3,244 acres of cow-common on the north side of the river and still more on the south. Every morning, an hour before sunrise, the town cowherd would blow his horn on the meeting-house green. All cows had to be brought to the green. The cowherd led them out to the lush river meadows and brought them back "a little before sunset." Sheep must have "one person to follow them constantly." The wolves preferred lamb to beef.

Appleton acres had a "heavy growth of oak and hickory" when the first Samuel arrived. A river, "commonly called Mile Brook," ran through the tract, and on it Samuel Appleton built a saw mill, the first move of the settler destined to do well. Later he built a malt distillery which was an even better idea from a financial point of view. Settlers arriving later had to agree not to "damnify" Appleton's water rights.

The first Samuel's first dwelling was of logs, but soon the smell of sawn lumber from his mill was sweet in the air of Ipswich. Frame houses faced the village street. The General Court granted Ipswich two-fifths of Plum Island, or twenty acres, lying in the salt marshes, the rushes growing there to be used by the whole town for thatching roofs.

The Ipswich militia was already organized. In 1637, Lion Gardiner, leader of the "Company of Lords and Gentlemen," had begun a plantation at Saybrook, Connecticut, at the mouth of the Connecticut River. Pequots surrounded the fort he had built, killing anyone who came out to till the fields. Lion Gardiner blamed the Massachusetts Bay Colony for "raising these wasps about my ears." The Ipswich militia was a part of one of the three regiments in the colony, and Samuel Appleton was called upon to serve in the Pequot War. This Connecticut River tribe was totally destroyed. For this service he was given "a small parcel of land lying by the highway leading to his farm, by the Pequid lotts." This seems to have been the first Samuel Appleton's only military service.

The Agawam Indians near Ipswich "agreed to instruction in the Christian religion" in 1664. "Will you refrain from working on the Sabbath," they were asked through interpreters. "It is easy for us," was the reply. "We have not much to do any day and we can as well rest on the Sabbath . . ." This might have caused a faint twinge of envy among the younger settlers who listened to long sermons on the Sabbath and were usually at work at least "an hour before dawn" every other day.

In 1645, "youths from ten to sixteen are to be exercised with small guns, half-pikes, bows and arrows," the Ipswich court decreed. By this time, the second Samuel Appleton was twenty-one years old and his brother John was twenty-three, doubtless already well versed in the use of guns, pikes, bows and arrows. A few years later, John Appleton was "confirmed as Lieutenant of the troop of horse for the Essex Regiment." His brother appeared in the records much later, first as Lieutenant, then Captain — and very shortly as Major Samuel Appleton. Their father lived to see them parade wearing "gold lace on their hats, with red stockings and breeches of the same color."

In 1647, the General Court ruled that "if any young man attempts to address a young woman without the consent of her parents, or, in case of their absence, of a neighboring magistrate of the County Court, he shall be fined £5 for the first offence, £10 for the second and imprisonment for the third." Several prosecutions were tried at Ipswich Court but two young men of Ipswich managed to find favor with Samuel Appleton — Martha Appleton married Richard Jacobs and Judith married Samuel Rodgers. Sarah, the middle daughter, married the Reverend Samuel Phillips of nearby Rowley and she made a home for her father, who was twice a widower, and who died in 1670 at Rowley in the eighty-fourth year of his age.

Instead of becoming more and more like a peaceful English village, Ipswich was insecure.

"Arms may be brought to the meeting-house on the Lord's day," the Ipswich town court decided. "Each company of militia is to have two thirds muskets and the rest pikes," was the next order. "The pikemen are to wear corselets and headpieces." The General Court in Boston announced that "Every town is to have a guard set a half hour after sunset, to consist of a pikeman and a musketeer." In case of an alarm of Indian attack, "a musket shall be discharged . . . to all centinals who shall answer by going to the houses and crying 'Arm! Arm!' "

The year was 1676 and the month February, when the soldiers of every town were ordered to "scout and ward to prevent the skulking and lurking of the enemy about it, and to give notice of approaching

danger." So that there would be fewer hiding-places, it was "also ordered that the brush in the highways and other places be cut up. The
watch is not to disperse till sunrise, when the scouts go out."

King Philip, sachem of the Wampanoag, son of Massasoit, had succeeded in banding the Indian tribes together against the settlers and he
nearly succeeded in wiping out the New England plantations. The towns
along the Connecticut River were going up in smoke. Captain Samuel
Appleton was commissioned to command a foot company of a hundred
men and to proceed westward from Boston. Ten days later Captain
Samuel was commissioned major and "Commander in Chief of the army
of those parts." Major John Pynchon had resigned after the Indians had
burned his town of Springfield, Massachusetts.

On the nineteenth of October, 1676, the village of Hatfield was attacked. Major Appleton and his "army" reached the scene, up-river
from Springfield. There was an engagement during which his sergeant
was "mortally wounded by his side" and an Indian bullet passed
through the major's hair, "by that whisper telling him that death was
very near," as the early chronicler wrote. Letters still in existence show
that this second Samuel urged the people of Springfield to gather together to defend the remnants of their settlement rather than to try to
escape down the old Bay Path to Boston.

Although a hero to his fellow colonists, Major Samuel Appleton was
a person "facticiously and seditiously inclined and disaffected to his
Majesty's Government," according to Sir Edmund Andros. This royal
governor planned to combine the New England colonies under one head
— himself. He descended on Hartford demanding the Connecticut
Charter, did not get it, and that handsome document survived without
any damage or other evidence of having been hidden in an oak tree. The
Massachusetts General Court ruled that no governor had a right to levy
taxes without the consent of the assembly "chosen by the Freeholders."
So Governor Andros ordered the "ring leaders" fined and imprisoned —
among them the second Samuel Appleton. He went into hiding probably
in his son's house in Lynn.

Major Appleton "addressed the people from a rocky eminence" near
Lynn concerning their rights. But this was no way to avoid a King's
warrant, and the major was arrested and thrown into prison. The rock
near Lynn came to be known as "Appleton's Pulpit."

Records have been destroyed but Major Appleton seems to have been
"imprisoned in Boston jail" perhaps from the nineteenth of October,
1687, until the following March 7, when he was released on giving a

thousand-pound bond to "appear at the next court" and to be "of regular behavior." The bond was continued about six months but no further charges were made.

It became a family tradition that, in 1689, the once-imprisoned Major Samuel "had the honor of conveying Governor Andros to prison in Boston harbor." There seems almost too much poetic justice in this to be true but actually it is more than likely. As Cotton Mather wrote in his diary, ". . . a Strange Disposition entered into the Body of our People to assert our Liberties against the Arbitrary Rulers that were fleecing them." The "principal Gentlemen in Boston" met with Mr. Mather "to see if bloodshed could be avoided."

Even Governor Andros seemed to have noticed that something was going wrong. There was "a general buzzing among the People, great with expectation of their old charter back, or they know not what," he wrote. On the eighteenth of April, 1689, people "at the South end of Boston" said that those "at the North were all under arms and the like report was at the North respecting the South. About nine of the clock, the drums began to beat."

Around noon a message was sent to Andros "how unsafe he was like to be if he did not deliver himself and his fort." Andros left the fort, discussed matters in vain and was confined in Boston for the night under strong guard. The "Castle" surrendered next day, the *Rose* frigate struck her topmasts and sent her sails on shore. Major Samuel Appleton may well have heard the drums beat and have helped to escort Andros back to the Castle as a prisoner.

The second son of the second Samuel Appleton was born in 1664 and named Isaac. Like his father, he had the title of major and he had ample opportunity to serve. In 1689, the "Ipswich horse" were "ordered to Haverhill, as one place of rendezvous for forces going to meet the enemy." The following year Ipswich was ordered "to raise its part of twenty men . . . to strengthen Albany." European powers were fighting for supremacy in the New World and using Indians as pawns in their game. The disaster at Deerfield in 1704 exceeded the Hadley attack. But no chronicle of Major Isaac Appleton's exploits seems to have survived although it is always to be hoped that some ancient manuscript may yet come to light.

As in the days of the "Pequid lotts" it was still customary to reward military service with grants of land. More than three hundred years later, in 1971, there were to be 972 acres belonging to a member of the Appleton family. Three hundred head of pure-blooded Guernsey cattle would graze on Appleton land, and quantities of alfalfa hay would be grown by modern scientific methods. This land would be termed "the oldest working farm in the United States owned and operated by a single family." It is to become eventually a public reservation, the gift of Colonel Francis R. Appleton.

The Appletons, younger sons of British landed gentry, were land-hungry because manors and farms had been so often entailed, descending to eldest sons. They found it soul-satisfying to own acreage in a new country, but, as a general rule, they willed most of their grants to first-born sons in the English fashion. The second Isaac Appleton, born in 1704, had a farm, but the third Isaac, born in 1731, was going to need more land.

Men came to Ipswich with undeveloped tracts for sale, and the third Isaac, probably with his father's help, bought six shares in the new township. The "Great and General Court of Massachusetts . . ." had "granted unto sixty of the inhabitants of the Town of Ipswich, a Township of the contents of six miles square . . . to be called New Ipswich." [3]

This third Isaac Appleton was to be styled deacon, because of being elected by his fellow church members to a position second only to parson at a time when church and state were one. He assumed that he was going to live in Massachusetts but by the time he got to New Ipswich, the town was in New Hampshire!

Some very early real-estate operators had gotten hold of the enormous inheritance of a discouraged man by the name of John Tufton Mason. [4] His direct ancestor had been John Mason, at one time governor of Newfoundland and vice-admiral for New England. Along with Fernando Gorges, Governor Mason had been given a patent for the whole Province of Maine, and he held for himself alone a patent for the land between the Merrimack and Piscataqua rivers extending north to Lake Ontario and the St. Lawrence River. He sent workmen to Portsmouth to exploit the salt works, the fisheries and the fur trade. They were to build Mason Hall for him at Dover in this territory which he named New Hampshire. Governor Mason was about to embark for Portsmouth when he died in 1635. He had no sons but left his property to his daughter's two sons, Robert and John, provided they would take his name. John died young but Robert Tufton, of age in 1650, became Robert Tufton Mason and arrived in Portsmouth, New Hampshire, in 1681 to claim his inheritance.

He came too late. Settlers had acquired the land from the Indians and not only refused to pay rent to Robert Tufton Mason but literally ran him off. He fled to England, had his patent confirmed, returned to Portsmouth and spent the rest of his life involved in hopeless litigation. Robert's son, John, died and it was Robert's grandson, John Tufton Mason, aged twenty-one in 1738, who inherited the grant. He had no accurate record of the extent of his property but he was out of patience and out of cash. He probably had no idea how many thousands of acres he sold but he kept enough mountainous country to provide his descendants with bear-hunting for several generations. After a wrangle with the Massachusetts Bay Colony, men "ran the line," cutting with an axe the letters N H for New Hampshire on one side of huge trees in virgin timber, and M for Massachusetts on the other.

New Ipswich, New Hampshire, is almost due west from Ipswich, Massachusetts. It is really not far away, perhaps fifty miles, as the crow flies — but the Ipswich share-owners were not crows. They traveled by ox-cart. Even today, over two hundred years later, an Ipswich gas station attendant said he didn't know where New Ipswich was and that he had never been there.

Deacon Isaac Appleton set out for New Ipswich "about 1750." The exact date is said to be uncertain but at any rate he was lucky not to have started two years earlier. Indians attacked the town, carrying off a farmer and his family. Other settlers fled to a fort on Battery Hill in nearby Townsend, leaving only one man, Captain Moses Tucker by name, who refused to leave his newly completed log cabin. When the settlers returned they found him safe, the other cabins still standing — but the meeting-house was burned down. They must have thought with new appreciation of the Christian Indians of Ipswich. But they must also have understood. Powder and bullets for the defense of frontier towns were usually kept in the meeting-house.

Isaac Appleton was about twenty when he arrived in New Ipswich. A new meeting-house, where he was to become deacon, had been built. His six shares as a New Ipswich proprietor entitled him to some choice land just off the road to Peterboro — a town whose first permanent settlers had arrived only the year before. The Appleton farmhouse still stands on the right side of a road leading into a little valley where a river runs. Today deer still come down to browse on meadow grasses, but Isaac had to clear most of his land with infinite labor. Logs were needed to build the first dwelling, a little south of the present house on Appleton Road. Barns had to be built, eventually of such huge proportions that livestock could be sheltered, and corn and hay laid up for the long winter, when snow filled Deacon Appleton's Ipswich River bottom like a brimming cup and the close-crowding hills were white. Spring freshets had to be reckoned with — but New Ipswich had water power to turn their saw mills, their grist mills — and eventually their textile mills.

Deacon Isaac was twenty-nine when he married Mary Adams of Concord, Massachusetts, in 1760. Their oldest child, a son named Isaac, was

Appleton Farmhouse, New Ipswich, New Hampshire

born in New Ipswich in 1762. "Our mother was twenty when I was born," he said, when he, himself, was over eighty. He lived to be ninety-two.

So Mary Adams was eighteen, when her spinning wheel, her feather bed, her quilts and chests, filled with whatever household goods her parents gave her, were loaded into a cart, and she journeyed northward, up into the hills to her new home. "There were only five houses in New Ipswich" when she came, she told her son. Mary and Isaac Appleton of New Ipswich had twelve children.

In 1771, the nine-year-old Isaac watched the militia drilling on the village green just as all Appletons back to the first Samuel had done. "I saw them choose their first officers, their Sergeants and their Corporals," he said. His father was chosen second lieutenant and in 1775, when news came of "the Concord fight," Lieutenant Isaac Appleton helped rouse out the militia and then rode with them over the hills and down to his wife's home town. His brother Francis, who had come to New Ipswich about 1770, and lived "on a right of land north of his brother," also served in the Revolution, for, as an early chronicler put it, "he went to the capture of Burgoyne where he lost his horse." This is not to say that he had the horse shot under him — he just mislaid it somewhere around Saratoga. "He was subject at times to a remarkable aberration of mind," although "amiable, pious and industrious," the chronicler said. Absent-minded people would have sympathized.

Deacon Isaac resumed his farming as soon as possible, having no vocation for a military career. His first son and namesake, born in 1762, inherited the farm and tilled the soil as an oldest son was expected to do. The second son and second child was Joseph, born in 1764 and named for his mother's father. According to New England tradition, he was practically fore-ordained to go to college and become a minister. He graduated from Dartmouth in 1791 — at the age of twenty-seven and his brother Moses, the fifth son, nine years younger than he, graduated from Dartmouth that same year. It is possible to glimpse an unwritten story of family loyalty — an older brother putting off his own education to help a younger one. Joseph Appleton died in 1791 — the year of his college graduation. His younger brother went on to receive a degree in medicine and practiced in Waterville, Maine.

Samuel Appleton, third son of the deacon and future merchant of Boston, "for several years assisted his father in carrying on his farm" according to the New Ipswich town historian. He was also "an industrious scholar" in 1787, under "that famous teacher Mr. Hubbard." As a matter of fact, the little town of New Ipswich was organizing one of the earliest academies in the country.[5] Eleven neighboring towns were brought into the project, all banding together with funds for a building and for salaries. They promised to "support and maintain a school for and during the term of five years," each town "to pay an equal share and proportion." Nothing quite like it had ever before been attempted.

In 1789 a small wooden building with a bell-tower was built on a hill. The trustees effected a deal with Dartmouth College whereby students from New Ipswich Academy "shall be indulged the privilege of studying in said Academy . . . for part of their time . . . and students so indulged, upon producing a receipt of money paid to the trustees of said Academy shall have the sum carried to credit their account for tuition which they shall be charged at said College . . ." In 1789 Samuel Appleton received the first teacher's certificate issued by New Ipswich Academy.

John Hubbard, preceptor of New Ipswich Academy, certified that Samuel Appleton was "well acquainted with English Grammar and well capable of keeping an English school . . ." That Samuel Appleton was "possessed of abilities sufficient to instruct a school in reading, writing, orthography, English Grammar and Arithmetic" was further attested — this time by the local minister.

About 1818, Charles Barrett wrote to Samuel Appleton, Esq., now of Boston, "We have built an elegant Academy, 45 by 36 feet, two stories high, with a handsome Apparatus and Library room; but the great misfortune is, we have no Apparatus or Library to put in it. In addition to building the house, we have added $1,500 to the fund. In fact, the Academy would now be upon as respectable a footing as any in the State, had it a pair of small Globes and a small Philosophical Apparatus and Library . . ." It was said that "Mr. Appleton responded nobly." The Academy got the globes plus one hundred books for the library and large gifts in cash as the years went by.[6]

But meanwhile, in 1788, young Samuel Appleton had no money nor had he, as yet, that teacher's certificate. Charles Barrett was an agent for lands in Maine, once part of the Mason Grant, and Samuel was on his way to take up a claim. He had not been to Boston again since his uncle took him there to help sell farm produce. Long after, he told the story in his own words.

"My next visit to Boston was made in May, 1788. I was traveling from New Hampshire to Maine to take possession of a lot of land which was promised me in the forests of Lincoln County, on condition I would build a house and bring into cultivation a certain number of acres within five years. I came to Boston to take passage in a wood coaster, to Camden, and to add to my stores. For my summer's campaign, I bought in Boston, half a barrel of pork, a bushel of white beans and a keg of New England Rum . . .

"In November, ensuing, I returned from Camden to Boston, having paid my passage in helping to load the sloop with wood. We arrived at Boston about 6 o'clock on Saturday evening. On examining my finances, which was easily done, I found I had not money enough to keep me over Sunday in Boston. I therefore immediately set out for my Grandfather's in Concord. There had lately been heavy rains and on arriving at the

Concord River at about 12 o'clock at night, I found the water about a foot deep, this side the bridge. I pulled off shoes and stockings and waded through and an hour after, I found myself safe at my Grandfather's door where I was warmly welcomed." During the next winter Samuel Appleton was given his teacher's certificate and got himself a job in a school in nearby Temple.

"For two or three years after, I frequently passed through Boston, coming and going from my old home in New Ipswich to my new establishment in Maine." Every winter he taught school.

About sixty years later, the people of the town of Appleton, Maine, asked Samuel Appleton to give them a bell for their church. They thought that their village had been named for his father and they knew that "Samuel Appleton Esquire" was now well-to-do. He set them right in a most businesslike way. "You say the reasons of your asking the boon from me, rather than any other person are 'First that the town of Appleton was named in honor of my venerable father and to commemorate the name of his family.' I think there must be some mistake in this. My father, Isaac Appleton lived and died on a small farm at New Ipswich, New Hampshire.[7] I do not think he was ever in the State of Maine, or ever heard of the town of Appleton." Then he went on to tell a little of what it was like to try to develop a tract in Maine.

"I took for myself a lot of land, more than two miles from any other settlement, and for some time carried my provisions on my back, going through the woods by marked trees, to my log-house and home, at that time. . . .

"As I should be very sorry to give a bell that might sound my praises under false pretences or impressions, I therefore most respectfully decline complying with your wishes."

The people of Appleton, Maine, were somewhat distressed. "The farm upon which you commenced in your young days lies about three miles from the new meeting-house and is now under improvement," they wrote. They withdrew their request and hoped Mr. Appleton did not think that they were trying to deceive him. "Had we succeeded in getting it by such means it would have sounded only our dishonor."

Samuel Appleton was pleased with this reply and referred to the first letter. "Your second reason for asking me for a bell was, that if you were not wrongly informed, I could make this gift without the least possible injury or inconvenience to myself. To this, your second reason I now reply, that, through the kindness of Providence, in my pecuniary affairs you were not wrongly informed on that subject; and if you will procure a suitable bell for your new meeting-house, and send me the bill, I will with the greatest pleasure, pay the amount."

And again, Samuel Appleton recalled his homesteading in Maine. "I am happy to hear that a meeting-house is erected and that the gospel is preached within three miles of the place where I spent three long summer seasons, during which time, I never heard the sound of a church-going bell, or ever heard a sermon, or the voice of prayer: there being at the time, no place of worship within twenty miles of my humble dwelling." [8]

The loneliness and the magnitude of the task he had undertaken were too much for Samuel Appleton. "In 1790," he wrote, "I having amassed by my various Exertions, from one to two hundred dollars, had an offer of a co-partnership, by a worthy, established merchant of Ashburnham." This is a town in Massachusetts right on the New Hampshire line. Five highways met there in hilly farm country, but there was not much industry except a wood-working shop for making furniture. But Samuel Appleton was much happier in Ashburnham. He said that to be a merchant had always been his "hobby."

"I now visited Boston very differently from what I had done before, say on Horse with saddle-bags, often lined with 50 or a hundred silver dollars." That jingle of silver dollars was an exhilarating feeling but when the accounts were settled at the end of the year, "I found we had only made about enough to meet our expenses," he said. "This would not do for me — and we most amiably dissolved our co-partnership." Samuel Appleton got back his original investment but had nothing for his labor "save a little knowledge of Country Shopkeeping."

Samuel now (in 1792) opened a store at the foot of "Burying-ground hill" in New Ipswich, he said. "I kept a great variety of goods in a small way, . . . sold a great deal of Rum — often treated my customers with grog . . . filled many a lady's snuff box for a copper — lost money by it but was considered generous and gained custom for other articles." About two years later, Charles Barrett, the rich man in town, took him into partnership.

In November, 1794, "I came to Boston to seek my Fortune," Samuel Appleton wrote. He was still only twenty-eight years old. "I wished to hire a shop for the retail trade but found it very difficult to procure one in a good situation. After a few days of fruitless search, William J. White offered to sell me his lease of a small shop of about 20 feet by 18. Five hundred dollars was the rent, on condition that I would buy his stock at cost, which he figured at about $2,500. He was honest enough to say that he didn't think the goods worth two-thirds of that because they were not imported but bought in Boston." Samuel wanted that business and "agreed to take his lease and his goods on his own terms."

Cornhill was the most popular place to shop. It curved from the corner of School Street to intersect with State Street which led directly to Long Wharf and continued to Dock Square and Market Square. On the corner of State Street and Cornhill was the Old State House and on the square was Faneuil Hall. There were market stalls on the square where country people came to trade. Rather loftily, his younger brother Nathan said that Samuel sold goods to country traders.

But Samuel Appleton delighted in cobblestoned Cornhill after the cart tracks around New Ipswich. There was a smell of the sea in the air and the smell of tar on ropes and rigging. Old North, Old South churches, and King's Chapel were all nearby and the sound of churchbells striking the hours on weekdays and calling the faithful on Sunday made him realize that this was Boston. There never was, there never would be, a city quite like it, although eventually, Samuel Appleton was to feel at home in London.

But the twenty-eight-year-old Samuel knew that, unless he wanted to go back to the uneventful life of a small town or the loneliness of the Maine woods, he would have to make a go of his shop in Cornhill. It was a good idea that he had arranged for his younger brother, Nathan, to help tend store. Who but Nathan could be trusted completely, who would work for next to nothing and take care of customers properly? Part of the time at least, Samuel would have to be off buying goods at auction to sell to country people "for cash or short-term credit, for a small profit." Nathan was fifteen by now and plenty old enough to go to work.

THREE

THE YOUNG MERCHANTS

NATHAN APPLETON did not exactly jump at the chance to go to Boston. While Samuel offered no reminiscences of early school days, Nathan offered several. There was "the Widow Tillick" where he was sent when he was very small, but it was no playschool which she kept at her house. He remembered that she taught him his letters by pointing to them with a "fescue." The alphabet, in New England, was presented in rhyme to the effect that, "In Adam's fall, we sinned all," and very shortly Nathan could read through to "Zaccheus he, did climb a tree, His Lord to see."

On his first day at the New Ipswich town school, Nathan was scared half to death by seeing a big boy, who happened to be a cousin of his, "severely flogged." He remembered that he and Rebecca Barrett were the champions at every spelling bee at town school. Later, it would be a mystery to him why his oldest son, Tom, could never spell although sent to the best private schools. But it was in mathematics where young Nathan really shone. He went "through cube root" and was looking for new worlds to conquer by the time he was about ten. The town school master had to confess that cube root was the end of the line as far as his own knowledge was concerned.[1]

The next step was New Ipswich Academy where there were lessons in Algebra, and long sessions of Latin and Greek. There were also "exhibitions" — plays, actually, in which Nathan had the lead, once as Belcourt in *The West Indian*. This was Richard Cumberland's most popular comedy, produced in London in 1771. In New Ipswich, New Hampshire, about 1792 or so, Nathan Appleton played a young gentleman who inherited great estates in Jamaica and had come to London to learn the secret of his birth. Belcourt pursues the first beautiful girl he sees on the street, there are incredible misunderstandings, villains are punished, boxes of diamonds tossed around and the thirteen- or fourteen-year-old Nathan Appleton, as Belcourt, finally wins the "amiable Louisa" at the end of five acts in forty-eight scenes.

Nathan next played a much more demanding part — that of the comedy lead as Marplot in *The Busy Body*. This play was written by Susannah Centlivre, around 1709, and it was long and complicated. Nathan enjoyed himself all the way. Some of his lines were more representative of London than of New Ipswich village, perhaps. When he sees his friend enter the Lady Isabenda's house, he says, "Gad, I'll watch. It may be a Bawdy-House and he may have his throat cut." One of Nathan's classmates as Sir George says, "I am so humbled in my Pretensions to plot upon women, that I believe I shall never have courage enough to attempt a chambermaid." Marplot almost succeeds in wrecking his friend's chances to elope by demanding to "see the monkey." It is really Sir George hidden "behind the Chimney board." Marplot then almost succeeds in wrecking Isabenda's chances by exposing another of his friends as an imposter. There was suspense, however improbable the plot, with Nathan playing the part of the unintentional villain. He was "cuff'd, kick'd and beaten," as he declared in the last scene, and it is to be hoped that his schoolmates did not take their parts too realistically. In the last act, Marplot is rewarded with "a large inheritance" and a chance to recite an epilogue, thirty-eight lines long. Further rewards came later in life when Nathan Appleton addressed Congress — his early experience in memorizing lines serving him well and his self-possession when appearing in public never deserting him. Mr. Hubbard, first headmaster of New Ipswich Academy, put on plays "in a very superior style," everybody declared.[2]

Nathan, Isaac Appleton's seventh son, was ready for college before he was quite fifteen. "In August, 1794, I made the journey to Hanover, on horseback," he wrote. He handed over a dollar, took the examinations and was admitted to the freshman class at Dartmouth. For a little while, he mingled with the group of students, some his own age, some in their twenties as his brother Joseph had been — and then he turned the horse's head toward home.

"It had been decided previously . . ." that he "should become a merchant rather than a scholar," Nathan said. In October or November, 1794, "I took my departure for Boston. At that time a stage ran from

Boston to Groton. I was allowed a horse as far as Townsend, with my brother Eben to take him back." The ten-year-old Eben, youngest of the Appleton boys, watched as Nathan "footed it" out of sight over the hills, "a pocket-handkerchief" in his hand, knotted to hold all his clothes except the clothes on his back. Before long it would be Eben's turn to take the road to Boston.

Nathan arrived at Groton early in the afternoon but the Boston stage had already left so he had to wait till morning. Another day's journey lay ahead and "on passing Charlestown bridge, the evening lamps were lighted."

Samuel had already found Nathan a boarding-place near Quaker Lane where "a very old couple" were hospitable to young men. Eliphalet Hale was there; he had been at New Ipswich Academy along with Nathan and now took him under his wing, teaching him "the first principles" of double-entry bookkeeping. Eliphalet Hale worked for John Cushing — already famous in the China trade and for dressing his servants in Chinese costume. Nathan figured that if double-entry bookkeeping were required by the Cushings, the Appleton brothers needed it. He "managed to buy *Mair's Treatise*" and soon opened a set of books for his brother that was "the equal to anything in any well-known merchant's office.

"I have always attributed a great portion of the failures which take place to a want of attention, or a want of knowledge in the proper principles of bookkeeping," Nathan wrote. It is to be feared that Samuel was not sufficiently impressed. He was off to Europe to buy goods, willing to trust figures to Nathan while he yielded to the spell of sailing-ships, outward bound.

In 1798 business was at a standstill in Boston. In all the narrow waterfront streets there was the smell of burning sulfur, considered the only protection against yellow fever. Since there was little to do at the shop, Nathan concluded that this was the time for him to go to a smallpox hospital! "I permitted myself to be inoculated for the smallpox at Dr. Aspinwall's hospital in Brookline," he wrote. Inoculations were sufficiently dangerous because the form of smallpox induced was not always mild and the methods primitive. On the other hand Nathan did not have yellow fever.

And as at his boarding-house, Nathan made a useful friend. This time it was Joseph Story, future Supreme Court Justice, now about to graduate from Harvard. Joseph Story knew about some French people living in Boston. At Story's suggestion Nathan went to board in the family of

Francis Sales, where he could speak French every day. "That delightful and sunny representative of Southern France, that living Gil Blas in hair-powder and pig-tail," eventually went to Cambridge to teach French at Harvard. Nathan Appleton was a border in the Sales family for a year or two. He soon spoke French fluently.

"I became of age in October, 1800," Nathan wrote: "My brother proposed that I should become a partner with him, on terms which I considered liberal and which I accepted." In 1802, Samuel came back to Boston and Nathan was in England, "shut up in a stagecoach which has only two small windows — hurrying from post to post by night and day . . ." as he negotiated for goods to be sent to Boston for his brother Samuel to sell.[3] Eben had taken Nathan's place as clerk and keeper of books.

Nathan attended strictly to business and became "reconciled to living without the sun." He had been abroad in 1799 when he established credit with a French banking firm in Leghorn and recommended the fast lading of ships for that port, just liberated from a Napoleonic embargo. He had traveled rapidly through Paris and London but this trip in 1801 seems to have been his first really long one. He could not be said to like England. The condition of the labor, especially in textile towns, shocked him. Class distinctions annoyed him and he hoped that Americans would never be so "debased" as to take money for waiting hand and foot upon a traveler, pleasant though such services might be. As to "curiosities" in museums, he had no time for them and preferred a good roast beef dinner to "Roman antiquities" any day.

In 1802 business was not good, no matter how hard this Appleton partner worked. "It was the time of the Consulate; and Napoleon never stood higher in public estimation . . . as the restorer of peace" but "caution and curtailment were impressed upon me in all my letters from home," Nathan said. "The day after the proclamation of the ratification of the peace, in April, 1802," he decided to leave rainy England and set off for the Continent. He embarked at Harwich, took a brief tour through Holland and Belgium and then hired a cabriolet in Brussels which he kept all the way to Paris.

Paris in June made Nathan Appleton forget about business at least for a while. He wrote in French to his brothers back home. The gardens and the promenades were beautiful, the museums were full of "curiosities" which he found he enjoyed. Better still there were theaters and "all sorts of amusements everywhere."

Biggest show of all was "that great man, Bonaparte," Nathan thought.

He was lucky to catch a glimpse of him "when he reviewed his guards of which there are six or eight thousand. Except for these reviews, which he holds each month, it is very difficult to see him. He hides from the eyes of the public." This, Nathan thought, was because Napoleon, as first consul, was acting too much like a king. "The French consider him their sovereign and like his government."

Samuel and Nathan changed places again and it was Nathan's turn to report from Boston. On July 20, 1804, he mentioned that "the death of General Hamilton in a duel with Colonel Burr is the general topic of conversation. An Eulogy is to be delivered in this town by H. G. Otis."

But for the most part, Nathan wrote only of imports and exports. It seems incredible that he could have bought and shipped out so many barrels of potash and pearl ash, produced among the Atlantic states, or that Great Britain could use so much potassium carbonate. But lye was essential to the finishing of fine wool. Where the sheep grazed in England the trees could not grow, but in pioneer New England trees must be cut and burned to clear land for farms. The American colonies had been forbidden to manufacture goods, but in the earliest days directions had been sent to them for producing fine quality lye by boiling down ashes. The process was long and tedious, requiring iron cauldrons and rakes and scrapers — these wrought-iron tools surviving to puzzle later generations. The expression "to rake and scrape together" had meaning for the Appletons of New Ipswich who must have found potash light and easy to transport and to exchange for much needed goods and even cash. The Appletons of Boston found potash and pearl much easier to sell by the barrel than to produce — but like all trade, this one was not without risk.[4]

"I shipped 50 bbls. pott. and 40 bbls. Pearl ashes at 43/6 and 42/ amount $2,388.47," Nathan wrote his brother on July 20, 1804. "I have been induced to ship pretty largely of ashes, thinking the prospect good."

But by September, 1804, he was saying, "I am sorry to hear that Pearl ashes are doing so badly — although I think there can hardly be a loss on our shipment." He put "53 bbls. all Pearl" on board the brig *Hannah* which "cost about 40/." Business was bad and no mistake, Nathan admitted. "Of the goods received by the *John Adams* and the *Two Pollies*, I have made some sales but purchasers are not very sharp-set and no article will bring a good price . . ."

Then, along with a sudden change in the wind, business picked up everywhere. Samuel sold the potash in Liverpool and Dublin for a good price and put the profits into manufactured items which arrived on time, the weather for trans-Atlantic sailing being right for once.

On November 10, Nathan wrote, "I have now the pleasure to inform you of the arrival of the *Polly* from London; the *Venus* from Liverpool and the *Olive Branch*. . . . By these vessels, I judge we have in, the whole of our goods for this season. . . . Business since my last has been very good — scarce ever better. . . . Money, to be sure, continues scarce but our remittances from the country are quite as good as I expected although a great part of them are in *Butchers notes* which I cannot now get discounted." In the collecting of country promissory notes, Nathan excelled, though he did not say so. "Take sales altogether, I do not think we ever made them to more advantage. . . . The lowest advance I have sold any woolens in town is 37½ to 40 per cent . . ."

"I have determined to take myself a tour to the Southward this winter," Nathan told Samuel. "I think the prospect for making remittances in cotton very good — and I am induced to go myself in preference to sending Eben, by the strong inclination which I have to visit that part of the country — and the persuasion that our business here will not suffer at the hands of so good a manager as Eben." It is to be hoped that Eben Appleton, now twenty, read this letter, because he was rather self-effacing where his two older brothers were concerned.

"Goods of most kinds sell so well here, that I do not know that I shall take any," Nathan went on. But he was "preparing to be able to take a considerable sum in cash . . ." At half past three, on the afternoon of the twenty-eighth of November, Nathan was on board the "ship *Warrington*" bound for Savannah with a fine northwest breeze.

The breeze was too good. A short time after they dropped the pilot, the ship struck on a reef, and Nathan had an item for the first page of the journal he kept. The pilot was called back, suggested a kedge anchor and the *Warrington* was pulled off the rocks without injury, but it was eight o'clock in the evening before the ship was under way again. Three days later, they spoke a fishing schooner from the Banks and traded some beef and rum for cod. After that, the voyage was a series of head winds, high seas, hail and lightning. The owner and two other men, besides Nathan Appleton, were the only passengers. Nathan wrote with pride that he was the only one not seriously seasick. "I am liable to light touches of nausea," he admitted, "which generally discharge my stomach and are attended with little disagreeable sensation and no loss of appetite." On December 18, they saw land, the seacoast, "a level plain with trees which present the appearance of a fence of palisades."

The pilot came on board but "the tide set too late to carry us up before dark." On December 20, with the pilot still aboard, the *Warrington* had made no progress toward Five Fathoms, the Savannah wharf for vessels drawing more than twelve feet. It was on a sand-spit three miles from town anyway so the four passengers "had the long boat prepared and at 7 o'clock, with 3 pairs of oars, set out with the tide." It took three hours to row to the Savannah town dock. The *Warrington* made it to Five Fathoms three days later.

Savannah did not appeal to Nathan Appleton. The sand in the streets went over his shoe-tops. At his first lodgings, his landlady, proud of her clientele, told him that Aaron Burr had stayed with her "a fortnight" — that he was "constantly uneasy, slept little and avoided solitude as a pestilence." This was interesting but did not compensate for the cold winds that blew through the house, and Nathan moved nearer town. At "Colonel Stillman's" lodging house, he found "a number of planters and members of the legislature . . ." All they talked about was "dueling and pistol-shooting."

On December 25, Nathan noted rather dismally that "Christmas is much more noticed at the Northward." Business was "at a standstill" to be sure but "the only amusement appears to be shooting and there is great abundance of game in the vicinity." Nathan never did care much for hunting, however. He preferred to observe and was disappointed not to see any alligators, having been told that the river was full of them, from five to six feet long. "At this season of the year they remain nearly torpid at the bottom," Nathan said.

Two days after Christmas, gunboats arrived at Savannah. "The first is the most clumsy, unseemly mass of wood ever to set afloat in the form of a vessel and in her passage from Charleston was nearly lost in good weather. She was several times half full of water. Number two is schooner-rigged and quite a handsome vessel," Nathan wrote in his diary.

Nathan "looked at cotton" but was glad he had not brought goods for sale. A hurricane, the previous August, had devastated Savannah, ruined much of the planters' crops and left the planters poor and in debt. He bought some rice and some choice Sea Island cotton which was in such short supply he knew it was bound to go up in price. On January 2, 1805, "Took leave of Savannah with very little regret," he wrote. But soon after he reached Charleston, Sea Island cotton had advanced and he was pleased with himself for buying at the bottom of the market.

Charleston fared much better in the young Boston merchant's estimation. In fact, he gave it his highest praise when he said that "the city approached by water, bears a very considerable resemblance to Boston." Nathan described "windows of the second stories coming down to the floor" in houses, a style evidently new to him but eventually to be a feature in his Beacon Street parlors. He thought that there was "a very considerable degree of grandeur and magnificence displayed in the shops." Straight and regular streets pleased him this time in contrast to Boston where almost no street could be called straight. "King Street," he said, "is of very great length and is a place of great business as it is the market of most of the cotton which comes in from the country in wagons."

Charleston shocked Nathan Appleton none the less. "Here for the first time, I saw the horrid sight of the sale of human flesh," he wrote in his journal on January 8th. It was "a sight at which human nature, unprompted by custom, must ever revolt. 'Tis a sad spectacle — some of the poor wretches look with trembling round on each bidder to see which one is to be their future master, while the unfeeling auctioneer with cutting taunts and jeers is adding insult to injury. This might be a solitary instance, but it was certainly true. Others, with an indifferent stare, appeared wholly unconcerned at their fate and it is fortunate for these poor wretches, if, as their manner certainly indicates, they are really destitute of any feeling. Cargoes of them are now offered for sale in this place to the present disgrace of the United States and probably future destruction of many of its citizens. . . . What madness — or rather mad avarice can induce these people to encourage the further introduction of the seeds of future evil! In fact only one vote was wanting at the last session of the legislature to have repealed the act."

At this time, Nathan Appleton was twenty-four years old. When he, himself, became a legislator he made every effort to end slavery by legal means. The violence of certain abolitionists made him remember his prophecy. He lived to see the "destruction of citizens."

Aside from this unhappy and lasting impression at the slave market, Nathan had a good time in Charleston. He went to a concert where "at nine o'clock commenced dancing" with "a number of very fine young ladies present" — Miss Rutledge in particular. There was a picnic, where "the supper is furnished by each individual supplying a dish — say ham, tongue, chicken etc.," which struck Nathan as a fine idea that he would try out at home. And to sum up his social life, "Charleston certainly contains many fine girls and their manners are free and pleasing," he said.

There was business of course. N. Appleton bought at Charleston 50 casks of middling quality rice at $4.50 each. He saw a Liverpool price clearance of five dollars in December and noticed with pleasure the favorable prices — particularly "the great advance on rice." He was in two minds "whether to ship or sell here" where the asking price had already gone up to $5.50 and he thought it would go higher. Sea Island cotton had been "an excellent article" — continuing to advance. On February 4, "Took leave of Charleston with considerable regret, as I could not but be pleased with this place."

Since he wanted to see the country, Nathan chose to return home by stage-coach but, beginning with his three-mile ferry trip over the Cooper River, the trip was tiresome, the weather cold and wet, the country "a raw, sandy plain covered with wood, mostly pitch pine with here and there a live oak." After crossing the Great Pee Dee River, "Ashley's swamp" was "a very unpleasant place to pass, the water almost over the horses' backs." He saw nothing of the great plantations for, although they could be reached by road, the rivers were the highways to their door.

Stage-coach passengers got "bacon and cornbread, homiemenie and peach brandy" when they stopped for meals. Sometimes the tablecloth appeared to have been "steeped in the gutter." At Georgetown, South Carolina, the stage-coach passengers were told they must get on as they could, because the next stage had been discontinued! Nathan hired a conveyance costing him thirty dollars for a forty-mile trip. But at last he entered the state of Virginia and now it was a different story. He "breakfasted at a handsome and good house and dined in an elegant style" even if the roads were not a great deal better.

On February 14th, Nathan "viewed the capitol, the seat of Government" at Richmond and approved of everything he saw including the style, "after the model of a Greek temple," and "a marble statue of George Washington."

Nathan was prepared to find Washington "a city only in name" but "the houses are so scattered that there is no such thing as a street," he declared. "A fine, broad *road*" was called Pennsylvania Avenue, which reached "the Capitol of which only one wing is yet built." But he thought when they got around to finishing the job, it would do honor to any nation. The "President's house" was "a very fine building of free-stone." He dutifully attended to his sightseeing until he discovered that the impeachment trial of Supreme Court Justice Samuel Chase, for undue severity, was going on, Aaron Burr presiding over the trial. Now every day he began his diary with, "attended the trial."

On February 21, 1805, Nathan described the scene. "The Senate Chamber is fitted up in a theatrical style for the occasion, and with the display of taste and beauty, which occupy the temporary boxes, presents at the same time a gay and solemn spectacle. Colonel Burr presides with much dignity and the greatest silence prevails. Judge Chase is venerable and dignified."

He listened and commented upon the style, reasoning, "ability and grace" of each lawyer — or the lack of these as the case might be. It was as though he were studying his own future role in Congress, and he left Washington for Baltimore on March 2, hating to have to tear himself away. "Hear with much satisfaction of Judge Chase's acquittal," he wrote on March 3.

"With the appearance of Baltimore, I am on the whole much pleased," Nathan wrote. But in his praise of Philadelphia, Richmond was almost forgotten. "Philadelphia is unquestionably the finest city in the United States, containing 70,000 inhabitants and is perfectly regular. The houses are wholly of brick and a very great number of them are very elegant and magnificent . . ." Such was the verdict of the young Boston merchant.

"New York is much less regular than Philadelphia but appears much more lively," Nathan decided on March 12th. "Broadway is a finer street than any in the United States" but the theater "neither inside nor out appears to much advantage" although there was some very good scenery. He went to the Academy of Art in New York and looked at casts "but having seen the originals" in Paris, the academy "was not so particularly interesting." There was a painting he liked. It was called *Cupid Stung by a Bee!*

In New York, Nathan went to a dancing party "where was quite a brilliant collection of ladies who were gay, tasty and conversable." The next evening he met "Miss Pell, the chick for whom Mr. Gray is sighing so loudly." On March 18, he boarded the sloop *Alonzo* for Newport and Providence, but got tired of slow progress on Long Island Sound and left the *Alonzo* for the stage at New London.

The stage "took up a very pretty girl going to a boarding school in Providence." Completing his survey of cities, "Providence is pleasantly situated and from the elevated part of it has a very fine view," Nathan wrote, but he was beginning to long for home. On March 20, his final diary entry read, "Went to turnpike road which continues to Boston." It was "very fine and expeditiously we got on, and I noticed with pride the greater dispatch, cheaper fare, better carriages and horses than on any part of the frontier road. A nearer approach to Boston brings a thousand pleasant reflections . . ."

At a boarding school in Boston there was another "very pretty girl" whom Nathan had yet to meet. She was studying at the Berry Street Academy. Her name was Maria Theresa Gold.

FOUR

NATHAN AND MARIA THERESA

MARIA THERESA GOLD was born on November 7, 1786, in Pittsfield, Massachusetts. Her father, Thomas Gold, was a prominent Pittsfield lawyer and a Yale graduate. He married Martha Marsh, daughter of a doctor, and they had ten children, all of whom they educated — even the five daughters. Maria, the oldest girl, went away to boarding school in Hartford when she was twelve.

Many very proper letters from Maria to her father have survived.[1] In 1798 she said she was "obliged to attend school early and late." The only lessons she mentioned, however, were in needlework. She "had got a screen" to embroider but was "going to work a pocket book first." There was one complaint. There was no "forte piano" at school and Maria thought there ought to be if she was ever "to learn music."

By 1802, Maria Theresa was at the Berry Street Academy, Boston. This early coeducational academy was near the Old State House and Faneuil Hall, the street name later changed to Channing Place. William Payne was owner and headmaster. He had been a tutor, then teacher and private-school proprietor on Long Island, New York, and now in Boston, with varying success. Elocution was his passion, several of his students, Judge Theophilus Parsons among them, owing much to his instruction at a time when oratory was greatly admired. In a stable behind his combined school, boarding-house, and home, William Payne had "a mimic theater, with stage and pit." Here students performed elaborate plays which were remembered in Boston long after the built-over stable disappeared.

Addressing her father as "Honored Sir," Maria told how much she loved the school. "The situation in which you have placed me is very pleasant and the family are very amiable. I have that attention paid me, which I never experienced in any other boarding school before; and if in the course of my studies I should make such progress as to merit the approbation of my amiable parents, I shall think myself completely happy." There was a "forte piano" at the Paynes' school, but the first thing a student had to learn was to tune it. Another thirty years would have to pass before young Jonas Chickering of Mason Village, New Hampshire, near New Ipswich, would solve the problem in Boston, his grand pianos having a cast-iron frame. Maria Gold's teacher encouraged her, but Maria thought, if she couldn't learn to tune a forte piano, she had better take up the "gitarr."

The amiable family who paid so much attention to Maria consisted of Mr. and Mrs. William Payne, three sons and four daughters. The second son, John Howard Payne, was born to fame. He came to be called the first American Hamlet and, toward the end of his life, while adapting *Clari, or the Maid of Milan* for use as an opera, he wrote "Home, Sweet Home." [2]

In December, 1802, "John stands by me and says I must not forget to present his respects to you," Maria told her father. "Perhaps you recollect this amiable child, the youngest but one of this charming family." John had organized a boys' club called the "Federal Street Band." They wore blue-and-white uniforms the exact replica of the Boston Light Infantry and this was the year when the eleven-year-old John Payne marched at their head in the Fourth of July parade, wearing his captain's uniform, his plumed helmet and carrying a sword.

Eloise Payne was Maria's best friend, the one who went shopping with her to buy a pelisse and to try to find a furrier who would make over her old muff. At the cost of only nine dollars, Maria acquired a large and elegant muff of very good "furr." Eloise and the other Payne girls, Lucy, Sally and Anna, were friends of Maria Theresa's for many years.

Maria reported on her studies. "Respecting my Geography, I think I have a handsome knowledge of it. Arithmetic I have attended to diligently and as far as I have gone, do perfectly understand it; Grammar I have paid attention to also." Maria had "made rapid progress in Music" and before long she thought she could go on with it "without the assistance of teachers and tune the instrument also."

Dancing lessons were extra at the Berry Street Academy. "I shall have a bill to pay Mr. Turner as soon as my quarter is up," Maria warned her father. "I think I have greatly improved my dancing since I have been at his school. I have become acquainted with a minuet and many other steps that I did not know before." While thinking about how she loved dancing, Maria suddenly forgot that she had begun her letter, "Honored Sir," and wrote, "Indeed Papa, your daughter has been called an elegant dancer by good judges."

Maria proceeded to sketch in her social life. Lawyer Gold of Pittsfield knew various judges — though not necessarily of dancing. First and foremost was Judge James Sullivan. He was justice of the Supreme Court in 1776, appointed on a committee to reorganize the laws of the new Commonwealth of Massachusetts in 1780, and in 1786 a member of Congress. In 1797 he ran for governor of Massachusetts, but the Federalists defeated him. While all of this impressed Thomas Gold, his daughter Maria couldn't have cared less. The judge had nine children, six of them sons, and at this time three were young and unmarried. Maria was invited to the Sullivans for Thanksgiving dinner. The whole family was there including in-laws.

She was "treated very politely indeed," she told her father, much to his satisfaction. "Mr. B. Sullivan invited me to the subscription ball which is composed of the first people in this town, as I did not like to go with Mr. Sullivan alone, Mrs. William Sullivan invited me to go with her and Mr. William Sullivan wrote me a very polite letter to take tea with them on that day and go from there with them." Maria was being discreet and wanted her father to know it. Bant Sullivan — always known by his middle name because his step-brother was also William — was just twenty-one and most attractive.

William and Sarah Swan Sullivan were practically bride and groom, having been married in May, 1802. Sarah's mother and her sisters Hepzibah and Christiana were also at the Thanksgiving party. Their father Colonel Swan had been imprisoned in Paris for debt! Having lost his wife's fortune, he made another, handed it over to her and was then imprisoned falsely, in his opinion. Mrs. Swan sent him all the money he wanted and he was allowed to live in his own Paris apartment. But he refused to let his wife bail him out and set him free to come home. Mrs. Swan was the only woman member of the Mount Vernon Proprietors, the land syndicate developing Beacon Hill. She gave each of her daughters a house on Chestnut Street as a wedding present. So Maria Gold went first to tea on Chestnut Street and then to the ball.

"Mr. B. Sullivan accompanied us; I found the ball very brilliant and very much crowded," Maria said. Perhaps there wasn't room enough for her elegant dancing to be properly admired. But she met the Mason girls whom she had known in Williamstown the summer before. Susan, Miriam and Anna called on her at Mr. Payne's boarding school next day and invited her to Sunday dinner.

"They sent their coach after me and I was handed into one of the most elegant houses I ever saw," Maria said. Their father was Senator Jonathan Mason. Susan Mason, who married Maria's doctor, John Collins Warren, became one of Maria's close friends. Jonathan Mason gave Susan a house on Park Street when she was married in 1803.

Thomas Gold, in 1806, sent a younger daughter Elizabeth, always called Eliza, to Mr. Payne's school, and Maria considered herself in charge. "I hope the little advice which I am capable of offering her will not be lost," she said. "I am confident she will *yet* become the elegant and accomplished woman you desire her to be." Maria had been at home for a while but now she was back in Boston.

Very casually, Maria mentioned that "Mr. Appleton is with us and in good health." Since there was no explanation of who Mr. Appleton was, it seems that her father already knew him and also "Mr. S. Appleton" who had gone to England.

"Mr. Appleton has just been informed that his father is at the point of death. This information has given him much uneasiness — his spirits are much depressed. We hope he may yet have more favorable news." Isaac Appleton died in New Ipswich, February 25, 1806 — the day after Maria wrote this letter to her father.

Out of the twelve children of Deacon Isaac Appleton, nine survived him. His wife was still living, and probably Aaron had been helping his father on the farm, but Isaac, his father's namesake, had married a Dublin girl and had gone to that nearby town to live. The girls had married and scattered, with the exception of Mary who married Joseph Barrett. Moses was a doctor in Waterville. The name of Appleton was no longer often met with in New Ipswich. It was Samuel Appleton of Boston who saw to it that the name should not be forgotten when he endowed New Ipswich Academy — on condition that it be thereafter known as Appleton Academy.

At the Paynes' school and boarding-house in 1806, Maria described the young ladies as being as charming as ever. She had not less than a dozen around her while she wrote, all chattering about Cooper, the handsome actor who was playing in Boston that season. Maria saw Thomas Abthorpe Cooper in *Macbeth* but she did not happen to men-

tion that she and the young ladies took turns reading aloud from
Alonzo and Melissa, or The Unfeeling Father — A tale based on Truth.
It was a tale all right. That there was any truth in it seems unlikely, but
this often-pirated work by Isaac Mitchell was said to be the most popular Gothic novel written in America. Maria also omitted to tell her father
that Nathan Appleton signed himself "Alonzo" when he addressed her
in verse! [3]

In the novel, the hero was engaged to Melissa until his father lost his
fortune. Melissa's father broke off the match and tried to force his
daughter to marry Alonzo's rival. The time, according to the story, was
the American Revolution. Many scenes were laid in a castle on Long
Island Sound in Connecticut, where ghosts abounded and the draw-
bridge had a lock and key. Alonzo endlessly attempts to rescue Melissa
but is foiled by her "Unfeeling Father."

Believing her dead, Alonzo visits her supposed grave where he is told
of her funeral, "attended by eight young ladies for pall-bearers, all
dressed in white with black ribbons and the bells tolling." Here, in an
early edition of this novel, now at the Beinecke Rare Book Library,
Yale University, there is still a little yellow violet pressed between the
pages.

Of course Melissa was not dead — it was the grave of her cousin.
Alonzo had met Benjamin Franklin in Paris who helped him restore his
father's fortune. Melissa's father relents — everybody cries at Alonzo
and Melissa's wedding — and so did the girls at William Payne's boarding school. Everybody knew by this time that the handsome Nathan
Appleton was Maria's Alonzo. In her letters she signed herself "Mira"
rather than Melissa, perhaps because Nathan found it better suited to
his poetry.

By early 1806, Nathan Appleton had asked Thomas Gold of Pittsfield
for the hand of his oldest daughter in marriage. Thomas Gold was by no
means the "Unfeeling Father" but he was not pleased. With all those
accomplishments, geography, the forte piano and the minuet; with all
those prominent Boston friends — Sullivans, Masons, lawyers almost all
of them, why had Maria chosen a farm boy! Then there was the matter
of education. Nathan Appleton, although admitted to college, had turned
his back on Dartmouth and kept store. His father and grandfather were
farmers and no one as yet had said anything about the Appleton coat of
arms. The Golds could have produced one. [4]

Thomas Gold was a Yale graduate and so was his father, the Reverend Hezekiah Gold. [5] Maria's great-grandfather, also a Reverend Heze-

kiah, graduated from Harvard. Maria's grandfather, the second Hezekiah, was a Congregationalist minister in Cornwall, Connecticut. His claim to fame included the fact that he could "lay more green rail fence than any of his parishioners" but his "noble farm" was so successful that some of them objected to paying his salary of £65 and ten cords of wood. Sarah Sedgwick, his first wife, was the mother of five children — Maria's

Thomas Gold Mansion, Pittsfield, Massachusetts, scene of Maria Gold's marriage to Nathan Appleton and of Longfellow's poem, "The Old Clock on the Stairs." (Photograph courtesy of the New York Public Library)

father among them. This Sedgwick family connection brought affectionate relatives into Maria Theresa's life. Catherine Maria Sedgwick, the future novelist, attended the Berry Street Academy.

Disregarding her father's disappointment, though probably aware of it, Maria Theresa Gold set her wedding date — April 13, 1806. This was a Sunday — perhaps the most convenient day for Golds to gather in Pittsfield. In any case, no one could say that Nathan Appleton wasted a weekday getting married.

The Thomas Gold house on East Street, Pittsfield, was originally a farmhouse with a huge chimney and a keeping-room where Maria's mother still loved to sit even after her husband had added a parlor with white-paneled fireplace wall, wainscot and French landscape wallpaper.[6] Eventually, improved finances and changing tastes brought about extensive alterations, perhaps by that gifted country builder, Asher Benjamin. There would be a portico in the Greek style, more rooms for an expanding family, and a beautiful staircase with carved balusters, and a landing where a tall clock stood.

All of this could hardly be achieved in time for Maria's wedding but she had five sisters plus a cousin on her mother's side who had been adopted into the family. One girl, Martha, never married but all the rest were brides in this house, and there was always a clock on the stairs.[7]

Maria eventually told her little daughter Fanny that the clock had "seen" her wedding. It was Fanny Appleton Longfellow who suggested to her husband the subject of one of his best-loved poems, "The Clock on the Stairs." He described the Thomas Gold house on East Street as he saw it.

> *Somewhat back from the village street*
> *Stands the old fashioned country seat.*
> *Across this antique portico*
> *Tall poplar trees their shadows throw.*
> *In that mansion used to be*
> *Free-hearted hospitality.*
> *Here great fires up the chimney roared*
> *The stranger feasted at his board . . .*

The Thomas Gold house was doomed to be remodeled by subsequent owners until it ended in neo-Gothic style with wooden towers and battlements. Then it was torn down to make way for a public school, its poplars uprooted, its gardens bulldozed into asphalt-covered playgrounds. Part, at least, of the staircase was stored in a barn which eventually burned, but the clock descended to Fanny and stands not on the stairs but in Longfellow's study, Longfellow House, Cambridge.

In that letter-writing age, someone must have described Maria Gold's wedding and some day such a letter may still be discovered. Perhaps there was a wedding journey or perhaps it was journey enough for Nathan and Maria to drive to Boston, to their new home, number 2 Park Place.

This pleasant-sounding address brings up pictures of Boston Common bounded on one side by Park Street. But Nathan Appleton was not yet ready to move to the country. Park Place was "near Board Alley" and led out of Hanover Street. It was at the North End, still a fashionable part of town where merchants' houses had been built complete with a captain's walk on the roof where the owner could carry his spyglass to look for the topsails he would recognize, or where his wife, with a nagging fear in her heart that she might be his widow, would look to see if his ship came in. Current in New England's speech was the expression, "if my ship comes in."

Hanover Street was one of Boston's oldest thoroughfares. Garrison houses, reminiscent of Indian warfare, were still standing. No one minded if there were a tavern or two. Side streets extended toward Copp's Hill where there was a fine harbor view or ran directly to the docks, drays of merchandise rumbling over the cobblestones. Maria could walk everywhere she wanted to go — to Berry Street Academy, to see Eloise Payne, and in June to walk with her to Gilbert Stuart's painting room on Summer Street. The young Appletons had as yet no need to keep a carriage.

In September, 1807, Mrs. Nathan Appleton wrote to her mother in strict confidence. Maria was pregnant, evidently a little frightened and she wanted her mother to be sure to come to Boston to be with her before the child arrived. Either Maria failed to keep her mother's letters or her mother found that the remaining nine children left little time for writing. It was Maria's father who answered, first explaining that he had invaded no privacy but had been given "a summary" of Maria's news. He had advice to offer.

"My anxiety at the moment would prompt me to offer you the best counsel of my heart. . . . You have hitherto taken much exercise and employed your time industriously. . . . It has procured to your delicate frame much strength and firmness, qualities indispensable to such as may be Mothers." This kind of life "has given you a cheerful mind — discreet sociability and a happy flow of spirits. . . . Keep the Piano in good tune — see to it moderately, it will soothe and quiet all your passions and keep you in good humor with yourself . . ."

Maria was to remember "that the accouchement will fill your excellent companion with unutterable joy and your affectionate parents and numerous relatives with unbounded satisfaction . . ."

Of course Maria's mother would be with her. "The time must be at your designation . . . write us soon and fix the day. . . . You need take no trouble about your Mother's conveyance. If the season proves favorable, she will go by chaise, if otherwise, by stage."

The summons for Mrs. Gold never came. Maria had a miscarriage which left her ill and depressed. She and her "amiable companion" would have to wait a while longer for children and they were both disappointed — though not without hope.

The year 1807 was difficult for a young merchant, and Nathan Appleton's ability proved itself, in that he suffered less than some others, older, more experienced but less alert than he. In June, the American frigate *Chesapeake* sailed out of Hampton Roads, on a shakedown cruise. Just outside the three-mile limit she was hailed by the British frigate, *Leopard*. Nothing was ready for action aboard the *Chesapeake*, but when the *Leopard*'s boat came alongside with orders from the British in Halifax, Commodore James Barron refused to muster his men for inspection and possible seizure of British seamen. The longboat returned to the *Leopard* with this reply and the *Leopard* opened fire at close range. Three men on the deck of the *Chesapeake* were killed and eight wounded including the Commodore. A lieutenant on the *Chesapeake* ran to the cook's galley and returned with a live coal in his hand which he tossed into the touch-hole of one gun. Out of her forty-four-gun armament, this was the only one fired. There was nothing for the *Chesapeake* to do but strike the colors.

The young Nathan Appletons shared the consternation that swept over Boston when the news reached them. Their friend, Judge James Sullivan, a Jeffersonian Democrat, was now governor of Massachusetts and favored the Jefferson Embargo which followed the taking of the *Chesapeake*. His son, William, became a Federalist, as were the Appletons and most of their other friends. Bitter feeling between the Sullivans, father and son, caused grief to both of them. In Boston, generally, the two parties had gotten along reasonably well, but now rivalry broke out and there were arguments on the dignified Exchange and in the taverns. Street boys threw mud at the carriages of the merchants. Then the temper of the people began to change. Merchant ships, forbidden to sail, rotted at their wharves. Shipyards were empty. Fishing fleets went out to the Grand Banks no more, and for the country people there was no sale of potash. Farmers' families raked and scraped in vain. Judge Sullivan lost his next election.

There were failures other than those of importer-exporters. Among them was the bankruptcy of William Payne and the breaking up of his school. Hard times had reduced pupil enrollment. Mrs. William Payne, the former Sara Isaacs, descendant of the first Jewish family on Long Island, died early in 1807. Her husband lost her guiding hand so essential to a man of his flamboyant temperament. The little theater had been expensive to maintain — there were debts and mortgages. John Howard Payne, now fourteen, was sent to work in a New York counting-house where he was of no use at all. When he managed to get on the stage in New York, Bostonians still shook their heads over him.

But in 1809, John Howard Payne was back in Boston as juvenile lead in the popular play called *Norval*. He had been "wonderfully successful in New York," Maria Appleton wrote. "I hope he may have the merit to satisfy even the fastidious taste of a Boston audience — as this has proved to be his ruling passion and he is rendered unfit for anything else."

Maria's schoolmates, the Payne girls, "were all scattered among their friends and yet undetermined how they shall dispose of themselves." Nancy Payne was visiting Maria. All inadvertently however, Maria was responsible for a little typically Bostonian scandal and a blighted romance for Lucy, the oldest of the Payne sisters. Maria asked Lucy to dinner one night with one of her brother-in-law Sam's friends. Nathan Appleton told the story.

"Lucy was highly pleased" with Sam's friend, Bourne. For a while it looked as if she might "dispose of herself" by becoming Mrs. Bourne. She "construed every civility into an offer of marriage" and even told her friends she was engaged. But the young man now said "he had no object but amusement." He got himself engaged "to a Miss Hall of Medford." Nathan had "never seen the lady — but report gives her a most excellent character." A few months later, Nathan told another chapter of the story. "Mr. Bourne can hardly overcome his chagrin at being jilted" by Miss Hall. Maria might have felt it served him right.

The Payne family solved some of their problems when Anna and Eloise opened a successful school in Newport. Lucy (still husband-hunting) and their father lived with them "doing nothing" as Maria Appleton put it. But John Howard Payne had "begun to pay his father's debts," from his earnings on the stage.

Maria must have been sorry to leave her friends in the neighborhood of Park Place and Hanover Street but she was as happy as her husband to find herself the mistress of number 54 Beacon. Her summer with her parents in Pittsfield had restored her health and she was eager to begin enjoying life. "How soon is Eliza to be with us?" she asked her father in

November, 1809. "The season of gaiety has commenced with uncommon brilliancy and spirit. I trust, if my sister has not lost all relish for amusement at the Town, I shall not long plead for her consent to join us." Eliza soon arrived.

At first all did not go well with Eliza in Boston, however, "I am perfectly satisfied with the attention paid her," Maria wrote, "although she sometimes complains that it is not sufficient — but the truth is, she has been so much flattered at home that she is not satisfied with anything short of exclusive attention here. This, she should not expect in a place so distinguished for brilliant and accomplished Dames as B."

Maria said that her younger sister talked too fast, sometimes mispronounced words and "likewise makes use of vulgar expressions." She and Nathan had "taken the liberty to point out these defects" and at first Eliza took it badly. But they "laboured incessantly" so that by March, Maria felt that she and her husband had not "laboured in vain." Eliza's "figure is considered finer than anything we have amongst us. She would in truth be a fascinating creature, were she a little more precise in her manners and conversation."

In early March, Samuel Appleton was back in Boston after having spent most of the last ten years abroad. He found rooms for himself and announced that he was tired of the importing business. Maria had her own idea of why her brother-in-law had come home. "Mr. S. Appleton is often with us," she told her father. "He is now looking for a wife. I think he shows a great partiality to my fair sister — but my husband says she is too good for him. I know not whether he will marry — or return to England."

Samuel Appleton was forty-three years old — Eliza not yet twenty. A few weeks later, "Eliza Gold is with us," Nathan wrote his brother Eben, "and really makes herself quite conspicuous by her dancing and exuberant spirits." Samuel was still in Boston.

On May 24, 1810, Nathan Appleton dissolved partnership with his brother Samuel. In the legal document, signed in Boston, articles of co-partnership were "made and concluded between Nathan Appleton . . . and Daniel P. Parker and Eben Appleton of said Boston, merchants, at present in trade under the firm of Appleton and Parker." Business was to "commence on the first day of August, next . . ." Nathan was to contribute his stock of goods and also "the goods and effects of the late company of S. and N. Appleton." After dividing "the receipts with his late partner, Mr. Samuel Appleton," Nathan was to invest "the sum of fifty thousand dollars" in the new company. Daniel Parker and Eben

Appleton each put up sixty thousand dollars and it was "also agreed that one of the parties should live in England."

Eben was in England already and once more there were romantic complications involving the Gold family. Harriet, that cousin of Maria's who lived in Pittsfield with Maria's parents, thought that Eben Appleton was going to marry her. Maria said that she was "sensibly grieved" to hear that Harriet's affections "were deeply engaged" but she thought her cousin would get over it. As to Eben, "we are disposed to believe that it is in his power to say something in his own defence." Evidently Maria's father had taken her to task. Eben said nothing. He married an English girl.

Nathan Appleton's business letters would now be addressed to Eben Appleton, Liverpool, England. There was always a bit of news other than financial. In July, 1809, "The principle speculation going on is in Church building," he said. Members of the Old South had seceded because their minister's sermons contained too little about the fires of hell. "They are building a very elegant church at the head of the Mall" — on the corner of Park and Tremont streets. Their new minister "a famous Dr. Griffin" was "said to be a perfect Salamander" — so sermons would be really hot. In fact, the site of this church soon came to be known as "Brimstone Corner."

In March, 1810, Nathan sent a draft of "12,500 pounds sterling" to Eben. He usually headed his letters with the name of the ship by which he was sending them. This time the heading was "by a run-away." The ship bound for England would slip out of the port of Boston against the law.

James Monroe had been in London working to bring about better relations between England and the United States. Madison was now President and Monroe had gone to Washington, D.C., to try to push through a bill abolishing the non-intercourse act of 1809. "I have delayed giving orders till Monroe's bill shall actually pass but intend to make them out directly," Nathan told Eben. The bill failed.

John Quincy Adams had been appointed minister to Russia at St. Petersburg. He was soon to sail "in a ship of Mr. Gray's — who calculating on protection, loads her with coffee and sugar," Nathan wrote. Both French and British frigates and privateers roamed the seas making prizes of each other's merchantmen but Nathan figured that Eben could find a fast-sailing and lucky vessel so he sent "a large order for Nankeens" to which Eben was to "pay particular attention." This durable yellow or sometimes orange material was used mostly for men and boys' pantaloons and was sure to be in demand in Boston.

In May, 1810, Congress decided to permit trade with France and Great Britain, but they gave Monroe the power to invoke non-intercourse against either nation, should search and seizure of American merchantmen continue. The thing to do would be to get as many cargoes as possible for Parker and the Appletons on their way across the Atlantic before fleets of vessels arrived to glut the market. Nathan urged Eben to move fast.

Summing up this difficult phase of his career as a merchant, Nathan Appleton wrote, "I continued business with my brother with varied success but on the whole with an average of prosperity."

The Colburns, who had rather pointedly ignored their new neighbors, the Appletons, changed their tune during the winter of 1810. "Mrs. Colburn, last evening, gave a very splendid ball at which Mrs. A. and myself were present," Nathan wrote. Maria had caught cold, her cough lingering on, and this was the first time she had "ventured out of an evening and I am happy to find that she has received no injury from it."

In that official autobiography of his, Mr. Appleton wrote, "In 1810 I visited England on account of the health of my wife." Mrs. Appleton, who had arrived in Manchester, England, by the seventh of July, gave her private and unofficial account of the voyage. She had enjoyed every minute of it. "In fact, the good people considered me a wonderful sailor — for there was not another passenger on board but what was more or less afflicted. As I was always well, I endeavored to amuse the sick by reading to them, during the week, plays and interesting biography. On the Sabbath, I gave them a sermon." Maria did not say whether she read these from a volume of published sermons or whether they were of her own composition.

The Appletons landed in Liverpool where Eben lived in "a neat little house 3 miles" from the city "where they experienced all the pleasure of retirement with the advantages of town." They liked Mrs. Eben Appleton, the English sister-in-law. "She is a pleasant, agreeable woman" who had style, Maria said. Eben did not mention Cousin Harriet Gold. " 'Tis a subject which he evidently avoids. I have been as silent — for I am sensible that no good can come of it. He conducts himself with propriety, attends to business and his wife."

In Manchester, Maria caught cold "from riding in the rain." While her husband visited the great textile mills, she coughed and stayed in bed.

She "hoped to go out soon" because she wanted to see the goods "in those immense warehouses which darken my windows," she said.

By July 28, 1810, the Nathan Appletons were in London. "I have devoted my whole time to looking after goods," Nathan wrote to Eben. "Most fancy goods are so very dear that I am almost afraid of them. I have some ribbons, bonnets, shawls etc. preparing to ship by the *Golen*. . . . I have purchased a quantity of fancy muslins, Imitation shawls enough . . . and pretty cheap." Handsome shawls in imitation of those made in India were copied in Paisley, Scotland, and worn by both men and women — so perhaps these are what Nathan referred to.

N. Appleton, as he signed himself, also bought "300 bales of cambrics, considerably better" than he saw in Manchester, and "650 bales of Carlisle Ginghams at six and a half to eight cents a yard — a very durable article." Back home, Mr. Parker had sold his goods well but Nathan expected that "business will not be good in Boston this season." He told Eben that "if goods in Manchester fall considerably, I think you may keep buying moderately." He and Maria had "pretty much concluded to go to Scotland."

Maria was enthusiastic over Edinburgh. She said it "defied her powers of description." She found "many Americans there who were so kind and attentive that it was with real sorrow" that she parted from them at the end of their stay. Among these were Mr. and Mrs. Francis Cabot Lowell and their children. Maria was particularly grateful for the company of Mrs. Lowell, the former Hannah Jackson, because Mr. Lowell and Mr. Appleton talked of nothing but textile mills.

For some time, Nathan Appleton had been angry and frustrated by the various embargoes that had plagued his business. Why should a country as young and vigorous as the United States be almost totally dependent on foreign manufactured goods? There was cotton in the South, and ingenuity in New England along with water power and even iron of sorts. He was not the only American thinking along these lines but he was among the first, as was Francis C. Lowell.

The two men must have already known each other well. Both were Boston merchants — perhaps business rivals. Francis C. Lowell bought and sold cotton, dealt in foreign exchange and discounted notes taken out on purchase of cargo. There was even a distant cousinship between Lowells and Appletons.

Mr. Lowell had spent several weeks in Lancashire observing the operation of cotton mills. As long as he made no drawings and took no notes, the guarded secrets of improved machinery were considered safe from him. Mr. Appleton had done the same thing except that he was concerned with prices, rate of production, quality of products — and profit margin.

"Whilst in Edinburgh, I saw a good deal of Francis C. Lowell, Esq. who was there with his family," Appleton wrote for his autobiography. "We had a good deal of conversation upon the subject of the cotton manufacture and he told me that he had determined to make himself fully acquainted with the subject with a view to the introduction of it at home."

Mr. Appleton told Lowell that he would go along with the idea and put up some money. At least, that is how he told the story of a chance encounter between two Americans in a Scottish parlor.

FIVE

MR. MADISON'S WAR

WHEN AMERICANS WENT ABROAD, in the days of sailing ships, they usually stayed at least a year. Of course no properly conscientious New Englander would admit going merely for pleasure. The journey must be for health or education. The Francis C. Lowells, after leaving Edinburgh, went to Cheltenham, where water with a high sulfur content had been found in the time of George III.[1] The king and the royal princesses made Cheltenham Springs fashionable. Mr. Lowell had been threatened with a nervous breakdown[2] and for some reason he hoped that the horrible-tasting water would improve his health, although history fails to indicate that it did George III very much good. On his way Mr. Lowell just happened to visit a few textile mills.

Nathan Appleton went abroad for his wife's health. He chanced to look in on his partner, Eben Appleton, and to buy some goods to be sent to Boston. Maria's education benefited. Remembering those geography lessons, Maria said at first, rather anxiously, that she had not seen enough to be able to report on "the soil and inhabitants" of England. The Appletons stopped at Stilton however and Maria commented favorably on Stilton cheese, the product of that area. At New Castle-on-Tyne she had become properly aware that the city was famous for its manufactures.

But at Burleigh House, built in the reign of Queen Elizabeth, as Maria told her father, her eyes were opened to the possibility of knowledge far beyond the range of William Payne's boarding school. The centuries-old deer park, the magnificent house and the finest collection of pictures in the kingdom gave her a new outlook and completely new interests.

The long sightseeing journey was accomplished in a series of coaches, which jolted over cobblestones at each town, smothered the passengers in dust on country roads or tried their patience when the big, lumbering vehicles crawled through quagmires. Nathan remarked that their speed was nothing like that of John Gilpin although they had taken the same road out of London.

Bath was chosen as the health resort for Maria. Only a few of the Roman Baths had been excavated and, as yet, no one, including Maria, cared about going that far back in history anyway. It was the Pump Room, built in the Palladian style, that everyone came to see. There were carpets, paintings, a fancy clock, chairs, couches — and soft music. And of course there was an indoor fountain where people drank the water containing the usual sulphates, plus lime, carbonates and chlorides. At Bath "the only really hot springs in Britain" gushed out of the ground. There were various buildings where visitors could take baths, but Maria became very ill.

On December 10, 1810, Nathan told his brother Eben about it. "The uncertainty about my going to London arises from the state of Maria's health. I am sorry to say she has been quite ill ever since we arrived here. She has not been out at all — her illness partly from a cold and partly from a more serious cause and I am not without fear that she may be confined before her time."

Soon after this, Maria lost the child that she and Nathan had hoped for. It was on December 21, 1810, that she wrote to her father — five months after her previous letter. "Once more, Dear Father, I have the pleasure of addressing you after so long an interruption to our correspondence, and of acknowledging the receipt of your affectionate letter, which was in truth an exquisite treat for it found me recovering from a long and painful illness — a prey to melancholy and depression of spirits." [3]

In Bath, England, on the twelfth of December, the Appletons had news by the *London Dispatch* of the non-intercourse proclamation. They were "disheartened but not surprised. This puts a new face upon the state of affairs," Nathan wrote his brother. "You will of course make every exertion to get the goods off as soon as possible. I suppose Parker will make large remittances — for my own part, I have no doubt that all goods shipped in March will be admitted — you had better hurry everything as much as possible. This proclamation I think will secure

American vessels from French capture and I would not be in a hurry about insurance — for the *Orion* is a good ship. I would have everything shipped by her that can be got ready."

As soon as Maria was able to travel, she and her husband went to Liverpool. They were there at the end of January when Maria wrote again. "The recent death of the Princess Amelia, youngest daughter of his Majesty, has put the Country in mourning, and this event, combined with the indisposition of the King and the many failures which have followed in quick succession have cast a general gloom over the country." The Appletons were going back to Bath for a while and then to London.

In London, Nathan insisted that Maria buy some new clothes. She needed something to cheer her up. They sailed from Liverpool, and arrived safely in New York, June 21, 1811. Again the sea voyage had done wonders for Maria. "She walks every morning before breakfast," her husband reported, "and her cheeks are acquiring a ruddy hue." With pride and with his usual humor, he added, "Maria finds the ladies of New York astonishingly old fashioned. She can hardly walk down the street without attracting as much attention as an Osage Chief."

Back in Boston by the middle of July, they found 54 Beacon "in very good condition — and the situation as delightful as ever." Eliza Gold had gone back to Pittsfield, and when the Appletons returned to Boston there was news of her. She was engaged to Charles M. Lee "of Utica, New York, a young lawyer of much promise." [4]

"Samuel is in very good spirits — enjoying the world as well as any man can — cares little for money as he finds himself rich enough." This was Maria's report, so if the exuberant Eliza had broken his heart, it was whole again. He bought a large farm in Cambridge, near the Common, planted a garden with fruit trees, and later his tenant made him "a dandy duck pond." His brother Nathan thought little of this investment and of other parcels of real estate that Sam acquired, but whether he wanted more money or not — Sam's fortune increased.

Along Cornhill, business was not good. "The credit of shopkeepers never was at so low an ebb . . ." Nathan found, in July, 1811. No one had any idea whether there would be importations in the autumn. Congress was not in session and it was anybody's guess whether "intercourse will be opened" and "how much time will elapse before the repeal takes place, *if it takes place at all!*" He thought the goods he and Eben had sent over would average about forty percent mark-up and that bad debts might "take over half the profit."

"My present opinion is much more favorable to see an adjustment with Great Britain than when I first arrived. . . . I think the more eligible mode of availing ourselves of an early repeal will be by shipping the goods to Halifax where they can be introduced at short notice — or sent to Montreal as may appear best. As this mode will subject the goods to considerable expenses, we have not great opinion of it." He and Mr. Parker had "however concluded to authorize" Eben to ship goods "not to exceed £5,000 in staple articles. . . . By going into Yorkshire," Eben ought to be able to "get the goods very low; low-priced woolens are at present in great demand and must be higher during the winter." As it turned out, Nathan Appleton was following the right course — but for the wrong reasons. There would be no "adjustment with Great Britain."

In September, 1811, Nathan visited Canada. He told Eben to continue to ship to Halifax where he planned to hold goods in storage to wait for a better market. "From all accounts, business is as bad in Canada as anywhere else," he found. "Ashes are dull. . . . Some smuggling is carried out but not, I apprehend, to any great extent as they are vigilant on the look-out and several seizures have been made."

By February, 1812, Samuel Appleton was back in London. Ever since his youth he had loved to wander and again he was bored with Boston. Once more, he was the recipient of Nathan's letters. "I informed you of the sale of part of the *Ann's* cargo to the amt of upwards of $130,000 and Mr. Hinckley has since sold the Hare skins and goat's wool at barely cost and charges." David Hinckley, merchant, figured often in Nathan Appleton's letters at this time. Mr. Hinckley had now gone to Baltimore to attend to the auction of the *Roxanna's* cargo. Nathan looked for a profit on the "Brimstone, Shumack Claret and Greek wine, brandy, opium and various other articles . . ." This appears to be the first and almost the only mention of opium as an article of importation by the Appletons. The tragic results of its use were not then recognized, and doctors prescribed it all too freely for all kinds of illnesses.

Letters from Nathan to his two brothers continued with alternating hopes and fears concerning the opening or the closing of American ports. They shipped 39 bales of New Orleans cotton by the "brig *Thomas*" and 133 bales "on board brig *William and Martha*." A few days later, the price of New Orleans cotton had increased ten percent. The *Roxanna* set out, this time "with 3,500 barrels of flour for Cadiz." Referring to a letter from Samuel which reached Boston the fifth of April, "I am happy to find that your former good luck attends you,"

Nathan told him. For his own account, he, too, had been lucky. Ships with Appleton cargo had almost all come in.

In Boston the Nathan Appletons had a still more important reason for feeling lucky. On March 31, 1812, their first child was born. "Maria brought us a fine boy on Thursday last — they are both doing remarkably well," the boy's father wrote. The baby was named Thomas Gold Appleton, and years later this famous Boston wit gleefully referred to himself as having just missed being an April fool. In 1812, his father could hardly believe their good fortune as he was able to report, "Maria has fine health and the boy grows apace." It all seemed too good to be true.

War was declared between the United States and Great Britain on June 18, 1812. "This horrible madness has been perpetrated! We stand gaping at each other, hardly realizing that it can be true — then bursting into violent execrations of the madmen who have sacrificed us." Nathan wrote, speaking for most of New England, reeling from the unexpected blow of "Mr. Madison's War."

Nathan wrote to his brothers, not knowing whether letters would ever reach them — offering the latest mercantile news and his best advice concerning the Appleton cargoes. "It is expected there will not be a British force on our coast equal to our own under 14 days — during which it is to be hoped some of the homeward bound ships will arrive. The *Roxanna* is in danger, the *Ann* not quite safe [but] as she is to wait at Smyrna for new fruit there, there is some chance that she may there hear of the war. . . . We are all depressed and disconsolate when we reflect on the ruin brought upon our country."

Boston had been a ship-building seaport since the days of the Revolution.[5] The *Constitution* was built in Hart's private shipyard. Her bolts and spikes were made by Paul Revere, of drawn copper, drawing being a new hardening process. After two rather embarrassing failures when crowds gathered to watch her launching, and the *Constitution* refused to leave the ways, she was finally set afloat on Columbus Day, 1797. Money to buy the site for the Charlestown Navy Yard was not appropriated until March 1, 1801. In 1803, the *Constitution* was ready to take off for Tripoli — Paul Revere having made plates with which she was coppered. "The carpenters gave nine cheers, which were answered by the seamen and calkers because they had, in fourteen days, completed coppering the ship with copper made in the United States." It was in the Mediterranean that she earned her name "Old Ironsides" but it would appear that she should have been called "Old Coppersides."

On July 28, she was back in Boston after her escape from a British squadron. Eight frigates, including the *Constitution* and the *Chesapeake,* were repaired at the Charlestown Navy Yard during the War of 1812. The private shipyards were busy building privateers, thirty-one in all. Harbor forts were repaired and a volunteer militia organized.

For some time business in Boston proceeded as usual. The British granted licenses for American ships to sail — the price of a license being from one to two thousand dollars. Ships passed the American blockade and slipped into American ports — if lucky. If stopped and it could be proved that the goods aboard had been bought before the declaration of war, the ships were allowed to proceed, tie up and post a bond until proof of their claim could be established — when the bond was refunded. Of course there were exasperating delays, causing wharfage charges to mount and perishable cargoes to spoil. At Halifax, the *Union* was delayed until "the *Union's* British license arrived," Nathan told Eben. "The *Union* got in from Halifax day before yesterday," he wrote on October 25, 1812. It was "a lucky escape." She had calicoes aboard which he supposed would bring "100 to 125% profit . . ." The *Roxanna* almost slipped into port but an adverse wind sprang up, she grounded and was caught, brought in safely but bonded.

In February, 1813, Nathan anxiously reminded Samuel of "the necessity of sending out evidence that the goods of the *Swiftsure* and *Roxanna* were purchased before the war was known . . ." He was preparing "petitions" for other ships but in all cases "nothing will be done till we get evidences from England." In this same letter, he announced that he and Parker had "concluded to dissolve partnership as we have nothing to do and our affairs are so snug that it will be a work of no difficulty." Careful bookkeeping and avoidance of excessive borrowing had paid off.

"I can hardly suppose that the war will continue very long," Nathan went on to say. Samuel would "be able to judge from the temper of the British people. At any rate, when the state of the market warrants it, I wish you to purchase for me £5,000 worth of goods, or if you choose, to buy £10,000 on our joint account — it will be agreeable to me. . . . The money should be invested in staple goods which are cheapest, either cotton or wool — say cambrics largely — calicoes, shirtings, ginghams, shawls, printed vestings, flannels etc. . . . Most of the goods you sent out this year were very well suited to this market — woolens which cost very low, might do very well."

Three weeks later, Nathan added a page to this letter which he had not found a way to send to England. ". . . We have lately learned the capture of the *Sarah* by the *Constitution* — another splendid victory. We are apprehensive our port will now be blockaded." Chesapeake Bay was so closely blockaded that "even licensed vessels are not allowed to pass."

The "temper of the British people" was not improved by too many glorious victories on the part of a navy they regarded as having no rights of its own on the high seas. By the end of May, 1813, the British men-of-war *Shannon* and *Tenedos* were watching Boston harbor.

The *Chesapeake* had come into Charlestown Navy Yard on April 9 to refit and recruit a crew. She sailed on the first day of June and almost immediately engaged the *Shannon*. The two frigates were out of sight of the town but the sound of cannonading was heard, and people along Hanover Street rushed up narrow stairs to captain's walks on housetops or climbed Copp's Hill for a wider view. All they could see was smoke rising. Longboats were hastily launched. After a while, slowly and sadly men rowed them back again. The ill-fated *Chesapeake* had been taken.

Said Maria Appleton, writing to her father, a week later, "You have undoubtedly seen in the papers all that is known of the capture of the *Chesapeake* — 'tis a most unaccountable affair. Even the capture of Fort George does not console our citizens. . . . Much as it is to be regretted, it will on the whole do us good for we had become almost as haughty and overbearing as the British — that Pride which caused the War, if not checked in us, would end only in our destruction . . . but at how great experience have we purchased this wisdom." Like her husband and her father, Maria was a staunch Federalist.

The Nathan Appletons had a private reason to be thankful and happy. Maria's second child and first daughter was born on October 18, 1813. The baby was named Mary. Again, mother and child were strong and well. Gratefully, Maria spoke of the invaluable blessing of health for which she fervently thanked God.

A schooner arrived in Boston in January, 1814, with Madison's message, announcing that the United States had accepted the British offer of negotiation, the conference to take place in Gutenburg. Not yet realizing how much easier it is to get into a war than out of it, Nathan Appleton was once more sure that the end had come. Seven months later came the successful British foray upon Washington which was unguarded because it was supposed to be too far up the Potomac to be attacked. The inhabitants "ran off into the woods," the President's house was burned — that pre-White House, free-stone building Nathan had admired in 1804.

New York was to be the next British target, but the harbor bristled with guns, many of them, like those on the *Constitution*, made in Great Britain. Boston suddenly began to wonder if fifteen heavy cannon on Governors Island and ten on Charlestown Point Battery would really protect the town. By June 27, 1814, "a general sense of alarm prevailed." A conference was held about "the sinking of hulks" in Boston harbor. Hulks of old ships were made ready and it was arranged that ten companies of artillery would come to Boston from neighboring towns, at the first alarm, to help out the Boston militia. A "temporary gun house" was built on Boston Common. By the end of August there was "volunteer digging." Fort Strong was built at East Boston, a battery was set up on Dorchester Heights and other defenses built in Roxbury and Cambridge. A notebook was entitled "Mechanics of the Town" ready to "co-operate by manual labour in the measure for the Defence of the Town and Naval Arsenal . . ." The list was headed by Paul Revere — then seventy-nine.

The British advanced upon New York along Lake Champlain, the route made memorable by Burgoyne. This time their defeat was not at Saratoga but at Plattsburg. Boston was not attacked and the only sound of guns had been those of the *Chesapeake* and the *Shannon* — until the morning of February 13, 1815.

On Monday, an express arrived "in the incredibly short space of thirty-two hours from New York." The British sloop-of-war *Favorite* had arrived in New York harbor under a flag of truce, with the treaty of peace "already ratified by his Britannic Majesty." It had been signed in Ghent, December 24, 1814.

Now the guns around Boston were fired — salute followed salute. Bells were set ringing and on Pearl Street, the dignified Eliza Cabot pounded on doors. "Do you know why the bells are ringing?" she demanded. "Why, for fire, I suppose," Mrs. Quincy, the senator's wife, said. "No, it's *Peace! Peace!*" [6] On went Miss Cabot, breathless — possibly even without her bonnet!

Seamen organized a parade, six horses pulling each dray loaded with men, their leader wearing a sign that said "Peace." The volunteer fire companies roused out their bands and filled the streets with band music. The news came early on a Monday morning and the "whole day was given over to rejoicing."

By nightfall ships' crews were signing on and ships' stores were loading. It was all premature as far as Nathan Appleton was concerned. Nearly a month later he wrote cautiously to Eben who, with his family, had been visiting at 54 Beacon but was now in Liverpool again. "No doubt you will have been a long time anxiously looking for arrivals from Boston before this reaches you — and truly the delay has been very great since we had certain intelligence of peace, but it had not been thought safe to go to sea any sooner."

The news in this letter was probably not wholly a surprise to Eben. Nathan had been disillusioned about the business of importing-exporting for some time. He had realized profits during the war, in large part from goods warehoused in Canada and permitted to come into the United States, coast-wise or overland, by various means. But there had been too much anxiety, too many embargoes.

"In revolving in my mind what course to take to avoid the necessity for labourious personal attention to business, for which I am becoming intolerant — and the other extreme of having no regular established business — I have finally concluded a partnership concern with the two Mr. Wards . . ." Benjamin C. Ward and William Ward were two "very industrious, worthy young men." They were to do all the wholesale buying and selling for Nathan Appleton who would "invest $40,000 and as much more as they put in," as capital for the new firm from which Mr. Appleton would receive "½ of profit after paying interest and $1,000 for their extra services."

". . . Mr. William Ward goes to England in the *Milo*," Nathan said, and, if Eben had set himself up as a commission merchant, as he had proposed, he was to negotiate funds for Mr. Ward. Nathan wanted to know the amount of his own available funds abroad. He thought he had about £7,500 with London bankers and perhaps four or five thousand pounds more "coming in." William Ward was to "proceed to Paris for the purpose of purchasing French goods . . ." and Eben's advice would be appreciated.

"Our manufacturing establishment in Waltham is just getting under way," Nathan wrote, and Eben already knew that his brother had discovered a new business interest. As far back as September, 1811, Nathan had reported that "manufacturers are increasing pretty rapidly but as little capital is invested in them, they make their way gradually. I think, however, a large establishment with all the branches connected, would be sure to do well, particularly with a good number of workmen from England.

"There is a deficiency in dye works and bleaching. There are two cotton spinning factories at New Ipswich and another going up. King and Everett have also got a factory under way at Fletcher's Mills. S. Batchelder is concerned in a factory and manufactures a good many goods for which he finds a ready sale," Nathan said. On his trip south in 1804, he had befriended a man whom he had just met again. "My Buford chap is weaving at New Ipswich and highly delighted with the country. He says he earns a dollar a day and can get board for $1.50 a week." His employers "give very good accounts of him, so that I am glad I have been the means of so much bettering his condition."

"A large establishment with all the branches connected," which Nathan Appleton had mentioned in 1811, was the key innovation to be carried out at the Waltham mills. They were the first textile mills to be built with all the processes from raw cotton to finished cloth combined under one roof. This system plus the improved machines under construction formed the solid foundation upon which the American textile mills were to be built at the beginning of the Machine Age.

Eben, when he next went to Manchester, was to "buy and send out to us a few lbs. of cotton twist of different numbers, from 15 to 60, with a few pieces of grey calico of the different qualities and the same bleached, in the rough. They will be very useful to us to calculate how we can compete with them." Eben was also to send "the exact prices of each" and, if he should encounter some British textile workers in need of a job, "a good bleacher would, I think, meet with encouragement" in New England.

Waltham was a small farming community on the Charles River, nine miles from Boston. There was low-cost land available plus a defunct paper mill for sale when Francis C. Lowell got back from England in 1812. He and his family had taken passage just before the declaration of war, and their ship was captured by a British frigate and taken to Halifax. Mr. Lowell's baggage was searched three times so it was just as well that he had not jotted down notes or sketched plans of textile mills. The Lowells finally reached Boston in a miserably dirty little coast-wise ship which they hired at an exorbitant price. Mr. Lowell went right to work to raise capital for a mill.

Money for the new venture was almost impossible to come by.[7] Mr. Lowell's Cabot uncles refused to have anything to do with the project, because they had been disastrously involved in a mill which had been built in Beverly, Massachusetts, in 1788. In this early mill a pair of horses driven by a small boy in the basement walked around and around a huge wheel. Wooden gears and pulleys relayed this horsepower to the carding and spinning machines in the building overhead. The product was an extremely coarse cloth. George Washington said in his diary that he had breakfast with George Cabot and rode out afterwards to see the mill. The Cabot family gained personal satisfaction from their claim to a mill pre-dating the famous Slater mill at Pawtucket but that was about all they gained. The Cabots turned their attention to importing cotton cloth from China with gratifying results. Certain outspoken remarks were said to have prejudiced other investors against Francis Cabot Lowell's project.

Patrick Tracy Jackson, however, was all enthusiasm for the scheme. Born in Newburyport in 1780, he had been apprenticed to a Newburyport merchant when he was fifteen; super-cargo on a merchant ship before he was twenty, then captain's clerk and finally captain. After three voyages, he retired from the sea, and set himself up in 1808 as a merchant in East and West India goods. In 1811 he was almost bankrupt, but by 1813, he was able to raise $20,000 to put into Francis C. Lowell's project. Mr. Lowell was married to Jackson's sister, Hannah, and Jackson had married a Cabot, so that family interests were at stake when he agreed to drop everything else and manage the factory.

Mr. Francis C. Lowell and "Mr. Patrick T. Jackson came to me one day on the Boston exchange," Nathan Appleton said in his pamphlet, *Introduction of the Power Loom*, written "at the request" of friends in 1858. These men said they had bought Bemis' paper mill and a water power in Waltham and that they had obtained an act of incorporation with a charter authorizing them to raise $400,000. They were only going to raise $100,000 until the experiment should be fairly tried. The purpose of Patrick T. Jackson's conversation on the exchange was to get N. Appleton to subscribe $10,000.

N. Appleton said he had yet to see an American cotton mill in practical operation. So far those New Ipswich mills had never made any money. But theoretically, the business ought to succeed. He wanted to see the experiment fairly tried so he was willing to take $5,000 worth of stock. At that time, if a company failed, the investor not only lost his cash but also was liable for the debts of the concern in proportion to his holdings.

Nathan Appleton's commitment was among the lowest, but he was chosen one of the directors of the Boston Manufacturing Company, which was on its way by February 13, 1813. The new company's first step was in the right direction. They hired Paul Moody, a mechanical genius, to translate the knowledge that Mr. Lowell had in his head into wheels of cast iron and spindles whittled out of wood.

Paul Moody was born in 1779 of educated parents in Byfield Parish near Newbury. Six of his brothers went to Dummer Academy as did the young Jackson boys. Paul, who was about the same age, would have none of it. He was apprenticed to a mechanic when he was twelve, became a hand-weaver when he was sixteen, working for the Scofield brothers of Newbury who had a factory which turned out coarse woolens by primitive methods. In 1812 he worked for a firm making carding machines and, when the Boston Manufacturing Company offered him a job, he was a master mechanic, thirty-five years old and considered a successful man. The challenge of building something new was what appealed to Paul Moody. Most of the work would consist of adapting and improving existing machines, but there was ample room for invention and he was to hold several patents.

Mr. Lowell "was for some time experimenting at a store in Broad Street" where he "employed a man to turn a crank," Nathan Appleton wrote. Over a year went by before any machine was built and ready for operation. Other manufacturers had power looms of sorts — Mr. Lowell bought one for a hundred dollars and another for two hundred. He and Moody made models — one after another.

"It was not until the new building at Waltham was completed and other machinery was running, that the first loom was ready for trial," according to Nathan Appleton. "Mr. Lowell said to me that he did not wish me to see it until it was complete. . . . At length, the time arrived. I well recollect the state of admiration with which we sat by the hour watching the beautiful movement of this new and wonderful machine, destined as it evidently was, to change the character of all textile industry. This was in the autumn of 1814."

In different parts of the Waltham factory other machines were working beautifully — almost all of them with improvements. Mr. Appleton told what he termed "a pleasing anecdote." He said that "Mr. Shepherd of Taunton had a patent for a winding machine which was considered the best extant. Mr. Lowell was chaffering with him about purchasing the right of using" Shepherd's machines "on a large scale, at some reduction from the price named. Mr. Shepherd refused, saying, 'You must have them. You cannot do without them as you know, Mr. Moody.' "

But Paul Moody had been watching the patented machine at work and he said, "I am just thinking I can spin the cops direct upon the bobbin." A "cop" was a mass of coiled thread wound by Mr. Shepherd's machine. As soon as Moody suggested eliminating the winding machine, everyone saw that it could be done. " 'You be hanged!' said Mr. Shepherd. 'Well, I accept your offer.' 'No,' said Mr. Lowell, 'it is too late.' " As usual, Mr. Lowell made "the numerous mathematical calculations necessary . . . and Mr. Moody carried them into effect."

Mathematics had been Nathan Appleton's delight ever since he was a small boy, but he was not especially interested in mechanics so it was understood that he would not go out to the mills often. However, after the jubilation over the success of the new machines had died down, a serious problem confronted the Boston Manufacturing Company. Their product didn't sell! Nathan Appleton was called in.

Mr. Lowell explained that here was a difficulty he hadn't thought of. Nathan Appleton said he would see what he could do and told the story later. "At that time, when the Waltham Company first began to produce cloth, there was but one place in Boston where domestic goods were sold. This was a shop in Cornhill kept by Mr. Isaac Bowers, or rather Mrs. Bowers." Mr. Appleton went to see Mrs. Bowers who said "everybody praised the goods and had no objection to the price . . ." They just wouldn't buy American-made cotton sheeting even though it was thirty-seven inches wide instead of a yard like the goods from India which it was supposed to imitate.

Appleton suggested that "a parcel of goods" from the new mill be sent over to B. C. Ward and Company, that new firm in which he was a partner. He asked what the price ought to be, and Mr. Lowell said he would take twenty-five cents a yard. "I soon found a purchaser, in Mr. Forsaith, an auctioneer, who sold them at auction, at once, at something over thirty cents. We continued to sell them at auction with little variation of the price," Nathan wrote. His co-partners, B. C. Ward and Company, became permanently the selling agents for the mills and Nathan told what happened next.

". . . I found an interesting and agreeable occupation in paying attention to the sales and made up the first account with a charge of one percent commission. This was purely a nominal charge for the time spent in a pleasant occupation — and not an adequate commission but satisfactory under the circumstances. This rate of commission was continued and finally became the established rate, under the great increase of the manufacture. Thus, what was at the commencement rather unreasonably low, became, when the amount of annual sale concentrated in single houses amounted to millions of dollars, a desirable and profitable business."

"I was content with a moderate fortune," Nathan Appleton had explained, when he handed over his importing-exporting business to B. C. Ward and Company. Now, "by accident," as he called it, Benjamin C. and William Ward, those worthy young men, were on the way to become really wealthy — and so was Nathan Appleton.

SIX

WILLIAM AND MARY ANN

WILLIAM APPLETON acquired his first Beacon Street address in 1814. He was twenty-eight and about to marry Mary Ann Cutler, aged twenty. Maria told her father about it. "William is pledged and will be married the first of January. He has taken the house next to ours and it is now furnishing for their reception." Mrs. Nathan Appleton approved of William's choice. "Everyone acquainted with the parties believes it to be the best bargain William ever made."

Cousin William seems to have been looking the field over because, about six months earlier, Maria had observed that he seemed "in good spirits although Miss L. has pledged her faith to another." That William loved a good bargain was no news to anyone.

When William first came to Boston, he had lived with How and Spear who kept a West India goods store. In 1807 "I went into business with N. Giddings, we kept at the Corner of India and Central Streets, the only store occupied in the street," he wrote. "Our business was the buying and selling of West India goods and crockery ware." William was in partnership with N. Giddings until 1809 — the year after his cousin Nathan bought 54 Beacon.

"Then considering myself worth about four Thousand dollars, I bought the ship *Triumphant* at Salem for five-Thousand dollars . . ." The triumphant William sailed on his ship to Fayal, a ship-owner at the age of twenty-three. He felt pride and anxiety in almost equal parts. In Fayal, William put the *Triumphant* under Portuguese colors and sent her off to Liverpool, taking passage himself in "Mr. Heard's ship." John

Heard was a prominent East India merchant of Ipswich, his son a life-long friend of William's. They got as far as the English Channel when, "the wind being adverse," they put in at Kinsale, a port on the south coast of Ireland. From there they went to Cork and Dublin, then to Holyhead and finally to Liverpool.

At Liverpool there was news for William. His ship, the *Triumphant*, had been captured by a French privateer! For two weeks, William grieved, not only for the loss of his entire fortune plus a thousand dollars he had borrowed, but for the first ship he had ever owned.

Then William received a letter. The *Triumphant* had been "retaken and brought to Plymouth, England, where I went to take charge of my property," he said. Here was proof that he was not only a natural-born trader, but born lucky — not that he ever dared to believe in his good luck without worrying about it.

William Appleton stayed in England until July 10, 1810. For the first time, he mentioned working with his cousins, Samuel and Nathan. He loaded about ten thousand pounds worth of goods, "for account of my-self and Parker, Appleton and Company," on the brig *Eliza* and sailed for Boston aboard her. "These goods and another importation" he sold, and at the close of the year 1811, he found himself worth ten thousand dollars.

England was struggling to maintain her supremacy at sea against Napoleon's expanding power, so William loaded two ships with naval stores for England. He went back to England himself and was in the visitors' gallery in the House of Commons when he heard debates concerning England's insistence upon her right to search American vessels. "Orders in Council concerning American ships would be repealed," he learned. Feeling sure that this meant the end of embargoes, William went out and bought goods. He had thirty thousand English pounds' worth of cargo on the high seas or loading when the War of 1812 was declared. Now his mental anguish was almost past bearing. He went home on the *Roxanna*.

"When I closed out my importations, I thought myself worth sixty Thousand dollars and I did not attend to any business of importance during the war . . ." William said. His ships had come in, their cargoes selling at a tremendous mark-up. What he did not say was that the nervous strain had been too much for him. He was taken very ill, and his cousin Nathan's wife, Maria Theresa, took care of him.

Years later, at Christmastime, William wrote a thank-you letter. "To you, my dear Mrs. Appleton, I am much indebted, which I shall ever

Number 54 Beacon Street. First Beacon Street home of Nathan Appleton, and later the home of William Appleton. Entrance on the right. The next house to the right, Number 53, was built by Mrs. Samuel Appleton. (Photograph courtesy of Holman's Print Shop, Boston.)

remember. Beside the usual acts of courtesy which I have always received from you in an uncommon degree — there are others of a more
important character.

"Well do I recollect your kind attentions, eighteen years since, when
you took me to your home and nursed me with a sister's care . . ."

To cheer William, young ladies were invited to call on him at 54
Beacon Street. He was small, frail-looking with deep-set, intense eyes,
and a fine Roman nose. If William had ever cared for "Miss L," he
forgot about her when Mary Ann Cutler appeared on the scene. She
was a cheerful girl, full of good health and good spirits. It didn't take
her long to come down from her step-father Jonathon Amory's house
on Park Street to the Nathan Appleton house on Beacon Street to entertain the young invalid, and as soon as William was well enough he
could "walk her home" after dark.

Up on Park Street, Mary Ann had three half-brothers and three half-
sisters. Her mother had been Mehitable Sullivan, daughter of Governor
James Sullivan. Mary Ann Cutler treasured a letter writen by her father
to "Jonathon Amory Tertius," in 1795.[1] In it James Cutler expressed
his thanks to Amory for taking over "the cares and exertions which our
mutual concerns must involve." Mary Ann was five when her father
died and seven when her mother married Jonathon Amory.

Mary Ann's mother was an out-going sort of person, always giving
parties and asking Mary Ann to help entertain callers. Mary Ann played
minuets when her young half-brothers and sisters gave a dance. She
played psalm tunes on Sunday when everybody gathered around to
sing. William Appleton described Mrs. Jonathon Amory, his future
mother-in-law, as a "lady of much energy, of character, commanding
in her appearance and of a strong mind."

In Maria Appleton's parlor, Mary Ann was glad enough not to be
asked to play the piano. She really loved music but it was a relief to
find that William would rather she left the piano alone. That William
really disliked music was something she had yet to discover, but for
the present it was obvious that they couldn't hold hands if her hands
were on the keyboard.

Wedding plans were made in Mrs. Jonathon Amory's parlor, secretly,
yet in the midst of callers and inquisitive relatives, one of whom Mary
Ann described as "lynx-eyed."

"It was the Sunday evening before New Years day, or else it was
New Years evening in the drawing room after tea. Mother and I were
writing on scraps of paper to each other about fixing our wedding day,"

Mary Ann remembered. They decided on January 9 which was a Monday.

William Appleton's comment was as follows: "I engaged in a matrimonial speculation, the whole result of which is not ascertained. In January, 1815, I was married."

The convivial Sullivans gave parties before the wedding as did the elegant Amorys. Mary Ann "appeared as a bride in a purple pelisse and white bonnet with feathers." There were dinners where "hot turkies, ducks, partridges and a profusion of delicacies of every description" were served with fine wine to accompany each course. Some of the gentlemen got "seriously gay." [2]

Maria Theresa's father seems to have heard about it — perhaps from the young Sedgwicks who were there — and he wrote one of his sermonizing letters. Maria defended herself. "Our temptations to excess are great," she admitted, "but I think we are not so dissolute and abandoned as you imagine.

"William and his wife are settled near us. They go on swimmingly. The more we see of her, the more we are disposed to admire. They seem to be well matched."

During the spring of 1815, William went back into business. He began the building of ships, his first being the *Telegraph*, the *Courier* and the *Minerva*. He also sent on board the brig *Amsterdam* ten thousand dollars in French and Spanish gold — half for his own account and half for his cousin Nathan. "Should the war rage on the continent, I suppose it will bring a great price," Nathan said. "At any rate, there can be but little doubt of its doing as well as exchange at the present rate." A little later, the Appleton cousins sent twenty thousand Spanish dollars to Liverpool, by the *Panther*.

Nathan told of another of William's ventures. "A new insurance company is incorporating — to be in underwriting what the New England Bank is in banking. William A. has been very active in getting it up — it is very popular and shares in great request."

On July 1, 1815, Nathan told his brother Eben that "William is making money by speculative business — his family prospects are sufficiently promising." Mary Ann was now noticeably pregnant.

William and Mary Ann's child was born October 21, 1815, and named William Sullivan Appleton. Mary Ann was still in bed when her husband left her on November 7. "I was attacked by the dyspepsy, so called," William said. He could keep nothing in his stomach and was afflicted with what he called "that vile complaint of my bowels and with these difficulties I contended till Autumn." [3] He sent for Dr. Warren who gave him emetics and purges until William looked as if a light breeze would blow him away. Before long he weighed only 116 pounds and was sensitive about it, expecting to be laughed at. Quite possibly those simple twelve-course dinners everyone indulged in were to blame, but no one seemed to notice that William's dyspepsy was worse every time one of his ships failed to make port on time. Dr. Warren did what all the other doctors did when baffled — he sent William on a journey for health, and Charleston, South Carolina, was the place where everyone was going. The elder Mrs. Otis was already there, "half of Boston" or, in other words, most of Dr. Warren's patients, would soon arrive.

William wrote love letters to Mary Ann, not quite a year after their marriage.[4] "The time shall not be long, my dear Angel, that we are separated and then we shall enjoy life more (if possible) than before we were torn from each other. If any persons were ever more happy than we have been, no one ever will be than we, when I again reach the arms of my much beloved Mary Ann. In my sleep, I imagine myself with my wife and boy and when I awake feel much disappointed to find we are many thousand miles from each other . . ."

William tried hard to write cheerfully. "I have improved so much within the two or three days past as to think myself almost well. I enjoy my meals as formerly and feel no ill effects from them. I drink a little wine which sets perfectly on my stomach. I have just returned from riding. I am not very strong, very little *liveliness*; had it not been for the unfortunate cold I took when I came on shore, I should have been very smart by this time. I am quite satisfied and hope we shall be thankful for this and many other blessings we enjoy."

He had just received a letter from Mary Ann which he said he had "read more than twenty times." Mary Ann had told him how much the baby enjoyed being given a fig to suck. Nobody said anything about cooking or even washing the figs which came from Smyrna. "I cannot help thinking how that dear little rascal would look, sucking a fig," William told her, "but I don't believe he is as pretty as when sucking" (here William put in some dashes) "you know what.

"I received a letter from our good Mr. N. Appleton," William continued. "He says you keep your spirits up and behave manfully, that's a good girl." William wanted Mary Ann to write at least a few words every night and send her letters twice a week.

Nathan dropped by to see Mary Ann every day. He put her letters aboard the best coast-wise sailing ships he could find and brought her a letter from William every time one was sent to his office. Maria's sister Frances was visiting and "Mrs. Appleton has been so kind as to spare Frances to me at night," Mary Ann said. And on November 13, "Mrs. Appleton was to see me for the second time, looking very beautiful."

Perhaps Maria Theresa was wearing some of the new clothes her husband had ordered for her from London. Eben was to "see to them — four dresses of Merino cloth, two for daytime, cut high in the neck, two for evening in the latest style." The London dressmaker who had made her clothes in 1810 had "promised to keep her measurements." Nathan also ordered a warm winter coat for Maria, saying that blue or brown material would do but what he really wanted was a "bright bottle green" with bonnet to match, "richly trimmed but not gaudy."

The Nathan Appletons were especially happy just now. Their third child and second son, Charles Sedgwick Appleton, was born on October 9, 1815. Maria and the boy were both well. Their little Mary was just a year and nine months older than Charles while Tom was now three years old. Everyone spoke of Tom Appleton as being an unusually handsome child and to compliment Mary Ann they told her that her baby William looked like him. "Between ourselves," Mary Ann wrote her husband, "our baby is somewhat handsomer." She thought their child looked "everyday more like his father and he likes to be petted as much as his father."

Toward the end of November, Mary Ann moved up the hill to her mother's house on the corner of Park and Beacon. She didn't want to go but the strong-minded Mrs. Amory insisted. It was true that Mary Ann's cook had left to get married and the baby's nurse had gone to take care of another newborn baby. Benjamin, Mary Ann's houseman, came only by the day to look after the fires which were kept burning constantly in several rooms. Next door, Maria Appleton had been frightened one night — "almost sure she heard people going in and out of the house." She had awakened her husband but "he did not hear any noise — or rather did not care sufficiently to know whether there was a noise or not." It proved to be their houseman "who had got up very early and was stamping about the kitchen."

Mary Ann wrote from Park Street on December 7. "When I first came here, I told mother I was going to get a load of wood, and if she pleased, should tell Benjamin to convey it into the closet in my chamber. She said I must not give myself the trouble about it for she had happened to say something to father about wood and he observed that he had already provided for my wood. I did not dare to say any more."

Mary Ann was once more a daughter in the house instead of her own mistress. She appreciated all the Amorys tried to do for her but from now on her letters would be full of social occasions, where she had to play the piano for dancing parties and on Sunday evenings she played those psalm tunes again. She said little Willie made a face at psalm tunes. One night she had to sit long at table helping her step-father entertain his "Fish Club." But she had had the honor of sitting next to Mr. Otis who made himself very agreeable.

On the eighth of December, "There is no less than twenty-one people in the family," Mary Ann wrote. "Mother has her hands full." And on January 11, 1816, "Mother is going to have a *monstrous* party. There is about 320 people invited and a great many answers have come and scarcely any regrets." The whole family had to move up to the third floor. The entire second floor "was to be used for supper rooms, the night of the ball.

"I have the room I used to occupy before I was married and I assure you I feel quite at home in it and I think it the pleasantest room in the house. It is the upper chamber over the little parlor. But, pleasant as it is, I would not come back to it and leave that in Beacon Street."

The next day was spent making "jelly blanc-mange and all the good things for the party." Mary Ann walked down Beacon Street with one of her half-sisters to her own house, "to get Mother my knives and forks, plates and so forth for her party."

Of course the ball was a great success. Two hundred people arrived but Mrs. Amory's "large parlors" held them all. William's comment arrived a few weeks later. It must have been "a monstrous nuisance to move all one's beds as you say Mother did, but I suppose you ladies find it good fun."

William wanted to know what had become of the barrel of sweet potatoes and the hams he had sent to his mother-in-law. "The sweet potatoes you were so good as to send us, we have never seen," Mary Ann replied, "and we don't find there were any on board the vessel. . . . Somebody must have taken a fancy to them and eaten them; Father sent twice to the vessel but could hear nothing of them." Of course William had words with the ship's captain. Then the potatoes plus the hams were found—in Mrs. Amory's cellar. They had been delivered — but nobody told her, and because of the party she had failed to check those many below-ground rooms: the wine cellar, the root cellar and all the rest. The potatoes and hams were eaten and enjoyed, but the efficient Mrs. Amory was embarrassed. It was said that Maria Appleton was afraid to go into her own cellars for fear of rats. But Mrs. Amory was of sterner stuff.

William forgave his mother-in-law and engaged in some long distance persiflage with Mary Ann. He urged her to go to parties and to dance more. When she danced only twice, "I think, if I were situated as you were, I would not have acknowledged, even to gratify my husband that I could only get an old widower and a married man to dance with me. But, my dear, you shall find your husband more attentive than all the beaus when you get home."

"I have received this morning my dear husband's letter," Mary Ann replied. ". . . I have read it over and over again and have scarcely had it out of my hands since I received it. It has been backwards and forwards from my hand to my bosom all day. Do not laugh at me, my dear, they have all been laughing at me today for being so choice of your letter and for appearing so much elated at hearing from you. I endeavor generally to conceal my feelings when my spirits are very high or very low, but when I hear from you unexpectedly, as I did today (for I did not expect a letter till tomorrow) it was impossible for me to help expressing the delight . . ."

William did some business for Nathan while in Charleston and sent messages to Nathan in his letters to Mary Ann. Because she was really interested in business, which most women were supposed not to understand, her cousin Nathan teased her a little. He said he would send his friends to her for the cotton prices and the latest market news. It pleased William when Mary Ann wrote to him that his ship *Quincy* had outsailed the *Milo*, making the passage from Liverpool to Boston in twenty-two days. He had not supposed she knew he owned the *Quincy*.

At last the time came for William to start home. On March 29, 1816, "I fear I shall not sleep at night when I get nigh you," he wrote. He hired a carriage and a man to drive it because he could "get on much faster" and he equipped himself with "plenty of bread, chocolate and sugar," determining to eat nothing he could buy en route except eggs. Since lodgings were so apt to be dirty, he brought his own sheets with him.

Somewhere beyond the Pee Dee River, "at a house where I stopped this day, a woman was nursing a child about as old as our William and

I was so much pleased at looking at the little dog that I would have kissed him if he had not been as dirty as a pig," William wrote.

All along, William had tried to believe that his health was improving. But on the way home, "I do not expect to get so well but that you and the little boy and myself will have to travel most of the summer," he now admitted. "I have some thoughts of getting a light traveling carriage in Philadelphia for the purpose. What do you think of it? Write me in your next. You know we can sell it in the Autumn and it will be much cheaper than to hire."

Needless to say, Mary Ann approved of any plans that included her and the baby. "If you intend to ride a good deal (and if it is less expensive than to hire) it will be pleasant to have a carriage that we should feel at home in, but to tell you the truth I am not *ambitious* to ride in my own carriage until I am forty years old; or thirty at least," Mary Ann replied.

William wanted to know what else, besides a carriage, he might bring from Philadelphia. "You say you intend getting bonnets for us all," his wife commented. "I don't know whether you include Mother or not but she said sometime since she would very much like a white chip bonnet from Philadelphia." Mary Ann thought William would do well to ask a friend of theirs to take him to "the most tasty milliner." For herself, she wanted "white chip" because she thought it "prettier than any other kind of dress bonnet." And if he were going to get something for the baby, "let it be silver bells and coral."

"Our dear little William" was prettier, more pink-cheeked, his blue eyes brighter than ever. That he was an unusually happy, sweet-tempered child, not only his mother but everyone else agreed.

This was Mary Ann's last letter to her husband before his return from South Carolina. Pasted into a letter book now at Baker Library, Harvard Business School, her letters and William's tell a love story of two people whom the outside world never considered at all romantic.

In all his letters, William tried to encourage Mary Ann with good news about his health, but in his diary he wrote, "I returned in much worse state than I left. The summer was passed in traveling, a most miserable existence; very great irritability, but God knows not without great suffering."

Business was bad in Boston. Five firms failed, all of them owing money to the Appletons. "September 30, 1816, Monday. A pleasant morning; rose early and went to my Store to make arrangements for sailing in the Ship *Roxanna* for the Mediterranean," William noted in his diary. He had kept his promise to Mary Ann. She was going with him — along with his doctor. There was quite a party to see them off: the Nathan Appletons, Mary Ann's mother, two of her sisters, a half-brother and his wife. William said his spirits were good and that he was much strengthened by seeing Mary Ann show so much fortitude. She hardly shed a tear.

William's weight was down to "103 lbs." His diary during the voyage was for the most part about his diet — whether "4 Oz. of beef and a small biscuit in the whole day" would be better than milk, figs and a glass of wine, or whether to "have done with wine and milk" and just eat rice and herring.

William had nothing to say about Mary Ann's diet or her state of mind but they had left their little boy with her mother. Assorted aunts, uncles and cousins lived at Mrs. Jonathon Amory's, among them Tom Amory, only three years older than Willie Appleton and very fond of him. Of course there would be letters from home but they would have to follow by sailing-ship. Her little boy could climb the stairs alone — he was cutting teeth. The news her sisters wrote her finally reached Mary Ann. But when, after many months, she was told that the little shirts she sent to the baby were too small, she might have lost her fortitude and cried. He was growing up without her.

William wrote a letter to Maria Appleton, addressing her with unusual informality as "dear Maria Theresa," and calling her "my dear cousin." He was "indulging in the hope that the time will come when we can again, with unparalleled freedom, run in and see our best friends. Oh the happy hours we have passed with you! I must not think of them. I shall become melancholy!"

William saw very little in Sicily that met with his approval. "There appears to be two grades among them, no medium between the prince and the beggar." He looked in vain for the equivalent of the hard-working, self-respecting middle-class Americans with whom he was familiar. "The great folk seem very fond of their ease. Their principal amusements are riding and going to the opera and gambling. In fact, they seem to go to the theatre to gamble, a vice the ladies are said to be very much attached to."

The average day of a Sicilian prince called forth William's scorn. "They repair to the playhouse at nine o'clock, they have supper in their boxes or in adjacent rooms prepared for the purpose, called conversation rooms, where they gamble till two or three when they retire. They rise about ten, take very little breakfast, then ride a short time, dine at two, take a siesta till four and again resort to the Marina where they ride till nearly dark. Thus ends twenty-four hours . . ." William looked over the ladies. They never took any exercise, they were fat, they had bad complexions and "stupid faces."

By the end of March, William and Mary Ann had taken a villa outside Palermo. They had a garden full of fruit and flowers with a view of a mountain he thought "could compare with any part of Monadnock." He liked to watch the goats "jumping from cliff to cliff in search of food" but he always managed to worry about something — this time for fear the goats would fall!

William said he knew nothing would interest his cousin Maria Theresa more than an account of his health. He was better. "I also trust that I am not quite as excitable as when I was in Boston, but this is a subject too mortifying for me to dwell upon" — and he wanted Maria to thank her husband for his kindness.

In his diary, William said that Dr. James, who had sailed with him, gave him "35 drops of Laudanum" to regulate his stomach, along with "oil of cinnamon." He had a severe attack of what could have been gallstones, but recovered although three doctors who had been called in despaired of his life. As soon as he was well enough to go out he "took Mrs. Appleton to see the dead Bishop" whose body was "placed in an easy chair or throne" in a church in Palermo. William counted the number of candles burning, the number of lamps lighted, and the number of musicians playing appropriate music around the corpse. His "spirits were pretty good" he said but he would "leave Palermo with little regret." He thought he had gained more "in ten weeks than at any other time" since he had been sick.

During the rest of his European trip, William Appleton had various attacks of what, in one case, he called "Cholera morbus." But every time he recovered, he found things he could count, such as musicians and candles; costs he could estimate and objects whose value he could set down.

William and Mary Ann came back to Boston in 1818 and their second child, James Amory Appleton, was born on the twenty-ninth of October. Their house on Beacon Street, which they had rented from the Colburns, had been sold. Mary Ann's mother urged them to live with her but they took lodgings. In the autumn of 1819, William bought his cousin Nathan's house, number 54 Beacon Street. They loved it dearly and all but two of Mary Ann's ten children were born there.

News had come to the William Appletons while they were abroad of the birth of Nathan and Maria's fourth child, on October 17, 1817. "Mrs. N. Appleton calls her baby Frances Elizabeth," one of Mary Ann's half-sisters had written her. The Nathan Appleton children never bothered about the fact that the William Appletons were cousins. Mary Ann was always "Aunt William" to them just as, in 1819, there would be an "Aunt Sam" on Beacon Street. Fanny Appleton, although born at number 54, never remembered any home but 39.

William summed up his adventures. "During my absence, I expended some ten Thousand dollars, which sum I made in shipments from Sicily to the United States and in goods from England to Charlestown."

In 1819, William went "into business with Messrs Paige and Chase, which continued six years. I made by that concern about thirty Thousand dollars and carried on considerable business on my own account, my health feeble, yet able to attend to Business."

William also summarized Mary Ann. "My good Wife is happy and deservedly so; she is all that any reasonable man could wish, ever finding friends and so fortunate as to have no enemies. I have been better satisfied with her the last year in troubles and anxieties than in prosperity; she has strong powers of mind not brought into action on common occasions; take her all in all, her husband and friends have cause to be proud of her."

SEVEN

SAMUEL AND AUNT SAM

NATHAN APPLETON was about to set out on a business trip to Pittsfield on New Year's Day, 1819. He had some presents, a box of books, and some Boston newspapers to take to his wife's family. Maria made him wait while she finished a letter to her father.

"Our brother, Samuel, you will perceive, has finally turned Benedict. He wears his chains as gracefully as any man can who is learning a lesson he ought to have learned by heart long ago. The Lady he has chosen appears to be precisely suited to his taste and I have no doubt will make up his long arrears of happiness."

Sam's bride, Mrs. Mary Lekain Gore,[1] was thirty years old. She was a handsome woman with sparkling dark eyes and dark ringlets. Her late husband, John Gore, had been a Boston merchant but he and Mary Lekain had been married in Albany and he died there. He had a first cousin, John Gore, Jr., also a merchant of Boston, and both John and John Jr. were nephews of the spectacular Governor Christopher Gore of Massachusetts who shocked his conservative friends by his high style of living and his coach with liveried out-riders. Mrs. Mary Gore herself had no objection to a bit of style.

Heading his letter, Boston, 26 September 1818, Nathan wrote to Eben about Samuel's plans. "Brother Samuel is about going to house-keeping soon — he has purchased Mr. Cotting's Palace on speculation." [2] Eben, although again in Liverpool, England, had been in Boston recently and knew exactly what Nathan meant. What Samuel had bought, however, was not a palace but "an unfinished free-stone mansion" or the excava-

Mr. and Mrs. Samuel Appleton in their home at 37 Beacon Street. Artist unknown. (Photograph from the collection of the late H. W. L. Dana, Courtesy of the Longfellow House Trustees.)

tion for one on the upper corner of Walnut and Beacon streets where the Cotting palace was to have stood.

Uriah Cotting was a real-estate plunger. His speculations amounted almost to a one-man urban renewal project as he bought whole districts in several areas of Boston, tore down old buildings dating before the Revolution and planned — at least on paper — rows of three- and five-story warehouses.

In 1814, Cotting's "greatest work" according to his contemporaries, was the building of a mill-dam and a road running across the Back Bay marshes at the foot of Beacon Street, across the dam and directly to Brookline with a branch heading for Roxbury. Perpetual tide-mills were expected to produce water-power for lease to the Boston and Roxbury Mill Corporation while the horse-drawn traffic would pay toll to Cotting and his associates. A multi-colored plan of the project was printed. The legislature granted a charter.

Too late, there were warnings in the papers that "the beautiful sheet of water which skirts the Common would become a mud basin, reeking with filth, abhorrent to the smell and disgusting to the eye." When stock in the scheme went on sale, "the street was blocked by the throng of persons eager to make an investment . . ."

Uriah Cotting was rich! In 1816, he bought of Dr. Joy, a lot 248 feet deep on Walnut Street and 75 feet wide on Beacon, for twenty thousand dollars. He was already assessed for unfinished houses on Walnut Street. He had conveyed, at one time or another, 1230 parcels of land on forty-one streets and wharves. He had piled mortgage upon mortgage when he began his mansion. Some say he had proceeded as far as the first story when his debts caught up with him. Others say that he pulled down what he had built to avoid taxes and to re-divide his land, the better to sell it. Uriah Cotting never lived to see the mill-dam project completed. "Important pieces of land were sold for five or ten dollars more than the mortgages on them" when Cotting died "of rapid consumption" in 1819. Samuel Appleton got Cotting's "sightly Beacon Street corner" close to the bottom of the market — whether with or without portions of a free-stone mansion.

There seems to be no photograph of Samuel Appleton's house. At the time of Samuel's death, however, Nathan Appleton ordered a tall wine pitcher to be made of coin silver. On one side it was ornamented with an artist's rendition of Sam's house. It resembled 39 Beacon except that the entrance was much more elaborate. There were columns beside the first-floor windows and flanking the drawing room windows as well.

Pitcher, coin silver, over 13 inches high, with representation of Samuel Appleton's house and a miniature bust of Mr. Appleton. (Courtesy of the Longfellow House Trustees.)

The pitcher itself is astounding. Not an inch is left undecorated. Bunches of grapes in full relief ornament the handle while the lip is an acanthus leaf. And just under the lip is a little silver bust of Sam Appleton in person!

It was said that Mr. Appleton "ever found delight in gratifying each wish of his wife with almost boundless indulgence." He would have liked his memorial wine pitcher that his brother gave to Mary Lekain Appleton.

When, in 1845, Aunt Sam went to Paris to find a cure for her crippled knee, "I wish you to be liberal with yourself," Sam wrote her. "I think you can at least work up to advantage the hundred bales of cotton per *Versailles* and if that is not enough, try your credit, as you will probably never visit Paris again. My motto, you know is 'make hay while the sun shines'."

Sam had had little practice in writing letters except for business reasons. But in 1845, he wrote to Mary as though he were her young lover rather than her husband, married to her for twenty-seven years.

"The nights seem as long to me as are the nights to her whose lover is absent. This is prose, and very prosey it is, of the partial lines, viz,

> *"Long as for him who works for debt, the day,*
> *Long as to her the night, whose love's away*
> *Long as the years go, winter seems to run,*
> *When the brisk minor pants for twenty-one."* [3]

Samuel Appleton said he "never could write a long, sentimental letter, in my best days," but he was doing pretty well.

"I want to hear you talk. I want you to ride with me, this pleasant weather. The country looks charmingly and I want you to enjoy it with me." By this time, the road on top of the mill dam was completed. Young men raced their sleighs over it in winter, passing each other with hardly an inch to spare — upsetting every so often. But in summer Samuel Appleton's barouche was seen among other carriages as they "jogged along at an easy pace."

Unlike his cousin William, Sam had not the least trouble with his digestion. Aunt Sam acquired a gifted cook whose efforts she directed and praised so that masterpieces almost daily emerged from the kitchen. Important dinners were given at frequent intervals for political figures such as Daniel Webster, distinguished foreigners such as Louis Agassiz and stars of the theater like John Howard Payne. Nieces or nephews were often guests.

There was "a delightful dinner at Aunt Sam's as usual," Fanny Appleton wrote, after a theater party to see "the heart-breaking tragedy of 'King John' which however, only gave us a better appetite for Aunt Sam's oyster-tastee, duck and the most fragrant coffee in the most graceful of cups." At the head of the table, sat Uncle Sam "resplendant in a new garnet velvet dressing gown." On Thanksgiving Day there would be roast goose with apple sauce.

Isaac Appleton Jewett, the nephew who most often visited the Samuel Appletons, testified that "never was such coffee, such breakfasts and such dinners as in that famous mansion."

Fanny agreed with her cousin Jewett — as he was always called. But she reminded him that Uncle Sam's mansion "has a protecting genius that overrules all ordinary domestic disasters."

Aunt Sam loved to give parties for children. In 1835, she gave a May Day party with Fanny to help her.[4] "It was the prettiest scene I ever saw," Fanny declared. "The house was adorned with a profusion of flowers and a charming wreathe of multifloras and violets hung suspended between the folding doors." Fanny said she made that wreath herself. "Little Eleanor Gardiner was chosen queen and crowned with flowers" but the boys had had about enough of behaving like "young courtiers." A fight broke out over the choice of a king. It was in "true political spirit," Fanny said, when George Lyman was finally chosen. "Cheering for their majesties was very vehement."

Samuel Appleton had tried previously to retire from business but he had gone abroad again after all and continued his import-export business. At first, he was not interested in American manufacturing. On the list of the first subscribers to the Merrimack Company, "N. Appleton" appeared as owner of 180 shares. A week later, the board of directors agreed to open the list to more subscribers and William Appleton bought 25 shares, Eben Appleton 15. The name of Samuel Appleton was absent, as of December 1, 1821. However, according to the history of New Ipswich, Samuel already had an interest in a mill in his native village.

In 1820, Samuel Appleton and Charles Barrett, Jr., and others were incorporators of the New Ipswich Waterloom Factory. They built a new mill on the site of an old one with a fulling-mill above it that they already owned. The New Ipswich Waterloom Factory went into production in 1821 for the manufacture of sheetings but it was successful "for several years" only.

There were other earlier mills in New Ipswich, and during a brief period of prosperity before rapid, low-cost transportation mattered, the Barrett mansion was built in town. There was French landscape wallpaper above a white painted wainscot just as there was in Thomas Gold's house in Pittsfield and in Aunt Sam's Beacon Street mansion. China and silver, displayed in corner cupboards, were in the most fashionable classic styles. Another similar house was built next door for a son of the family. These houses are still standing in New Ipswich, New Hampshire. Owned by the Society for the Preservation of New England Antiquities, the mansion house is open to visitors. In the wide entrance hall in this older house is a marble bust of Samuel Appleton and there is another like it in the library at Appleton Academy. If painters of portraits are more to be relied on than sculptors, this Akers bust, of which several copies were made, did not resemble Sam.

When Charles Barrett died, the New Ipswich Waterloom Factory was sold at auction to "a company in Boston," not named in the history of New Ipswich. The problem of transporting raw material to the mills and finished products from deep in the country to a good market had been solved, not in New Ipswich but by the Merrimack Company. Samuel must have realized that he would have done better to go into the Merrimack Manufacturing Company whose first move was to buy out the Proprietors of Locks and Canals on the Merrimack whose original purpose had been to make the river navigable to Newburyport. Their Pawtucket Canal had never been developed beyond a narrow waterway around the Pawtucket falls for the passage of rafts of logs and lumber. The canal income "hardly averaged 3½ per cent per annum" which, as Nathan Appleton put it, "made the purchase of the stock an easy matter." New locks and dams were built, the old canal enlarged till the water was "sixty feet wide and eight feet deep, which it was estimated, would furnish fifty mill-powers." A "mill-power" was figured to be equal to about sixty horsepower. A mill would pay the canal company at "a price fixed on, of four dollars a spindle, or $14,336" for enough power to run a textile mill. The new canal with its series of new locks and dams cost "upward of $120,000."

An agreement was made "with the Boston Manufacturing, or Waltham Co." for machinery for two mills. As it was all-important to the Merrimack Company to have the use of the patents of the Waltham Company, and especially to secure the services of Mr. Moody, it was finally agreed to equalize the interest of all the stockholders in both companies, by mutual transfer at rates agreed upon. The Waltham Company was paid $75,000 for all their patterns and patent rights and the release of Mr. Moody from his contract. "The first wheel of the Merrimack Company was set in motion on the first of September, 1823." Samuel Appleton had backed the wrong mill when he built in New Ipswich but later he owned large blocks of stock in the mills along the Merrimack.

As for the Barretts, it was going to take more than just a few years of success to support two handsome mansions and the elegant style of life that went with them. In 1850, the Appleton nieces and nephews were astonished to learn that "Uncle Sam has lately bestowed $20,000 on the heirs of the friend who first advised him to come to Boston." This friend was the elder Charles Barrett — the big man in the little village when Samuel Appleton was a boy.

In 1823, in a private journal, Samuel wrote down a New Year's resolution. "I promise, during the following year, to spend the whole of my income, either in frivolity, amusement, public utility or benevolence." To the New Englander, a law more sacred than any of the Ten Commandments was that, everyone, rich or poor, must "put away something" each year. Luckily Sam Appleton's friends and relations knew nothing, at the time, of his intended spending spree. William, who counted up and gloated over his increased gains each year, would have been horrified.

In 1828, Sam had to back-track a little. Stockholders in the mills were assessed by the directors for a percentage of their holdings to pay for additions and improvements. Samuel promised himself to set aside enough money out of dividends to pay assessments. Aside from that, the plan to spend money remained in force.

It was estimated that Mr. Appleton gave away half of his income every year. Perhaps coming under the head of "public utility" was his donation of ten thousand dollars to Dartmouth College. In presenting his gift in 1843, Samuel Appleton said he hoped that Dartmouth would continue to "dispense simplicity, purity and truth." He compared Dartmouth to an "emporium," dispensing these qualities. Possibly there were those who thought it undignified to compare Dartmouth with a shop selling a variety of goods, but Appleton hated pretentiousness — and no one was disposed to quarrel with the cash. In 1849, Samuel Appleton received an honorary degree of A.M. from Dartmouth.

The New Ipswich Academy became the Appleton Academy as the result of a gift from Samuel Appleton. A new four-story building with Greek pillars and a small, perfectly proportioned cupola was built, and

Appleton money was added to the endowment fund. This building burned but a similar building has replaced it where, in the library, stands the bust of Samuel Appleton, his long side-curls forward of his ears. Under the right light, this white marble bust seems to have a look of private amusement as if Mr. Appleton knew that long hair could become a controversial subject between future students and their elders. The values that he stressed, simplicity, purity and truth, are still highly regarded at Appleton Academy while fashions swing full circle in the course of more than a hundred years.

In 1833, Samuel Appleton agreed to buy fifty shares in the "Western Railroad." That Sam considered this a gift rather than an investment seems strange but all the Appletons wanted a railroad through the Berkshires to Albany on the grounds that it would benefit Boston commerce and the prosperity in general of everyone in town. Many people doubted that a steam engine could be powerful enough to climb the Berkshire hills hauling a train. The railroad project met with so many difficulties that for a while it seemed as if Samuel Appleton were right — he had made a gift. Then — also for a comparatively short time — his gift paid off and he had a profit which could be given away again.

Boston had long been considered a city of intellectuals, but the establishing of a public library was surprisingly slow in coming. In 1847, Mayor Josiah Quincy, Jr., offered fifty thousand dollars for a public library building if ten thousand dollars in gifts could be subscribed. Nothing was done. There were those who said that the public could not be trusted with valuable books. Samuel Appleton thought otherwise and gave a thousand dollars although most of his friends continued to collect their private libraries or to support the Boston Athenaeum where a man could read in peace, all women-folk excluded.

In 1844, Samuel Appleton addressed the managers of the Boston Female Asylum. "Many years ago," he told them, he had been asked to contribute money to this organization. At the time, he had not been able to afford a great deal but he had received a letter of thanks, "couched in such flattering terms that it has left me your debtor." This debt he paid by enclosing a check for a thousand dollars. Needless to say, Miss Abbey L. Wales, in behalf of the managers, wrote an even pleasanter letter.

The Female Asylum was one of the earliest organized charities in Boston. They built "a larger and more comfortable house" for the orphan girls who lived and went to school there. Mr. Appleton sent them another thousand dollars the following year and directed that the money be placed in a "permanent fund, the interest to be expended annually in medals, books, money or anything else the managers might think proper, amongst the most deserving girls . . ." He might have been thinking of his little nieces, happy and protected, showered with pretty gifts on birthdays and Christmas, when he wrote, "A present, given to an orphan girl of eight or ten years, for her good deeds of good behavior . . ." might have a "beneficial influence on her conduct through life." Writing to his wife, Samuel said, "I have sent my letter to Mrs. Wales, Secretary of the Boston Female Asylum so there is another thousand dollars gone, never mind, I have plenty of dollars left."

The work of Charles Francis Barnard in behalf of Boston's street children, early attracted Samuel Appleton's support and sympathy. This young Harvard Divinity School graduate, born in 1808 and ordained a Unitarian minister, decided to devote his life to uncared-for children. In 1832, he "gathered a class of three waifs" in Miss Dorothea Dix's front parlor. From these three the word spread fast, that there was a good place to spend part of Sunday. In winter there was warmth and free food. In summer there were country excursions, and the children had no objection to learning to sing hymns and listen to Bible stories. Charles Barnard had a talent for working with children and by 1836 there were 730 waifs who went to the "Warren Street Chapel."

Sitting in pew number two, in King's Chapel, Mr. and Mrs. Samuel Appleton heard about and approved the work of Charles Barnard and they were indignant when the Unitarian Society refused to support the Warren Street Chapel. It was never Samuel Appleton's way to broadcast the amounts of his benevolences so there is no way of knowing how much he gave, over the years, to the Chapel but he could be depended upon. Mr. Barnard organized the children's Fourth of July Floral Parade with Beacon Street on their line of march and a pause at number 37 to give Mr. Appleton a basket of flowers. If they heard he was ill, they came to sing for him. And Aunt Sam could be depended upon to have refreshments passed around.

Aunt Sam had her own favorite charity. She worked for the "Widows Aid Society" and the "House of Industry" where women who could not leave home to go into domestic service or work in a small shop, could sell "needlework." They made children's clothes to measure, caps for ladies, like Aunt Sam's beautifully frilly affairs — and night caps for everyone.

Public charity consisted in placing "paupers" in almshouses. As far as possible, families took care of their own less fortunate relatives, and it was the women of leisure who began to organize the first private "Societies." Mrs. Nathan Appleton held a meeting in her parlor, to start the "Widows Society." The Boston Female Asylum was organized at the home of Mrs. Jonathon Mason and one of the by-laws read that only "with the consent of their husbands," could these ladies receive "donations" for the Asylum, and that their husbands must be held "accountable for the money." The paid director had to be a maiden lady.

Of course it devolved upon the Appleton men to look after the women in their own family — if widowed or unmarried. They acted as unofficial trustees, and in 1844, for example, Samuel Appleton instructed his sister Dolly, whose husband, David Everett, had died in 1813. "Your property in my hands is now paying good dividends and interest," he told her, "so you may let your charities and expenses be on the liberal side without encroaching on principal." He sent his sister a check for three hundred dollars of her own money, which Mr. Barrett was to cash for her. "I cannot think of giving much advice to you," Samuel wrote — and then proceeded to advise that in her "givings" she should "remember our relations." But Dolly was to "loan" rather than give "to Mr. Preston who married our grand niece, one hundred dollars to enable him to buy farming tools." Dolly should "take a note for the same, on interest to be paid annually."

As to charities, Dolly knew "ten times as well as I can tell you, the benefits of charity as held out in the Bible," her brother told her. But Samuel rather hoped that the New Ipswich orthodox minister was not going to get too much of a hand-out. There was a bone of contention between both Samuel and Nathan, who were Unitarian and their Ipswich relatives who believed in fore-ordination and infant damnation.

This matter came up in connection with Isaac Appleton Jewett. He was the son of Nathan and Samuel's youngest sister, Emily, who had married Moses Jewett of Burlington, Vermont in 1804. Emily had a little girl, Harriet, who died before she was two and in 1809, her son was born and named for his grandfather. Emily also died in 1809. Moses Jewett went "out West" and settled in Columbus, Ohio, but the problem was what to do with the baby. His grandmother Appleton took care of him as long as she was able, and when his aunt, Dolly Everett came back to New Ipswich from Marietta, Ohio, where her husband had died in 1813, she took charge, especially where Jewett's religion was concerned. When Samuel Appleton married, the New Ipswich Appletons thought they knew what to do with Jewett.

Considerably to everyone's surprise, "I do not think myself a suitable person to take charge of I. A. Jewett," Samuel wrote. "I have not that orthodox piety which my mother and sisters think ought to be implanted in young minds. I am willing to give him a thousand dollars towards a college education, should you and his father think that would benefit him — you may inform his father of this."

This somewhat severe letter was written to Samuel's sister Mary, known to nephews and nieces as "Aunt Barrett." She was by no means a favorite. Whenever she visited Boston she made the children recite the early orthodox catechism and, if they could not do it, she made them learn it. Little Fanny Appleton was particularly terrified of her and even in 1832, she wrote in her diary, "[We] went into Aunt Sam's several nights in succession and were nearly talked to death by Aunt Barrett."

By this time Isaac Appleton Jewett was over twenty-one, a most personable young man and master of his own fate. His father had remarried and his Uncle Sam had for some time regarded Jewett as almost an adopted son. He was just as restless as his uncle had been, had literary aspirations but no very settled occupation. Aunt Sam was sure she could find the right wife for him, and various young ladies were introduced, enjoyed his persiflage and mock-gallantries but got nowhere with him. He was most useful to his Uncle Sam in answering letters, many of which were solicitations for charity. He compiled an Appleton genealogy to please his uncle but would not live at 37 Beacon Street — making visits however, from time to time.

Fanny Appleton summed up the situation in 1848: "Jewett is still at Uncle Sam's, who want to keep him, but he fights shy, not willing to accept any cage, even of golden wires."

The furnishing of number 37 Beacon Street, must have come under the heading of "frivolity and amusement" for Samuel. In 1838, there was "Yankee papering" on the drawing room walls, but the ceiling had "frescoes" according to Fanny Appleton who thought this was "incongruous."

The fashion of marble statues, some life-size and over, some "table size," was in full swing. Uncle Sam was already "going the whole chisle" in 1835, Fanny said. Not only were gods and goddesses standing around hallway and parlor on pedestals, but "Uncle Sam's bust frowns down in Cato-like majesty." This first so-called likeness was by Horatio Greenough.[5] The process of being "busted," as irreverent young people called it, must have amused Uncle Sam for, nearly twenty years later, he had himself again immortalized in marble.

"Mr. Akers, a young sculptor from Maine" had been modeling Longfellow and visiting his somewhat unwilling sitter at the same time. Fanny took Mr. Akers over to see her Uncle Sam, who invited him to one of those lavish dinners. "Mr. Sam Appleton's is a great head for him and which he is quite ambitious to undertake," Fanny reported. Akers got the job. Fanny said she planned to watch and criticize the sculptor's efforts — but she went on a trip. Samuel Appleton must have gotten some of that amusement he planned on.[6]

Also under the heading of frivolity came "Aunt Sam's fountain" which threw "a golden ball in air." Aunt Sam's clothes and jewels were frivolous, amusing and pure pleasure for her husband. She went to a tea given by "Mrs. Otis, the Lady Mayoress" where "she looked very much like a duchess," in a rich garnet-colored dress. In 1837, Aunt Sam, now well over forty, "looked younger, if possible." Her husband gave her a diamond pin, perhaps for her forty-fifth birthday. It was selected for her by nephew Tom Appleton, whose impeccable taste was one of the few things his Uncle Sam approved of without reservation. The diamond was "far the largest and purest stone I have seen in London or Paris" — for £100, Tom wrote. The jeweler was both famous "and trustworthy."

Somewhat to his dismay, Samuel Appleton was elected to the Massachusetts State Legislature from 1828 to 1831 and was "presidential elector" pledged to Daniel Webster in 1836. He was no orator; the legislative duties he would take seriously because of his New England conscience — so the honor would cut into his time for frivolity and amusement. But he believed with all his heart in a protective tariff to help develop American manufacturing. Most of his old friends who were still merchants with ships at sea were on the other side. And this, too, was hard because Samuel was a friendly man, unused to incurring enmity.

Nevertheless, "I, Samuel Appleton give it as my firm opinion and belief that the manufacturers . . . have added to the growth of Boston and the increase of its commerce," he wrote. "I therefore consider it of the utmost consequence to the Merchants of Boston, if they consult their own interest, that they encourage the manufacturers of Massachusetts and New Hampshire.

"Only look at the articles imported for manufacturing purposes." He enumerated "hides, rags, barrells, wool, flour, hemp, dye woods of various kinds, madder, barks and many different kinds of dyestuff. The above-named products are imported from foreign ports and solely for our manufacturers."

Samuel Appleton was right but not even he could foresee how many products his own country could eventually produce.

EIGHT

BUILDING A CITY

WHILE HE WAS GROWING UP in New Ipswich, Nathan Appleton must now and then have dropped a hook and line into the trout brooks that tumbled out of the hills around his father's farm. But farming is a dawn-to-dark occupation, except in winter when the Appleton boys were glad to get time off to go to school. It would have to be Nathan's oldest son Tom who had leisure to become a sportsman and to write home about salmon fishing in Scotland. In 1821, Nathan had no idea that there was fine salmon fishing at the Pawtucket falls on the Merrimack River, scarcely twenty miles from Boston.

Mr. Appleton went on his own kind of fishing expedition, in 1821, however.[1] Demand had outstripped the capacity of the Boston Manufacturing Company, so Patrick T. Jackson and Nathan Appleton hired a horse and chaise and set out to look for a river with a waterfall. They had a letter from a man in Amherst, New Hampshire, who said he knew just the place, and they met him "at a fall of the Souhegan River, a few miles from the Merrimack." One look was all they needed to tell them that the falls were not nearly high enough. On their way home, they passed the Nashua River but nobody said anything about a waterfall "which has since been made the source of so much power by the Nashua Company. We only saw a small grist mill standing near the road, in the meadow, with a dam of some six or seven feet," Nathan wrote.

When Jackson and Appleton got back to Waltham however, they found Paul Moody all excitement. He had been on the same errand and had discovered a place where "the whole power of the Merrimack poured down" in a fall of over thirty feet.

Appleton saw the Pawtucket falls for the first time in November, 1821. "A slight snow covered the ground." Patrick Tracy Jackson, Kirk Boott, Warren Dutton, Paul Moody and John W. Boott were there. These were to be directors of the new mill project. They "perambulated the grounds" around the fall. There was a bridge over the Merrimack, three or four houses, a tavern and a store. This was East Chelmsford. The men looked at each other and somebody said that one of them might live to see the place contain twenty thousand inhabitants.

Jackson felt that his engagement at Waltham would not permit his taking the management of a new company, but that Kirk Boott would like the job. Thomas M. Clark, of Newburyport, agent of the Pawtucket Canal Company, was given the job of buying up the shares of that practically defunct concern. He then turned his attention to buying farm land around the falls for the Merrimack Manufacturing Company. Current prices were paid. A farm of a little over a hundred acres was sold for eighteen hundred dollars, for example, but of course there would be those who felt cheated when the news came out that East Chelmsford was to be a factory site.

Paul Moody made a chalk drawing of the falls area and now the air was filled with excitement as it was clear that the falls could support not one but several factories. Chalk drawings became pen and ink sketches, sketches became a plan for a city.

Before the building of Lowell, no city had been planned on a totally new site, to rise in such a short time — not on a harbor or on a hill that could be defended — but just on a waterfall. Each generation of city planners goes to work with confident hopes of avoiding past mistakes and creating something close to perfection. Nathan Appleton and the others "perambulating" the grounds beside the Merrimack were no exception. Nathan wrote of their hopes and fears.

"The introduction of the cotton manufacture in this country on a large scale was a new idea. What would be its effect on the character of our population was a matter of deep interest. The operatives in the manufacturing cities of Europe were notoriously of the lowest character for intelligence and morals . . ." But Appleton was not worried. "Here was in New England a fund of labor, well educated and virtuous . . ." Profitable employment could bring nothing but good, and he had been feeling anxious for some time because there was "little demand for female labor" now that machine-made textiles had taken the place of

Early view of Lowell, Massachusetts. (N. Phelps Stokes Collection, Prints Division, The New York Public Library, Astor, Lenox and Tilden Foundations.)

Pawtucket falls. (Prints Division, The New York Public Library, Astor, Lenox and Tilden Foundations.)

homespun. He remembered the widows and "female orphans" who had such difficulty finding a means of livelihood. Boarding-houses would be established at company expense. Respectable women would be found to take charge of them and there would be every provision for religious worship in the new city.[2]

In December, 1822, Messrs. Jackson and Boott were appointed a committee to build a suitable church of stone, not to exceed a cost of nine thousand dollars. This was an Episcopal church because Mr. Boott wanted it that way, but the company also gave "liberal grants of land to other places of worship."[3]

Country girls "were readily induced to come into these mills for a temporary period," Appleton wrote. It was not expected that they would stay any longer than to earn enough money to help out the family at home or to use when they married to help establish a home of their own. It was all too idealistic a dream — a sort of industrial Brook Farm — but while it lasted there were encouraging results. The girls banded together to sponsor an adult education program, inviting lecturers to come to speak at the various churches. They edited a paper called the *Operatives Magazine* which later merged with another, called the *Lowell Offering.*

Lucy Larcom, poet, writer and teacher made the *Lowell Offering* famous. Her widowed mother had brought her and her sister to Lowell where they worked in the mills. Lucy used part of her earnings to continue her education, to go west to teach — and eventually to write about the Machine Age in its early days.

The twelve-hour working day was shockingly long and it is a mystery how the *Lowell Offering* could ever have been written, except that Lucy Larcom and others were allowed shorter hours once in a while — with pay cuts to match. But girls who grew up on a farm were accustomed to working long hours, cooking, scrubbing, minding younger brothers and sisters, raking and scraping to make potash. At home, hand spinning and weaving were almost a form of recreation. At the factory, at least at first, these girls found it almost play to walk back and forth tending machines that did spinning and weaving. While some were said to be afraid of the machines, others had their fair share of Yankee ingenuity and mechanical aptitude.

In winter, on the farm, the boys had less work to do but the girls' work was never done. They managed to go to school along with their brothers just the same. Two generations were to come and go; operatives, most of them from Ireland, would take over Lowell before there were mill girls who couldn't read. When that time came, a granddaughter of Nathan Appleton would go to Lowell to teach them. She and some of her friends were early social workers.

From the beginning, the Lowell mill girls and the new city which was being built for them attracted attention from writers on social problems. For a while, comment was most favorable. Captain Basil Hall, formerly of the British navy, came expecting to find little to his liking but in his *Travels in North America in the years 1827 and 1828,* he was full of praise. "On the 12 of October, we made an expedition from Boston to the largest manufacturing establishment in New England, or, I suppose in America, at Lowell on the banks of the Merrimack," he wrote. "This river had been allowed to dash unheeded, until the recent war gave a new direction to industry." Captain Hall had taken part in the War of 1812. He thought that "the spot" which he "now saw covered with huge cotton mills" had been "only a few years ago" inhabited "only by painted savages." Chelmsford villagers might not have entirely liked this! He was taken to see "the hydraulic works" and marveled that "a stream capable of giving motion to forty or fifty cotton mills was brought through the forest to a reservoir, from whence it was distributed at pleasure to the numerous establishments starting up on every hand."

But Captain Hall's mind was mostly on the mill girls. They "work only from daylight to dark, having half an hour to breakfast and as long for dinner," he exclaimed. Overseers were not brutal, there was no dirt and foul air. "The whole discipline, ventilation and other arrangements appeared to be excellent, of which the best proof was the healthy and cheerful look of the girls, all of whom, by the way, were trigged out with much neatness and simplicity and wore high tortoise-shell combs at the back of their heads."

The former naval captain wondered if the Lowell mill girls were really as nice as they looked. "I was glad to learn that the most exemplary purity of conduct existed universally amongst these merry damsels — a class of persons not always, it is said, in some countries, the best patterns of moral excellence," Captain Hall wrote. He spent the night at a local hostelry and next morning at six was "awakened by the bell which tolled the people to their work and on looking from the window saw the whole space between the 'Factories' and the villages speckled over with girls, nicely dressed, and glittering with bright shawls and showy-coloured gowns and gay bonnets, all streaming along to their business with an air of lightness and elasticity of step, implying an obvious desire to get to their work."

In 1842, the Rev. Mr. William Scoresby visited Lowell. Like Captain Hall, this Britisher had also been to sea. He was briefly captain of his father's whaling vessel but was now a clergyman. Mr. Scoresby wrote of his visit under the title, *American Factories and their Female Operatives, with an appeal in behalf of the British Factory Population and suggestions for the improvement of their condition.* Having "deposited my travelling bag at the Merrimack House and ordered dinner . . ." the visitor went over to one of the factories to watch the girls come out. "Several hundreds of young women, but not any children issued from the mills immediately within view." Mr. Scoresby could hardly believe that small children did not work in the Lowell mills. Lucy Larcom had gone there to work when she was eleven years old but all that was changed. Even in 1827, mill owners had built three schools in town.

The reverend gentleman proceeded to describe Lowell mill girls. "Altogether orderly in their manner and very respectable in their appearance," he found them. "They were neatly dressed and clean in their persons, many with their hair nicely arranged and not a few with it flowing in carefully curled ringlets. All wore, (being in the height of summer) a light calico-covered bonnet, a sort of caleche, large enough to screen the face and with a dependent curtain shielding the neck and shoulders. . . . There was not the slightest appearance of boldness or vulgarity; on the contrary, a very becoming propriety and respectability of manner, approaching with some, to genteel." Mr. Scoresby then proceeded to scold British factory girls for going around without bonnets and for "levity of behavior on the streets." He quoted passages from the *Lowell Offering* but humorously remarked, "Really these factory girls are too learned."

As the demand for American-made textiles increased, a larger labor force was needed. Brick dormitories with kitchens and dining rooms were built close to the mills. Matrons continued to watch over the girls as though they were at boarding school. Small wooden cottages sprang up, with a matron, a matron's parlor and incredibly small bedrooms where girls slept, four or five to the bed. Again, this was not very different from life in a country farmhouse. But the demand for labor gave agents an opportunity to go into the hinterland even as far as Canada to bring in girls. They were promised meals and free transportation to Lowell only to be jolted over the roads in a covered van, given nothing to eat and forced later to pay the agent for use of the vans. They often found wages not as represented but they were an intelligent, articulate group. By 1844, Sarah Bagley, a mill girl since 1836, published the *Voice of Industry* — a labor publication. This early labor leader said that the

Lowell Offering was subsidized — because mill owners had helped the girls with expenses. There seems to be no proof that Lucy Larcom and her friends were ever subject to censorship — but times were changing. The *Offering* lost subscribers. The *Voice of Industry* was new.

In 1844 the Lowell Female Labor Reform Association was organized. The girls wanted a ten-hour day and more money. There were walk-outs and stockholders' meetings were called. Nathan Appleton voted to increase wages and cut dividends. When it came to cutting dividends, William Appleton opposed such a measure, of course. Wages were increased however while increased demand for American-made textiles took care of dividends. The ten-hour day was refused.

Eventually, Nathan Appleton was said by some writers, long after his death, to have been a hypocrite, whitewashing evil conditions, hiding exploitation and telling lies. There is no justification for this point of view in any reliable document. Lowell, as he saw it, was to lead the world into a better day of prosperity for people whose lives had been as hard-working as those of his parents, his brothers and sisters. In later life he was grieved to discover how difficult it is to create prosperity for everyone even in such a city as he dreamed that Lowell was to be.

From Nathan Appleton's point of view, the first thing to do was to manufacture more and better cotton cloth. "I was of the opinion," he wrote in his *Introduction of the Power Loom and the Origin of Lowell,* "that the manufacture and printing of calicoes might be successfully introduced in this country. So not only must there be new spinning and weaving machines but a cotton-printing machine must be devised." Francis Cabot Lowell had died on August 10, 1817, at the age of forty-two. His loss was a sad one and now, when further innovations were needed, he would be missed all over again.

In Europe, textiles were no longer printed with wood blocks. Machines carrying several engraved cylinders distributed different colors. "The engraving of these cylinders was a most important part of the process," Appleton explained. Now it was Mr. Boott who went to England on a tour of observation, and he proved able to uncover secrets just as Francis C. Lowell had done. "The art of engraving cylinders was kept a very close mystery and all exportation of machinery prohibited" but plans came back that Moody could work with.[4]

"Dr. Samuel L. Dana was employed as a chemist." This was all Appleton had to say about a most remarkable man.[5] There were to be American manufacturing secrets, too, so that it would be wise not to tell too much. Samuel Luther Dana was a Harvard graduate who had served in the War of 1812 and then returned to take his medical degree. He had a practice in Waltham but began to experiment with chemicals until he had produced a bleach which greatly improved the appearance of sheeting turned out by the Boston Manufacturing Company. He was thirty-one when he gave up his medical practice to manufacture chemicals in a small plant he owned and operated. A trip to Europe to study dyes further advanced his skill so that he was just the man for the Merrimack Print Works.

"Through the superior skill and talent of Messrs. Boott, Prince and Dana, the printing of calicoes at the Company was brought to the highest degree of success," Nathan Appleton wrote proudly. Dr. Dana's success was the result of his discovery that the addition of cow-dung to dye made colors brighter, but that sodium phosphate made from bones could be substituted for the "bulky, undesirable animal excrement." The dye-workers at Lowell must have appreciated this improvement.

Dr. Dana worked for the Merrimack Company for the rest of his life. His ever-inquiring mind led him to wonder about the way the "lead-service pipes" at Lowell were bright inside and dull on the outside. He found that the lead in the pipes was being dissolved "by the action of gases from driven wells." He was still a physician and when he warned that drinking this water would cause lead poisoning, he was ahead of his time and a benefactor to Lowell.

The factories on the Merrimack were still surrounded by farms, and Dr. Dana became interested in farm problems now that cow-dung was no longer a cash crop. He wrote several pamphlets, such as *A Muck Manual for Farmers* which Lowell factory girls could take home to the farm when their year or so in the mills had ended.

The factory buildings were much admired as they rose among the green meadows beside the Merrimack. The machine shop was three stories high with half-height basement windows peering out above ground and a steep slate roof with a bell-cupola to crown the ridge pole. The bell, deep-toned and authoritative, regulated the lives of all within its sound.

In 1824, the village of East Chelmsford became the town of Lowell. Nathan Appleton chose the name. The petition before the Legislature to "set off a part of Chelmsford as a separate township" was ready for a vote, Appleton said, ". . . but it was a matter of some difficulty to fix upon a name. I met Mr. Boott one day who said the question had narrowed down to two, Lowell or Derby. I said to him 'then Lowell by all means,' and Lowell it was."

Nathan Appleton and the calico printing machine, by George Peter Alexander Healy. (Courtesy of the Lowell Public Library, Lowell, Massachusetts.)

Nathan Appleton had his heart set on bringing his brother Eben home from England to take part in the development of Lowell. Samuel had built a house there which he was "fitting up," Aunt Sam wrote, in 1821, "not that he expects to move there but for the sake of employment." He too expected Eben to live in Lowell. Then Eben refused.

"He says he may come in the fall" Aunt Sam wrote, but her private opinion was that "it's very doubtful if he comes at all. You know, his wife is not pleased with the country. Nathan came in with tears in his eyes" to talk over the bad news.

Nathan could not understand how Eben could resist Lowell. A description of the town in 1825 seemed to him no more than just, and not at all too flattering.[6]

"On the banks of the Merrimack are already three superb factories and two immense piles of brick buildings for calico printing. In front of these, on the banks of the factory canal, which is fenced in and ornamented with a row of elms, are situated the houses of the people. They are handsomely and uniformly planted with flower gardens in front and separated by wide avenues. There is a beautiful Gothic stone church opposite the dwelling houses and a parsonage of stone is erecting. There is a post office, fine taverns, one of which is a superb stone edifice of the same material and perhaps two hundred houses all fresh from the hands of the workmen. The ground is intersected with fine roads and good bridges. The whole seems like enchantment." Directors of the Merrimack Company had just appropriated five hundred dollars for a public library, a handsome sum for the period, but building had probably not yet begun.

Eventually, George Peter Alexander Healy would paint Nathan Appleton's full length portrait, standing in front of the calico printing machine. It was a handsome picture of an undeniably good-looking man, his mouth firm but at the same time sensitive, hair still thick and curling over his ears to meet the sideburns above a stand-up collar. The family said it was a wonderful likeness, Appleton said it flattered him — and his children teased him by calling it "The Great Manufacturer." The Lowell Public Library was to receive this portrait.

In his pamphlet, *The Origin of Lowell*, Nathan Appleton wrote of the workers at the mills. "The contrast in the character of our manufacturing population with that of Europe has been the admiration of most intelligent strangers. The effect has been to more than double the wages of that description of labor from what they were before the introduction of this manufacture . . ." He was proud also of the price of cotton yard goods manufactured in America. In 1816 Waltham sheeting sold for 30 cents a yard. In 1819 it went down to 21 cents and by 1826 the price was 13 cents a yard, still with profit for the producer.

It was during this sunny period of early industrial progress that Nathan Appleton decided that he needed a new house. On the two lots he and Daniel P. Parker had bought in 1816, there was a farm house known as the upper Copley house. This was not where John Singleton Copley is assumed to have lived but a tenant house the artist had owned. Appleton and Parker tore it down and in 1818, they were ready to build a pair of town houses to be numbered 39 and 40 Beacon Street.

Thirty-nine Beacon Street was Nathan Appleton's home. For a long time it was attributed to Bulfinch but Alexander Parris was the architect and builder, a young man born in Hebron, Maine, where his father died when he was three years old.[7] As a boy, Parris was apprenticed to a carpenter and builder. During the War of 1812 he was a captain of engineers at Plattsburg and came to Boston when the war ended. Parris was thirty-six when he built the David Sears mansion. The Sears house, part of which is now the Somerset Club, was a good advertisement for the newly arrived architect. In 1819 he built St. Paul's Church on Tremont Street, with its columns and deep portico in severe Classic-Revival style, and that same year he got the job for the Parker and Appleton houses.

French windows such as Nathan saw in New Orleans opened from a small parlor and from the big front parlor on the second floor so that people could step out on an iron balcony which ran all the way across the building. The two drawing-room windows were rather far apart. A description written almost a hundred years after the house was built, speaks of the distinctive curves in each floor plan, the wonderful marble mantels and mahogany doors, unsurpassed in Boston. A beautiful spiral staircase wound its way to a small dome of glass.

In the front entry, the floor was tiled in black and white marble. Overhead here and in some of the rooms the plaster had been molded into classic designs. The vestibule had wallpaper called *Views of Italy*, designed by Dufour of Paris about 1815 and brought from France.

Nathan Appleton had a few words with Richard Walsh, the contractor, concerning plaster.[8] "In September, 1819, we made a contract with you to do the plastering and stucco work on the house we were then about building on Beacon Street at the following rate, 15 cents per yard for plastering for paper. Twenty cents for plastering for paint, 20 cents a yard for stucco ceilings, 20 cents per foot for plain stucco covering and all other work in stucco or plastering in proportion to this price, we finding the materials.

"The work was completed to our acceptance in the course of the year 1819, previous to which time we had paid you on account, the sum of 3,200 dollars. You have demanded of us a further sum of about $800. We believe that we have already overpaid you about $900, according to the contract." In answer to Walsh's demands for eight hundred dollars more, this letter proposed that Walsh return the nine hundred overpayment. By 1823, the affair was still unsettled.

There were more touches of luxury in Daniel Parker's house than in Nathan Appleton's. Parker's entry floor was laid in marble of several colors, not just black and white. He was more lavish with wallpaper and the banisters for his curving staircase were more heavily carved. On the newel post a small ivory counter was set into the wood. This indicated a paid-up mortgage. Nathan Appleton had no such symbol. When necessary, he mortgaged his house to pay for further investment in Lowell.

On April 8, Maria Theresa wrote to her father beginning with excuses for not letting him hear from her "for the last five months." She explained that "the cause (viz. the arrangement of our new establishment) is diminishing in magnitude every day.

"The spring has opened upon us certainly not in a smiling mood — nevertheless we enjoy it in a greater degree than usual, simply because we are in better health. Our children, with one or two exceptions, have been perfectly well all winter. I have had some ill turns but they have been of a milder nature than formerly and much less frequent." It seemed as if the new house, all bright with new paint and paper, looking out on a new and different part of the Common, was going to be a lucky place.

Maria wrote again in September to tell her father about her life in the new house. The small living-room across from the drawing-rooms on the second floor was a delightful place to entertain callers, while the big rooms and the handsome dining-room provided the opportunity to entertain on a grand scale. Maria Theresa had been "unusually occupied with company for the last three months. Ever since June there has been a constant succession of strangers and we have scarcely a day without some friend to dine or take tea with us — and very frequently I have had occasion to make dinner and evening parties, which always consume much time, both in preparation and in putting affairs in order afterward . . ."

Nathan had been elected to the Massachusetts Legislature in 1815 and 1816. In 1821 he was elected again which perhaps accounts for the "succession of strangers" as well as friends who came to the new house down the hill from the Bulfinch State House. Appleton's special interest was a protective tariff for the Massachusetts manufacturers.

Invitations to 39 Beacon Street were reciprocated and Maria said she had been "more into Society than usual." Then there were the children to keep her busy even though their dearly beloved Margaret never deserted the nursery, taking them all into her loving Irish heart. Tom was now nine years old and reluctantly applying his nose to the grindstone of Latin grammar at the Boston Latin school. Mary was willing enough to study French with a French political refugee who came to the house to teach her the language of diplomacy. Lessons were carefully chaperoned because the daughter of one of Nathan's friends had fallen in love with her Italian teacher. The results were tragic. Exposed as an imposter, the Italian had killed himself in Miss Hinckley's parlor. Nathan Appleton had done what he could to protect the girl, both from her father's wrath and from scandal.

Charles Appleton was now (in 1821) just six years old. Fanny was four. "I am now a little indisposed," Maria wrote her parents. "I had a miscarriage last spring — and being just as far advanced again (say six months) I am threatened with the same accident." Dr. Warren made her stay in bed for two months — but the accident happened again anyway. Maria was determined not to be an invalid if she could help it. She wanted to enjoy her new house, and go to Nahant or to Pittsfield in the summer. Most of all, she wanted to see the newly built city of Lowell she had heard so much about.

In 1824, the Appletons set out for Lowell in a two-horse closed carriage.[9] They went first to New Ipswich, where they picked up Mr. and Mrs. Samuel Batchelder and their little girl, Isabella, just five years old. Years later, Isabella told about it. She had never seen such a handsome carriage before. Tom Appleton, "boylike, rode on the box with the coachman" and willingly got down to get her a drink of water every time they stopped. He was her "first hero," Isabella said. Appleton and Batchelder rode together in the Batchelder's two-wheeled chaise, with the trunk strapped under it. This was so that the two men could talk business. Mr. Batchelder had been running a New Ipswich mill since 1811.

The men drove ahead but stopped and ordered the carriage to stop, so that everybody could see the falls. This was Isabella's first view of "a blue river dashing in white foam over the rocks in the July sunlight." They spent the night at Tyler's Stage Tavern near the Concord River bridge. Later the Stone Tavern was built and considered the height of luxury.

Travelers from Boston to Lowell who had neither a two-horse carriage nor a two-wheeled chaise, took the public stage for Amherst, got off at Billerica and waited for the Billerica-to-Lowell stage to pick them up. By 1825, there was a direct Boston-to-Lowell stage, drawn by six horses, making the run once a day. The trip often took five hours. The Middlesex Canal carried freight only, but it froze over in winter when freight went over the road by ox-cart.

When it became obvious to the mill owners in Lowell that something must be done about transportation, the Boston-to-Lowell railroad was "the first of the Boston railroads to be organized and the first to begin operating," according to Nathan Appleton. He would have liked to claim a first for the nation but "the city lost its railroad lead in 1826 (losing to South Carolina) because of the need to educate the public."

A contribution to the *Boston Courier*, commenting on the larger project of the Boston and Albany railroad in 1827, declared that "every person of common sense knows that it would be as useless as a railroad to the moon."

In 1829, the Massachusetts Legislature appointed a committee to study the practicability and expense of a Boston-to-Lowell railroad and came up with a dismal report. When the organizers were finally allowed to proceed, there were few takers of the original shares of stock, offered at five hundred dollars. William Appleton, however, bought fifty shares and the Locks and Canals Company offered the railroad a bonus of $100,000 when the work should be completed.

Rails were imported from England and laid over stone sleepers which were supported on parallel masonry walls sunk in the roadbed. It was some years later before anyone noticed that British rails, fastened to wooden ties, laid over ballast, gave a much smoother ride.

A steam engine was imported from the Stevenson works at Newcastle-on-Tyne, along with a British engineer to run it. The Lowell Machine Shops, having built every sort of textile machine, copied the railroad locomotive, probably with improvements. Of course the machine shop needed the right man for this job, and Nathan Appleton excelled in finding people. George Washington Whistler was a perfect choice.[10] A West Point graduate, he had been assigned by the government to help locate and build the Baltimore and Ohio. He resigned from the army to become engineer for the Proprietors of Locks and Canals at Lowell. A little over thirty at the time, he had resigned with the rank of first lieutenant, but around Boston and Lowell they always called him Major Whistler.

When the American locomotive was finished the British engineer was told to run it. He claimed it wouldn't work and then very suddenly found himself out of a job. Major Whistler was famous for his short temper. An American engineer was hired and "after that, Lowell locomotives did as well as the English," according to Charles Francis Adams who wrote about it for *The Memorial History of Boston*.

Locomotives had names, the way ships did, so it was decided to name the new engine the *Patrick Tracy Jackson* in honor of the fact that he was an original subscriber to the railroad with 124 shares. At the Merrimack Company there was an artist employed to design prints. Perhaps he had the job of painting the name in gold on the locomotive — but it was too long. *Patrick* was as far as he got and the engine would be affectionately known as the *Pat*, anyway.

Nathan Appleton would have liked to claim exclusive credit for the calico printing machine at Lowell as well as for the railroad but he was too careful a narrator not to present the entire picture. "The business of printing calicoes was wholly new in the country. It is true that after it was known that this concern was going into operation for that purpose, two other companies were got up — one at Dover, New Hampshire, the other at Taunton, Massachusetts, in both of which goods were probably printed before they were at the Merrimack Company." But printing to any degree of perfection took time, Mr. Appleton explained. He was clearly of the opinion that neither Dover nor Taunton mills could approach the perfection of Merrimack.

Eben Appleton and his family came to Lowell, after all. Eben's youngest daughter, Caroline, was a great friend of her cousin Fanny's and told what it was like in 1835 in Lowell, while the railroad was being built to carry printed calico to Boston.[11]

"This surprising railroad!" she exclaimed. "The word is on every tongue and a sight for every eye, an excuse for every idler! The front of our house looks more like a fair than the entrance of a quiet residence like ours. Such a procession of stages, carriages, carts and vehicles of all descriptions! With little trouble, we could walk over their heads. I often contemplate this concourse in nervous fidgets." Caroline was expecting every day to see some children belonging to the Irish workmen crushed in the traffic because "nothing frightens them. They are now under the horses' feet, now on the track and now sitting on top of the steamers."

After weathering a severe depression, there were new mills; the

Appleton Company and the Lowell Company formed in 1828, the Suffolk, Tremont and Lawrence companies in 1830, the Boott Company in
1835, with the Massachusetts Company to follow in 1839. The planned
town became the city of Lowell in 1836 but before that it was famous
as a showplace.

Andrew Jackson visited Lowell in 1833. His chief impression of the
famous mills seems to have been that two thousand five hundred mill

*Mill girls at work on looms in Lowell, from a bank note
vignette. (Courtesy of the New York Public Library.)*

girls, marching two abreast in his honor, formed a parade two miles long.
They had on white dresses, blue sashes and carried parasols. Jackson's
pronouncement was said to have been "Very pretty women, by the
Eternal!"

When Charles Dickens visited Lowell in 1842, his impressions were
varied.[12] It was a large, populous, thriving place. "Those indications of
its youth which first attract the eye, give it a quaintness and oddity of
character which, to a visitor from an old country, is amusing enough."
Dickens took exception to the mud in the streets which he said was
almost knee-deep. Everything built of wood seemed to him flimsy but
he approved of brick. "The very river, that moves the machinery in the
mills (for they are all worked by water power) seems to acquire a new

character from the fresh buildings of bright red brick and painted wood among which it takes its course; and to be as light-headed, thoughtless and brisk a young river, in its murmurings and tumblings, as one would desire to see."

Dickens defended the mill girls against the British point of view concerning factory workers in England. "These girls . . . were all well dressed; and that phrase necessarily includes extreme cleanliness. They had serviceable bonnets, good warm cloaks and shawls: and were not above clogs and pattens. Moreover, there were places in the mills in which they could deposit these things without injury; and there were conveniences for washing. They were healthy in appearance, many of them remarkably so, and had the manners and deportment of young women . . . not of degraded brutes of burden . . .

"The rooms in which they worked were as well ordered as themselves. In the windows of some, there were green plants which were trained to shade the glass . . ." Dickens also visited boarding-houses where mill girls lived and he marveled over the care with which boarding-house keepers were chosen. Their character was closely looked into.

The fact that the girls were depositors in the Lowell Savings Bank astonished Mr. Dickens. As to the *Lowell Offering* written by the mill girls — he declared that it would "compare advantageously with a great many English annuals." There were pianos in the boarding-houses and many of the girls knew how to play them.

Dickens knew about Jackson's visit, only the way he heard it, there had been three miles of girls instead of two. He knew that the girls had been "all dressed out with parasols and silk stockings."

Anticipating comments from some readers, " 'How very preposterous! . . .' " for girls of their station in life, Dickens wrote that he "would beg to ask what their station is? . . . It is their station to work and they *do* work. They labour in these mills twelve hours a day, which is unquestionably work and pretty tight work too." But "for myself, I know of no station, in which the occupation of today is cheerfully done and the occupation of tomorrow cheerfully looked to . . ." that is not "humanizing and laudable."

Mr. Dickens had no kind word to say for the Boston and Lowell railroad, however. "The cars are like shabby omnibuses but larger: holding thirty, forty, fifty people. The seats, instead of stretching end to end, are placed cross-wise." This, of course was not the proper British arrangement. "In the centre of the carriage is usually a stove fed with charcoal or anthracite coal, which is for the most part red hot . . ." The train stopped at lonely way-stations where Dickens could see no reason for anyone wanting to get off. Then it roared "like a mad dragon" through the main street of some populous town, waking the echoes, scaring the horses and dashing on "pell-mell, neck-or-nothing, down the middle of the road."

The builders of Lowell had all seen factory conditions in Great Britain and they were gratified by Mr. Dickens' comments and proud of their city. They all believed that a big city was as much better than a small one in the same degree that a railroad is better than a canal. Eben Appleton's daughter expressed the optimism of the period. She didn't mind the crowds in front of her house. "It is delightful for me!" she exclaimed. "Something new at last!"

NINE

GROWING UP ON BEACON HILL

THERE WOULD EVENTUALLY BE TEN CHILDREN at William Appleton's house. The Samuel Appletons were childless. The Nathan Appletons had eight children in two installments. Not a Beacon Hill Appleton of the first generation had gone to college but the boys of the second generation knew that Harvard awaited them.

Maria and Nathan's oldest four were the first to encounter the doubtful joys of education. Tom and Charley went to Mr. Green's Latin School where they took considerably less interest in the language of the Caesars than their father had done. They could not be said to overwork in school but they were among the best skaters on the Frog Pond and their sled, "Nimble Dick," was the fastest on Boston Common.

Among large families of children, death was a frequent visitor. Maria had been so often disappointed by miscarriages that both she and Nathan watched and worried over Tom. When he was twelve he had measles, often a fatal disease, and he was slow to recover. The following summer he was sent to New Ipswich to live with people named Davis and help with the haying. The idea was that he would gain strength by being out-of-doors — and go part-time to New Ipswich Academy.

Master Thomas Gold Appleton did not like the idea and he proved to be an eloquent letter writer. "After breakfast, which was simple . . . I mowed a little with my host, Sam and another, but very poorly." Swinging a scythe wasn't as easy as it looked, but Tom developed an appetite. Dinner was also "simple." In the afternoon they got in "an exceeding large load of hay" and Tom, who was riding on top, "struck

very nearly the beam" over the barn door. He "rested awhile" and supper
was "simple."

Tom's aunt, Mrs. Barrett, knew it was her duty to keep an eye on
him. She "mentioned my going to Bible class on Wednesday at the
Academy, where I don't want to go," Tom told his father. A few days
later, "I went to that den of tyranny, a school. . . . I recited a lesson
in Sallust and was pretty well worn out before I came home."

Tom now put his really excellent mind on the problem of how to get
away from New Ipswich. "The last two days were exceeding hot. I
understand a man in Pepperell died a-mowing and three in Chelmsford
last week." Since his parents worried about his health, this ought to
do the trick.

But Nathan Appleton was not afraid his son would die a-mowing. He
merely commented unfavorably on Tom's spelling. "As to spelling, I
never was an extraordinary caracter [sic] that way and for a dictionary
there is none in this house," Tom replied. He then proceeded to comment on his father's handwriting. He had not been able to read the
words his father said he had misspelled.

"The way I read your letters are 1st, I see what the sence [sic] is; 2nd,
I find out one or two letters in a word, 3rd, guess at it, and there are
a good many words in your letters I can't make out at all."

Tom has not exaggerated. Nathan Appleton's writing was difficult
at best and frequently indecipherable. He freely admitted this, laid it to
a lack of early instruction and admonished Tom who continued to spell
badly and to campaign to come home.

Trying a new tack, "Mother would be shoked [sic] to see the ants
running all over the cheese and butter, the pies nibbled by rats," Tom
wrote. He left this letter lying around, Mrs. Davis read it and was upset.
Tom said he was sorry he had hurt her feelings. The ants were "mostly
in the sugar," anyway.

In October, 1825, T. G. Appleton, aged thirteen, went to Round Hill
School in Northampton, Massachusetts. This famous school was noted
for two progressive ideas in education. "Gymnastics" were taught and
flogging was never resorted to. Nathan Appleton still remembered the
time when he saw his cousin flogged at school in New Ipswich. He
hoped gymnastics would strengthen Tom. Mr. Appleton already knew
the school directors; Joseph Green Cogswell, whom he termed "the
Mathematician" and George Bancroft, former tutor in Greek at Harvard.

"Old Bancroft," as his students called him, was twenty-five when
he opened Round Hill School with Cogswell who was thirty-nine. After

taking the degrees of Master of Arts and Doctor of Philosophy at the University of Göttingen, Bancroft tutored a while but found college "a sickening and wearisome place." Attempts at the ministry were equally dreary and he was not going to find school-keeping easy.

Cogswell, after graduating from Harvard, sailed as a super-cargo out of Ipswich. He found life on shipboard monotonous so took up the law which was worse. Becoming a merchant, adventures with brigands ashore and pirates at sea provided too much excitement, so he became a student at Göttingen where he met "little Bancroft."

Many brilliant men were to look back upon Round Hill School as a high point in their youth. John Murray Forbes,[1] just a year younger than Tom Appleton, described school grounds that "covered perhaps a hundred acres, with fine woodland and views of the Connecticut Valley, Mt. Tom and Mt. Holyoke." No student ever forgot "Croneytown." Forbes described it. Tom was there when it perished. "In parties of twos and threes, we burrowed into the hillside, made a low chimney and front door looking south, with height enough to stand erect and a real lock and key. Here many rabbits and an occasional partridge, the product of our traps or our bows and arrows, were cooked and many an ear of sweet corn roasted, especially on Saturday afternoons." Young John Murray Forbes freely admitted that he was one of the best archers among the hundred and fifty boys but that T. G. Appleton was a sucessful competitor.

"I have great need of a box of tools, especially a hatchet, a saw, a spade and trowel," Tom wrote his father almost immediately upon his arrival at Round Hill.

The disaster to Croneytown can be linked directly with the fact that the boys at the school were hungry! They had feasts at Thanksgiving and Christmas when they were given wine. One of them drank too much. On one occasion Mr. Cogswell shot three deer and everyone feasted. But between feasts, meals were as simple as in New Ipswich. Day after day there would be no meat and no second helpings.

More important still, hunger was used as a punishment! Tom described the system. "We have two bells to call us at meals and if we are not in our place at the time the procession moves, we lose that meal; we also lose our meals if we are not at prayers, either in the morning or evening." On Tom's schedule of a day's proceedings, fifteen minutes was the length of time allotted for each meal. Transgressors were sentenced to stand at a side-table during meals where they got only enough food "to support life," according to Tom.

Early photograph of the Nathan Appleton house at 39 Beacon Street, entrance at the right. (Courtesy of Holman's Print Shop, Boston.)

An example of Nathan Appleton's handwriting.

(partial translation)

Boston, Friday Oct. 3 43

Dear Fanny
    I enclose you the letter by the steamer—as I had **none**—I opened Thom's   What a horrid hand he writes—. It is I think a sad mistake to consider illegibility fashionable. I am sorry to perceive that your beautiful plain hand is somewhat degenerating . . .

(Courtesy of the Longfellow House Trustees.)

Sam Ward, son of the New York banker and Julia Ward Howe's brother, was a classmate of Tom Appleton's. Omitting any mention of his own sins, Tom told what happened to Sam Ward, who "talked back in Latin class" and was sent to his room without any dinner. Sam demurred, was told to hold his tongue — which he did not do. Worse

View of Round Hill School, Northampton, Massachusetts, probably by Francis Graeter, 1826. (Courtesy of the Forbes Library, Northampton, Massachusetts.)

still, he tried to slip in to dinner anyway, was caught, ejected and his punishment increased to no dinner for a week.

Out at Croneytown there was food! About the middle of January, 1826, Mr. Cogswell observed that boys were absent from meals even when they were not being punished. According to Tom, Cogswell "soon suspected something and at last discovered the whole affair by his cunning and sagacity. One unpleasant and moist evening, Cogswell told the boys not to go down to Croneytown although it was Saturday. Some few, not understanding . . . went down there. He, although one would

think he would be detained by more important business and the un-
pleasantness of the weather . . . went, and surprised them all in their
holes. In one of the houses, they were enjoying themselves on a pudding of their own make, little expecting such a visit. Hearing his knock,
thinking he was a boy, they opened the door. How greatly they and
he were astonished and how soon the pudding went under the bench,"
Tom left his father to imagine.

It had been forbidden to buy "sausages, flour, potatoes, apples etc.
from the people of the neighborhood." Rabbits and partridges were
snared or shot out of bounds for the most part. Berry-picking, if done
out of bounds, was forbidden, as Tom later discovered to his sorrow.

"Saturday evening presented a dismal sight," Tom wrote his father
on January 15, 1827. "About 30 houses utterly destroyed from the face
of the earth and their inmates sent forth to mourn the loss of their
property. The destroyer came and that which was before a flourishing
village, rapidly increasing in houses and inhabitants, was soon reduced
to nothing but a heap of ruins. . . . The axe and club first demolished
the houses and then fire was applied to consign them forever to ob-
livion . . ."

Comment from Tom's father was predictable. "I regret the destruction
of Croney Village because I had a curiosity to see it but if, like Sodom,
it worked iniquity — destruction ought to follow." Tom never said
whose pudding went under the bench but his account of the affair had
a ring of eye-witness reporting that his father tactfully overlooked.

Most of Maria Theresa's letters to Tom were full of exhortation.[2] He
was to study the scriptures daily — and not to forget to brush his teeth.
News about the younger children was a little more interesting to Tom.
Mary was "pursuing her various studies with her usual closeness of
application. Fanny is the same gay, thoughtless creature, without a
trouble or a care in the world with the exception that now and then
Charlie gets the largest piece of toast or cake — and then she declares
her grievances in no uncertain terms."

All of Tom's letters home were entertaining. There was the one about
the ride in the light wagon, for instance, when the horses "became
outrageous . . . ran smash against a large elm tree" on the road to
Northampton, "shattering the wagon to pieces. . . . The injured boys
are fast recovering. I believe it was reported in the village that three
were killed and seven badly wounded." Shocking and sad was the
story of the boy who, after being told that both his parents had died,
tried to hang himself but was cut down in time and "had no memory

of it afterwards." Tom's gift to the school housekeeper of a dress pattern of Lowell-printed plaid was typical of him and pleased his father.

Not surprisingly, however, Nathan Appleton wanted to hear something about Tom's studies. "In your next, give us a touch of Algebra and I should like also a bit of philosophy — suppose you let us know why it is our duty to be virtuous . . ." Tom said he didn't know how to introduce either subject in a letter.

Tom Appleton was fourteen on March 31, 1826. In August, his father dropped a bombshell. "What do you think of entering college next commencement? In the first place, are you prepared in your studies — in the second, had you better remain where you are another year?"

Tom was certainly not prepared but he was not going to say so. He opened a campaign to stay at Round Hill. "You asked my opinion about Charles's coming here," he began. "I think on the whole, it would be a very good thing for him, as here he can have good exercise, study in abundance, many little boys to play with etc.

"One great disadvantage and the only one that I can think of that small boys have here, is that most of them have no brothers to help them when they get into difficulty and there are many occasions when a small boy needs the advice of an older brother." Charles would be eleven in October.

Tom won his argument, George Bancroft was pleased because he was going to have two Appleton boys and wrote Tom's father that all was well with Tom's "condition and prospects" but the young man was going to have to go back to Greek.[3] "I always regretted his abandoning Greek. His taste is strong for letters and I was afraid for him that he would be so much pleased with the outer courts of letters that he might linger among them rather than penetrate the inner recesses. His mind is more fitted for literature than business and I was afraid for a season that poetry and drawing and polite studies would take him from the severer pursuits . . ." Tom was going to get Greek and more Greek.

Nathan Appleton received a communication from Tom. A boy could be a university student without offering Greek for admission. Mr. Appleton checked. It was true that "according to a late regulation" students could study what they pleased in college classes but they would get no degree. Tom countered. "I can not clearly perceive the advantages attending a degree," he wrote. He had to go back to Greek.

Charles Appleton arrived at Round Hill School in January, 1827. "A boy here learns to be a man and also learns the wickedness of the world. I see a good many bad deeds in the boys and it learns me how bad the world is and I shall know it, when I am a man, coming from here," Charley told his father in his first letter home.

The Appleton boys roomed together, not in the brick house, but in a smaller wooden building recently completed. Tom had asked for a certain room because it had a stove in it. They got the room but not the stove. After all arguments failed Tom asked his father to write to Bancroft — who was angry. Bancroft said, "I need not expect any more from your influence than my own." Tom reported, "His arguments were little more than that I *might* commit evils which had been committed by other boys."

Other boys had probably been caught cooking on their stoves. Tom had sent money to his friend, Robert Apthorpe, to buy food in Boston and send it to him at Round Hill School. The box was confiscated by Cogswell when it arrived which was a major tragedy for Tom and Charley. But they finally got a room with a fireplace, if not a stove.

In May, 1828, Tom wrote cheerfully to his father. "I am dashing away at Homer at the rate of 11 miles an hour, blinding Miss Polly Phemus, sacking cities, falling in love with goddesses with the greatest celerity." He entered Harvard the following September.

Charles was heart-broken to have Tom leave him. "I have been with him all the time at school and I do not know how to get along without him." He described his new quarters, "a small room with a tolerable large quantity of cracks to let Mr. Wind rage in. On the right hand side as you enter there is a fireplace large enough to do honor to a Lilliputian and to nobody else and bricks to serve as andirons. . . . The plaster, being very rotten, has got sundry holes . . . the window for a wonder remains unbroken." There was a closet full of firewood.

Charley was homesick but there never was a happier college undergraduate than Tom. His letters now were to Charles and definitely not intended to be read by his father. "I have not a very laborious time. Reading, studying, visiting, *eating* etc. alternately occupy my time." Tom sent Charley "a meat box" which he hoped "old Joseph won't steal." It was amazing how fast his money went in Cambridge. He had spent a dozen dollars before he knew it and was now broke so he could only send three sheets of chocolate and other guzzlings for Charley's friends.

Charles was doing well in his studies at Round Hill but asked if Tom's examinations had been hard. "The details of the examination which you desire would be quite uninteresting in a letter and there are plenty of more agreeable subjects," Tom told him. He described his room in Cambridge with its fireplace, a table covered with a green cloth, his crimson rocking chair, "divers books, novels, etc. in scholastic confusion," and on the walls, some of his own works of art.

Tom's next letter took up duck-shooting on the Charles River. In another, he told of "a squabble" on muster day in Cambridge when "the soldiers and townsmen" were rather "fly" and the students "grubbed down their valor with nothing but their fists."

"You had better come to college," Tom advised his brother. "It is a fine place and full of fun."

But Charles knew that his father wanted to have a son in business. "I long for the time when I must enter a store, for the thoughts of being under Mother's eye, of passing a pleasant evening at home and lastly of home itself, are very pleasant," Charley told his father. "But I would rather wait till I am fifteen . . ." He was at the head of his Latin class and grateful for permission to go back to Round Hill School for another term in 1830, although he would always be a little homesick.

Appleton girls were not sent away to school. Fanny was ten years old when she announced, "I now go to Miss Peabody's school, and I like her very much, though I have to walk in the cold a great way, as it is in Franklin Place."

Elizabeth Peabody of Salem, with her sister Mary, had come to Boston to make a second attempt to start a private school. Their first school had failed for lack of pupils but this time, with the help of Dr. William Ellery Channing, the famous Unitarian, they had "daily applications" for more scholars than they "could receive."

Miss Peabody, writer, lecturer, Transcendentalist and founder of the kindergarten, with long years of crusades ahead of her, was at this time only twenty-three. Mary, her quiet assistant, was to be, eventually, the wife of the crusading Horace Mann but she was now just twenty-one.

Elizabeth Peabody's ideas of education for girls were even more advanced than those at Round Hill with their gymnastics and no flogging. "If it is best for the minds of boys, a classical education is best also for girls," Miss Peabody declared. "There is no sex in intellect." So ten-year-old Fanny Appleton was expected to take Greek with Miss Peabody who had studied it with Ralph Waldo Emerson.

Unfortunately, Fanny did not realize that, as a mere girl, she was not supposed to be bright enough nor strong enough physically to study the classics. She didn't bother to work very hard at Latin and seems to have skipped Greek altogether. Miss Peabody's ideas took root however. When Fanny was twenty or so, she read Mary Wollstonecraft's *Vindication of the Rights of Women* although the people at the lending library were shocked because she even knew there was such a book. Much to her annoyance, Fanny would one day be called a bluestocking.

In 1827, Miss Lizzie Peabody was not pleased with Fanny's efforts, however, and addressed Mr. Nathan Appleton on the subject. "I feel a great deal of interest in Fanny, indeed — and not the less for her faults. . . . From these considerations, I have thought, Sir, of a plan for her benefit. Will you let her come to me the first four days in the week in the afternoon instead of the morning? I have two scholars in the afternoon, only, and although the time will be a little shorter than at present, she will have more of my personal attention . . .

"I shall give her long lessons, that will occupy the morning hours and I think you will perceive immediate improvement. Her chief difficulty is that she learns her lessons with so much facility that they do not serve the purpose of disciplining her mind or of occupying her time — thus leaving her mind to the invasion of every evil."

Just what kind of mischief Fanny got into, Miss Peabody didn't say. But ten days later Tom got a letter from Fanny. "I suppose you think it rather strange that I have not written you a letter this term; but I have not the time."

Fanny also went to a Miss Mallet's dancing school. She told Tom that Miss Mallet heard he was going to be a poet. "You must not be a poet," Miss Mallet had said, "because if you were you would turn out to be poor . . . poets always turn out poor. Therefore," and this time it was Fanny's own advice, "I think you had better not if this is the case." Miss Peabody would not have approved.

Almost exactly a year later, Fanny addressed her brother Charley at Round Hill School, in a very grown-up manner. "As I have got some leisure, I think I had better improve the time. I am glad you are coming home so soon, as I long to see you. I expect you will be grown a great deal and I hope you will not be so thin as when you were here before. . . . I hope I am not such a romp as you think me. I do not associate with boys and therefore I do not know anything about Edward Motley as I have not seen him . . ."

Edward was Charley's best friend, the younger brother of John Lothrop Motley, now at Round Hill School. The Motleys lived at 7 Walnut Street, just up the hill and around the corner from 39 Beacon. The Appleton boys loved to play-act in the Motley attic, Tom and Lothrop (the future historian) wearing flowing capes, feathered hats and brandishing wooden swords.

Charley had asked how things looked back home. There was no snow and she loved "slay rides" Fanny told him. Number 39 was no different. The outside had been "painted over again with red paint but that is nothing new, as it was red before."

During the summer of 1826, a new drawing master had come to Round Hill. His name was Francis Graeter. He was a German refugee and he got the job because he showed Bancroft a landscape he had painted — of Round Hill School.[4] Tom Appleton disapproved of Graeter because there were no lithographed scenes handed out for pupils to copy. The new teacher said "he shall take us out into the fields and make us copy the first thing we see," Tom complained. He had just described new methods and a new school of art.

Only later did Tom tell what happened next. Graeter took his pupils out to "Licking Water," the brook that ran through Round Hill property. Each boy sat down to sketch, their teacher, with his own sketch book, out of sight. It was hot. Tom pulled off his clothes and took a swim.

Somehow, he managed to get dressed again just before Graeter appeared and asked to see Tom's drawing. Tom had hastily turned to a drawing he had made under the previous teacher. It was a palm tree out of a familiar copy book.

Graeter's expression was of polite interest. He asked Tom to show him which tree he had drawn, and they set out through the woods. Long later, Tom remembered that he figured he could tire out the new teacher. But Francis Graeter had the long stride of a mountaineer, so on and on they went. It was Tom who got tired. "Well, I guess that tree was somewhere farther South," Tom said at last. Graeter solemnly agreed and they turned back toward the school.[5]

The following year, Francis Graeter went to Boston to try to sell some of his landscapes, and Miss Peabody gave him a job, teaching in her school. Fanny Appleton learned to draw very well indeed — as her sketch books proved when she drew castle walls, cottages, bridges, and roads in Switzerland. She took lessons from other teachers, so Graeter should not be given all the credit, if certain rather primitive landscapes are his.

Mary was actually the student in the family. She was the best French scholar in her class. When Tom, to his dismay, failed to make the first group in French at Round Hill, his father said that it was because he had let Mary help him too much while he was in school at home. In

1826, Mary was "studying the Socratic dialogues" and keeping Fanny "pretty tight to her studies." But Fanny, according to her father, was "pretty much the same sort of rogue."

Miss Peabody's school was so successful that she took Mr. William Russell as a partner.[6] He was an elocution teacher, down on his luck, whose elegant manner and high-minded conversation at Dr. Channing's deceived everyone. Mary Appleton took elocution lessons of him. Lizzie Peabody had him keep the books and invited him to use tuition money "for his needs." His needs absorbed most of the funds before Miss Peabody even thought of checking up on him and he departed. Elizabeth and Mary Peabody had to close their school.

The Appleton girls and many of their friends then went to George Barrell Emerson's school. Begun in 1823, it lasted until 1855 and was largely responsible for two generations of highly intellectual Boston women. Mr. Emerson was a pioneer, lecturing on "The Education of Females," and helping to organize the "Boston Mechanic's Institute" for instruction in the sciences. He worked with Horace Mann in behalf of Normal Schools.

A French exercise book of Fanny Appleton's[7] was labeled "Chez Monsieur Emerson, 11 Chestnut Street." At the top of one of the pages was the notation, "39 mistakes." There were extenuating circumstances. The entire passage had to be written in the historic past — an almost obsolete tense with many pitfalls.

Maria and Nathan Appleton's third son was born October 1, 1826. They named him George William. His older brothers and sisters were as delighted with him as with a new toy, their father said. He was strong and healthy and letters were full of his prowess, but he lived only until the following twenty-fifth of May. Maria believed that God had chosen little George William to come to Him, unspotted from the sins of the world. Still, it was hard not to remember how they had all loved and enjoyed the child. Mary began to keep house for her mother who was not well.

The girls went out to see Tom's room in the off-campus house where he lived. "His room was in great confusion and when Mary asked to fix it, he told her it was useless as it would be just as bad next minute," Fanny wrote to Charley. It was Charles who "had habits of neatness," along with Mary. Fanny would one day be an absent-minded housekeeper and feel guilty about it while Tom blissfully enjoyed the clutter.

Charles wrote to his mother from Round Hill School in July, 1829. The girls were away, he did not say where. "I suppose you are now the only tenant of our once noisy and thickly settled house and if the letter of an affectionate son can chase away the solitude of the house for a little time and give you some pleasure, it shall be done. To be sure, roguish Fanny and sapient Mary are sometimes troublesome to you, likewise myself when I am rarely at home, yet remember Mother, that we are children and children will always plague their parents . . . therefore this is my excuse for acting foolishly.

"I think that a good journey every summer will do you considerable good, more so than all the medicines you take, because they alleviate the body for a time but at last weaken it . . ."

Maria took journeys in summer whenever she could but she could not follow the remarkably wise advice of her thirteen-year-old son Charles concerning medicine. Nevertheless, she was at a grand ball in 1830, "looking quite splendid and very handsome besides" in a new dress. It was her first appearance in company for quite a while.

All this was in a letter Mary wrote to Tom, telling about a party that she went to at the Sears's house. Tom was supposed to be there but failed to turn up. "We could only think of two reasons for your not coming; one that *as usual* you had forgotten all about this most important affair, and the other that you had been suspended as Mother thought you would be." Mary was tempted not to go herself but "Monsieur Gilbert, the friseur" had come to the house to curl and dress her hair and she didn't want "his labors expended in vain."

Tom was "not to be amazed at my minute details of my *first ball*," Mary went on. "We entered the ballroom at ½ past nine and I was for a moment perfectly enchanted with the gay scene that looked to me like fairy land. Mrs. Sears and Miss Anna looked very beautiful among all the other handsome ladies. I only had a short time to gaze around before I began to dance . . . and thence forward had full employment to the end of the evening without ever getting into the supper room."

Mary got tired of being asked whether she was going to Washington or not. On November 1, 1830, Nathan Appleton had been elected to Congress. "Oh how you would have laughed to see — or rather, hear, the speeches and congratulations. I believe the people thought we were all coming out to receive the felicitations on Father's election . . ."

Charles had written to his father from Round Hill, the previous June. "I have begun bookkeeping again this term on a new plan which is said to be the best going. This is my last term and I hope I shall improve, at least I shall try. Business, I suppose, is gradually becoming better and will be in a very flourishing state when I enter the store." When

Congressman Nathan Appleton left for Washington in 1831, Charley reported regularly. Domestic cottons were declining fast; a big order came in from New Orleans — but by January, 1832, "Business is dull as usual, not a vessel for three weeks to Philadelphia."

During the spring of 1832, Tom escorted his sisters and Aunt Sam to Washington. "Mary as manager" planned it all, "I am to be pilot, groom, overseer of luggage, beau and head-waiter — as occasion may arise," Tom said. The idea had been that their mother would take this trip with the whole family so that they could all visit Congressman Nathan Appleton in Washington. But as the time for departure approached, Maria Theresa was not strong enough to take the journey so Charley stayed at home to look after his mother. Aunt Sam chaperoned the girls.

The travelers were in Baltimore on their way home, on May 17, 1832. Tom wrote his father, setting down on paper what was one of his most outrageous and most often-quoted puns! "Soft shell crabs are here in all their glory and we have them for dinner regularly. No wonder Crabbe was a poet; every crab is full of poetry."

TEN

CONGRESSMAN NATHAN APPLETON

NATHAN APPLETON was elected to the Massachusetts General Court in 1815, 1816, 1821, 1824, and 1827. His was a familiar figure as he climbed Beacon Hill, first from number 54 and then from number 39, to the new State House, during sessions. He said that the first speech he ever made in public was against a tax on insurance companies. Both he and his cousin William were doing well, investing in this growing business.

At first a Federalist, Mr. Appleton observed by 1827 that "party spirit ran very low." He was amused to see former political opponents "harmonizing" at the Exchange Coffee House. Their harmony was promoted by a new political party "not friendly to Northern Interest," soon to become the alarmingly successful Jacksonian Democrats. Mr. Appleton made a speech "approving the protective system" which he said was "anything but an ultra one" and in 1830 he was asked to be a candidate for Congress to work on a protective tariff.

It was a "close contest" between Nathan Appleton and Henry Lee of Beverly, the merchants' candidate. Henry Lee was the brother-in-law of Patrick Tracy Jackson, one of the prime movers, essential to the success of the Lowell mills. He had been on a voyage to Calcutta when the War of 1812 broke out and he lived in India for several years. As a Boston merchant, he had not that sixth sense in business which enabled the Appletons to profit under adverse circumstances so he failed in business several times.

Lee's backers had not expected him to fail in politics. When Nathan Appleton won the election to Congress, the excessive surprise of some of the people at the Sears' party was what especially annoyed Mary Appleton.

"I took my seat in the twenty-second Congress, December, 1831," Mr. Appleton wrote, but he left home before Thanksgiving. He was fifty-two but felt himself alone and homesick like a schoolboy in Washington. Repeatedly, he begged his family to write to him and they did — seated around the table in their old schoolroom, now called the green parlor and passing the pen and paper from hand to hand. Maria wrote less frequently, being all too often in bed, wracked by what she called her influenza cough.

Tom had been "admonished for excessive absence from prayers, recitations and Sabbath exercises" at Harvard. He had been a member of the Knights of the Square Table which joined forces with the Porcellian, fellow members in this famous club being Lothrop Motley and Wendell Phillips. To his mother's surprise and his father's great relief, Tom graduated from Harvard in 1831.

Although officially studying law in Cambridge, Tom had a better time at home along with his brother and sisters. In his first letter to his father in Washington: "We are . . . well off for fun and comfort as ever, bating your loss, of which we are hourly reminded by some inadvertant recurrence to your returns from business by one of us. Alas! Ye keyhole now awaits in vain for ye tinkle of ye wonted key! Ye capacious armchair now remains unfilled. And ye blooming turkey weeps through her oysters for ye skillful weapon of its departed carver." Tom was nineteen.

Charles was now living at home and going to the counting-room as a clerk. He was so lonely for his father that he wrote of a dream he had. Coming home from work, "wearied and fatigued," Charley dreamed he saw his father in the parlor wearing the "well-known brown coat and clay-colored pantaloons, shirt collar (or as Mother insists upon calling it, 'Dickey') over your ear. I rushed forward to embrace, crying 'Oh, Pater noster!'" Then Charley looked up to see his father's "beloved face, and nothing was to be seen but the well-rubbed mahogany arm chair."

Charles was sixteen and the one who wrote the most about his mother. On December 15, "She does not cough nearly as much as she did but we do not intend to let her leave her room until she is perfectly well." He kept his mother supplied with novels to read. On December 30, "Dear Ma came downstairs, yesterday," Charley wrote. "She is already looking out for lamplighters."

The lamplighters would be along on New Year's Day for their annual

Thomas Gold Appleton, in academic robes, painted in Rome by Robert Scott Lauder, circa *1834. (Courtesy of the Longfellow House Trustees.)*

hand-out. So would the chimney sweeps, their efforts required by city ordinance, their pay gratuities from householders. Then there was the "Watch" whose hourly "All's well" Bostonians had always hoped to hear echoing through the dark streets ever since Colonial times. It was a man's task to pay these people, so Maria worried about doing it herself and giving everyone the right amount. She sent Charley to the office — or the "store" as they called it, to get her some cash because, of course, she hadn't any.

Everything was charged and bills rendered annually. Maria was angry with Murdock, the provision merchant because his bill was $180, which she said was outrageous. Maria wrote to him to send her monthly accounts hereafter, so she could "examine them."

"Mother has offended Mary, the cook," Charley wrote. She ordered "some clipping and we dine sometimes like anchorites.

"Business is dull, as usual. Not a vessel for three weeks from Philadelphia." But yardage from Appleton mills brought good prices.

"I know you will have to rub your spectacles with your kerchief before you finish," Charley said at the end of his letter. He thought there must be "cotton wool" in the ink he was using. "I imagine I see you inquiring where they are and on examination finding them on your nose. Do you send your servant after them — left in the House of Representatives?"

"This is Thanksgiving Day and I have no letter from home," Nathan Appleton told his family. He was at Gadsby's, a famous hostelry for members of Congress where, to quote his children when they visited him in the spring, "the pleasures of the table" included "tinned butter" and "soup à la cockroach!" When Webster arrived, he and Appleton each took a front parlor at Gadsby's and had their meals served to them together, first in one and then in the other parlor. At least, it was less lonely.

Mr. Appleton called on President Jackson on the fifteenth of December, 1831. "He had his spitting-box beside him — and the rats were only wanting to make the whole scene conform to caricature." The cartoon Nathan referred to showed rats with the faces of the cabinet members, fleeing from Jackson whose chair was collapsing. Appleton disagreed with Jackson on so many points that he and the President just talked about the weather.

When a newly elected member of a political group, large or small, first appears, he is given as obscure a position as possible. Nathan Appleton was appointed to the Committee for Invalid Pensions. Mr. Appleton was still feeling indignant about it when he wrote his memoirs at least twenty years later.[1] "Considering that I was the representative of a greater commercial interest than any other individual in the House, and withal, a practical merchant, this appointment could be considered in no other light than a spiteful revenge upon the city of Boston for having disappointed the administration in the choice of representative."

The gentleman from Massachusetts had come to Congress to see that some sort of protective tariff bill would be passed over the opposition by Southern states. The delegate from Virginia introduced a resolution to inquire into the minimums recognized in our revenue laws. "A sort of desultory debate, during the morning hours, had gone for several weeks" when it occurred to Mr. Appleton that he might make a short speech. He consulted with Webster, who agreed, got some figures together and watched for his chance.

George McDuffie, representative from South Carolina, made "a most strenuous appeal against further debate" on the subject of minimum tariff on January 21, 1832. "I did not choose to let the opportunity go by," Appleton wrote. "I undertook to show that South Carolina was the author of the system of minimums, which was only another name for specific duties and a system capable of defence." This form of import duty had been introduced by South Carolina in 1816, Mr. Appleton pointed out, and he praised South Carolina for good judgment, until McDuffie, a violent free-trader, could hardly contain his rage.

When the gentleman from Massachusetts spoke of McDuffie's "strenuous appeal" he was putting it mildly. A *Portland Daily Advertiser* reporter had a little fun describing the McDuffie style.[2] "Sir, (a thump on the desk upon a quire of paper, heavy enough to echo over the whole hall) sir, South Carolina is oppressed (a thump). A tyrant majority sucks her life-blood from her (a dreadful thump) yes, sir (a pause) yes, sir, a tyrant (thump) majority unappeased (arms aloft) unappeasable (horrid scream) has persecuted and persecutes us (a stamp on the floor)."

The *Boston Daily Advertiser* described the Nathan Appleton style. "Mr. A is an unassuming gentleman in his manners in debate and the last man who would be guilty of a breach of courtesy . . ."[3] McDuffie, however, claimed that Appleton had insulted him.

According to the *Boston Advertiser and Patriot*, Nathan Appleton had promised "the most full and complete information in relation to the subject of manufactures." He would then "call upon South Carolina to say whether she is prepared to break down or cripple any part of the nation's manufacture which she has done so much to bring into existence and in whose prosperity I believe her so deeply interested . . ."

One accusation was that mills made too much money. Appleton pointed out that only a small proportion of the factories made as much as a twenty percent profit, while "every new ship that touched the water could command a profit of seventy five percent over the cost of building it, which was the work of only a few months."

When McDuffie of South Carolina was ready with his rebuttal, "he chose a place to deliver it, directly by my side and to make it exceedingly personal," Appleton said, but when this speech was finally printed, he was amused to see that the personal remarks had been left out. Thumps and shouts were transcribed into print only by a jeering press while Mr. Appleton's figures cut right through mere oratory.

In letters to his family, Nathan expressed his discouragement. "I am not in a merry mood and here no jokes are found nor a good game of whist." But as soon as his speech was published in Boston, friends began to congratulate him.

"You mentioned that only one person had praised your speech to you at Washington," Tom wrote on January 30, "but let me tell you that I have already received a dozen compliments for you. Everyone was hungry for it and all are full of praise."

Early in 1832, the Cherokee Nation sent deputies to churches all over New England to plead for their rights. Two came to Boston where Tom, taking his father's place as host, presided at a dinner for them at 39 Beacon Street. Fanny explained to her father that the guests of honor were Mr. Ridge and Mr. Boudinot, her mother's cousin.[4] This was Elias Boudinot, born in Georgia among the Cherokees and sent by missionaries to Cornwall, Connecticut, to be educated. He took the name of the school's benefactor and married Harriet Ruggles Gold of Cornwall. At this time, Maria Theresa's cousin-in-law was editor of a weekly newspaper published in Georgia, written both in English and Cherokee. Fanny was more taken with Mr. Ridge, Boudinot's cousin and " a young Cherokee Chief." He was "an extremely interesting youth," she said. At dinner he was "vastly agreeable and sang us several real Indian songs."

The Appletons "made a large party" to go to church to hear the Indians speak. Their plea was to keep their Georgia lands and continue to live there instead of being sent to lands in the West which, as yet, no one else coveted. Fanny told her father about the meeting. "Mr. A.

Everett and Dr. Beecher spoke, but their eloquence was tame after the speeches of our Cherokee friends. . . . Mr. Ridge brought in your name in connection with Webster and Everett in a way which called down thunder."

It was early spring when Tom and the girls began to plan for a visit to their father in Washington. "Mary and I have some gowns buying. Mother is as yet undecided, I believe, whether to go or not," they wrote.

Maria Theresa did not go, for Charley was quite right when he said she had not the strength to attempt the journey. She wrote to her "dear Husband" that she had been feeling better lately, able to come downstairs after another bout of coughing and high fever. Charley had been "devoted and kind." She hoped "the young party" had arrived safely in Washington, referring to Mary, Fanny and Tom with Aunt Sam as the girls' chaperone.

On April 19, the young party had gotten as far as New York. Outside their hotel, all was "rain and mud and inside, yawns and somniferousness." Fanny wrote to Charles about it. Numerous Gold cousins called on the Appleton ladies and Charley would have been amused to see "such divers entrances of servants and mysterious whisperings" until at last Aunt Sam's "bold demands for Champagne were listened to and a bottle was produced."

They had a private sitting room, but while Fanny was writing her letter, "Mary and Aunt S. are going to try a Highland fling, in the lower drawing room." Fanny said that, in spite of the rain, New York "looks very fine and is truly an immense city." It was even better at night, "excessively brilliant with its gas lights." There was a fine view from the window, which she had been trying to sketch but she thought the weather vane on a nearby church steeple had "rusted North East."

At last "when the vane turned round, the clouds vanished," and "carefully wrapped in our Buccleuchs,[5] we plodded the streets and shops to see how fast money could be spent and to see the fine inhabitants of this good city." Mary added a postscript. She was "having a dress or two made here which must be sent on to Philadelphia." There was no mention of Tom but he spoke for himself from Philadelphia — in praise of crabs.

Both girls wrote impressions of Washington to their mother, to Charley, and to friends back home. Mary described her father's angry opponent, McDuffie of South Carolina, as "a thin gentleman, who looks very much like a Methodist preacher, lays down his words with gymnastic emphasis, extremely in the style of Dr. Beecher."

Fanny did not like having to go to the Capitol so much, "a somniferous place father has wished us to visit often and we got well tired of listening to these stupid debates which we took no manner of interest in." She thought "this Houston trial" [6] was "somewhat more attractive than the Tariff and Appropriations bill . . ." although she took care not to tell her father this because she wanted to please him.

Sam Houston, now fifty-nine, was tall and commanding, sometimes dressed in buckskins and always carrying a hickory stick. The future hero of Texas had used this walking stick to beat up Congressman William Stanberry of Ohio, whom he happened to meet about eight o'clock one evening on Pennsylvania Avenue. Congressman Stanberry had claimed — according to Houston, that Houston used undue influence to get a contract to supply the Cherokee Indians with food on a forced march westward. Eventually, Houston was reprimanded for caning, but it was pointed out that he had not pulled a gun.

The fifteen-year-old Fanny Appleton was already interested in Cherokees. But she complained that in Washington nobody ever talked about anything but politics. She would have to "become quite a politician" [7] she was afraid and meanwhile, "We have not been to a single party yet for the wise reason that there have been none."

The girls called at the President's mansion, and Mary, who was an ardent Cotton Whig, felt disloyal when she wrote, "I do not feel very bitter against the poor President, for we paid him a visit the other day and I found him polite enough. He reminds me, somehow or other, of an armadillo, for he had a tattooed look. His hair stands off his face in a most horrent attitude. He had the courtesy to rise" and spit tobacco juice in the fireplace instead of using the spittoon.

By May 11, the deplorable lack of parties had been corrected. Mary and Fanny had a chance to wear their new dresses and to write to their school friends of strange customs. "The most elegant refreshments here, at parties, appear to be cut oranges and torpedo crackers," Mary wrote. The oranges ruined her white gloves but the torpedo crackers "highten much the gaiety." The girls were home again by the end of May.

Charles had had no vacation but in June he went to Lowell with his uncles Sam and Eben and "Uncle William." Uncle Sam pleased Charley immensely by having him take his father's place as a "mill proprietor." Together, they gave "a grand dinner" with wines brought from Boston.

"I think it is not likely you have heard much about the factories for some time," Charley wrote his father. "The Suffolk mills look very well

. . . the Tremont mills are finished all but the machinery which is making and will be put down immediately. The Lawrence foundations are laid."

Charley said that the cholera was constantly talked about. "Chloride of lime is to be smelled everywhere and I should think Satan and his imps were squatting or had been, in all the alleys and recesses, so confoundedly does it smell of brimstone, which lime so much resembles." In the mill towns up the Merrimack, it was "almost ludicrous to see the quantities of filth which alarmed people are pouring into the streets" and covering with chloride of lime.

In all this long letter, written for his father's enjoyment, there was one sad comment Charley could not leave out. "Mother's cough continues and is very distressing. I cannot conceive how she has bourne it so long or how she will, much longer." Charles hoped that his father could return soon "to ease Mother of domestic responsibilities" so she could "get into the country for good." The girls had been in the country at Newton where their mother joined them from time to time.

"On my return from Congress, I found New York a deserted city on account of the Cholera," Nathan Appleton wrote. "On coming into Broadway from the Battery, all was silent as death; not a person to be seen. On reaching Bunker's Hotel, the only person visible was a member of Congress from Connecticut, like myself on his way home."

Mr. Appleton reached Boston late at night on July 18. The family had come in from Newton "to receive him . . . Mother's cough very bad." But it was not until the second of August that he could persuade Maria Theresa to go to Pittsfield where Berkshire air always seemed to help her. Her father had died in 1827. Three of her sisters were also dead, two in childbirth and one of tuberculosis. But her mother was in good health, always happy to have someone to look after. Martha, Maria's oldest sister still lived at "Elmwood" the beautiful house on the Sudbury road. She had become somewhat eccentric, delighting in attending to everyone else's business instead of her own. Tom escorted his mother to Pittsfield but returned in ten days which was as soon as he could politely leave his grandmother and his masterful Aunt Martha.

The young people stayed alone in Boston with their father who took them to Nahant on weekends where the girls walked along the cliffs with "beaux" — as they called every eligible young man. Tom and Charley fished for tautog. The girls spoke regretfully of leaving Newton, Fanny especially missing "a sweet walk with Dr. Lieber" of an evening.

Dr. Francis Lieber,[8] was a thirty-two-year-old German refugee whose tales of adventure were like no others Fanny and Mary had ever heard.

He had fought under Napoleon, and after Waterloo, while continuing his university studies, had been arrested as a subversive character. He enlisted in the cause of Greek liberation but his group was refused food and shelter in Greece and robbed by bandits. Reaching Rome "ragged and penniless," Lieber got a job as tutor to the German ambassador's son. At the age of twenty-three he published his first book, which was on his Greek adventures. By 1829, he had begun his encyclopedia, eventually to be the nucleus for the *Encyclopedia Americana* and he had married Matilda whose father had hired him as her tutor, in England. In 1832 he was in Boston for the second time — having gone back to England to claim his bride. During the winter of 1832, he was Mary Appleton's tutor in German. He would one day write remarkably affectionate letters to her.

Charley Appleton had his own opinion of the brilliant German scholar. "Dr. Lieber is a funny man," Charley said.[9] "We took a long walk, ankle-deep in dust and in fields. He sang several German songs as loud as he could bawl, and made a lot of milk punch which he drank and became rather ridiculous."

On the fifth of September, "Charles, Fanny and I under Father's care, set out for Pittsfield," Mary wrote in a journal she and Fanny were keeping. Three days later, in the afternoon, they arrived "in high glee" and "found Mother looking very well."

Mary and Fanny's combined diary was full of horseback rides, and excursions to Stockbridge and Lebanon Springs where the health resort was nearly empty. The Shaker settlement just beyond they saw, and exclaimed over "such neatness." They visited the round barn and the dairy where the smell of fresh cheese gave them "furious" appetites.

Often, Nathan and Maria Theresa went with their children, "father in the carriage with mother" being a frequent entry in the journal. It was a sort of honeymoon, reminiscent of their first ride together after their wedding in Pittsfield. Maria Theresa was more beautiful than ever, less painfully thin, her cheeks a more natural rose rather than flushed as in Boston. They had been alone together very little since big business claimed Nathan.

Maria Theresa kept no diary. In her letters to her father, she often spoke of a "painful illness" when one of what she called her "accidents" occurred instead of the birth of an expected child. These left her "a prey to melancholy." Her father, although a demanding parent, somewhat jealous of her husband, wrote when she was thirty-eight, "While you suffer and enjoy little, Mr. Appleton is happy and enjoys much. He hardly knows what it is to suffer or experience privation. If you can so manage yourself as to pass 40 years, you will no doubt experience pleasure as much as he does."

Maria was now forty-six and it seemed as though that happy time had come. "You will take on flesh and be robust," her father had prophecied. "Keep along as well as you can and look forward with confidence to the time when you will enjoy uniform health and good spirits." This Maria had tried to do, always telling Nathan that she believed she was better.

After a long and tedious journey, the Appletons arrived safely at 39 Beacon Street, around the first of October. And now the next session of the legislature came nearer. Nathan had a talk with Dr. Warren who said that Maria ought to get through the winter pretty well. A journey south might be the thing later on. Since it was next to impossible to rent a comfortable house in Washington, Charleston was recommended. The doctor promised to keep in touch. Nathan and Maria said goodbye.

The Washington scene was all too familiar when Mr. Appleton returned in December, 1832. Incredible as it seemed, the national debt had been paid off. The powerful Southern bloc endorsed the theory that import duties would bring too much revenue to a government already rich in public lands, for sale in the West. Mr. Appleton had a new opponent, Richard Henry Wilde, Congressman from Georgia.[10]

Mr. Wilde, born in Dublin, Ireland, was an almost entirely self-taught lawyer from Augusta, where his widowed mother kept store. He became attorney general for Georgia and served five terms in Congress. Upon retirement, he became a noted student of Dante and in 1832–33, when he encountered Nathan Appleton, there was a dark secret in his life. He wrote poetry! He was soon forced to admit that he wrote "My Life Is Like a Summer Rose." The song had been set to music and Mary Appleton could have played it on her harp!

The Gentleman from Massachusetts made "a most important speech" in which he said that opposition to the tariff bill on the ground that the government didn't need money, was nothing but an excuse. The opposition, moreover, had exaggerated the amount the government would receive, by about $95 million. Appleton said the forecast in revenue from import duties was "too monstrous to need refutation."

Mr. Wilde was insulted. He accordingly made insulting remarks, misquoted Mr. Appleton, but "retracted" next day, "acknowledged himself wrong and made a very handsome apology" according to the Boston Daily Advertiser. "Mr. A. was happy to receive the apology . . ."

Mr. Wilde was insulted all over again however, by the preamble to the Report of the Massachusetts Committee on the Tariff, and refused to permit it to be printed. Mr. McDuffie of South Carolina was not entirely out of the picture — he was at a Carolina convention helping them to rattle sabers, announce that they would nullify all acts of Congress, and secede. He said he would "repair to Washington and cause the knees of the tariff men to smite together."

On the whole, the 1833 session of Congress was more lively than the previous one. Nathan Appleton approved Jackson's firm stand against nullification and he had been given much more important work to do. The impending tariff bill was in large measure his own effort. But, as before, he longed to be at home.

Tom wrote a cheerful letter telling of the young horse his father had bought in Pittsfield. "I have just returned from a ride on our steed. Yesterday [Jan. 5, 1833] Aunt Sam was afraid to accompany me with him in the chaise, dreading his stall-fed gaiety. He went, however, charmingly. So this morning I thought I would join Uncle William in a canter." Tom trotted his horse down to 54 Beacon Street, but something didn't quite suit him. "While I was off my horse fixing myself and Uncle William holding him, he got frightened and broke away from his hand and dashed over the country, Uncle William after him with his quaint boots, tight fur cap with long lappets, looking like some Sir Paladin, running down a fugitive foe. I walked home, and found, when I reached the stable, that steed and Uncle had both returned safely, he having hired a vagabond to ride my horse, when caught."

Fanny told her father that Mary and Charles had gone off to a party together — Tom had gone she knew not where — and she was left to sit by the chimney corner alone. He teased her in his next letter. Did she want a new dress and was that why she had refused the invitation Charles and Mary accepted?

Charles said that society was a bore. His father "received" no account of one of the parties "except from the misanthropic Charles — who dispatched it with a single growl."

John Howard Payne, the charming schoolboy Maria had known at the Berry Street Academy, turned up. He was now forty-one, author of several plays in collaboration with Washington Irving. The "first American Hamlet" had made some money but could never keep ahead of his creditors. He was now on his way to Washington because he had "an offer from a land speculating company to go free of expense to Texas to examine some land and make a report . . ." He knew "about as much of the qualities of land as a gentleman in the moon," he said, but these people wanted him to induce emigrants to settle in Texas. Aunt Sam gave him a big dinner party even using her silver service. Charley told about it. John Payne "let us into all the secrets of the London stage. He said he had heard of Mary's being the Boston belle." Of course John Payne remembered Maria. After dinner the Appleton young people brought over Maria's portrait by Stuart to show him. She was not at Aunt Sam's. She was ill again.

Maria Theresa's good health had evaporated almost at once. Dr. Warren [11] called on her three days after she got home from Pittsfield, and in Fanny's words, "The Dr. bled Mother, confined her to her bed and soon after blistered her, put her on a fruit diet, custards etc."

Maria Theresa lay on her bed with a thick poultice of mustard and other ingredients on her chest while painful blisters developed which were supposed to be drawing off the congestion in her lungs. Dr. Warren had blistered her before, "which reduced her strength much," but this was the first time there was mention of his bleeding her. Three days later, "Mother was bled again."

But as so many times before, Maria rallied, came downstairs and even walked in the sunshine on Beacon Street during an unusually mild autumn. The Warrens were such friends of Maria's that her portrait hung in Mrs. Warren's bedroom and the doctor was doing the best he could with the knowledge available. On the last day of January, "Mother is so feeble that she has been obliged to keep her bed except for two or three hours," Fanny wrote. "Dr. W. writes to father."

A "furious snow was falling" in Boston. Steam packets were stormbound, coaches were stuck in drifts and mail service between Boston and Washington was slow at best. Nathan Appleton started home as soon as he got the doctor's letter.

On the seventh of February, Dr. Warren did not think his patient would last the night. Her feet and hands were much swollen. She sang a hymn in her sleep "in a clear sweet voice, although she had great difficulty in speaking."

Word reached Pittsfield sooner than any news could get to Washington. On the night of the seventh, Grandmother Gold arrived "in a dreadful storm of wind and snow." She did not try to see Maria that night but when morning came, "Grandmother, Uncle William, Mrs. Warren etc." gathered at Maria Theresa's bedside. It was the scene required of these deeply religious people.

Maria Theresa made "not the slightest complaint." In the evening she "called all her children to her bedside" and told them to walk in the way she had taught them, to be faithful to that religion which was her rock of trust in that hour of death. They were to fulfill all their duties and realize all her hopes for them. She ended by asking them never to forget her but to let her memory be sweet and consoling to them.

On the ninth of February, Maria continued much the same with great difficulty of breathing. In the evening she called her servants to her and told them to be true to their religion. Margaret, the children's former nurse, sat with her that night. The tenth of February was a Sunday. Maria was calm and watched the sunrise. She asked the children why they were not in church and sent Tom away from her open window for fear that he should catch cold.

At two in the afternoon Maria had a sinking spell but Dr. Warren was able to help her. She suffered great distress for want of breath but refused any medicine that might relieve her pain, lest it put her to sleep. She kept her eyes on the clock, expecting that the time would come when her husband would arrive and she did not want to be asleep when he came.

Nathan had been traveling night and day as fast as horses could carry him. The special post-horses he had hired were being changed at the edge of the city of Boston when a messenger rode out to meet him. Maria was dead. He arrived at home "much agitated and fatigued — overcome with grief."

ELEVEN

FIRST JOURNEY

MARIA THERESA WAS BURIED in the Appleton vault under St. Paul's. It was all over and Nathan Appleton was fortunate to have important work to do. On February 20, 1833, he left his daughters with their grandmother Gold and, with Tom and Charley, returned to Washington.

Mary was housekeeper and at this point also keeper of the journal. Dr. Lieber called on his way south and Mary gave him a box to take to his wife. It contained some of Mary's party clothes, "my French pink moiré silk etc," she said. The girls were in mourning. John Howard Payne took Fanny and Mary to see his "old family mansion" and Fanny said that "with greatest interest did I retrace the scenes of my mother's younger days. I fancied I discovered the word 'Maria' cut upon the wooden frame of a window, in a room I imagined to have been hers."

Mary took painting lessons from Thomas Doughty, now in Boston, having exhibited his silvery-blue, romantic landscapes which prepared public taste for the Hudson River school. Fanny, putting on a huge apron, "marched down to Tom's room fully determined to accomplish wonders" with Tom's oil paints and a "card" or sketch board she had bought for herself. "But I did not find all things as I anticipated; brushes wanting, and paints used up," she said. She needed turpentine but, not knowing what she ought to have, she tried a bottle labelled "Poppy's oil" with which she attempted to mix her paints. It smelled like castor oil and she gave up in despair. The girls went nowhere except to Aunt Sam's.

For Charles, the trip to Washington with his father and Tom, was his first glimpse of the world beyond New England.[1] "I saw the Capitol before we came within sight of the settlement and thought it truly grand but the town hardly merits the name of city," he said. "We are nicely settled at McCarthy's with all the big dogs. Mr. Webster and co-patriot Frank Gray share our apartment." Mr. Webster was "very affable and agreeable etc and has no gravities or pomposities. I had yesterday the greatest intellectual treat I ever enjoyed, two great speeches from Mr. Webster and Mr. Clay and was well rewarded for standing up about three hours in a stifling crowd.

"Mr. Webster's speech was grave, full of arguments and now and then a burst of sarcasm and eloquence. Mr. Clay evaded Webster's questions or answered them slyly. He is, however, in my opinion more ready and eloquent as to language, than Webster and has truly a magnificent voice — the best I ever heard. He undertakes to say his bill will not destroy manufacturers. . . . His principle object, however, is peace, the most important of all objects in the end. So he is not so bad as we supposed . . ."

Charlie "went afterward to the House. Everything was head over heels. They did an immense quantity of business as you will have seen in the papers. Father says I have seen more done in one afternoon than he has seen in all his Congressional life." Charlie thought that Henry Clay looked like "some old farmer" and that Calhoun was rather "flunky-looking." Arthur Middleton of South Carolina was "bearded like a pard with red moustache" and McDuffie would make "everybody's hair stand on end when he spoke next day."

Knowing how lonely Fanny must be, Charles tried to make her laugh. He called her "the infant of the family" in this long letter, but explained that "every family must have an infant, even if sixty years old." This was ridiculous, he said, "Now that you are five feet ten, have been to Washington in your life, are half housekeeper, have studied under Mr. Emerson and wear corkscrew curls."

Tom had not honored Congress with his presence. "He turned his steps, wherever we went, to any place whereon was pasted 'Gallery of Paintings.' This was like a loadstone to the pole, even in times of hurry or business." Tom was seeing himself as an artist these days. He was tired of Harvard and had previously written to his father that he believed he could read law at home because it was a waste of time to ride over to Cambridge to lectures even though the new horse from Pittsfield would have been just the "steed" for it. Soon he was tired of Beacon Street and now he was tired of Washington.

"Tom left us for New York to embark March 29 on board the packet ship *Philadelphia*," the girls wrote in their diary. He had persuaded his father that what he needed was study in Europe but his sisters felt deserted and still more lonely. "This movement was very sudden and unwelcome to us," the girls said.[2]

Nathan Appleton wrote a letter of farewell[3] to his much-loved oldest son who would be twenty-one on the last day of March. ". . . In the first place, above all things take care of your health, which if not delicate — is not of that robust character which will bear to be trifled with. I have great hope the sea air will improve it — accompanied by rigid temperance." Tom's father suggested "a beverage of water only" and would recommend "a trial of it for a period of six months.

"The most common danger to which young men going abroad (or staying at home) are exposed to is that of excess social parties. It is, in your present health, all important that you should keep far from the borders of this danger. . . . If difficult to accomplish otherwise — such parties should be avoided altogether . . .

"The summer will be most favorable for traveling — the winter for studying — you will want to perfect yourself in the French language and I should think it may be well to take lessons every day during your stay in Paris. . . . I would recommend to you a course of lectures on the civil law at a convenient time — and on other useful branches . . ." Tom could be relied on to study French every day in Paris — but not with teachers accredited to the Sorbonne. As for lectures on the civil law — the "convenient time" never seemed to come.

In the matter of money, Tom's father wrote, "there is no reason why you should deny yourself whatever is comfortable and respectable but both are best promoted by a guarded, well-regulated but not niggardly economy. As a general rule, it is not wise to expend more or less than the respectable young men you fall in with." The lovable and generous Tom would find plenty of respectable (more or less) friends willing to let him foot their bills.

But now, his father took up the matter of women. "It is very desirable to cultivate female society, when you have an opportunity of getting into it, of a proper character — which is not always easy for a stranger. In this respect you will have some advantages which you should cultivate." Tom had letters of introduction to "Messers Bates, Wiggin, Aspenwall etc. in London and Welles in Paris" — all of them bankers, commission merchants or import-exporters. Not a painter, not a poet among them! Tom managed to lose his letters of introduction on the dock in Liverpool. He said the customs man was to blame. Someone picked them up and very kindly mailed them so that various Londoners expected that Mr. Nathan Appleton's oldest son would appear at once. Tom did not turn up and later, when he got around to making a few calls, it took all his charm to thaw the ice. For once, Tom's father was angry with him.

But Nathan Appleton, in his letter of fatherly advice, had reserved a last important warning. "I would recommend caution in making acquaintance with theatrical people — I mean writers."

Young Oliver Wendell Holmes was on the *Philadelphia* passenger-list along with Tom. He was going to Paris to study medicine, had not as yet published any poetry and was not yet called a "wit." He and Tom exchanged puns all the way across the Atlantic. These two "respectable" young men became friends, although to their annoyance as the years went by, each was sometimes credited with the witticism of the other.

Tom's letter from his father ended with the words, "Great expectations are made for you — many hearts are attached to you. . . . I have great confidence in your discretion, and wishing you may realize all our hopes, and the best of Heaven's Blessing, I bid you an affectionate adieu." This oldest son would try hard to please his father but in the end he would have to be himself.

After winding up affairs in Washington, Nathan returned to 39 Beacon Street, not only to find a pair of sad, forlorn-looking girls dressed in black, but the news that his brother Eben was dying. Eben with his wife and children, Sarah, Samuel Appleton Appleton, William, and Caroline, had been living in Lowell. He was successful in the work his two older brothers had cut out for him and particularly fond of Samuel for whom he named his oldest son. The Appleton young people spoke of Uncle Eben as "so gay and cheerful." He was unconscious on April 29, 1833, so that there was no proper death-bed scene which the assembled relatives regarded as a major part of the tragedy.

William Appleton of 54 Beacon wrote of the death of his "much esteemed cousin" Eben. "He was one of the most popular men I ever knew; he was deserving of the good will of his friends and acquaintances; his talents were far above the common order; he was rather playful than otherwise, better calculated for a literary life than a merchant." While the almost totally humorless William did not entirely condemn playfulness, it was clear that he thought little of a literary life.

Mrs. Eben Appleton returned to England, taking their oldest child.

The others chose to stay, all of them finding room in Aunt Sam's house and heart — especially Samuel Appleton Appleton.

Affairs at Lowell kept Nathan busy for some time but he had promised his girls a trip, Charley to come along and also Fanny's school friend, Emmeline Austin. Charles would look at waterfalls with his father, estimating potential water power while the girls raved about the beauties of nature. He and his father would get taken through factories to see if any were more efficient than those at Lowell while the girls would complain of a factory view from their hotel window.

On the third of June, 1833, the family departed on board the steamboat *President* and arrived in New York twenty-four hours later — a "fast trip," Mary and Fanny wrote in the journal they were still both using. On the fifth they took a fast Hudson River paddle steamer to West Point where they acquired a young cadet escort to show them the sights. All tourist attractions were called "lions" in the Appleton sisters' private language. When they had done their duty by a building, a view or historic site, they had "killed" the "lion." Mary said that the parade at West Point was too short but very pretty, the dress, however, of the cadets very unbecoming. They "killed" the West Point "lions," including the "Drawing Academy" and got on board another Hudson River boat bound for Albany.

Obviously this journal was intended to be read by the girls from Mr. Emerson's school and in the sewing circle where Emerson scholars who had come out in society made garments for the poor. Mary, being the oldest, kept the journal until she got tired of it when Fanny took over.[4] Sometimes, they alternated. There was more about "beaux" than about history. Mary said their "interest was excited by the appearance on board of a most exquisite youth with fierce moustaches and a guitar." They commented on "Moustache" as they called him, all the way to Saratoga.

After a night in Albany, the Appleton party took a round trip to Saratoga. We "proceeded to a barn, where we got into a railroad car, seeing 'Moustache' in the distance. At first we were quite alarmed at the rapidity with which we went but as no boiler burst and no accident happened we began to enjoy this mode of conveyance."

They found "Congress Hall" at Saratoga, "cold and cheerless, its immense halls scantily filled with company." Fanny was alarmingly thin, her father thought, and he took her to all the different springs and made her at least taste the water.

One evening "Moustache" got out his guitar and sang to the girls "divers sentimental songs, none of them the newest, chiefly Mr. Lynches 'Leaf in the Fountain,' and 'Love and Friendship'." They found out that "Moustache" was from New York, that his name was Lispenard Stuart and someone told them that he was "renowned in New York for his splendid equipages and unmanageable horses." Emmeline was surprised that a young man could be "such an exquisite as to wear moustaches and yet be so unpretending in his manner."

Mr. Appleton must have been glad when, by pre-arrangement, Mr. and Mrs. Dutton joined the party. Mrs. Dutton would make a good chaperone for his schoolgirls and they took to her at once, saying she reminded them of Aunt Sam. Warren Dutton, director and former president of the Merrimack Manufacturing Company, would provide Nathan Appleton with intelligent conversation — about water-power, factories, canals and locks.

When the Appleton party left Saratoga, the girls were late to breakfast and "Father was furious" but they made their train. As they traveled up the Mohawk by coach, even the girls were impressed by locks and canals at Little Falls, cut through solid rock. Along Trenton Falls a path had been cut for sightseers.

Mary, Fanny and Mrs. Dutton found themselves "in a deep curious ravine, high rocks on all sides and a black treacherous-looking river glinting along in this most gloomy solitude." Mrs. Dutton and Mary were frightened and turned back. It was not Fanny's style to turn back from anything. She and Emmeline, with a guide, went on clinging to chains set in the rock but finding them of little support. Rain fell in torrents. They came to a cascade where the water ran off the path with "fearful velocity," Fanny wrote. It was not a place "for giddy nerves! But the second fall was very fine, the water of a most beautiful amber hue." They made it to the top of the fall "by a staircase cut in the rock, very insecure and steep." Mrs. Dutton and Mary had gone ahead to a hotel at the top of the fall and came out through the hotel grounds to look for them, "the greatest heroines of the century."

A long overland coach journey almost directly west from Utica brought the Appletons to Rochester and at last to Niagara Falls. When the girls were not watching young men (they caught sight of Lispenard Stuart at a hotel in Canandagua) they were observing fashions. In Rochester, they found "country fashions mixed with city elegance." Streets in Buffalo were "filled with Swiss and Indians" who wore "white blankets with black borders, universally and the men even turn them

into frock coats. They all have red sashes and feathers in their hats."
Squaws wore "embroidered pantelets" and had "ornaments" pinned "in
front of their dresses." The girls went shopping for Indian moccasins.

By the twentieth of June, the Appleton party had reached the "large
and commodious hotel . . ." so "provokingly situated overlooking mills."
The girls, wrapped in their Buccleuchs, set out for a walk, found a long
wooden bridge leading "directly over the violent rapids. . . . Emmeline's
romance was sadly provoked by the appearance of mills and artificial
water works. Factories and Niagara! What profanation, what sacrilege,"
Fanny wrote. But once over the bridge, they found themselves on Goat
Island, which she had no hesitation in calling "the most lovely spot in
creation."

Fanny had been admiring "the paintings that have been taken lately
of this wonder of nature which certainly seems to baffle utterly all
powers of art." [5] The girls got out their sketch books anyway. All travelers also described the falls and the girls did this too, sparing no
adjectives.

When they left Niagara, "this lion of Nemean size and grandeur was
at last slain," Fanny wrote. "And I, at fifteen, had seen Niagara."

The Appleton party returned to Rochester via Lockport where, of
course, they stopped to admire the locks, "six in number and curiously
enough constructed." For the first time, Fanny became aware of what
life on what was then the frontier would be like. Lockport was the most
dismal place she ever visited. Endless forest hemmed in the narrow road.
Then came the clearing. "Nothing to be seen in every direction but
stumps, stumps, stumps, encircling the very doors of the houses and
blackening the fields, hills and meadows."

The travelers had come to Lockport to take the lake steamer, *United
States.* "A mysterious Englishman" tried to get acquainted with the girls.
He "talked and stared and blazed" — this last referring to his red face
and they made fun of him among themselves, calling him "Asmodeus."
They knew that Asmodeus was the evil spirit exorcised by Tobias on
advice from an angel. Quite probably they had read the translation from
the French of Alain René, by Fielding, called *The Devil on Two Sticks.*

As the steamer turned east along the shore, Lake Ontario became
rough. Fanny walked the deck with Lucy Nichols, a Boston girl she met
on the boat. Mary and Emmeline took refuge in the lounge and now
"Asmodeus" began talking to Fanny and Lucy about Mrs. Trollope.

Everybody talked about Mrs. Trollope's *Travels in America.* That
English lady's acid remarks were prompted in part by her business fail-

ure in Cincinnati where she had built what she called a "bazar" in Greco-Moresco-Gothic-Chinese style. Nothing else in America came up to it, and the Appleton girls talked about and quoted Frances Milton Trollope all the time. But by now, Fanny was feeling seasick and any subject poor "Asmodeus" could have chosen would have been wrong. He next "declared that he had hoped to have the pleasure of *picking me up* for some time," Fanny later wrote. This was not the correct approach to a Boston girl!

Next morning at Oswego, Fanny came into the dining saloon "starving" and asked for milk. "There's none but what's on the table and that's gone," a stewardess told her. The Duttons had had enough of the lake steamer and left, promising to meet the Appletons at Burlington on their return. Finally, the *President* reached Ogdensburg where the starving Fanny and the rest had breakfast.

Then they learned that their steamer would tie up for several days. This was too much for Nathan Appleton who hated delay. He hired a coach to take his family along the lake shore to Hogansburg on the edge of what is now the St. Regis Indian Reservation. They were getting into the smallest most uncomfortable of coaches when "to our horror and dismay, just before setting off 'Asmodeus' marched up to Father and requested a seat as there was no other means of conveyance. . . . Dad could not refuse and in he got, his blazing visage reddening still more in the insufferable warmth of the day, our narrow quarters" and the bad road.

The cold looks from the girls should have cooled him off and finally he did seem to get the message because after a while he "rode mounted on the box." The road was corduroy, another new experience for the Misses Appleton of Beacon Street.

Upon the Duttons' departure, Mr. and Mrs. Charles G. Loring of Boston had joined the Appleton party. Fanny and Mary described the lawyer and his wife. "Mrs. L. has a most cadaverous and spectre-like appearance and seems like one's idea of the tomb with a ghostly grin and unnaturally bright eyes. . . . Mr. Loring was a bit too much . . . what with his sentimentality and loquacity." But after a good meal and some rest the girls changed their minds about the Lorings. Mrs. Loring had a delightful sense of humor and her husband had only been trying to cheer them up. After that noon meal they "set out again in high spirits and . . . even cracked a few jokes."

At St. Regis, the girls were shown into "a somewhat capacious apartment . . . with two low beds and a long bench instead of chairs." Fanny, Mary and Emmeline got ready for bed but, "While performing certain necessary ablutions and other offices of the toilet," they were "suddenly transfixed with horror." They thought they saw a face peering in at them from a huge hole in the wall, "formerly occupied by a stovepipe but now empty and having direct communication with the next chamber." They were sure it was Asmodeus.

"Our terror was however soon allayed by the discovery that Charley was the sole occupant of that room and that his black coat it was, that had alarmed us." Charley had stuffed his coat into the hole in the wall so that the girls wouldn't keep him awake with their chatter. But Fanny said their room was really like some of those in Mrs. Radcliffe's haunted houses.

They spent Sunday at St. Regis where the Indians were "very numerous and well off." They watched canoes filled with squaws crossing the St. Lawrence to come to a St. Regis church, "simple and pretty but quite rude. . . . The devotion and respectful order of the Indians who knelt on the floor, entirely wrapped in their blankets and appearing completely absorbed by their occupation of telling their beads," impressed Fanny. "They all knelt gracefully as they entered, crossed themselves and arranged themselves on opposite sides, the men and women." The service was conducted in their Indian language "by a French Catholic Priest with Indian assistants, interrupted by the shrill, piercing chorus of the squaws, with which the more agreeable voices of the men blended . . ."

On Monday, July 1, the steamer *President* arrived much sooner than expected. They might have avoided the mud-covered corduroy road but the Appleton party was glad not to have missed seeing the Indian town.

Although once more on board the boat and on their way to Montreal, there were portages where everybody disembarked and climbed into coaches which swayed and pitched into gullies. At one point a heavy thunder shower came up, and the Appletons saw lightning cross the road and hit a tree right in front of the horses. When the girls got out of the coach, at one portage, poor Mary fell in the mud. "Mrs. Loring lost all her gravity and could not restrain her merriment when beholding Mary who looked just like a mermaid rising from a muddy cave."

After resting a day in Montreal, the girls were off to see the "lions": the cathedral, a nunnery, the garrison. They marveled because all the houses were of stone. For the first time in their lives they saw beggars in the streets, but after attracting crowds of them by being lavish with coins, they learned to harden their hearts.

Now the Appletons acquired new traveling companions; the Crosbys of New York with their daughter Kate and their son, Johnny — who was "a beau for us, to rid us of the uncuttable Asmodeus," according to both Mary and Fanny. All the young people went to the "barrack yard" to watch the "British troops performing their manoeuvres." The Appleton girls were "enchanted" with the band music but thought the officers conceited, "strutting about and attitudinizing." But Kate Crosby was "crazy about redcoats."

In Montreal, the girls "ransacked the stores" for Indian moccasins to buy for all their friends. But they found only a few because the Indians, "fearful of the cholera, had not brought in any moccasins this year." The Appletons were aware of the danger of contaminated water. In Montreal, they drank only wine.

At a Montreal luncheon party, Fanny confessed that the wine "got into my head in such a degree that dizziness and faintness almost prevented me from getting downstairs without assistance. There was a good laugh at my expense." But Johnny Crosby gave Fanny his arm "and hummed songs, wild and sad, in the carriage, all the way back to the hotel."

At half-past seven that night, the Appletons embarked on the steamer *St. George* bound down the St. Lawrence for Quebec. The girls promenaded the deck, admired cloud effects by moonlight and a lunar rainbow. But Fanny was "low spirited and melancholy." By morning she was very ill and so was Kate Crosby. Mrs. Crosby was taken ill next day. They had all been "devouring ice cream" in Montreal. In Quebec, the girls ate ice cream that tasted like cauliflower, they said. Illness recurred. Not liking ice cream, Charley, Johnny and the men of the party were not ill — yet it never occurred to anyone that contaminated raw milk in the ice cream could cause trouble. It was not the dreaded cholera or they might not have survived.

Nothing dimmed Fanny's enthusiasm for Quebec, however. She had heard "the approach to Quebec extolled to the skies," but the view was more beautiful than she ever imagined. Hotels were all filled but they found a lodging house with a garden and "ascending therto in a coach, I passed through a *gate* for the first time and entered a walled city," she wrote. The diary was all hers now, Mary having lost interest.

At noon after dinner, "the gentlemen remembered it was the Fourth of July and ordered a bottle of Champagne." They all drank to " 'Our Country' and then to 'The Country we are In'." Poor Asmodeus, spurned but still their shadow, was at the same lodging house and the Appletons invited him to join in their celebration. Johnny Crosby ordered another bottle of champagne. Mrs. Loring got into a laughing fit. In this merry mood, they set off to explore the city.

The barracks were closed to visitors but Nathan Appleton knew the right people to get the Appleton party a permit, and the Crosbys knew some Highland officers. As a result they were all invited to see a special parade.

"The whole regiment of Highlanders performed the most curious and beautiful maneuvers in a huge courtyard. . . . The running motion of this immense body of soldiers was more exquisite than can be imagined," Fanny said. Oddly enough, the sound they made was "like the shaking of bags of wet sand or wet clothes! They passed between, through and by each other and when disorder appeared to be greatest, they all arranged themselves in regular columns. After all this difficult maneuvering, they all began firing. . . . Emmeline and I protected ourselves behind the gents. They fired directly before us, around us and across us and the whole air seemed to be filled with a thousand flashing reports and ringing guns. The effect was perfectly stunning and it seemed, if I had been shot, I should never have known it."

Of course there was a trip to the Montmorency Falls. Two girls were in a calèche, the others in a barouche, and N. Appleton in a gig with a business friend. Charlie rode horseback and so did the uninvited Asmodeus, who fell off his horse into the mud.

On the way home, "We talked, laughed and sang and I was never happier in my life," Fanny wrote. She rode with Johnny Crosby and they sang "Nobody, Nobody, No," and "Alan-a-Dale." Although late for dinner, Asmodeus appeared, "with his golden whiskers arranged with the most studied care and elegance and twisted into numberless, fascinating little pet ringlets . . ."

Asmodeus had offered Fanny his arm as they climbed a steep path at the falls and she had told him she could take care of herself, thank you. Now she invited Johnny Crosby to take a walk on the ramparts with her. They found a gun embrasure where she could balance her sketch book. It was "a very romantic and perilous position, for we were at an immense height over the town and could look into chimneys and streets," she wrote. They saw the steamer headed upriver with "Nicholses, Lawrences and last but not least, the most welcome sight to us — Asmodeus." They could hear "the thundering shouts of crowds of immigrants on board . . ." They "waved hats and kerchiefs and never were adieus wafted on the breeze from more joyful hearts!"

There was room now at the hotel so the Appletons changed their quarters. Officials and businessmen called on Mr. Appleton. Charley and the girls were invited to tea parties and dinners but by the ninth of July they too were off up the St. Lawrence. In Montreal, they "joyfully established" themselves in their old quarters at Goodenough's Hotel.

There was one more treat in store. Mr. Brigham, another of Mr. Appleton's many business friends, took the girls to Mt. Royal in his famous coach and six. There were twelve passengers inside and four outside, Mr. B. in a gig with their father.

On top of the coach, for the return trip, were Mary, Fanny and Johnny Crosby. To Fanny, not yet sixteen, everything was "immense." From this "immense height" on top of the coach, "the six horses looked like rats, prancing before us. We were in ecstasies — never did I enjoy a delightful afternoon more or a ride so much. . . . We sang all manner of songs, got into a gale of spirits . . .

"On returning to the city, we were amused by the excitement we produced; old Frenchmen held up their hands with amazement, or leaned out with horror as we looked in on them in their upper stories and were on a level with their visages in the narrow street . . ."

The Appleton girls and Charlie spent the evening in the Crosbys' hotel parlor, "reclining on the *floor* and conversing gaily. . . . The day was finished by a furious waltz on the piazza and we retired."

The return journey was by way of St. John and Lake Champlain to Burlington where the Duttons were waiting. But just as they left Montreal, Fanny had another bout of debilitating illness. "With the help of Johnny's arm," she reached the inn at La Prairie. On board the Lake Champlain steamer she felt better and then, just as she was looking forward to a whole day, the last one with Johnny, "faintness and headache and all that grim tribe of horrors assailed" her. When she crawled back on deck, "Seignor Johnny tried every art to amuse me and at last succeeded. . . . I enjoyed this bright and sunny afternoon amazingly."

Then they separated. The Crosbys stayed on the steamboat while Fanny sat in a carriage on the dock, "nearly one fourth of an hour, waving my handkerchief and looking unutterable things. We all continued waving, shading our eyes and giving tender and farewell glances till the turn of the road took me out of sight of the steamer . . ."

On the twelfth of July, "How forlorn it is to feel sick and miserably and to awake in a dismal country inn with dismal country accommodations!" Fanny wrote in her diary. But her spirits soon revived as the long coach journey began and she found herself "once more riding over

New England State roads and enjoying . . . the mountains of Vermont."
She was sure that, if she ever saw Switzerland, it could be no more
beautiful. At Montpelier, blasting was going on and "an immense rock
coolly deposited itself in the dining room, coming through the roof" of
the hotel. It missed the Appletons.

The "Gulph Road," [6] along the second branch of the White River,
was as spectacular as anything the Appletons had seen anywhere. Sometimes they could see waterfalls, deep in a gorge below the road, sometimes they could only hear the water, and their coach driver obligingly
stopped at points where they could glimpse a cataract. Fanny's diary
gave such an accurate account of the journey that the route may be
followed today by leaving the great six-lane highway and winding back
and forth under it on the old roads. Skiers now visit the Randolph,
Vermont, area.

One evening at Randolph "a charming little village buried in the
mountains" the Appletons walked out from the inn to a nearby hill.
While "the others scrambled to the summit to enjoy the view," Fanny
"sat on a rock with Papa" and they spent a quiet hour together "watching the blue smoke of the village curling upward in the distance." This
was the last entry in Fanny's journal of a first journey.

TWELVE

"YOU WILL HAVE
BUT THREE CHILDREN"

TOM APPLETON'S JOURNAL of his voyage aboard the *Philadelphia* reached his family in August when they were back in Boston. He had been becalmed, the second day out, and "right sound did our lazy ship sleep all day; but thanks to her light build, did not snore as some do," Tom began. He and Oliver Wendell Holmes were not the only punsters aboard. A storm sprang up and when a hen was swept overboard, T. B. Curtis of Boston thought that she would meet with foul weather. The morning after the storm, Tom said that he got out of bed in a hurry to find out whether they had perished or not. The breakfast table literally flowed with milk and honey — but Tom enjoyed his meals and was not seasick. He wrote a sonnet about a nautilus and said he wished he could ride a whale down under the sea and leave his card on a mermaid.[1] He had left cards on plenty of Boston girls. A mermaid would be someone new.

Having so fortunately lost his father's letters of introduction, Tom called on no bankers in London and met no wealthy young ladies, the daughters of such gentlemen. He had time to go to the opera however and to comment on the long faces of people riding in Hyde Park as if in a sort of "gaudy funeral." A bit of sightseeing and he was off for Paris.

"'Why did I waste my substance — why did I lose patience, money, comfort and time in the smoke of the island of Babylon — when dear, delightful Paris was within a jump!" he wrote. He grew lyrical over fountains in the Tuileries where "gold fishes leap from their circular oceans." He loved the "quantity of glass" — the houses all open with gleaming windows — the cafés all mirrors.

Tom met a friend in Paris who took him to see another friend and "what was my astonishment to find that friend was Sam Ward" of Round Hill school days. Sam had grown a pointed beard and a moustache so that "with his disguise of a perfectly French manner, no one would doubt he was French."

"You seem to be running pretty rapidly through the race of novelties," Tom's father told him.[2] "You should be quite ready to return by spring." But as to "getting down to hard study, I see little chance of that. Perhaps, however, you will soon be satiated with the lighter vanities and desirous to retire into the studious cells of the profession of law." Tom went to Switzerland on a walking tour.

Tom had been given money to buy a watch for Fanny in Paris — but of course it would be better to get it in Switzerland which would require this trip. The watch must be "a delicate and elegant one according to your taste," his father had said, and nobody had ever questioned Tom's eye for elegance, whatever his interest in the law. Charley needed a watch too but on being asked about it, said that it would be his turn to go to Europe the next year and he would like to choose a watch for himself.

Here was just the suggestion Tom needed. Why shouldn't he stay abroad during the coming winter and meet the family in Paris the following spring? His father set him straight. "I doubt if you will be disposed to give yourself seriously to hard study. Your presence at home will be very advantageous to your sisters and your absence very irksome. I have no idea of taking them to Europe next year — the objections, I think, are insuperable." So Tom, who was a born diplomat, headed for Heidelberg in October, where hard study was the custom — at least for some of the students.

In October, Henry Clay visited Boston. "Our distinguished senator and statesman has been received with great pomp and éclat in this bustling city," Fanny told Tom, taking her father's place as family letter-writer.[3] "Such a ludicrous entré as he made here! Cannons thundering, rains pouring, to usher in half a dozen shut-up funeral coaches and six demure, meek coachees and sleek, dripping steeds." The procession passed under the Beacon Street balconies but no one was outside in the rain.

Charley took up the tale. Henry Clay was given "a very splendid dinner at Aunt Sam's and went to Lowell with a party of ladies and gentlemen — amongst them Mary and Father." They spent the day tramping over factories" . . . and devouring all the eatables they could find." Henry Clay admired Lowell, that "famous boast of Yankeeland and declared that the tariff would need no other champion than Lowell itself, if it could be transplanted, as it is, to the region of the Nullifiers."

While "Mary and Dad" were gone, Fanny was housekeeper with her cousin, Fanny Wright from Pittsfield, to keep her company.[4] They found it "a pretty forlorn business" and they had all given up hope that Tom would come home in time to brighten the season by bringing his friends to Beacon Street.

On January 5, 1834, Tom's father wrote, "I observe you plead for a longer run than spring. I am disposed to grant whatever is for your real good. . . . I am not disposed to be hard, or disturb your discretion — but you must be aware that we feel deeply the loss of your society and I trust you will find that enough of an inducement in favor of home — to give it preference over any more lounging and idling abroad." His father would like an account of Tom's expenses. "There is an extreme scarcity of money although everything in the commercial world is in a state of prosperity. It is my wish that you should always incur every expense which is becoming the character of a gentleman; of course 'extravagance' is not so" — but Tom could have more money if he needed it.

"Mr. Sears writes Uncle William that he has met you in Germany — and that you have much improved in manners and appearance," Tom's father added. Tom could not have cared much for this rather doubtful compliment from a Beacon Street neighbor, but in any case, he had already left Heidelberg. The German language was altogether too difficult. He approved of German beer, however, and bought himself a German pipe. By the time he got his father's permission to stay abroad, he was in Italy, setting up his easel in the Pitti Palace in Florence in front of *La Seggiola* with permission to copy it "for all next month!"

When Nathan Appleton told Tom there was a scarcity of money, he referred to the situation arising from Jackson's refusal of a renewal of charter for the Bank of the United States. It was Jackson's idea that this Philadelphia bank was acquiring too much power, and the Boston Appletons found themselves on Jackson's side in the dispute.

William Appleton, one of the directors of the Boston branch of the Bank of the United States, was chosen to go to Philadelphia to tell Nicholas Biddle, president, that Boston was going to control its own business, with "a capital not to be withdrawn," and that he, William Appleton, "would not be the tool of any set of men." [5] Never noted for his tact but already famous for his business ability, he was just the man for this mission. "I found them, Messers. Biddle and Jaudon, quite prepared to meet my views," he set down in his journal. "I got the funds required and a promise that I might do anything I pleased in relation to the office in Boston."

At a public meeting in Boston, it was Nathan Appleton who was appointed chairman of a commission to proceed to Washington with a memorial to Congress concerning the Bank of the United States. On arriving in New York with Patrick Tracy Jackson and Henry Lee, they found "dissatisfaction with Mr. Biddle very ripe." To the surprise of the Boston delegation, Mr. Biddle himself appeared, and at a private conference, they told him "some home truths" to the effect that Boston would not sustain him in further pressure "against country and western banks by calling their loans, refusing to honor their drafts and suspending payments in gold." Biddle's "whole object was to coerce a charter" from Jackson by ruining or threatening to ruin small banks. "Mr. Biddle listened to us but we could get very little from him but the merest commonplaces," Nathan Appleton wrote. So the Boston committee went on to Washington.

A few days later, Appleton and his committee got a letter from James G. King, the "Almighty of Wall Street." Biddle had yielded — which eased the pressure on the money market. But "the arrangement was only for a month. After that, Mr. Biddle was reckless enough to renew pressure with even greater violence." Fortunately, "Congress adjourned soon after, when Biddle gave up the chase." Nathan Appleton wrote a series of articles on banking for the Boston papers, which he signed "Bullionite" and in which he denounced the suspension of species payments by banks as "merely a broken promise."

The so-called "Suffolk System" by which one Boston bank received a contribution of an agreed-upon sum from other banks and kept a gold reserve to guarantee its paper, had actually been the idea of Nathan Appleton during the War of 1812. This system was credited with having kept Boston banks solvent but he was so careful not to claim undue credit that his name was unknown outside of Boston at the time, even to those who praised the system.

Nathan Appleton had refused re-nomination to Congress, feeling that he had given up too much of his time to that exasperating group of lawmakers, during the last months of Maria's life. But in his last letter to his son Tom, dated April 12, 1834, Nathan indicated that this latest trip had been exhilarating. "I have been on a mission to Washington to carry an immense memorial to Congress and have concluded the matter by making a report of our progress to a great meeting at Faneuil Hall," he said. His report had been greeted with cheers but this was a point he left to Charley to tell.

Aunt Martha Gold had been acting as chaperone for the girls at 39 Beacon Street during the winter of 1834. She was a great talker, inclined to argue in favor of the doctrine of original sin. As her brother-in-law was a Unitarian and would eventually write a pamphlet upholding an opposite view, it is not surprising that Mr. Appleton enjoyed being away from home as much as possible. Writing playfully to Tom, Mary said that "beaux" also tormented their father. There was the "indefatigable Captain" who called on Mary and Fanny in the afternoon after having had too much wine at his noon dinner. "And the much more than half lunatic Mr. Gerry with divers others less known to fame." Did Tom remember the "preacher — isn't he a bore, outright and downright?" Charley tried to tease the extremely serious Aunt Martha Gold by declaring that he would get her married — perhaps to that preacher!

Mary said that she meant to "set up for a coquette" after she had "enacted the part of Miss Discretion and Sobriety" for so long. "Fanny, however, is coming on stage," she added. Their father would soon be doubly tormented.

Spring came to Boston but Tom Appleton did not. "Picture-dealers begin to find me out," he had written in May. Twenty-seven canvases, most of them copies of masterpieces, arrived in Boston. His own copy, which he called *La Seggiola* was among them. "We all think the *Seggiola* admirably well done," even Tom's father declared. "It stands in the library where I am writing this and Mary has just pronounced it exquisite." Tom rather agreed with this verdict but he had failed to make out a proper bill of lading as usual, although his father had previously explained the process in detail several times.

In June, Tom got permission to stay in Europe till October. "Charles sets off for Pittsfield with Aunt Martha," Tom's father wrote. Then Charley was to "go on to Saratoga for a few days." This was his first vacation in some time.

The girls went with their father to Newport, never neglecting for a moment their letters and diaries telling of people and places on their short journey, passing judgment as it was the duty of Bostonians to do. "Some of the New Yorkers are very rich and dress too much for good taste, at least in a place like this," they thought. "A gay widow appears every morning at breakfast with a fresh pair of white kid gloves. . . . As for beaux" the Appleton girls were "safe enough for the present" but they liked "the two Middletons" from South Carolina. One of the Middletons "has a great talent for sketching and draws admirably the groups in the dining room" of the hotel. Fanny "has the honor of being in the one he is about, now."

Picnics were fun, especially a "merry party and a nice fête champêtre on the grass inside of a picturesque ruined tower." Source of much subsequent archeological speculation, the so-called Norseman's Mill at Newport was to attract much attention — because of a poem written by Henry Wadsworth Longfellow, a poet Fanny Appleton had yet to meet.

"Bathing is the grand occupation here," according to Fanny. "I have only tried it once — with the Crowninshields. The ladies generally go about 10 or 11 A.M. down to the beach — there clothe themselves in the most grotesque costumes, some with gypsy hats and streaming hair.

"In the evening, we are very gay, waltzing kept up till midnight when, the gentlemen being left to themselves, sing glees, never failing to awaken the whole house. . . . Lately we have danced the Virginia reel and such-like antique jigs. They make great fun and *unstiff* people well. We also find certain games great promoters of merriment — especially Dumb-Crambo, which brings out people too much, sometimes. . . . Father has found it tedious enough."

More picturesque than the Norseman's Mill and more entertaining than Dumb-Crambo, however, was a certain fellow guest. This was Frances Ann Kemble, daughter of Charles Kemble, the celebrated Shakespearian actor.[6] Miss Kemble had just completed an extremely successful tour of the United States as her father's leading lady. The Appleton girls had seen her in Boston but her last appearance had been at the Park Theater in New York on June 20, 1834. Among other roles, she had played Juliet to her father's Romeo, but now, much to her father's dismay, she had found a Romeo of her own. She had married Pierce Butler, owner of an estate just out of Philadelphia and heir to a Georgia plantation.

Mrs. Pierce Butler "was visible evenings only" at first — because she was writing a book about her travels in America. But at night, "she waltzed and gallopaded most gracefully." Then after a few days, the actress was seen walking on the Newport cliffs clad in white muslin, "gloveless, with bare neck and arms!" She was even without a bonnet because she wanted to get a tan. But the Appleton girls said she was burned to "a bright mahogany color" and they were horrified. When they met her, after being properly introduced of course, they were soon "bound by the spell" that attracted everyone to Fanny Kemble. The friendship between the Appleton girls and Fanny Kemble Butler was to be a long one.

Tom came home at last, arriving on board the Packet *North American*, October 1, 1834. Joyful was his welcome from everyone with the possible exception of Uncle William Appleton at 54 Beacon. Tom was sporting a luxuriant moustache. Uncle William told him to get out of the house and not come back until he had shaved it off — at least so the story went!

Mrs. Thomas B. Curtis, who, with her husband, had seen a good deal of Tom in Europe, but had returned to Boston ahead of him, also had a report. "Our friend Appleton is one of the lions of society, having a great variety of Parisian and Highland vests, an English white top-coat and fancy studs from all parts of the world, exhibiting all the ruins of Rome in mosaic, and Berlin iron in every shape. In fact he is voted a fop; but he and I laugh at the report — it is but the whim of the day."

By February, 1835, Charley had a cold "which hangs on," the family said. He had not been to Newport at all during the summer, going only to Pittsfield to escort his Aunt Martha and on to Saratoga for a short stay. As usual, he had enjoyed everything. On the Connecticut River, the best steamboats were propelled by one wheel in the stern, stage coaches were tedious and roads were rough but scenery "at times romantic." Almost at once, he was back in Boston telling his father, in Newport, that business was not particularly brisk but that the Suffolk mills had declared a seven percent dividend while the Tremont mills made the same profit but "divided five percent."

For several years, Charles had always had what they called influenza during the winter. This March, when his cough was no better, he seemed surprised to be given a trip to Charleston, South Carolina. Letters home were full of enthusiasm with a touch of his own brand of humor. He had letters of introduction to cotton merchants which he did not lose but presented properly. He dined "with some aristocratic old maids named the Miss Pinkneys," who lived in "an old fashioned wainscotted house, plentifully furnished with mirrors, called 'Nullification Castle' . . . " The banner of the states' rights party had been delivered to the gallant "Nullifians here and an address made for the ladies."

Charley was fascinated by stories of Nullifiers being allowed to leave their meeting hall only by King Street in Charleston while the Unionists were told to go out by way of Meeting Street to avoid fights. Unionists broke down fences in order to get at their opponents while leaders on the other side "concealed their bruises from brickbats" and both sides tried to keep voters drunk and locked up until "marched to the polls." The Pinkney ladies were "desperate Nullifians but gave us a capital dinner, all light-made dishes" and Charley saw for the first time "plantains and banannas growing."

There was another "capital dinner" where salmon was served, "sent fresh from London, hermetically sealed." Charley liked everyone — especially a clergyman who was the merriest person he ever met, who "drank wine with gusto" and "denounced the custom of going to church twice on Sunday because, at the afternoon service, everyone slept and he thought it was better to do that at home." Charley was traveling with "Mr. Mason" but he did not indicate which member of that large family it was. Mary, at the same time, was traveling with Mrs. Mason and her daughters, by a different route. After considerable correspondence, they agreed to meet at Port Richmond and go home together. They were all in Philadelphia on May 14, when Charley wrote to his father and Fanny who were at home in Boston. "I have been here two days and have not written from having my time so fully taken up with shopping, riding about to see the buildings in the neighborhood, receiving visitors etc. but today, we who thought ourselves exempt from such mortalities, are kept at home by the pouring rain . . ." They were leaving for New York next day.

Mary had spent a day out at Butler Place at the invitation of Fanny Kemble Butler.[7] The Butler pre-Revolutionary mansion was about six miles from Philadelphia and Pierce brought Mary Appleton home "at dusk, bearing a load of flowers and passed part of the evening with us, arranging them," Charley said. And now, for the first time in his letters, he referred to a reason for his trip to Charleston. He had checked on the price of cotton for his father, to be sure, but he had gone because of his health. "Pierce Butler invited me to pass some time with him and promised every indulgence — thought it was the best place for reestablishing myself. I was infinitely obliged but refused, not liking to be among strangers (comparitively) — and I want to see Dr. Warren.

"I am better, have gained much strength and can walk all about town. My cough is not very troublesome, in spite of drafts etc. . . . I have a great notion of farming, think I should like it and it would do me good when I get well . . ."

In this letter, Charley mentioned for the first time a name familiar to the young Appletons — that of Harriet Coffin Sumner. "Miss Sumner called upon us. . . . She offers to do a thousand things for me — from which excuse me."

Almost exactly two months later, the next news of Charles Appleton came from his brother, Tom. Heading his letter Pittsfield and dating it July 13, 1835, Tom had spent an hour with Charley "this morning, and am very glad to be able honestly to tell you that he is *decidedly better*. . . . He asserts that he is far stronger and proves it by the length of his rides. He could not, when with us in [Boston], have sat a horse two hours. To be sure, as he ought, he usually walks the horse, though disposed to trot and canter. His only need is moderation. He has a rather awkward unwillingness to admit weakness, illness, fatigue or anything that seems unmanly . . ."

Only five days later, Tom wrote again. They had sent for Dr. Wright, Maria Gold Appleton's brother-in-law, who gave Charles laudanum for his cough. Tom now spelled out what no one had as yet mentioned — that dread word "consumption." Dr. Wright did not "consider the boy's lungs irrevocably shattered as Charles has not the hectic fever nor the night chills."

Mary and Fanny spent the summer at Pittsfield with excursions to Stockbridge and Lenox, to Lebanon to see the Shakers and to drink the water at Lebanon Springs. They rode horseback to their heart's content, even though "saddles and horses never match." According to Tom, the girls "ran up and down the hills, picking raspberries and getting brown and plump as partridges."

Nathan Appleton joined his children in July — forewarned by Mary that Augustus Gold wanted him to use his influence to get the Worcester Railroad to pass through Pittsfield. Because the family was all assembled in one place, there were no records of Charley's illness but he "endured the fatigues of the journey home beyond our hopes," in spite of the jolting stagecoach. Dr. Warren had not decided yet "about the advantages of foreign climes," for Charles, Fanny said. The doctor wanted to consult Dr. Jackson.

There were only a few weeks of false hope. Then it was decided to tell Charley that he was going to die! [8] "Though at first startling, it was a blessed comfort to witness the happy peace and perfect resignation with which the certainty of his fate was received. . . . On Saturday afternoon, he called us to him and spoke to us with cheerfulness and calmness indescribable and said to Father, 'You will have but three children.' "

On Sunday, October 25, the air was cool and invigorating and Charles seemed as well if not better than for some days. He thought he would like to take a drive but the doctor was late in coming so he put it off till afternoon. He walked, with his father's help, into the bathing-room for a change of air but "suffered much" from lack of breath. He asked to be carried around the house "and was conveyed in a sort of cradle of straw, all over the house, suffering apparently very little difficulty except in breathing . . ."

Back in his own room, "even difficulty in breathing did not disturb the serenity of his countenance for a moment," Fanny said. She rubbed his cold hands and when he saw that she was crying, he gave her "a strange look of wonder, almost of pity. He at last put his hands to his eyes and exclaimed, 'I can hardly see.' These were his last words and, like a happy child, he went to sleep."

THIRTEEN

EUROPE BY SAILING SHIP

NO ONE HAD FORGOTTEN that Charley's turn to go abroad to celebrate his coming of age would have been in 1836. To the surprise of the remaining children, Nathan Appleton decided to take them all to Europe and to give the girls the "grand tour" usually given only to boys. On November 16, 1835, there were not only three but five Appletons, plus cousin Isaac Appleton Jewett, who went aboard the sailing ship *Francis de Pau* in New York harbor.

William Appleton, in his journal, explained that he feared his oldest son was losing his health. The Nathan Appletons were pleased to have cousin Willie come along with them. He was a charming young man who would be twenty-one in 1836. Jewett, the son of Nathan Appleton's sister Emily, was also a welcome addition to the party for he was a cheerful, personable young man. Going from Boston to New York to see them off, were crowds of friends and Uncle William, hovering over Willie like a hen with one chick, Fanny commented. Aunt Sam had come to hover over Jewett.

A small steamer carried the Appletons and their friends from the wharf to the *Francis de Pau*, anchored below the city. Then this little steamboat went "puffing away for New York" [1] and the Appleton girls, their arms full of flowers and their eyes full of tears, waved goodbye from the deck of the *Francis de Pau* until the steamer was "lost in New York's chaos of masts." Then they discovered that the wind was unfavorable so that there would be no sailing until next morning. The girls dried their eyes and "settled their curls."

Both Tom and his father had crossed the Atlantic under sail before, but the girls and their cousins had some preconceived ideas they would have to correct. It was not quiet on board ship. They were unprepared for "the crowing of cocks, the gabbling of geese, the yawling of the sailors." And the ship's captain was not the rough old sea-dog the girls expected.

"But the captain!" eighteen-year-old Fanny exclaimed. "We are agreeably disappointed and fancy him vastly." After the five P.M. dinner, the first night on board, the captain offered Fanny his arm and they had "a most delicious promenade for two hours." He taught Fanny nautical terms and she passed on her new knowledge of "studding sails — the throat and the peak, the spanker boom and the lazy guy." Later, at supper, the passengers, of whom there were only fifteen, "became quite merry" over "Tom's stale puns" — according to his unappreciative sister Fanny.

Tom had brought along a bulldog named Brag which he seemed to think the Appleton party needed for a traveling companion. Everybody fell over Brag in their narrow quarters, while at first Brag felt called upon to pick fights with the captain's dog — named "Lowell out of compliment to our cargo of cotton," Fanny supposed.

There was a round-house on the deck of the *Francis de Pau* with a passage from it leading to the cabin below. Here the passengers gathered in the evening when the seas were calm. Jewett had brought his flute and played German waltzes; a Frenchman sang "spirit-stirring national airs" — Tom and some of the other men "concocted ghost stories" in the hope of frightening the girls. There was so little wind that the captain seemed likely to lose his bet with Mary Appleton that they would see land in twenty days.

Then the scene changed. On the twenty-second of November, "We are dashing like mad through the grey waves — ten knots increased to twelve." While almost all the passengers were below decks, miserably seasick, Fanny went out to have a look at the storm. She was the only one able to write about it. "Terrible sight. The gale drives on. Two sailors have just taken down the 'royal,' slipping it gradually by ropes from its giddy height to the deck. How they cling, like spiders, to their cobweb of rigging, regardless of this mighty rushing wind and the swaying of the ship so fearfully to leeward! The heavy sails echo with deep booming, to the roaring of the blast . . . they keep time like a muffled drum to the choruses of the sailors who are now reefing the mainsail and topsail!"

Fanny was hanging on tight to the taffrail, "awed, bewildered — till a mountainous wave broke" over her head, drenching her to the skin. "To be baptised by such a priest at such an altar — a child of the tempest!" she exulted. She stayed at the rail till her father came to get her, told her to put on dry clothes at once and have some supper.

Young William, although fond of activity, was not getting much sea air on this voyage for health. Jewett was no longer playing his flute. He said that he had cholera twice but it was nothing compared to this. Mary was as good a sailor as Fanny, taking her turn at walking on deck with the captain, but when he began to teach the girls navigation, it was Mary who understood logarithms and Fanny who gave up.

Tom and his dog were on deck most of the time. When one of the pigs, brought along as part of the live provisions, got away, Brag had something to bark about. Tom made a very good sketch of a pig being washed in a barrel prior to slaughter — showing sailors with brooms and including both dogs, Brag and Lowell. Nathan Appleton, also a good sailor, had little interest in scenes on deck, however. He stayed below and played whist whenever he could get anyone to take a hand with him.

On November 30, "Another tremendous gale last night," Fanny wrote. "The captain says he has lost, these last few days, a mainsail, foresail, jib and flying-jib. He wonders the yards stand so bravely in these heavy squalls." The captain told the Appleton girls that they "deserved Admirals for husbands" and sang Irish songs to them one evening "after the rest had retired."

The cry of "Land-ho" sounded from the maintop on December 5. Along the rim of a misty horizon, the Scilly Isles loomed, "a skirt of bonny England, my fatherland, the Mecca of my heart," Fanny wrote, suddenly remembering all the traditions of her English ancestry. A pilot boat appeared. "The first human face, the first human voice" from another vessel "that has greeted us since America faded behind. We imagined ourselves Columbus in a new world! What did the voice say? 'Where are ye from? Where bound? Send us a bottle of rum.'" The captain had a bottle of rum lashed to a spar and tossed overboard — as the *Francis de Pau* swept by.

The ship proceeded to Le Havre after an exasperating calm in the English Channel with "Barfleur light constantly on the horizon." There was one more gale, "winds roaring, sailors tacking constantly to keep the ship off the rocks." Fanny called it a voyage of nineteen days, not counting the two-day calm, so that the captain won his bet with Mary. But the mate, who had "expected to win his hat of Tom," lost that bet.

Le Havre "was like being transported into the many pictures, lithographs and sketches" the Appleton girls had seen all their lives. They were excited and thrilled but they were cold. At the hotel, the "giant cast-iron fire place" swamped the few "dwarfish sticks" that burned brightly, all the heat going up the chimney. Mr. Appleton "expatiated on the lack of improvements in this old world where such fire places could exist" and constantly sent the boy for more bundles of wood.

Then dinner was served. "But the fried sole! The omelette soufflé, the bread, the butter!" Tom "returned to his rhapsodies on la Belle France" and the cold room with mirrors but no carpets, fire but no heat, was almost forgotten.

The American consul, "Mr. Greene," soon called on Nathan Appleton. He said that Thomas Pennant Barton, Chargé d'Affaires under the Honorable Edward Livingston, had just sailed for the United States. Livingston had been trying to come to terms with Louis Philippe for a settlement of the "French Spoliation Claims." Having failed, he had already demanded his passport and had gone home. The Chamber of Deputies had finally voted to pay the claims but under impossible conditions, so that Barton also had just been summoned home. "There were great expectations of war between France and America" according to the "gentlemanly and agreeable Mr. Greene." He gave the Appletons "a splendid dinner with the best French dishes" and saw them off on their travels next day.

Also on hand to say goodbye was the captain of the *Francis de Pau* who agreed to take Tom's dog, Brag, to Paris with him, along with Lowell. Then "Father, William and I drove in a quaint carriage with all the windows in front and a droll postillion, red-jacketed and booted to his knees, bestriding one of our shaggy horses. The rest went in a vehicle open in front in the same style. 'Crack, crack, crack!' goes the postillion's whip" — and they rumbled off "at a very easy rapid pace." The young people peered out of the coach windows, eager to see every new sight. "Even the dogs seemed differently to bark!" Women wore scarlet petticoats and they had no bonnets on! The scandalized Appleton girls declared that "this unbonneted race can never have dreampt of influenza."

Reaching Rouen on December 12, "Father and the rest of the gents set forth after breakfast to explore some manufactures," while the girls walked out alone, guide-book in hand. This was to be their almost invariable pattern of travel. The girls "came unexpectedly upon a mighty cathedral" which almost took their breath away. Fanny thought it could "only be equalled by Niagara!"

On rode the Appletons, arriving at last in Paris in the rain. The Meurice, favorite hotel among Americans, had no room for them. They found that the captain of the *Francis de Pau* had indeed brought Brag to Paris but that the dog was missing. "The loss of that nice dog" made them "sad indeed." But the next day after a night in cold lodgings, Mr. Appleton was able to engage a suite of rooms at the Meurice "mirrored and curtained" in the French style but also carpeted and heated to please Americans. Four days later, in response to an advertisement in the papers with reward offered, Brag came back "like the Prodigal Son, fierce for food . . . and joyful was the meeting between us," Fanny said.

Tom decided that Brag might not be much of an asset during further travels, however. He gave his bulldog to the Baron de Poilly,[2] a friend he had made on his first visit to France and whose estate, Polambray, Tom had visited. This friend had figured largely in Tom's letters home and the girls were all agog to meet him. "The Baron has at last become visible," Fanny wrote. "He has the most remarkable appearance of youth, seeing that he confesses to fifty and odd; wears a flaming waistcoat and pants plaited round the waist, petticoat-fashion; is tall, very handsome and dandified and has a formidable array of moustaches and whiskers. . . . The Baron takes Tom under his wing to all the great characters, painters etc.; Madame Mirabelle amongst the rest, who is the Madame de Maintenon of the present day and collects all the wits and poets at her soirees." To these, it was understood, the Appleton young ladies were not invited. But they did become friends with the Baron's daughter, the Countess Fitz-James.

Americans from the diplomatic corps and those in banking and importing in Paris called upon Nathan Appleton. There was business to be done, and while this was going on they sent their wives to call on the Appleton girls. First on the scene was Mrs. Wiggin whose family was interested in Lowell mills. She said she must take Mary and Fanny shopping so they "deferred to her taste" and sent away the sellers of embroidery and millinery who had come to their hotel suite to "display their wares with such grace."

Mrs. Welles,[3] whose husband headed Welles and Company, the Paris branch of the bank of Samuel Welles of Wellesley, Massachusetts, took Mary and Fanny to the studio of Jean Baptiste Isabey.[4] He was a "charming old Gentleman with the gracious manners of a former age." Isabey was sixty-eight — famous for his paintings of Napoleon and recently popular for his miniatures. He had just finished a miniature of Mrs. Welles, which the girls admired. Nathan Appleton commissioned Isabey to paint his daughters and they felt it would be an honor because so many crowned heads had sat to him, not to mention wealthy Americans. Larger than most miniatures, this double portrait is now in Longfellow House, Cambridge, Massachusetts. It shows Fanny with soft brown curls framing her face. She looks a little like her mother, the lovely Maria Theresa whose portrait hangs near. Mary seems more of an Appleton with her blond coloring, her hair amazingly braided. Mrs. Wiggin sent her maid to do the girls' hair before the opera, so perhaps the maid was the architect of these coiffures in the miniature, where the girls appear, sitting side by side.

Of course sightseeing was not neglected. At the Louvre, Fanny saw "a great many copyists at work — several of them females. Was I not envious!" she wrote.

Several times, the girls attempted to catch a glimpse of Louis Philippe but he appeared rarely in public, fearing assassination. They were in Mrs. Welles' carriage going to Isabey's studio for a sitting when a crowd gathered to see the king on his way to the Chamber of Deputies. But his majesty "skulked out of the back door" and they caught only a distant view. There was not a single *"Vive le Roi."*

General Duff and his two sons called on the Appletons — while Mrs. Wiggin waited in her carriage to take the girls shopping. Lady Duff was the aunt of Fanny Ingles of Beacon Hill fame whose sparkling presence and joyous waltzing had enlivened many a party at Aunt Sam's. One of the young men, "Attaché Duff," undertook to impress the Appleton girls with his sophisticated airs — laughing at Fanny's enthusiasm for the Louvre.

Then off went Mary and Fanny with Mrs. Wiggin — "amused at her way of doing things" — not sure she took them to the most distinguished couturiers. But she got tickets for them to *Norma* declaring that to be in Paris and not see Italian opera would be like going to the moon and never asking for the man in it! She was "very zealous" in their behalf and the opera proved an unforgettable experience. Fanny and Mary had never dreamed of such a voice as that of Guiditta Grisi.

Now the invitations came in. "Dined with Mr. Welles at half past six and nearly starved with the meager fare which proves what we have heard about his economical display of wines etc.," Fanny told. "The

Mary and Frances Elizabeth Appleton, painted in Paris, 1836, by Jean Baptiste Isabey. (Courtesy of the Longfellow House Trustees.)

whole dinner party was made up of the Welles personal clan — Mrs. Wiggin, Smith and ourselves. . . ." So much for Father's business friends. The Duffs were most desirous that the Appleton girls be presented at court but because there was at the moment, no American Minister to France, not even Attaché Duff could arrange it. Mrs. Welles said they weren't missing anything. The court balls were "woefully stupid, the royal family sitting up like sticks as no one was allowed to speak to them."

Of course Nathan Appleton took his party to see the Gobelin tapestry factories — which at this time his daughters were inclined to rate higher than a court ball even though they were sometimes bored with their father's business. They saw "huge looms with weavers at work" copying some "enormous pictures by Raphael, with splendid, gorgeous colors." Fanny thought these tapestries must outlive some of Raphael's paintings, and unfortunately some of them did. Fanny's taste, although deplorable concerning imitations of Raphael done in silk and wool, was no worse than most of her contemporaries. The weaving technique, which Nathan Appleton admired, was truly remarkable. Many an American tycoon would buy a modern Gobelin for his new palace in Newport. Only a few would pick up a faded old tapestry made entirely by hand in years gone by.

Christmas for the Appletons was "anything but a merry day." Mary was "confined to her room with a cold" while Fanny and cousin William were still trying to get over "a regular Boston influenza." Jewett had departed for Marseilles, thoroughly disgusted with Paris. Then it was New Year's, 1836. "Instead of lamp-lighters and bills" as on Beacon Street, "bon-bons and cards showered down" on the Appletons on the rue de Rivoli. This was gratifying and Tom had done his best by his sisters. He had taken them to the old Palais Royale, then housing "a splendid arcade — a square of shops and cafés, each side, as long as Beacon Street." It was a "blaze of brilliancy completely bewildering." But by now all the Appletons, including Tom, were ready to leave wintry Paris.

There was frantic last-minute shopping. Dressmakers surrounded Mary and Fanny "like harpies," they said. Their new cloaks were much admired but the girls had no idea that they had bought so many clothes until it came time to pack their luggage. Almost at the last minute, "who should call but Mr. Rouhette," the French teacher of Tom and Mary's "juvenile days." He was unchanged, with "his elegant little bows, diamond ring and gold pencil case. . . . It was a scene worthy of the stage,"

Fanny said. Mr. Rouhette "entered, rushed up to Tom, kissed him on both cheeks and would have done the like to Father, if Father had not divined his purpose," in time to dodge!

The elegant Attaché Duff made a farewell call bringing a bouquet of artificial flowers with bon-bons among them. He talked "with fastidious indifference" about Fanny's adored Guiditta Grisi and told the girls they would "never look at the Louvre again" after they had seen Italy. Fanny was indignant. "Happy the days of greenness when we can open our eyes with unfeigned awe before a Cathedral or a Raphael and when Grisi's notes can summon a thrill of unschooled excitement," she wrote.

The Countess Fitz-James sent Tom a parting gift — a journal in which to write down his poetry and another for sketches and comments — all enclosed in one handsome case. The Baron had already taken Brag to Polambray where Tom would one day visit not only the Baron's large family of children and grandchildren — but also his dog who lived to a good old age.

Mr. Appleton had acquired carriages for a long European journey. On January 22, 1836, they left Paris in the rain — having arrived in the rain! "Our two vehicles make quite a show," Fanny said. "The largest is a sort of man-of-war on wheels, green as the sea, without and within, deep, roomy and comfortable with charming accommodations for books, before and behind and in pockets at the side." Mr. Appleton had hired a French maid for his daughters. "Adèle rides in solitary dignity on a sort of rumble seat behind the big carriage where she is no small adornment to the establishment," Fanny said. The second vehicle was equally delightful according to Fanny, and "bears in its rear the factotem, the General of the expedition . . . in fact the courier. And he, the short, the strutting, the ever-grinning, the all-important François." He was valet to the men of the party as well as courier.

"Paris with all its life and its gaiety, its splendor and its meanness, its comforts and its mud" faded in the distance. At dusk, the Appletons reached Fontainebleau, "explored" it next morning but found "an air of melancholy gorgeousness which floats one back to the days when kings *were* kings." With "no small thrill of pleasure," the girls found Aunt Sam's name in the guest book at the inn, written when she was there in 1833. Kings and queens might come and go but they were of minor importance compared to dear Aunt Sam!

"Wearisome, wearisome is this carriage life although we roll along as on velvet," the young Appletons discovered after two days of rain. Then the weather cleared. Tom, Fanny and William were in the big carriage and "merry enough was the eating of our chicken, as we mounted a high hill, with bright sun gleaming." From the inn of the night before, they had brought along roast chicken and wine. Tom had a tremendous appetite, "a shower of wings, drumsticks and crumbs fell from either window as they came, bare and meager from his unsparing teeth," Fanny said. The patient horses "toiled up many a slippery hill and down they dashed into many a vine-clad valley" with the girls and Thomas Gold Appleton, that litter-bug of the nineteenth century!

After a change of horses, their coach climbed another hill while Tom, Willie and Mary finished "with enthusiasm" their bottle of Burgundy. Whether or not Tom threw this bottle out of the carriage window, Fanny did not say.

On January 27, "it begins to appear quite natural to arise, not with but before the lark and meet the dawn on the road," Fanny said. Not that she liked early rising any better than she had on trips to Canada when her father had been "furious" for fear his girls would miss the train. She always exclaimed loudly against it as being against nature. The young Appletons were enjoying their journey to the hilt, however. At almost every inn where post-horses were changed, they rushed to some nearby spot to sketch something. Like modern tourists, all festooned with special cameras, lenses and light meters, Mary, Fanny and Tom were never without sketch book, pencils and water-colors.[4] There was never time enough to finish a sketch but they often worked on them at night, adding shadows, distant hills, or improving the outline of a peasant girl at a town well. It does not appear that cousin William sketched very much, and there would be times when Nathan Appleton must have wondered why someone didn't repair the tumble-down castles. But at last they reached Lyons where the whole party was as excited over silk mills as even Mr. Appleton could wish.

"The manufacture is an immense establishment and very curious," Fanny wrote. "After a time, I began to comprehend the art. They were making rich shawls and beautiful figured satins. The pure, glossy silk looks like spun silver as they wind it off on spools — which reminded me of Lowell. We were amused to see a man . . . turning the big wheel for the machinery — instead of a stream of water. Yankees can beat them in the utility of the 'Great Manufacture' — as they us in the 'variation' and ornamental."

The Appletons left Lyons by steamer, putting the huge carriage and the smaller one on deck — and sitting in them every day during the long journey down the Rhone. The steamer stopped at night, passengers going to an inn to eat and sleep, then "at the barbarous hour of half past five in the morning" it was back to the boat again. The country was flat but the impressive approach to Avignon made a dramatic climax as muddy river banks changed suddenly "to cliffs with castles and ruins and caves."

The travelers seemed unprepared for the beauty of the Palace of the Popes. Their carriages were taken off and stored for a few days while the Appletons made excursions in small, locally hired rigs. Vaucluse was the high point for the romantic Appleton girls. It seemed to Fanny that Petrarch himself must have created "the fountain in its cavern, to murmur dreams" of poetry and of Laura. She picked a leaf "from the laurel that Petrarch planted" and pressed it on the margin of her travel journal. At Avignon, she pressed a sprig of arbor vitae and wrote over it, "from Laura's grave." These remain, still faintly green, beside her journal entries.

Now it was back to the carriages again for an overland journey to Marseilles. Dr. Bigelow, of Boston, had assured the Appletons that the Maison Carée was one of the most beautiful Roman temples existing. Fanny found it "more unique than charming." But they stopped at a little inn near Aix where Tom and Fanny "scrambled up a hill behind the house" and found themselves "among curiously carved shrines" — the "extensive ruins of a fort and convent." They were enchanted because this was their own discovery. Back at the inn, there was another discovery. The wallpaper "with its Turks and fair Sultanas" was the same as the paper in Aunt Sam's breakfast room, back on Beacon Street!

All Marseilles was "a forest of masts" and the Mediterranean was so blue that "the sky looked pale beside it." Next, the streets of Genoa, as their carriage rumbled through the gates, were "literally lined with palaces" — their hotel a former palace. Fanny imagined herself "a highborn maiden who had a right to gaze into mirrors thirty feet high," lean on marble balustrades, listen to fountains — enjoy the perfume of orange blossoms — "and have perhaps a Romeo."

Turning southward, on their way from Genoa to Pisa, the Appletons stopped for an hour at Carrara. They found the town "one workshop, the chisle and hammer resounding in every street and the pavements strewn with snowy marble." Fanny was right when she said that the marble cutters had "produced more gods and goddesses than old Jupiter ever reckoned in his court." There was no time to visit the quarries, with their strange reflected tones of blue, green and gold, eventually the delight of landscape painters. "We consoled ourselves with the belief that the granite mines at Quincy were quite as fine," Fanny said.

All the Appletons were over-prepared for Rome. In school and at home they had read ancient history. In church, the Rome of St. Peter's ministry and martyrdom, of persecutions, catacombs and the early Christians, was the subject of sermons from time to time. On the first day of March, "Can I believe that tonight, I shall be in the Eternal City," Fanny wrote. At noon next day they "passed over Monte Cimino in such deep snow that a sleigh would have been acceptable." The Campagna looked cheerful after the snow — they "ascended a hill" and saw St. Peter's dome. Fanny thanked God in her heart that she had lived to this day. But having built a city of dreams, she could not fail to be disappointed by reality. She had forgotten that there was a modern city of Rome.

As they entered the Porto Popolo, they saw "gay barouches of smartly dressed ladies and whiskered Englishmen." Fanny thought herself back in Paris. Almost at once, Mr. and Mrs. Brooks called bringing William Payne with them. Seeing him reminded Fanny of "our merry days in Philadelphia" and she found him "as full of fun as then." Mr. and Mrs. Brooks immediately organized a party to see the Colosseum by moonlight, inviting several young men for Mary and Fanny. They "filled two carriages to take the Colosseum by storm," it seemed, and Fanny was disgusted with such a frivolous approach and resolved "against sentiment and romance . . . with such a cortège."

But coming suddenly upon it, "one huge mass rose like a wall to the sky" where, "through Time's finger-holes," she saw "here and there a star." Fanny's poetic imagination took over but she was still exasperated with Mr. Brooks because he had "brought along Byron in his pocket to compare the poetry with the reality — like a pattern of goods!" At first, St. Peter's seemed too big to Fanny but after she had heard music there, she was reconciled to the vast proportions of the basilica. Attaché Duff's prophecy was fulfilled after the girls had seen the Vatican gallery. The Louvre now seemed to have been "vault-like. How often have I seen casts and copies, how *new* was the effect of the originals," Fanny wrote.

Before long, the Appleton sisters had come to terms with modern Rome and loved it. They put aside their travel books, such as Mrs. Jameson's which "sounds so *flat* here," and took to re-reading Madame de Staël's *Corinne*, whose heroine, in search of poetic freedom, lived in Rome. Tom discovered a girl named Rosa Taddei, who composed rhymed verse on the stage, on subjects suggested to her by the audience. "Corinne exists!" exulted Fanny, because the "Improvatrice," her "eyes wild as though looking through all time," chanted verse after verse. "A harp struck up. Rosa's voice thunders forth tones as if her whole soul were in them" — just like Corinne, that early fictitious heroine of woman's liberation! Tom speculated that Rosa was in a trance, repeating what spirit voices told her.

There was a donkey-back expedition to the Campagna for a group of young people. Fanny's donkey-boy sang to her and picked violets for her. A girl named Harriet fell off her donkey and Fanny's donkey tried to run away. One of the young men said it was "an assinine expedition" — the pun being applauded. Fanny said it was "an expedition worthy of Mrs. Radcliffe."

Summing up modern Rome, "It does not live like others on the breath of whizzing manufactories and laboring steam engines, — but painting in all branches; sculpture in every variety, are staple productions. The noise of the chisle certainly accords better with its shattered columns and innumerable gushing fountains than would that of saw-mills and spinning-Jennies."

Nathan Appleton was an indulgent father, bent on giving his children and young William the grand tour in every sense of the word, but he must have wished he could see a few spinning-jennies. Fanny accounted for part of his time. "Went to see Father's bust at Wyatt's. Made a vast many alterations which the sculptor acceeded to good-naturedly."

Richard Henry Wilde, former Congressman from Georgia, called on Nathan Appleton.[5] The girls could not believe he wrote "that exquisite 'My Life Is like a Summer Rose'," because he was so "anti-sentimental looking." He was only on a visit to Rome but he had made Florence his home while he began his *Life and Times of Dante*. After leaving Rome, the Appletons spent some time in Florence where they revised their opinion of Mr. Wilde and forgave him his over-long monologues when he made Dante's Florence real to them. It was Fanny's turn to sit to a sculptor. She begrudged the time spent in the studio while Bartolini did more than justice to her corkscrew curls.

The Appletons had been encouraged about young William's health, and Nathan Appleton wrote to Willie's father suggesting that the boy spend another year with them. But in Florence young William was ill. They sent for a doctor whose report alarmed them so they set out for Switzerland at once. They were in Berne on June 20, which the girls found "excessively picturesque." Willie was better — sketch books were being filled so rapidly that Mary and Fanny had to buy new ones. That night they drove past the "picturesque towers of Thun," alighted at "a dashing new hotel beyond the town" and "rushed to the windows of their room to see the view."

After the noon meal next day, while Mary and Fanny "were puzzled what to sketch" but hard at it just the same, "Professor Longfellow sends up his card to Father," Fanny wrote in her diary. She hoped "the venerable gentleman won't drop in on us," although she had liked his *Outre-Mer*. The venerable professor, who had been twenty-nine on February 27, did not appear — he had been traveling in the other direction and went to Berne.

The Appletons put their two carriages in storage and took the steamboat to Interlaken. On July 31, a Sunday, Fanny was in her room writing letters and bringing her journal up to date. She was not particularly pleased to be called downstairs "to welcome . . . Professor Longfellow."

Longfellow was "a young man after all, or perhaps the son of the poet," Fanny wrote when she went back to her room to continue her journal. He was clean-shaven, undeniably handsome with fine blue eyes and a generous mouth.[6] Fanny Appleton had met her fate but for the moment she was not in the least interested.

At the hotel, there was the "young Count, so genteel and amiable a youth" who "brought in a band of blind musicians" one evening who "ground off waltzes." People from nearby hotels gathered and there was another German count, "rather well-looking but not over genteel," who waltzed Fanny almost off her feet while she screamed *"pas si vite!"* During the following evening the Appleton girls taught the Virginia reel to their friends of various nationalities. They "frolicked till eleven."

The day after his call, Fanny took "a drive and a walk along Lake Brienz with Mr. Longfellow — quiet and lovely — talk about the Tyrol . . ." she jotted down in the pocket diary she would later expand. There was a quadrille that evening and her partner was "a red-haired cockney who danced like a kangaroo." She danced a "highland reel with two Scotchmen" who were "very merry" and she "waltzed with both." The professor was there but he was no dancer. Fanny just "talked with Mr. Longfellow."

Of course Henry Longfellow was also setting things down in his daily record. On the day he sent up his card but did not meet Mr. Appleton, he wrote, "Good God, what a solitary, lonely being I am. Why do I travel? Every hour my heart aches with sadness." It was nearly a month later when he told of walking with Miss Fanny and watching while she "sketched the cloister and a cottage on the Aar." But when he put in an appearance at the Appletons' hotel that evening, he "talked incessantly with M. A." — Mary Appleton.

William seemed better. The mountain air relieved his "influenza," he could breathe more easily, so the Appletons decided to see more of Switzerland and then linger for a while in some other mountain village. They went back to Thun to pick up their carriages. The Boston Motleys, in their carriage, left Interlaken at the same time, taking Mr. Longfellow with them. Tom had gone ahead to Zurich, so at Thun there was extra space with the Appletons. "My lucky star placed me in the A's carriage with the two young ladies who are all intellect and feeling," Longfellow wrote. "We read the 'Genevieve' of Coleridge and the 'Christobel' and many other scraps of song; and little German ballads by Uhland, simple and strange."

"Mr. Longfellow, William and I in the big carriage," was what Fanny jotted down in her little record book. "Very pleasant morning. Know nothing of scenery, so liked listening to reading, German, Coleridge etc." They stopped near an old mill for lunch where Mr. Longfellow, Mary, Fanny and William sat on a log beside the mill stream and "had a very merry time." The professor did not mention this interlude but "read poetry as before" next day.

The Appletons parted company with the Motleys and Mr. Longfellow, to make a mountain excursion near Zug. The ascent on horseback was "steep like stairs." They took rooms, perhaps near the summit of Zuger-Berg — Fanny's notes are not too clear. In the morning a horn blew, there was a slamming of doors and scurrying of feet as everyone rushed to the summit to see the sunrise — "Jungfrau and all her maidens against a blue sky." After a good breakfast, they all started down the mountain, but Nathan Appleton was thrown from his horse, luckily on the grass so he was "unhurt" except perhaps for his pride. Fanny "now knew what eagles enjoy" and "felt like a bird" all the way. It was the last carefree experience for a long time to come.

William had not felt well enough to go up the mountain. In Zurich, the Appletons again consulted a doctor. "Worse news than we could expect. Mingle tears with my soup" at dinner, Fanny wrote. The Motley party of travelers had arrived in Zurich, and in the afternoon Fanny "walked with Mr. Longfellow, going up to a hill under some huge, dark linden trees — winds sighing and leaves rustling like continuous, dreadful thought." Even now, Fanny could not bring herself to write the dread word, "consumption," in her journal.

The Appletons hated "Le Corbeau," their inn at Zurich, and Mr. Longfellow improvised, as they left —

> *Beware the Raven of Zurich*
> *'Tis a bird of ill omen still*
> *A noisy and unclean bird*
> *With a very, very long bill.*

The town had also been crowded with "Italians, fleeing the Cholera" and William said he was well enough to go to a pleasanter place.

Fanny rode with William in the rain. It would have been considered a wrong-doing not to prepare William for death. Ever since childhood he had lived with relatives from time to time while his father traveled for health. He loved Nathan Appleton's children as though they had been his brothers and sisters so now he tried to comfort Fanny. He told her "how pleasant it was to die of consumption instead of a fever or an accident," and then, remembering some of his father's strong religious precepts, " 'Well — I suppose it is just as well that I have lived no longer, exposed to evil,' he said."

At Schaffhausen, William was "carried upstairs to bed." Setting aside plans for a further tour, Longfellow went to Schaffhausen with the Appletons. He took his turn, sitting with William, who was never left alone. But when Fanny had been with William and it was her turn to go out for a breath of air, he walked with her. The first day they "wandered off under some trees, sat down and had a long talk about Boston. . . ." On Sunday, they sat together with William "all morning" while Longfellow read aloud, and in the village "the bells rang like ours at home," Fanny said.

Sometimes William seemed better but his strength ebbed. Fanny had seen it all before. On August 15, "The wind was sweeping through the long avenue of trees" on the promenade beside the Rhine. "In the twilight stillness the rushing of the river mingled like a dirge" with the wind while Fanny and Longfellow "talked about Autumn, which he prefers to the rest of the year — so do I," Fanny wrote. They sat for nearly an hour on a bench under some trees and talked "about poetry and people and living in different places." Fanny said she wanted to live in the country where there were lakes and mountains.

"But now the rushing of the river and sighing of the trees undid me," Fanny confessed. This was as close as she came to admitting that she cried and Henry Longfellow comforted her. They sat talking till it was quite dark — "people occasionally passing like specters, lanterns hanging in the Casino gardens."

On August 24, William's "Happy spirit took its flight. Watching with such intentness every fainter breathing, it was some moments ere we were conscious all was over. Happy spirit, to regain thy angel's wing," Fanny wrote.[7] William would have been twenty-one in October.

Longfellow was not there. Just seven days earlier he had received a letter from Miss Crowninshield, "which decides him to leave us immediately," Fanny had written. "Quite distressed to have him go. He has been so kind to William and helped to keep up our spirits." Her understanding father took her to ride along the river. "Miss very much Mr. Longfellow" she wrote in her line-a-day book. Her father took her walking "down the valley."

Dr. Wainwright of Boston was in Schaffhausen when William died. It was a comfort to have him read the funeral service for the boy who was buried there, in Switzerland. Sadly the Appletons resumed their travels — eventually reaching Strasbourg.

FOURTEEN

APPLETONS AT THE COURTS OF KINGS

IN STRASBOURG THE HOTEL WAS FULL, but people were just leaving so the Appletons sat down in the salon to wait for their rooms. Fanny looked out the window and "suddenly recognized Mr. Longfellow in the street." [1] In her diary she had admitted that she had missed him. Now she had even more need of his sympathy because of William's death. But Longfellow was not alone.

Next day, the Appletons met Mr. Longfellow and his three ladies — Mrs. Bryant, "her fair blue-eyed daughter, rather pretty, Miss C — modest." Mrs. Bryant was the wife of William Cullen Bryant and "Miss C" was Clara Crowninshield. After breakfast in the hotel dining room they all talked together. Then, "they leave," Fanny wrote. And that was that.

How much the Appletons knew about Longfellow's private life, Fanny did not say. When he tried to lighten her grief during her cousin William's fatal illness, he might have told her the cause of his own loneliness — the death of his wife, Mary Potter, in Rotterdam. They had been married only four years when they set out for Europe so that Longfellow could study abroad before beginning his work at Harvard as professor of modern languages.

Longfellow had taken all his savings, sold some of his books and other belongings, and borrowed from his father to finance the trip. When two of his wife's school friends proposed going along and offered to pay their own and part of Longfellow's expenses in return for his escort (since young ladies would not dream of traveling alone) these extra funds were welcome. One of the girls was called home but Clara Crown-inshield remained and was the diarist of events.[2]

Clara was the illegitimate but acknowledged daughter of George Crowninshield, a dashing and wealthy sea captain. He sent Clara to good schools and left her a comfortable fortune in his will. Angry Crowninshield relatives failed to break the will but broke the scandal wide open. Her guardian, Benjamin Ropes Nichols of Salem, not only won her case for her but gave her a home in his own family. She was attractive, although not really pretty, somewhat unsure of herself, and Fanny Appleton's word "modest" described her well.

The Longfellows had been childless but in 1835, Mary was expecting a child. After a journey through Denmark, Sweden and Holland, they were in Amsterdam when Mary had "an ague fit." On October 4 it was raining, and the doctor said Mary had caught cold. The following night Clara, who had a room in the same entry at the hotel, heard a tap on her door. It was Longfellow who asked if Clara had a candle. She had burned down her bedside candle but found him another. "Is anything wrong?" she asked.

"Yes," he told her. "Mary is sick — worse than ever." Clara asked if she could help but he said "No — you can't do any good."

In his own journal Longfellow wrote of being up before daylight — "Mary being very ill. The very deuce to pay and all in the dark. . . . Sent for the Dr. in a hurry but before he arrived it was all over." Mary had suffered a miscarriage.

The doctor left Mary some medicine, and this seems to have been the extent of his treatment. On October 20 the Longfellows and Clara set out again for Haarlem and then Rotterdam. Here, Mary's strength suddenly failed and she told Clara that her "old troubles" had returned. There was excessive bleeding, fever and pain. The doctor in Rotterdam ordered poultices to be applied to her side and said that Mary would be well enough to travel in a few days. Although "deadly pale," Mary was eager to go. On November 29, 1835, after a brave fight, Mary Longfellow died of loss of blood and infection after her October 5th miscarriage.

Longfellow continued his studies but by the spring of 1836 he realized he must have a rest and a change of scene. He planned to take Clara along if a proper chaperone could be found but plans fell through and he left her in Heidelberg studying German in a German family near the Bryant ladies' pension.

The Bryants finally agreed to go to Switzerland with Clara, Mr. Longfellow providing escort. But Longfellow lingered with the Appletons at Interlaken. Finally, Clara summoned him. After all, she was paying at least part of the bills — a point Longfellow may not have told the Appletons. On August 30, Clara Crowninshield wrote in her diary, "Saw the Appletons of Boston." She and the Bryants, with Longfellow, took the diligence for Paris next day and sailed for home on October 12.

The Appletons planned to travel down the Rhine to see Germany before going back to Paris. But on September 14, in Mayence, the girls were seriously ill. They had been taking a water cure, the water tasting like that at Saratoga with rotten eggs added, Fanny said. Food also was almost inedible. Fanny was deeply depressed, remembering the touch of her mother's hand — longing for home. She was the first to recover, however, refusing to take any more "nauseous doses" from the doctor, his coat so sleek, his manner so solemn — and his horses so handsome, "one white steed to his chariot in the morning and two in the afternoon." He pronounced the illness gastric fever, which was as good a way as any to describe the effects of probably contaminated water, plus food poisoning.

Almost two and half dreary months passed before the Appleton carriage was at last dashing "along the gay boulevards" of Paris, "swarming with butterfly population." The girls recognized restaurants and shops along the rue de la Paix and the "sunshiny arcades of the rue de Rivoli" and at last the Hotel Meurice with its familiar inner court. They "felt a bounding thrill" which Fanny thought was "as strong, nearly, as if the State House and Beacon Street were before us." With "anything but tears" they looked their last at the traveling carriage, their "dear green ark."

After a brief stay at the Meurice, Nathan Appleton took an apartment for the winter, opposite the royal palace of the Tuileries. This palace, doomed to destruction within a few years, cut off all their sun but the girls did not complain. The golden damask walls in their apartment supplied sunshine enough. They adored their "boudoir with tête-à-tête sofas, rosewood cabinets and artificial flowers." In Mayence, while waiting for Mary to recover, Fanny had played billiards with her father and Tom. To her delight there was a billiard room in the Paris apartment.

Mrs. Wiggin put in an appearance wanting to take the girls under her wing again. "But we are old chickens now," Fanny said. The girls went to shops they had discovered for themselves ordering ball gowns with their father's full approval for he felt that his daughters deserved a little fun. Fanny was soon appearing in an enchanting pink hat, and humourously complaining that she met no one who noticed it. Jewett, who had been in Paris while the rest were in Switzerland, knew how to get "superb tickets" for opera and theater.

It might have been Tom who found a talented cook, so that the Appletons could give elegant dinners to bankers and diplomats and suppers for young people when everyone would "chat or play billiards, after."

During their first visit to Paris, there had been no American representative to the Court of Louis Philippe. Now everything was different. General Cass [3] filled the empty post of minister to France. Jackson man though he was, he and Nathan Appleton liked and respected each other. At first, Fanny was too ardent a Federalist to unbend, but she was soon admitting that Mrs. Cass "looked a little less Detroitish in a Parisian cap." Then, almost before she knew it, she found herself liking these Westerners, General and Mrs. Cass, and their son and daughters.

During their first trip to Paris, the Appleton girls had tried hard to catch so much as a glimpse of the king. Now General Cass saw to it that they would be presented at Court and gave Attaché Ledyard the very agreeable task of attending to everything. January 3, 1837, was to be the great day.

Fanny wrote up her journal that night. [4] She had been left behind like Cinderella in the chimney corner with no fairy godmother to take away her cold. Mary, in white crepe and roses, had gone off with Mrs. Cass. But Fanny was not without hope. The list of girls to be presented at Court was alphabetical. Fanny had it all arranged to go on the fifth with the Sears and the Walshes. Attaché Ledyard came to see her next day to cheer her up and plan for the next presentation. She gave him a cup of tea and they talked of the Sedgwicks of Lenox and the Duchess of Sutherland's diamonds.

On January 5 Fanny said to her cold, "you may go now, as one always hints to bores," and in high spirits, dressed for the presentation. "Roses trimmed my locks and blushed in my sleeves," she wrote. She had the honor of sharing the carriage of the ambassadress with Mr. Ledyard as her knight, wearing his attaché uniform.

Their names were recorded. Then a "noble staircase hung with many a chandelier rose high in air — five immense rooms opened before them" at the top of the stairs. The rooms were brilliant with lights, lofty and finely proportioned, rich in gilding and carving. They sauntered onward. Utter emptiness! Colder and darker were the rooms as they advanced. In the last room, a huge chandelier was standing on the floor while scarlet-liveried servants lighted the candles. Fearing delays, they had arrived too soon.

Mrs. Sears, her daughters Harriet and Ellen, Fanny Appleton and Attaché Ledyard wandered around, looking at portraits on the walls until they suddenly realized that the rooms were filling up. They hurried to the velvet-lined throne room which was already filled so they found seats in the third of the five big rooms, and half an hour later, "with no flourish of trumpets, not even silence . . ." they all "arose and courtesied in a wavering line," as his majesty arrived, bowing and smiling graciously. Louis Philippe was "old and fat and ruddy," Fanny said. He had "bleached white whiskers" and wore a "coal black wig." He paused for "many words to the Ambassadress and Mrs. Sears," but to the girls, "a bow and a smile and he passed on."

On the previous day, December 27, the king had been shot at on his way to the Chamber of Deputies. The bullet went over his head and lodged in the roof of the carriage. The duke of Orleans had a bleeding cheek from flying glass. Louis Philippe had been quite calm but the queen had cried. Now Fanny thought "how easily a dagger could have ended his persecuted days, from any hand in the throng, where merely elbow room was granted him."

After the king had passed, "surrounded by Maids of Honor, the Queen loomed in sight." She wore a "pale yellow dress and a blue velvet toque, one blaze of diamonds. And hideous enough she was, with her snowy ringlets and withered Austrian visage." The two princesses, dressed in red velvet, were better looking, and Fanny was quite taken with the "graceful, elegant Duke of Orleans" who stopped to speak to the American girls. At the end of the procession came "the boyish, light-haired Duke de Nemours," and the "Duke de Joinville, a tall, lanky school-boy." Fanny felt sorry for the royal family who must continue their weary round talking to the crowd of guests for the next three hours.

From now on, parties came thick and fast while the Appleton girls danced to their heart's content. The Welles family, bankers, gave a ball at which Mary was "seductive in blue tulle adorned with rose buds made of ribbon." She wore red and white wild roses in her hair and ornaments of turquoise and gold. Fanny's dress was white crepe with bouquets of roses on each side of the skirt and in the sleeves. The room was crowded with dancers, and she danced the first quadrille with Attaché Ledyard. Fanny also danced with the Count Rochefoucauld but remarked that some of her special beaux had not been asked to the party. They did not bank with Welles and Company.

There were plenty of American young men in Paris just now. To everyone's surprise, John Crosby, who had been such a beau of Fanny's in Canada, turned up. He had been married but was now a widower. One of Fanny's school friends wrote to ask if she had "renewed her flirtation" and would soon become Fanny Crosby.[5] There wasn't a chance. Johnny Crosby dined at the Appletons' apartment and Fanny played billiards with him. But he said that he hated the theater, so Fanny took Ledyard [6] to see the *Barber of Seville* with her.

The court ball was "the most magnificent spectacle that ever dazzled my eyes," Fanny said. There was a "delicious band"; Attaché Ledyard never left her side but found seats for the two of them in a balcony where they could see the whole show. They had a close view of the king and queen and watched the royal princesses, "dressed superbly and alike" who were constantly dancing with their "fore-ordained partners" — young officers of the national guard. Afterwards, Fanny heard that "our Ambassador's hopeful son took to his heels when demanded as a partner to a Princess."

Looking down on the scene, "nothing could exceed the brilliance of the effect," Fanny thought. "All the men were in dress uniform, the ladies garlanded with flowers . . . with all the starry firmament upon their heads in diamonds." Then she turned to look "from the dazzling light of the chandeliers . . . to the solemn, awful darkness of the terrace — where nothing relieved the blackness of the night but a glimmer of light at the Barrier d'Étoile and the firefly lamps of the file of advancing carriages . . ." The crowd increased.

In the crush, Ledyard gallantly escorted Fanny through the throne room, which was filled with diplomats, then to the next room where "groups of card players from all nations were seated as quietly as if nothing was going on. A solemn Turk in full costume was dealing." Fanny saw "Rothschild's sculpin visage peering through the crowd." Only the two largest rooms were reserved for dancing with a band and Fanny complained of this. "The ringing of the Postillion bells and whip echoed round the ceilings finely" she said, evidently enjoying these sound effects from the band but just as she was about to dance "we received a hint for supper." She and her partner parted because ladies were served first, then the men.

The ladies were shown into an ante-room where they milled up and down and waited. Even in her private diary, Fanny was too discreet to mention powder rooms. She watched the Countess Guiccioli "gliding about on the arm of a large dame dressed in Italian style." Somebody had pointed out the Countess, Lord Byron's mistress,[7] and Fanny was disappointed. The Countess was "a dumpy woman with auburn ringlets, fair complexion and light blue eyes, everything that Byron said he dispised" — at least according to Fanny Appleton. Byron had recommended a foreign mistress because after a man got tired of what she said, he could find entertainment in how she said it — but Fanny probably did not know this. She conceded, however, that the Countess looked younger than she had expected and had "plump white shoulders."

"At last the Queen and the Maids of Honor proceeded through our ranks," Fanny wrote. "And then, in one confusing, rushing mass, the dames flowed after her" into the supper room. "The disorder was disgraceful and lace and muslin and flowers sighed away their freshness in the contest . . ." But "no superlatives could paint the magnificence of the feast" when once those hungry ladies got into the supper room.

After the ladies left and after the servants had cleared away the first debris, the gentlemen came to the table. The king was not there! He had received an anonymous note to "beware," so Louis Philippe had left the ball. The Appleton girls got back to their apartment at five in the morning. The next night they went to another ball. At still another, the floor "was literally strewn with diamonds" when the necklace of a duchess was broken.

At their apartment, Mr. Appleton gave "quite a splendid feast to a dozen worthy Signors," Fanny wrote and she was "charmed with the elegant dancing" of the gentlemen. She also astonished Allyne Otis, her young Beacon Hill neighbor, now in Paris, with her "skill at billiards."

Also in Paris for a short time, was Horatio Greenough of Boston, already a friend of the Appletons. The sculptor had received his first big commission, a statue of Washington. This work, when finished, brought him more blame than praise because he had portrayed the Father of his Country as a Roman senator, somewhat insufficiently clad in a toga. In Paris, Mary Appleton sat to him for a portrait bust, although she wanted to take lessons on the harp instead. On the pretext of helping Mary to look cheerful, a crowd of young men gathered at the studio to watch proceedings. Among them, they perpetrated what they said was a "Dramatic Ode,"[8] beginning,

> Dear, dear, what can the matter be
> Mr. Greenough, you promised the likeness should flatter me

And the bust should be better than any made latterly
In figure and features and air.
And you took a great lump of clay, big as my bonnet
And you molded and pinched it and threw water on it
And who would have thought it, but now that you've done it
'Tis a fright that will make people stare . . .

There were several more stanzas in which the artist was supposed to declare that he always flattered his sitters and had made Mary "only too pretty." But after all the party-going, it was not surprising that Mary came down with the grippe. Greenough had to go back to Rome before the bust was finished.

On the sixth of March, the Appletons went to Ambassador Cass's last soirée of the season. The girls had been to a costume party where Mary represented "Flora," her dress sewn with flowers made of ribbon. Fanny had been a lady of Seville, her Spanish lace mantilla immensely becoming. "I danced much," she said. But now the Cass family were to go off on a Mediterranean voyage with Commodore Eliot. "A charming excursion, with so many beaux attached," Fanny said. She envied the Cass girls but the Appleton Grand Tour required a visit to Belgium, Holland, England and Scotland.

Attaché Ledyard came to say goodbye to Fanny Appleton. He was off to Marseilles to buy saddles and "other necessities" for the Cass party. He brought Fanny a bunch of violets. Fanny's Boston school friends had reported Boston gossip about her — that she was to marry her cousin Isaac Appleton Jewett, for example. They wrote of engagements and weddings at home, but in her diary Fanny commented, "I will enjoy my wings a little longer." And one evening, Fanny wrote, "Found poor Mr. Ledyard come to say goodbye once more." She wondered "if he will keep his promise to bring me home a willow-branch where the maidens of Judah hang their harps. Perhaps I may be inclined to accept it for my crest by that time!"

Longfellow, on his return to the United States, had called on the William Appletons. Aunt William wrote to Fanny about it.[9] "We have seen Mr. Longfellow several times socially. . . . I do not know what to think of him exactly, but shall endeavor to be more acquainted and think I may like him very much. . . . Your picture, which has attracted his attention always, during his visits, he likes very much — the attitude especially . . ."

One of Mary Ann Appleton's half-sisters had met Longfellow in New

York and wrote to Aunt William. "I hear good accounts of dear Fanny. You ask me how I like her beau? To tell the honest truth, he does not appear very interesting to me and I am disappointed in him although I cannot give you a good reason for it; but I trust it may prove a happy match, for she is as deserving of happiness as anyone I know." This letter would certainly have made Fanny indignant, if she could have read it.

Tom took Mary and Fanny to see the Paris Art Exposition, held at the Louvre. Among the painters showing their work was Isabey. "Our miniatures occupy a conspicuous place at the entrance," the girls wrote. They were surprised and pleased, not only on their own account but because they were fond of Isabey with his courtly manners and tales of by-gone days. It was a pleasure to see his work in a place of honor.

But now it was time to leave the Paris apartment where they had had so much fun and to set out once more in search of culture and education. Bales and boxes were packed to be sent home. Nathan Appleton, the ardent advocate of the protective tariff, was going to have duty to pay at the Boston Customs House. Other trunks were forwarded to London before the Appletons climbed into "a square American-looking carriage" with a mountain of luggage piled on top. Jewett was staying behind so he and Ned Motley grabbed a cab and tried to escort the Appletons out of town. After "a memorable chase" the cab horse gave up so the boys turned back. A few miles more and the Appletons' coach-harness broke — but the postillion had some string in his pocket to mend it. Of course it rained.

In Belgium, Nathan Appleton took his family to observe the manufacture of lace. He could see at a glance that American factories could make lace faster. Lace curtains, a sign of gentility, ought to sell very well if brought within the price-range of almost everyone. The girls were "tempted to no purchase" of Brussels lace. They made their pilgrimage to Waterloo, however, where "old women and boys fell upon" them with all sorts of relics, "real and forged that the ground yields," and they filled their pockets with bullets. Fanny "carried off a spread-eagle, once bright and shining from the cap of a French soldier." Her sympathies were "all with Napoleon" she said. They had their "portraits drawn" for their passports to Holland.

While still in Belgium, the Appletons parted with their American-looking carriage and after considerable delay found themselves "buzzing away with mad rapidity" by rail, "as if riding on a broomstick" over Holland's pancake-flat country. Railroad travel was "an awful violation of the laws of nature," Fanny thought. In Antwerp they dutifully visited the Bourse, "famous as the great 'Change' when Merchants were Princes."

Travel was now by public diligence. Every few miles, the driver pulled up his horses and a pretty girl came out of a house by the side of the road to bring him a glass of beer. The Appletons began to wonder how much longer the driver would be able to sit upon the box and not fall off. Houses in Holland "were of brick, an ugly material," in the eyes of the Appleton girls. Towns looked "like the busy parts of New York" — which, from Bostonians, was no compliment. But the Rembrandts were a revelation and a delight. At the Hague, Mary and Fanny were prepared to be even more thrilled by a work of art. It was rated as "the 4th greatest picture in the world." But it was *The Bull* by Paulus Potter, Dutch artist, 1625–1654. It looked like a bull all right — that was all they could say for it. "To immortalize such a subject is the highest effort of their art and taste!" exclaimed Fanny.

On Tuesday, May 2, 1837, the Appletons and all their belongings were "paddled away from the flat shores of the Lowlands . . ." The steamer *Batavia* was to carry them down the Meuse. It was "very pleasant, steaming down the river, reeds and windmills fringing the banks." There were Dutch ships with square prows, "scorning all speed," and on board the *Batavia* "it was good to hear orders given in English." At dinner, "Father welcomed with joy a boiled leg of mutton!" At last they "anchored on the skirts of London."

A young waterman rowed the Appletons to the Tower Stairs on the Thames and Fanny did not fail to imagine herself a noble lady of long ago being taken to the Tower of London. Climbing into a cab, the Appletons "drove on and on through the labyrinth of the city's dingy, ill-lighted streets, a human Pandemonium . . ." and arrived at the West End. Joshua Bates, American financier and head of Baring Brothers, had "a mansion in Portland Place." The Appletons "called him forth," late at night though it was, "to assure them of their arranged destination," the Cavendish Hotel in Jermyn Street. To their great relief, reservations had been made.

The usual calls from merchants and bankers were received. London seemed dismal after Paris, and Fanny thought about the Cass family, "now gliding over the blue sea of the South, sunk in cushions on deck — what luxurious idlesse . . . for the dreary months." Their father was constantly in conference with London bankers — on matters his children knew nothing about. He had a hard time hiring a suitable carriage and pair for his daughters, and at first the girls had to sit at their hotel window and watch the rain.

Tom, although officially still destined for the law, considered himself an artist and took his sisters to the galleries. Having admired the exquisite finish of the Dutch school and having developed a taste for cows if not for bulls as the right subject for a painter, Fanny was delighted with Landseer's "unrivalled animals. Such dogs and horses! His brush has extraordinary power in rendering the gloss and each particular hair," Fanny declared. But Turner came out badly in her estimation. He was professor of perspective at the Royal Academy and the girls were familiar with his illustrations for the poems of Byron and Scott. He was now experimenting with Impressionism. Fanny said he had carried his "dawby style" to a ridiculous exaggeration. Evidently fame had spoiled him so that the "gaudiest colors were thrown on anywhere without any attempt to form real objects."

Finally the Appletons had a carriage, and Regent's Park was their first enthusiasm. They saw "princely terrace mansions slightly secluded from the road, each with a private grass plot," which they thought rivaled old Italian splendor. "This immense sweep of columns and terraces encircles this beautiful park, so velvety green and deliciously springlike with buds on the hedges — combined palaces and rural beauty really expresses one's ideas of a city." Fanny's final accolade was reserved for Green Park, however, where she and Mary "alighted and strolled over its nicely rolled paths." Ahead of them was unoccupied Buckingham House. "Something in the slope of the ground in this Park, the winding paths, the range of houses and the two misty towers of Westminster Abbey over the trees" made Fanny say that it was "so like the Common beyond the Frog Pond and the Masonic Temple" back home.

Andrew Stevenson, a Jackson appointee, was minister to Great Britain. The Stevensons invited the Appletons to dinner. "Everything was in good style about the dinner, Virginia ham, American sweetmeats . . ." But Fanny was "truly vexed with our Ambassadress who puzzled her English guests with phrases and words not known in our best society." The only example Fanny gave was that Mrs. Stevenson had referred to her hairdresser as her barber!

At the Stevensons, the Appletons met "a quiet, genteelish Mrs. Nightingale, evidently romantic in her youth as her two daughters are named Florence and Parthenope." Fanny liked "Parthy" best — "a nice, modest damsel full of romance also for the 'Siren of the Sea' " — or Naples, formerly Parthenope. Tom was decidedly taken with Florence and when he later visited the Nightingales, his sisters hoped that he might marry the future founder of modern nursing, heroine of the Crimea and "Lady with the Lamp." Florence Nightingale had no such idea in mind.

British women were interested in politics, much to Mary and Fanny's surprise. "Politics, Bah!" wrote Fanny in her journal. The girls were on their way to St. Paul's when they "fell in with the Hustings. Roofs, sheds and houses near Covent Garden were covered with men and umbrellas in the pouring rain — shouting like a cotton mill in full spin. One victim of their popularity appearing to speak — the air was rent with cries. . . . His antagonist appeared and there was an equal din from the other party . . ." There were many "coroneted carriages in the mob." But the Appleton carriage was not near enough to see any "forcible arguments" such as "Brickbats and cabbages." At the next evening party a lady shocked Fanny by telling her that "ladies naughtily intermingled in politics and promised tradesmen their patronage or not — depending on their political party allegiance." The Tories had won, she heard.

Fanny gladly handed politics over as the exclusive domain of men but she did not approve of the famous London men's clubs. She and Mary were escorted through the Athenaeum Club rooms — "one of these magnificent and luxurious establishments, where bachelors find consolation for no home. Every comfort wealth can devise is here, a fine kitchen, a beautiful library, a noble hall where they can sit, read and chat *ad libitum*. A thousand members belong — with 25 guineas entrance and each year. . . . The ladies should set their faces at these retreats; petition Government! Most anti-marrying influences!"

On the twenty-fourth of May, came the birthday of Princess Victoria. After a dinner party that night, the Appletons set out for their hotel to dress for a ball. It would be the girls' first chance to display their French ball-dresses. But out in the streets an illumination in honor of the princess was going on. Her initials were written in flame-colored lamps or gas throughout London — "stars and crowns and the eternal 'P.V.' sparkled from every street while crowds gathered at every street-corner focus of light, like so many summer moths." At one corner, carriages stalled, six lanes across — the Appleton carriage solidly wedged among them. Hours passed. The mob increased and Ambassador Stevenson, who had been seeing the girls home, suggested that they get out and walk. But they were afraid to walk "amongst horses' feet and carriage wheels" and besides, having been to dinner, they were not wearing their bonnets! On the other hand, they were "unwilling to pass the night, or what little was left of it" stuck in the street and they were "vexed" because by this time they had missed the ball. "We finally sent for our hats and, dismounting, got home by side streets as best we might, on foot."

And now it looked very much as if the next court ball would be cancelled. "Their Majesties are both so ill there is no knowing how soon 'Long Live Queen Victoria' may resound in these sooty regions. Health and happiness to the English Rose Bud," Fanny wrote.

The Appleton girls began looking for a glimpse of the Princess Victoria. On June 1, they saw her, riding in a carriage with her mother. The duchess of Kent was "fine-looking" and wore "towering plumes . . . but alas for England's future queen . . ." Victoria was not beautiful — she was "a short, thick, commonplace-looking girl in white with a wreathe of roses, without a good complexion!" Poor, romantic Fanny thought every royal personage ought to look like a character out of the fairy tales she read as a child and now at last she had to conclude that "perhaps it is a royal distinction to be plain."

There was no use staying in London for the social season if the court was to be in mourning. On June 8, the Appletons set out to see the sights of England and Scotland. At Little Waldingfield, out came the sketch books. The church and the ancient Appleton family tombs were dutifully rendered in pencil and water-color. Stratford on Avon and Oxford, were "killed" as "lions" just like the sights in Canada, and Fanny, especially, lived again the tragedy of Mary Queen of Scots as set forth in many a novel the Appleton young people had read aloud around the fire in their own "green parlor" on Beacon Street. But even Fanny refused to believe in the blood stains where Rizzio died at Hollyrood Palace in Edinburgh. She suspected red paint.

On June 20, 1837, William IV of England died and Victoria became queen. The Appletons returned to London in August and Ambassador Stevenson offered to arrange a presentation for them. The girls decided not to go through with the ceremony but accepted tickets to "a kind of ante-room gallery," where they watched the queen's guests pass on their way to the reception room. It was "a mournful procession" Fanny said. "There were no plumes and jewels." Everyone was requested to wear unrelieved black and "one poor girl who had put on a white underskirt was sent back to change her dress."

During June, 1837, all the letters from girls in Boston had been full of descriptions of parties which took place every night and often there were two or three in one evening. Those Appleton girls needn't think they were having all the fun at those balls in Paris. Then came the financial panic.[10] Almost overnight the scenes changed. Sardonic jokes went the rounds. If a Bostonian met a friend in the street, the greeting was no longer "How do you do?" but "Who has failed?" Anything like a smile was such a phenomenon that barbers "began to charge extra for shaving such long faces!" Nathan Appleton was suddenly anxious about business. He and his family arrived in New York in August, after only a brief stay in London.

FIFTEEN

TWO BRIDES

"TRADE HAD BEEN CONSIDERED GOOD," William Appleton wrote at the end of 1836.[1] Wages were shockingly high, however. Those girls in the Lowell factories were getting two dollars and a half a week besides their board.

William figured that Congress was going to reduce import duties and that, although manufacturing had been "generally good and cotton very good . . ." people were holding on to their inventory for higher prices and "paying extravagant rates for the use of money." But a "reckoning day must come before the ensuing year closes." He sold his manufacturing stocks with the intention of re-investing when prices went down. William had just predicted the panic of 1837.

As to his personal business, William had been "as successful as in almost any year of my life," he said. "My property is worth sixty to seventy thousand dollars more than at the commencement of the year, after deducting twenty to thirty thousand dollars on flaxseed and sugar."

As the year 1837 ended, William Appleton's prophecy was fulfilled. "The last year has been one of change and disaster to the commercial world, such as has not been known during the present generation," he wrote. The Merrimack Manufacturing Company stock, which was around $1350 a share when William sold, went down to $950. "For myself I have been very fortunate. I do not know that I have lost anything by bad debts, directly. I have on hand a large amount of merchandise and some considerable adventures abroad. My present belief is that the voyages now under way will be profitable, in fact business will be good and stocks will advance, but I do not intend to extend myself . . ."

Jackson's hostility to the Bank of the United States had caused the President to withhold deposits of public money.[2] The feud between the government and financial interests had brought on the panic of 1833, and next, in 1836, Jackson had decreed that public lands must be paid for in coin. Very shortly, a trade balance against the United States caused further demand for gold and silver. The United States, at this time, produced neither, so that cash shipped abroad must come from the supply on hand, which was less than half the adverse balance. Van Buren, Jackson's favorite candidate to succeed him, was elected in 1837. New York banks suspended specie payments.[3]

William Appleton went to New York confident that he could get the banks to resume payment. But nothing could be done, and as a result the Boston banks also had to suspend. This was "a measure most affecting to me, mortifying in the extreme, but it is absolutely necessary for the protection of ourselves." [4]

The banking house of Samuel Welles failed. There would be no more beautiful but extravagant balls in Paris for wealthy Americans. In Boston, people sold their horses and carriages, dismissing coachmen and grooms. Mr. James G. King, of the New York banking house of Prime, Ward and King, went to London to see if he could convince the Bank of England to send over specie.

"It appears to me now that there will be no difficulty in banks resuming payment in May," William Appleton wrote in March, 1838. "We shall have a large amount of specie in that month which will put all right again . . ." Specie began to arrive, right on schedule. A ship from London arrived in New York and men went up and down the office stairs carrying little wooden kegs, marked "Prime, Ward and King." Mr. King's mission to London had been a success. The Bank of England had advanced "a million sovereigns."

But William Appleton had one more prophecy which proved all too true. "Before September, we shall be wondering why we were so much depressed. Things will get back to their former state and all will be well till we get in debt again in Europe."

In 1839, "the Bank of the United States, acting under its Pennsylvania charter, again suspended payment and proved desperately insolvent; carrying with it the Philadelphia banks who foolishly involved themselves in its fortunes — from which they were only relieved by a large loan from Boston and New York." This time, it was Nathan Appleton, rather than his cousin William, who told the story. "In arranging for this loan, I took an active and leading part. Philadelphia did resume, in consequence, on the 15th of January, 1841; but the Bank of the United States broke down after ten days' trial."

Nathan Appleton wrote a pamphlet entitled, *Remarks on Currency and Banking; having reference to the present Derangement of the Circulating Medium in the United States.* It was first published in 1841 and went through three editions. Subsequent histories of banking quote Mr. Appleton freely and usually without credit. Both on the scene and behind the scene, he and his cousin William were more important to Boston banking than anyone realized at the time.

In October, 1838, Mr. Thomas Gold Appleton was admitted to the Suffolk County bar. There must have been great rejoicing at 39 Beacon Street. Tom had an office, number 1-2 Tremont Row, duly entered in the Boston directories. One morning he was walking across the Common to his office as all serious, purposeful young American men were supposed to do. He met another newly admitted barrister. "Have you any cases?" Tom asked.

"No," said Tom's friend sadly. "Have you?"

"No, thank God," Tom replied.[5]

He kept all sorts of books in his office. It was a great place for reading poetry — anything except law. An office was perfect for writing poetry, essays, humorous items the newspapers published — anything except briefs.

While the Appletons were still abroad, Aunt Sam had written to the girls — "Your house begins to look beautifully clean; your drawing rooms are surprisingly improved by plain walls and the prettiest I know of." Eventually, another story and a half was added to number 39 Beacon Street. There were two more wrought-iron balconies and a group of three instead of two French windows on each bow-front level. The effect was handsome and still is today.

But in 1837, the clean, new look of fresh paint pleased Nathan Appleton very much. He must have been puzzled and exasperated by the reaction of his two motherless daughters. They cried! Their father had not realized how homesick the girls had been when they were so ill in Mayence. They had longed to find everything just as they remembered and here was the dear green parlor, no longer green, the double drawing rooms bare and brightly lighted.

The girls dried their eyes, however, and Fanny wrote to her friend, Matilda Lieber who would remember how the house used to look, "We are busy as possible giving our house a habitable look, hanging pictures and strewing knick-knacks that we picked up in divers nooks and crannies. We make quite a show of the beaux arts and begin to wonder where we shall put all our treasures — whether bits of marble dug up with our own hands from the palace of the Caesars . . ."

In spite of hard times in 1837, there were parties in Boston where the Appleton girls could wear their Paris ball gowns. The first of these Assemblies took place in Papanti's Hall in 1838 — after a hot discussion as to whether or not girls could look beautiful under those dreadfully bright lights supplied by gas. Those who thought that girls looked best by candlelight lost their argument. Papanti had gas chandeliers installed. Mary and Fanny Appleton were there, looking so lovely by gas light that a poem was written about them, said to be by "the Hon. Franklin Dexter."

The Honorable Frank Dexter had been the lawyer for the defense in a notorious murder case. His clients lost and were hanged but as a result, their lawyer became famous. He was about the age of Nathan Appleton, was married and had several sons. The girls must have hoped that it was a *young* Mr. Dexter who wrote:

> With lilies of the valley, one had
>   trimmed her dark brown hair
> While a crown of roses blushed around the
>   other's forehead fair
> And eyes looked out beneath these flowers,
>   each beautiful and bright
> The last were like the azure day, the
>   first as dark as night.

The poem went on for several stanzas to the effect that the two girls were on a balcony, gazing down at the dancers and dreaming of sights seen in Europe. The poem appeared in a paper, everybody knew that Nathan Appleton's daughters were the subject and who actually wrote the poem, but names were not mentioned, which made everything all right. Plenty of young men agreed with the poetic sentiments.

Banking affairs took Mr. N. Appleton to Washington, D.C., in the spring of 1838. The girls went along but it was not expected that they should be interested in finances since they could not, in their own right, control money. As to politics, of course they could not vote, but being from a loyal Boston Whig family they quite properly admired Webster and were indignant over the election of Van Buren. Fanny and Mary had something to say about a famous Washington hotel and a ball, however.

"Only think of surviving nine days (a nine days' wonder, truly) of Gadsby's unfathomable concoctions," Fanny wrote. Then there was the "hourly and untimely dropping-in of dawdling senators, grinding out a word a minute, an idea an hour."

The girls went to only one ball. It was so hot that tallow candles were fainting over the door tops, spilling wax on everyone, while grave senators, having had a "too partial preference for mint juleps," went "reeling through the Virginia reels." On their way home to Boston, the Appletons stopped over in New York where "pigs were elbowing fine ladies in the street."

Back on Beacon Hill at the end of May, the "sweet springtime was ripening so rapidly" that the girls could "almost hear and see" the flowers grow. They now took daily drives in a new carriage with beautiful horses which they called "a luxury specie payment." Evidently bankers' discussions had been understood, even by young ladies. But if they thought the carriage and pair had been bought because they had "hinted to Father," Mary and Fanny were wrong; there was a shock in store for them.

During the summer of 1838, Tom was officially at home with his father on Beacon Street. Fortunately, however, law clients continued to stay away and he found he could close his office to go to Newport — because of his health; Mary and Fanny went to visit Grandmother Gold in Pittsfield.

Mrs. Thomas Gold was "a fine old lady with a step as elastic as a chamois and a fresh young heart," Fanny said, writing to her cousin Jewett who had gone to Cincinnati to seek his fortune. Grandmother Gold drove around "in a broken-backed carriage with a steed somewhat worse for wear, through these lovely valleys which are very like Wales or Baden-Baden."

Since there were no old castles to explore, Fanny and Mary were building castles in Spain, "more habitable and less costly. . . . Father, as my special boon, is about to purchase some ground for a summer villa in the Stockbridge valley," Fanny explained. The girls had picked out the spot, having a view of the Housatonic, a grove of trees with mountains in the background. The fact that this plot of ground was only a mile from the Sedgwicks, commended the site even more than did the scenery. A railroad up the Housatonic was projected which in a year or two would desecrate these retired valleys, but would after all, "link them conveniently with towns, and yet at a safe distance from the afternoon bores," Fanny said. She referred to young men having nothing better to do than call on Beacon Street Appleton girls.

Other guests claimed Grandmother Gold's hospitality at the end of August so Mary and Fanny went to stay in Lenox at what they described as "a brick hotel with Grecian columns in front, looking forth, however, on a noble sweep of hill upon hill." They shared a private parlor with Fanny Kemble Butler. There was a joyful reunion because they had seen a great deal of Mrs. Butler in London. She had been staying with her father, Charles Kemble, at the Kembles' London town house where the Misses Appleton had their first taste of a literary circle, frequented by high society, stage people and fascinating adventurers.

In the Kembles' London drawing room, Trelawney, famous ex-pirate; hero of Greek wars and friend of Shelley and Byron, had fixed Fanny Appleton with his piercing eyes. This "dangerous person" had been "rather impertinent in his advances" but Fanny found him "really entertaining," she had confessed at the time. He was constantly harping on her "extraordinary resemblance to Fanny Butler — a notion which seemed to possess everybody." After her visit to her famous family, the former actress, Fanny Kemble, had returned to the United States with her American husband, Pierce Butler. The Butlers lived near Philadelphia but Mrs. Butler and her baby daughter were in Lenox to escape the summer heat.

At the Lenox hotel, every morning about nine, Mary and Fanny Appleton rose from their "straw couches" to go into the private parlor where they found "Mrs. Butler *en robe de chambre*" ready to sit with them. They were all "immediately in a frolicsome mood," laughing at everything, particularly "coffee served in a pitcher, taking it for beer!" Mrs. Butler "next dressed herself in riding costume — entirely in a gentleman's style . . . white pants, with a black velvet jacket and cap." [6] She was a superb horsewoman and loved to have Lenox people stop and stare. Mary Appleton often rode with her, long-skirted and discreetly side-saddle. Fanny went walking with Catherine Maria Sedgwick, "through the sun-checkered woods."

In the evening friends gathered, sometimes at the Sedgwicks, sometimes at the inn. "We laugh and we talk, sing, play, dance and discuss," as Fanny Kemble put it, rejoicing in "the absence of all form, ceremony and inconvenient conventionality whatever."

The Appleton girls were still in Lenox on the eighteenth of September when Fanny wrote, "you seem amazed, dearest Papa, at our being able to resist the temptations of tender partridges, delicious fruit — all other city comforts so long." They would be home soon but the climax of the summer was what certain Bostonians would have called a wild party! Seventeen young people piled into an omnibus, its seats covered with buffalo skins. The Appleton girls hired a barouche to ride in, "in case of rain," while Mrs. Butler rode horseback, her little girl on the saddle in front of her. Tom had joined his sisters in Lenox by this time and the other beaux were two Italian refugees, Albinola and Foresti. Miss Sedgwick and her sister-in-law were the chaperones.

Off they drove (or rode) through Great Barrington to Sheffield where they lunched, then on to Salisbury for the night. Fanny described Salisbury, Connecticut, as a quaint little village with two inns and a church, each inn having a huge ballroom! Next day it rained.

At first there were "long faces" but copies of Shakespeare and Byron were supplied by a Salisbury friend and "Mrs. Butler read nobly, Shylock — and with chat and frolic the day spun off . . ." At dinner the landlady served "a patriarchal turkey" which Albinola carved, nearly dislocating his wrist in the attempt. That night they all assembled in one inn and, having sent a mile for a fiddler, they had the merriest dancing in the ballroom, garnished around the walls with about a dozen grim primitive portraits.

The next day was bright and beautiful so they all journeyed to Canaan, Connecticut, in search of "newly discovered falls." Streams were swollen level with the bridges, and the falls were the equal of those at Schaffhausen, Fanny said. That night, back in Salisbury, they all enacted a carbonari meeting according to the directions given by Foresti who had been arrested in Italy for just such gatherings of conspirators, plotting to overthrow French rule in Italy. Fanny practiced her Italian with Albinola, a "useful beau" and found Foresti "amusing and a particular admirer of Mary's."

There was one more excursion, this time to Bissenbach Falls. Setting out in the omnibus, they climbed fifteen miles up a mountain road, "very wild . . . got out at a farmhouse, primitive to a marvel," where the omnibus was left and then "staff in hand marched to the fall," Mrs. Butler, and this time Fanny also, on horseback. After "much fatigue" they reached "a noble cascade, falling down a wild ravine." By this time, the Appleton girls were connoisseurs of waterfalls, their enthusiasm undiminished. They returned to Lenox sure that their three-day invasion of Salisbury "would become historic to judge by the wonder of the inhabitants." The girls went home to Boston, first engaging rooms at the inn for the next summer. Miss Sedgwick had already written some stories about Berkshire inhabitants which had made them indignant. Now the natives had still more to talk about.

In Boston assemblies began again. Tom joined a billiard club for which

Thirty-nine Beacon Street after alterations. The twin houses shown are now the headquarters of the Women's City Club of Boston. (Courtesy of The Bostonian Society, Old State House.)

he somehow found time while successfully avoiding all practice of law. The girls studied German with Dr. Charles Follen, German refugee and first professor of German at Harvard. He had married the delightfully independent Eliza Lee Cabot and had recently been dismissed from Harvard for liberal ideas. Dr. Follen was not the hard taskmaster that Lieber had been, and the girls began to enjoy German for the first time.

It would seem as if life at 39 Beacon Street were settling down to a familiar pattern. There were plenty of people who knew that changes were in the offing however, and one of these was Harrison Gray Otis. Writing to a Philadelphia friend,[7] he said that Nathan Appleton's contemplated second marriage was causing a sensation in Boston. Mr. Appleton was going to marry Miss Harriet Coffin Sumner — aged thirty-four. Nathan was fifty-nine. "But she is a nice woman — if he must marry." Only, "There's no fool like an old fool."

Miss Sumner was the daughter of Jesse Sumner of Boston — a former resident of Portland, Maine, and a distant connection of Charles Sumner. On her mother's side, Harriet was descended from a distinguished family of Coffins of Nantucket. Miss Sumner had tried to be sympathetic and helpful with the Appleton young people after their mother's death. She had tried in vain to do something for Charles in Philadelphia. And when she wrote to Tom while he was in Rome "challenging a correspondence" his reply was so elaborate as to suggest sarcasm. In no diaries or correspondence as yet available is there an account of Nathan's second wedding or whether his children attended. But it seems certain that their father's second romance came as a surprise to them. Their father was married on January 8, 1839.

"Our new Mamma is so amiable that it would be in vain to find fault, as yet, with her entrance among us," Mary wrote.[8] Harriet, or Mrs. Appleton, as her step-children called her, was going to have her work cut out for her, just the same. These three grown children had received a great deal of attention from their father and they were spoiled to a considerable degree. Mary, still nominally her father's housekeeper, would be expected to superintend the servants much more closely. The cook must produce better meals; more earnest efforts with broom and duster, mop and pail, must be expected of staff below stairs. Fanny must stop day-dreaming. She should learn to keep the household accounts as well as her own. Tom should have a home of his own.

In May, Fanny took over Mary's job as housekeeper while "Father and Mrs. A." went south, taking Mary with them. Over at Aunt Sam's, Fanny complained of hard work. The usually sympathetic Aunt Sam laughed and told her it was high time she learned to keep house because surely she and Mary would soon marry and must manage homes of their own.

Beaux were encouraged but the girls made fun of the young men who came to call. It was Miss Sedgwick who had suggested that the girls read Mary Wollstonecraft's *Vindication of the Rights of Women*. The book was published in 1792 so that it was by no means new, but it was practically banned in Boston because of the author's extra-marital experiences, her delayed legal marriage to William Godwin, and her illegitimate daughter who married Shelley. Among other matters, Mary Wollstonecraft wrote an exposé of laws permitting men to indulge in cruelty to their wives, and Mary Appleton said she looked into the book deeply. Fanny said she was afraid the book would make her more discontented with her condition, as a female, than she was already.

Efforts to promote a marriage for Tom were equally frustrating. Girls, some of them pretty, some of them rich, were paraded before him. But Tom had a formula. As each likely candidate married someone else, he would declare that his heart was broken. This could go on forever.

Cousin Samuel Appleton Appleton, Eben's son, set Tom a good example. He had been "staying in Marshfield with his August papa-elect, fishing together, drinking brandy out of the same flask," Fanny wrote. The papa-in-law to be was Daniel Webster, and Eben's son was going to marry Julia Webster. "Miss W. is a very fine girl though rather reserved," Fanny decided. She was the darling of her father's heart and Fanny became fond of her. But for now, everybody in the Webster family was off for England.[9]

Daniel Webster had over-extended himself in buying Western lands, partly in a company with Colonel Perkins, partly with Governor Cass and partly on his own credit. The panic of 1837 had "retarded" the sale of these holdings as Webster very mildly put it. He tried to go abroad in an official capacity but was blocked by Van Buren. But now his daughter was going to marry a man born in England, who had just happened to say he would like to be married there! For this purely social reason Daniel Webster and his family went abroad in January with "Agricultural lands of excellent quality in Ohio, Illinois, Michigan and Wisconsin" for sale. This departure left Webster plenty of time to peddle real estate because it was not until September 24, 1839, that Julia Webster married Samuel Appleton Appleton.

When summer came, the Appleton girls headed for Lenox again. After a short stay at the inn, they rented part of a house in Stockbridge, belonging to a local resident, Mrs. Yale, who took in washing. She was glad to provide some if not all of their meals and now and then she gave them cooking privileges. The girls hired what they said was "a nice barouche with two horses." Mr. Yale looked after the horses, and kept the barouche in his barn.

The sisters felt immensely independent and Fanny described their bachelor-girl quarters to the envious Emmeline Austin. "Behold me

Mary Appleton at about the time of her marriage, by George Peter Alexander Healy. (Courtesy of the Longfellow House Trustees.)

writing in a nice little parlor, with a straw carpet partly put down by our own fair hands, a bureau adorned with our books, a bouquet of yellow roses and laurel blossoms, Miss Sedgwick's picture, etc. . . ." This was in one corner. In another corner were "the seat and cushions of a divan on which we recline à la Turque . . ." It was very modern to have a Turkish divan but there were also two rocking chairs "of Puritan primness, a Lilliputian table and cricket" besides the big table where Fanny was writing.

"Our little drawing-room looks out on a beautiful amphitheater . . . of the Stockbridge valley with its white houses peeping out like buds in moss." There was also a dining-room and before many days went by Fanny was talking boastfully of "our lamb, mint-sauced," which was better than anything at the inn. Within a few days of getting settled at "Yale Manor," as the girls called it, nearly all the male summer visitors from Stockbridge, Lenox and Pittsfield had come to call. As Fanny said frankly, it was all so much more comfortable than being with her father and step-mother in Nahant and besides, they had "twenty times the independence."

Fanny described a few of the young men who climbed the steep mile-long hill from Stockbridge, to call. And then, without realizing how important he was to be, she added that there was "by way of a beau, this Mackintosh, a puzzle, not Chinese but English, who is supposed to be clever, having written the life of his father — as if any son couldn't do that with a good memory and decent filial affection. . . . He has quite a good face, laughs spasmodically — is constantly *absent* when *present* and jerks out his words like a badly working pump. I am rather piqued to analyze him, as, like most Englishmen, he has enough individuality to make it worth while." [10]

Robert James Mackintosh was not English but Scottish, and proud of it. His father, Sir James, could not have been easy to write about, because he was a brilliant man in two fields, medicine and law. His *Reflections on the French Revolution* and his lectures on "Laws of Nature and Nations" brought him recognition from the British government and he was knighted and given the post of recorder of Bombay. After a career in India, he entered Parliament, became a member of the Privy Council and wrote books on history along with numerous articles for the *Encyclopaedia Britannica*. Sir James had died in London in 1832, at the age of sixty-seven. His son Robert had been born in Bombay, December 2, 1806.

Robert had been traveling in the United States with a view to writing a book about it. He had also some not too difficult duties as an attaché to the British Legation in Washington. On his first call at Yale Manor, in spite of the long walk from the inn and "a heavy hill to climb" he brought the Appleton girls a file of French and English newspapers and reviews. The girls had more recent ones which he "carried off in triumph."

There were the usual Berkshire excursions which Robert Mackintosh promptly joined. Here was material for his travel book. The trip to "Ice Glen" was a wild scramble in the course of which Mary and Fanny had to tie their shawls around their waists and sling their parasols over their shoulders, Indian quiver style. The beaux thought they needed a good deal of help but Fanny said that Robert Mackintosh was awkward. Mary asserted her independence by trying to "climb through a hole in a huge rock." She got stuck half-way but "scolded off the gentlemen's officious assistance" and crawled out without help.

Fanny summed up her impressions of Robert Mackintosh. "I believe he is a good enough creature *au fond* — but such a combination of *gaucherie,* coolness and laziness I never encountered. He has such a horror of long words; blue conversation or anything that shall betray his ever having been an author, that he is not far from discoursing like the 'Artful Dodger'."

It did not occur to Fanny that Mackintosh might be registering a protest against the excessively intellectual group whom he met at Yale Manor. The whole Sedgwick family and especially Sedgwick in-laws and admirers, wrote essays, stories, poetry — using the longest words they could think of. They read their efforts aloud whenever they could get an audience. Right now they were collecting original poems and essays to be sold at auction at a "Fair for the benefit of the Lenox Ladies Sewing Circle." "Tell Father not to be anxious — *we* wrote nothing," Fanny wrote to Tom.

Tom said that in Stockbridge, the crickets said "Sedg'ick, Sedg'ick" when they chirped.[11] He joined his sisters after a visit to Pittsfield where he found his grandmother and sundry aunts and cousins "in their usual state of religious diversion and melancholy." He had already been to Newport where he had his hands full with so many young New York widows — at least according to Fanny. He found Yale Manor anything but melancholy, with not a designing widow around — but he sent to his father for more money.

Cousin Isaac Appleton Jewett appeared, having decided that his fortune was not to be made in Cincinnati but in New York where he planned to start a literary magazine. The city was too hot in August however so he took a room in Stockbridge to work on his article on the poet Milnes for Mr. Cogswell's review. At Yale Manor these days, there was "an amazing deal of edifying conversation, Jewett's mind being always active — Tom's generally at a hard trot," with Mary and Fanny "ambling pretty well when spurred by others."

But Robert James Mackintosh had gone back to Washington by this time. He had plenty of material about the bluestockings of Berkshire for his book, it would be presumed. Nathan and Harriet Appleton came by and their father promised to buy the girls a piece of land they wanted and build them a summer place. Mary and Fanny engaged Yale Manor for the following year.

On October 5, 1839, Mary and Fanny left Stockbridge to "stage it and railroad it home." It was still October, when Robert James Mackintosh made his appearance at 39 Beacon Street. If this was a surprise, a greater surprise followed. He and Mary Appleton became engaged to be married. "I love him as much as it is possible to love anyone in this world," Mary said.

At first Fanny was heart-broken. She and Mary had shared the same room, the same bed and the same secrets ever since she could remember. But she revised her opinion of Mackintosh. He was "so much improved in appearance that" she had to "concede him quite a handsome man — certainly happiness out-values the fountain of youth," she wrote. Robert was not yet thirty-three. Before long, in her diary, Fanny thanked God "for the good honest heart" that had been given to Mary.

It was a small wedding with only relatives and a few friends invited, "because of Mrs. Appleton's health." The bride's step-mother was expecting a child.

Fanny told about the wedding.[12] It took place at half-past-twelve noon, the day after Christmas. Mary was "simply dressed in white and looked charmingly, a whole Future in her eyes, sun-bright with Hope."

SIXTEEN

THE COURTSHIP OF
HENRY LONGFELLOW

HENRY WADSWORTH LONGFELLOW sat down to write to Fanny Appleton.[1]
Dating his letter January 8, 1837, he had no idea that Fanny and Mary
were ill in Mayence but pictured them as sailing down the Rhine, enjoying scenes that he had found romantic. He had translated the "Elegy"
by Friedrich von Matthisson for Fanny and said he knew she would
enjoy the "pleasing melancholy" expressed by the writer as he pon-
dered among ancient castle ruins. Longfellow sent his letter as "a sort
of Valentine" thinking that Fanny would receive it in February.

When Miss Fanny got home to Boston, Longfellow would like to help
her with German — that "musical tongue." But this not too cheerful
Valentine reached Fanny when she could not possibly care for pleasing
melancholy. She had lost her mother, her brother Charles, and now her
cousin William. The long-delayed letter reached her in Paris when she
was trying to throw off grief and be happy again — if she could.

Longfellow could not know how he had looked to Fanny as she
watched him from the shadows at the hotel in Strasbourg. She had
admitted in her diary that she had missed him. She needed the sympathy and understanding he had given her at Schaffhausen — and there
he was laughing in the sunshine with the attractive Mrs. William Cullen
Bryant and two young girls — one of them pretty. He had seemed just
a squire of dames. When she got back to Boston, she was sure she was
not going to read German with an old college professor. By that time,
Longfellow would be almost thirty.

Still feeling sure of his standing with his dear Miss Fanny, Longfellow wrote to George Ticknor, whose place he filled at Harvard. It was now September 28, 1837, and after a few items of Cambridge gossip, he said that there was nothing new in Boston except the arrival of the much-loved Appletons. Both Mary and Fanny had returned looking more beautiful than ever. There had been nothing like it since the Boston Massacre. Then it occurred to him that this might be an unlucky comparison. But surely it applied only to other men whom Cupid's darts might wound. He could mention two or three such "dandy-legs." Unfortunately, he did not mention their names but felt sure that he, himself, was not being over-confident.

After boarding for a while with Professor Felton and others at the corner of Kirkland and Oxford streets, Longfellow found two large, handsome rooms at Craigie House on Brattle Street, Cambridge.[2] This Colonial mansion had been built by Major John Vassal in 1759. After the Tory major fled to England, it became Washington's headquarters during the American Revolution. In 1837, it was owned by Mrs. Elizabeth Shaw Craigie who rented rooms to students and teachers so that she herself could afford to live in the mansion where once she had seen better days.

When Longfellow took rooms, he knew little or nothing of the history of Craigie House. His interest came later. In 1837, he said he felt like an Italian prince living in a villa. He told his sister, Annie Longfellow Pierce, that he walked up stone steps having big flower pots at each side, to reach the massive front door. The wide entrance hall led to a beautiful staircase with Longfellow's rooms to the left at the head of the stair. His first study looked out over the meadows to the Charles River. Longfellow assured his sister that her admiring gaze would fall upon the author of *Outre-Mer* reclining on a sofa, wearing a calamanco dressing gown and red slippers. The author regarded himself as a prose novelist just now.

The land around Craigie House was still farmed in 1837. Mrs. Craigie employed a farmer whose daughter Longfellow said was a giantess and also pious. Her name was Miriam. She brought him his breakfast of tea, toast and waffles every morning around eight. Along with fat Miriam came hordes of flies from the barns behind the house, which Longfellow killed with a sling made from a silk handkerchief. This was *after* breakfast, he said. Then he took a walk in the garden — then worked on books and papers or prepared lectures until the farmer's daughter brought him his dinner at five in the afternoon.

There was no mention in letters to his family in Portland, Maine, of Longfellow's morning calls at 39 Beacon Street. He went there often to help Mary and Fanny Appleton with their German. A note to "Madonna Francesca" referred to a delightful day passed with her on a Monday. There was the gift of a volume of German romance containing a minor work by Jean Paul Richter which she was to read. Professor Longfellow assumed that Miss Fanny would want to read a full length Richter novel full of descriptions of spring and blossoms. To Fanny, the minor work looked sufficiently difficult.

Again, as at Strasbourg, Longfellow could not see himself as Fanny saw him, and there was too much he didn't know. Attaché Ledyard for example, in his handsome uniform, had been much more fascinating to the twenty-year-old Fanny than a Harvard professor who, in her opinion, was too old to wear anything so gay as butter-colored gloves. A bunch of violets from Ledyard, although they faded too soon, was more romantic than a book in German, a language Fanny continued to dislike.

Longfellow thought that the right moment had come. On Sunday evening, December 10, 1837, he sat alone in his study at Craigie House writing a letter — not to Fanny but to her sister, Mary. ". . . And what have you been doing in the bright parlor? Shall I sit there no more and read from pleasant books? Are those bright Autumnal days gone forever?" Then he launched into German. "It makes me utterly mournful in spirit when I think and see that the beautiful dream there has ended. . . . Even now, greet my dear, dear Fanny whom I shall always love as my own soul . . ." [3]

Fanny Appleton had refused to marry Mr. Longfellow, and to his bachelor friends he confided the story until it became a rather too-well-known romance. Sam Ward of New York and Sam's cousin George Washington Greene of Rome heard all about the "Fair Ladie" whom Longfellow had met in Switzerland and had loved passionately from that moment on. Longfellow described Fanny as a woman "not only of talent but of genius, glorious and beautiful, tall and pale."

Greene was told that this "Fair Ladie" had given only friendship in return for Longfellow's love. They were good friends but Longfellow was still determined to win her love. By late July, however, he had made no progress. Longfellow still continued to call on her and sometimes they passed an evening alone together, "but not one word is ever spoken on a certain topic." The professor was not going to beg and plead but he was sure that his silence had nothing to do with pride.

Frances Elizabeth Appleton, by George Peter Alexander Healy.
(Courtesy of the Longfellow House Trustees.)

By July, 1838, Mary and Fanny were spending their first summer in Berkshire, reading about the rights of women. They had received wise counsel concerning the pitfalls of marriage from that maiden lady, Catherine Maria Sedgwick. And meanwhile Longfellow had determined upon an almost unbelievably ill-advised course of action. He was writing a novel to be called *Hyperion*.[4] His heroine, whom he named Mary Ashburton, was Fanny Appleton who was to be "painted" so as to make her "fall in love with her own sweet image" first of all and then to fall in love with the hero, Paul Flemming, alias Longfellow!

Paul Flemming meets the heroine at an inn where "presently a female figure clothed in black, entered the room and sat down by the window. She rather listened to the conversation than joined it; but the few words she said were spoken in a voice so musical that it moved the soul of Flemming like a whisper from heaven . . ."

Longfellow did not fail to describe his heroine, Mary Ashburton, further. "Her face had a wonderful fascination in it. It was such a calm, quiet face, with the light of the rising soul shining so peacefully through it. . . . And O, those eyes with 'down-falling eyelids full of dreams and slumber' and within them a cold, living light, as in mountain lakes at evening or the river of Paradise, forever gliding . . ."

This was the novel certain to cause Fanny Appleton to capitulate! One of the various things wrong with the plan was that Fanny was not the sort of girl to fall in love with her own image even if she recognized it — which at first she did not. Fanny told her friend Emmeline that there were a few good things in *Hyperion*. She liked some of the poetic comparisons which the professor's "scholastic lore and vivid imagination" had produced. But on the whole, it was a thing of shreds and patches with too many re-used college lectures in it. It still hadn't occurred to Fanny that she was being identified as Mary Ashburton and that people were talking about her!

Cousin Isaac Appleton Jewett very kindly woke Fanny up to the situation. He took a quick trip from Stockbridge to New York where he happened to meet Longfellow. The professor gave him a copy of *Hyperion* to take to Fanny along with "a rank Swiss cheese." Charles Sedgwick said that the cheese typified Longfellow's admiration for Fanny Appleton which was "as strong as it was disagreeable."

After Jewett left Berkshire, he wrote to Fanny that all his friends in Cincinnati were talking about her. In New Orleans where he went to give the cotton business a try, the girls paid a lot of attention to him, he said, because they heard that he was the cousin of the beautiful Miss

Appleton. Eventually there was a squib in a Boston paper which Jewett mentioned. He meant to jeer at Longfellow and flatter Fanny. But Fanny was furious.

Fanny was feeling especially disillusioned about men. Attaché Ledyard had become Secretary of the American Legation in Paris but he had neither brought nor sent her a branch from the willows of Babylon when he returned from the Mediterranean. She had been right about the romantic opportunities aboard ship. Henry Ledyard had married Matilda Cass.[5]

Hyperion, which Longfellow had been sure would make Fanny capitulate, had done just the opposite. She hated to be talked about. Moreover, it had been one thing to make fun of young men who called on her but now she suspected she might be laughed at — and that was different! Longfellow had hoped that the sale of *Hyperion* would pay off a last debt to his father and sales were indeed good. Then his publisher failed in business and half the edition was seized and held by the creditors.

"No matter. I had the glorious satisfaction of writing it . . ." Longfellow said. He thought he had won a great victory — not over Fanny, his "Fair Ladie" — but over himself. He was sure that he no longer loved Fanny Appleton.

On December 26, 1839, immediately after their wedding Mary and Robert drove out to Lexington in a sleigh. Eliza Lee Cabot Follen [6] had given them the use of her house for their honeymoon. She had gone to New York to see a doctor — her husband, Charles Follen, now a Unitarian minister in Lexington, Massachusetts, had gone with her. After waiting only a few days, Tom and Fanny went out in one of the Appleton sleighs to see the bride and groom.

"I found Mary as comfortable as I could wish in a sunny parlor with a big cosy-looking sofa and bookshelves in every direction and a nice coal fire," Fanny said. Mary and Mac had been taking tremendous walks through the snow and would be content to settle there for a month, if it could be." While the sisters talked, "Tom and Mac began a furious shuttle-cock game" of ideas and jokes.

"They gave us a very nice dinner of mincemeat and beefsteak; the snug dining room and fare bearing some resemblance to Yale Manor, tho' superior. Mackintosh thinks himself bound to return to his Washington duties soon, however. If it is possible for us to get ready, I should not wonder if we leave about January 13," Fanny said. The bride's sister was going to Washington with the newly wedded couple!

Fanny's next communication to her friend Emmeline came from Beacon Street and was dated January, 1840. "I am happy to inform you that Mrs. A. has a boy. She has had a dreadful time and the poor little wretch seemed very unwilling to enter this world and had precious little life in it at first but I have just seen it and it gave very audible proofs of its existence. It is about 2 hours old, I believe." "It" was William Sumner Appleton, born on January 11, half-brother to Tom, Mary and Fanny. Next would come Harriot, born November 16, 1841. This spelling of her name was taken from that of a Nantucket ancestress and she set great store by it. Nathan, always to be known as "Natey," was born February 2, 1843, and was the last of Nathan Appleton's second crop of children.

Mr. and Mrs. Robert James Mackintosh and Miss Fanny Appleton set out for Washington on January 13, 1840, as planned. They were on board a Long Island Sound steamboat "cutting through the ice," New York bound that night. Next morning they went to see Mrs. Charles Follen — Mary and Mac to tell her how much they had enjoyed the use of her house. She said she had been "near dying" from an operation but was better. Dr. Follen had gone back to Boston the previous night, planning to write his inaugural sermon for his Lexington church, on board the steamer. Eliza Lee said she had wanted to go with him but he urged her to stay and get a little more strength.

The Mackintoshes and Fanny Appleton told Mrs. Follen what a fine, still night it had been on Long Island Sound. Dr. Follen must have had a pleasant voyage on board the steamer *Lexington*. But it was the night that the steamer *Lexington* burned! Sparks from the smoke stack caught in bales of cotton piled on deck. The fire was almost instantly out of control. Dr. Charles Follen and nearly all of the other passengers and crew were lost.

When Fanny Appleton heard the dreadful news she said she almost doubted the goodness of God. She was sure the loss would kill Mrs. Follen, "a woman of such intensely excitable feelings and her existence . . . so completely merged in that of the good doctor." But grief did not kill Eliza Lee Follen. She had a son whom she prepared for Harvard along with other boys in the school she established. She became a leader in the Boston Female Anti-Slavery Society.

Had they known of the *Lexington* disaster, the stopover in Philadelphia would not have been happy. As it was, Fanny, Mary and Mac found Fanny Kemble Butler looking handsome in garnet-colored velvet. She teased the bride and groom with "gay, saucy speeches." Next morning, they were off early, "railroading it very comfortably" in spite of the cold weather, the cars, with closed windows and red-hot stoves, "being by no means bad conveyances," at least according to Fanny. The Appleton girls' last trip to Washington had been by coach and post-horses, most of the way.

After shivering in uncomfortable lodgings for a day or two, Robert Mackintosh rented a house on Y Street. Fanny said she had always wanted to live in the country and this was a country house. "Although this calls itself a street, the houses are as few and far between as old Ashburner's teeth or a sermon from Dr. Channing," she said.[7] Tom would remember Luke Ashburner of Stockbridge and everyone at Dr. Channing's church in Boston was bewailing the fact that he left the preaching to Dr. Gannett so often.

Fanny walked once "into Pennsylvania Avenue" where she saw fine liveried carriages and smartly dressed pedestrians. But snow covered the fields and when "the slosh and mud" subsided enough to let her walk at all she usually headed for Georgetown which she thought had a foreign and picturesque air with its views of the broad river.

"Robert, as I gradually get to call him, is the most devoted of husbands and Mary is as unexacting as a woman can be whose honeymoon is just waning," Fanny wrote to Tom. "I've got so accustomed to their tender endearments that I flatter myself to be very little *de trop* and as Mac is occasionally to be away on business . . . my society relieves Mary of the loneliness brides suffer." If Tom got weary of parental tête-à-têtes he was to join them in Washington!

Mr. Hudson, with whom Robert Mackintosh worked at the British Legation, soon called. He was "a very good-looking, merry sort of person but somewhat à la fat boy," Fanny said. Robert brought over an English subaltern to meet his sister-in-law and she said he seemed "extremely waggish." At first, she paid little attention to him because of an Austrian attaché, Mr. Friedrichstall, who had been "attaché everywhere and appears an amiable youth enough." The Austrian attaché continued to drop in of an evening while the facetious subaltern, Lieutenant Campbell, called even more often. "A man in such a constant state of effervescence," Fanny never beheld before. His specialty for the entertainment of ladies was a series of sleight-of-hand tricks and he told Fanny that his "thimble-ing" had been the delight of the duchess of Kent and caused her to compliment him greatly! Fanny was amused but not too impressed. The thimble-rig game was always a part of country fairs in Berkshire.

Attaché Mackintosh and Nathan Appleton's two daughters were invited to dine at the White House. The Van Buren dinner party was much less stiff and formal than Fanny expected, but she "nearly perished with the cold in the large rooms." The President did not get too high a mark from Fanny. He was pleasant and affable enough but she thought he had a "secretive manner . . . showing a cautious, diplomatic soul."

There were numerous dancing parties where the Appleton girls met men from the British Legation and plenty of other men besides. "Do you *sli-i-ide*" asked one affected young gentleman. Miss Appleton could and did waltz. She discovered a Washington innovation — a waxed floor which made waltzing all the more delightful.

But before long Lieutenant Campbell was assigned duties outside of Washington and had to take his effervescence and his parlor tricks elsewhere. Fanny was not taking Mr. Friedrichstall seriously, having become disillusioned with attachés in general. When Mary and Robert decided to sail for England, it was no great disappointment. Robert thought he could get a better post somewhere else, and Fanny agreed with him when he said that a three-years' residence in Washington was enough. A few weeks had been enough as far as she was concerned. By February 25, 1840, Robert, Mary and Fanny were "lolling on Mrs. Butler's nice ottomans" and by March 3, they were in Boston.

Mary and Robert sailed for England on the *New York*, from New York, but Fanny decided not to see them off. That widening of water between ship and shore would have been too much for her. They had invited her to go with them but she had refused. "I know it is much better that I should remain here (even if Father gave his consent which I am very sure he would never have done)" Fanny said. But Mary was now expecting a child and Fanny "often felt that she *must* be with her to take care of her."

It was not easy for Fanny to be happy without Mary but she did her best. Aunt Sam gave a dinner party for "Big Daniel" whose "ponderosity" oppressed Fanny as she sat beside him.[8] She asked him to tell her about "London society in general and its lions in particular — which got merged on his part into some dry squeezes of the hand, tender speeches and 'God bless yous' in his old vein." Daniel Webster also did justice to Aunt Sam's excellent meal but Fanny found time passing slowly.

Aunt Everett, Nathan and Samuel Appleton's sister, came to visit Sam during the spring of 1840. She was seventy and looked just the way Fanny remembered her. But she had to be told that the tall young lady was the little girl she had once "appalled with her long counsels," Fanny said. Aunt Everett came over to 39 Beacon one day and "wandered over the house, picking up the past and commiserating the many, many changes," Fanny said. "Tom completely puzzles the old lady with his waggery and goat-like addition of a beard. But Aunt Everett knits and goes to prayer-meeting as regularly as if she were in N. Ipswich." [9]

Charles Sumner began calling on Fanny Appleton. He had recently returned from Europe and Fanny gathered from his conversation that "no American of his age" had ever received "more attention from great people." He was "full of talk about literary lions, as he has been a Daniel among them." But Fanny hoped his "agreeableness won't grow rusty with his English clothes."

Berkshire summers at Yale Manor were now over for good. Where two unmarried girls in their twenties could live, daringly entertaining young men — a single girl alone could not. Fanny wrote to Mrs. Yale telling her to keep the furniture left behind by her former tenants and rent the rooms to someone else. Then she went to Newport with her father, Mrs. A, the baby, and Tom.

"Marine Villa" proved to be delightful. There was "a straw-carpeted, flower-perfumed drawing room and a pillared piazza." Swallows were building nests under the eaves and there was an eolian harp at Fanny's bedroom window. She could hear the distant sound of the sea and also the babbling of her infant half-brother, Willie, who had learned to hold out his arms to her so that she would pick him up. Father had time to "parade of mornings in the French-marquis *robe de chambre*, so useless in active city life," while Tom enjoyed going "hatless and strapless." Of course he never went out without his hat in Boston and his pantaloons were always strapped under the instep, outside his boots.

Cousin Fanny Wright of Pittsfield was invited to Newport to keep Fanny company. The girls decided upon a daring venture, not the equal of a Berkshire excursion perhaps, but fun just the same. They went to a local store, bought material by the yard and each made a "bathing dress." They actually went into the water, "our dresses with straw hats defying discovery of ourselves," Fanny said.

Tom sat on the cliffs with the girls and wrote poetry — then went fishing, promising them tautog for dinner. He came home with a handsome fish but Fanny suspected that he had caught it "with a silver hook" at the fish market.

They had taken the house for three months. Fanny reported that "Father seems fully content here and is busy writing a genealogical history of all the Appletons from Eve." But she, herself, had a copy of the *Dial* which she found much more interesting. There was much that was readable in it, she thought, and also some nonsense. As for Transcendentalism in general, Fanny would "only concede that there is *something* in it." A little later, Fanny met Margaret Fuller, probably at one of Miss Fuller's "Conversations" at Elizabeth Peabody's West Street book shop. Miss Fuller undertook to instruct her group of ladies on Transcendentalism, and Fanny said it was all so intellectual that "the air burned blue."

Early in September, Nathan Appleton and Tom left Newport "for this famous Whig gathering which is working like a tempest in a teapot in that quiet city of Boston," Fanny said. "Beds and boards are supplied for this Whig army. Some patriotic ladies had their garrets hospital-like with beds — some, though absent from town, give keys to their servants to open their houses." Fanny thought this was "a dangerous civility, for though a very good Whig, I know humanity is fallible and if spoons do disappear they can never complain as it might affect the interests of the party."

The political situation was curious. Massachusetts manufacturing people, favoring a protective tariff, were Whigs, of course. But so were the anti-tariff cotton planters. Bankers, who hated Jackson's fiscal policy, were Whigs so Henry Clay was the Appletons' favored candidate. But William Henry Harrison was nominated. When Harriet, the baby, Fanny and the servants, their carriage, and their carry-all finally got to Boston, Fanny found herself up to the ears in politics, whether she liked it or not.

Webster was making himself a stump orator for the Whigs, she found, but she said that "Harrison fever" was ludicrous. "Youths behind the counter wear log cabin brooches upon their shirt-bosoms and infants in Whig cradles were squalling to the tune of 'Tippecanoe'."

After Harrison was elected, and political excitement died down in Boston, there was a fair to raise money to complete the Bunker Hill monument. Fanny drew a cartoon for it, showing "a mock monument, half-finished, with a score of little *work-women* hoisting stones etc. and one solitary loafer slinking about it in an attitude of astonishment — a very well-designed satire, showing the necessity of women's work," — Fanny declared.

Fanny Elssler was giving dance recitals in Boston. Fanny Appleton, having seen the famous ballerina in Paris, was afraid the Boston performances would be a disappointment. But the dancer was even better than Fanny remembered, the recitals a sell-out and audiences wild with enthusiasm. "In the warmth of her German heart" Miss Elssler "actually insisted upon bestowing a thousand dollars for the Bunker Hill Monument," although there were those on the Monument Committee who thought they ought not to accept the gift of a foreigner!

Fanny Appleton was at the benefit performance. When Miss Elssler finished she made a speech, "pronounced in a sweetly timid accent, ending thus, 'There are two monuments which will rise together — one of granite on Bunker's Hill, the other of gratitude in my *heart*.' Thunders and thunders of applause followed."

Of course there was news from Mary by almost every trans-Atlantic mail. She and Mac were "comfortably situated at housekeeping near Regents Park in London," Mac having taken a mansion there for three months. On the eighteenth of October, Mary's birthday, a son was born to her and still the news from England was good. Fanny called Ronald Mackintosh her "Cockney nephew." But it was later learned that Mary had suffered some child-birth injury which no one seemed to understand. Weeks went by and she was still in great pain when she attempted to walk.

Fanny tried to remember that London doctors were famous. Surely some cure would be found for Mary. To pass the time, Fanny began to read Dante "with a warm-souled Italian" who "explained admirably the different allusions and took charming flights of fancy to *Bella Italia*." Every other Monday night there was dancing at Papanti's Hall on what Fanny described as "the nicest floor in the world, though a shade too elastic." It was set on springs! A huge circle was always kept open for waltzers, with people who still liked quadrilles doing the best they could around the edges — to waltz-time.

Early in February, 1841, James Winthrop Andrews, lawyer, described by Tom as "Fanny's adorer," wrote her a letter.[10] He went on at length about the rules of etiquette which he never broke but was breaking now. Next he took up the subject of Fanny's "diamond eyes" and "lips of ruby hue" and finally, before asking her father's consent and after begging her to show the letter to no one, he asked her to marry him.

Page after page of this remarkable document indicated that James Winthrop Andrews was sure that Miss Appleton could not possibly resist him. He would appear below her Beacon Street balcony — she was to give him a signal and he would know the happy news. Fanny did not appear.

As for Henry Wadsworth Longfellow — his passion for Fanny Appleton was dead, he told George Washington Greene. "Though on this account, I lead a maimed life; yet it is better thus than merely to have gained her consent — if it could have been done. So of this no more — no more. . . . Three of my best years are melted down in this fiery crucible. Yet I like to feel deep emotions. The next best thing to *complete* success is *complete* failure . . ."

The courtship of Henry Longfellow had not failed, however. Once more he was wrong — not just about Fanny but about himself as well.

SEVENTEEN

TO HIM WHO WAITS

THE S.S. COLUMBIA, one of the first of the Cunarders, left Boston May 1,
1841. The mail steamer would call at Halifax and then head out over
the Atlantic bound for Liverpool. Fanny and Tom Appleton were
passengers on their way to London to visit Mary.

Fanny had supposed that nothing could equal her first voyage by
sailing ship but she soon changed her mind.[1] It was quiet on board the
Columbia, there was no "bawling of orders . . . no racket of ropes nor
rushing about of sailors nor wearisome creaking of masts, as in a
packet . . ." In her letter to her father, mailed from Halifax, Fanny gave
steamship travel the ultimate praise in terms of a cotton manufacturer's daughter. The Cunarder's "easy, majestic motion would delight
you more than that of the Lowell water wheels."

History repeated itself, however, when Fanny "had a charming long
tramp with the captain" by the light of a "watery moon" with Boston
Light still visible on the horizon. "All the while the band played old airs
and the captain made civil speeches in any quantity" — offering to walk
with Miss Appleton whenever she appeared on deck and to order the
band to play nothing but her favorite tunes.

Halifax was in sight at nine-thirty Monday morning. Fanny saw
"tumble-down wooden houses embrowning the hillside." She thought
of New England towns with their sturdily built small houses, most of
them painted white. This shabby look must be the result of colonialism,
she felt sure. She and Tom decided not to go ashore.

"Young Cunard" came aboard, however, to urge Fanny to visit his sisters. She felt shy about being "thrust upon the privacy of a group of damsels," but he sent his carriage to the dock and escorted her "to his Papa's handsome mansion overlooking the town and shipping." The girls made Fanny feel at home while Tom and young Cunard went riding. Then the mail from St. John's was late, the *Columbia's* departure was delayed, so the Cunards asked Tom and Fanny to dinner. Fanny was embarrassed all over again because she had on her sea "costume" while the Cunard girls "arrayed themselves in full dress." Captain Judkins of the *Columbia* and Lieutenant Miller, described by Fanny as "Lord of the Mails," also came to dinner. Captain Judkins had been obliged to explain in writing why the new Cunarder had slackened speed for an hour between Boston and Halifax. It was because *Columbia's* boilers "boiled over."

Everybody back in Boston had read Richard Henry Dana's *Two Years Before the Mast*. Fanny was delighted when, after leaving Halifax, they sighted ten icebergs, the largest of which the captain "calculated to be a quarter of a mile long and eighty feet deep." It was fascinating to watch as "large masses fell from the icy cliff, splashing famously." Captain Judkins was less than pleased. He said they "might encounter these detached pieces" but Fanny could not wait to tell her friends that she had seen something that Dana described. The only trouble was that these icebergs did not seem to move as fast as Dana's did.

Many small ships, "chiefly brigs and barks crowded with immigrants" bound for Canada, passed the Cunarder on her way to Liverpool. Crowds of immigrants still seemed a strange sight to Tom and Fanny Appleton because the importation of labor had still to reach full tide, but their father, the pioneer manufacturer, had already changed their world, just as the first immigrant Appleton had helped to change the American colonies.

On May 15, the voyage was over. Tom and Mary went direct from Liverpool to London, impatient to see Mary and Robert Mackintosh. Mary "looked delicate and thin but very pretty." Robert was "looking remarkably well and is, to me, one of the handsomest men I have ever seen," Fanny said. Nephew Ronald was "the ultima thule of health and good nature."

The Mackintoshes had taken a house in a small court which opened out upon Regent's Park but was closed at the other end by a church with gardens behind it.[2] There were six mansions built as a gift from the queen to impoverished gentlewomen but usually let by them for the sake of revenue. Mary's address was "St. Catherine's," the atmosphere aristocratic but informal.[3] Fanny was astonished to see neighbors call on each other without first putting on a bonnet. Mary's nursemaid, "a young woman rather slight," carried the baby in her arms all day, out in Regent's Park. And Ronnie was "no slight weight." Fanny wished she could "make a shipment to America of English nursemaids for the well-being of juvenile Republicans."

Mary rarely felt well enough to go out but Mrs. Wedgewood and Mrs. Rich, two of Robert's sisters, entertained Tom and Fanny. At a "tea-drinking" at Mrs. Wedgewood's, Fanny met Thomas Carlyle who "began at once, in the strongest Scotch accent" to question her about Ralph Waldo Emerson, "lauding him immensely . . ." Carlyle had "a heavy, farmer look with rough features and hair, a slouchy manner but eyes soft and clear like Burns." He talked in a humorous fashion. Tom was vastly pleased with English ways and things, and "here to be sure, we get the cream of it," Fanny added.

When Derby Day came, Mary "had not the courage for it," but Fanny, Tom and Robert drove down to Epsom Downs with Miss Gifford, a cousin of Robert's, to keep Fanny company. They thought their "little, low phaeton" with its innocent appearance, would be perfectly safe. However, "all the dashing chariots with gay-jacketed postillions and coroneted hammer-cloths and the high coaches of the Four-in-hand Club showed divers aristocratic intentions of running us down and cutting us out of file when the press of vehicles became severe — which it does for three long miles before you arrive," Fanny told. "Poor Miss Gifford was dreadfully frightened and had cause — for the horses were champing at her bonnet and the pole of a carriage behind nearly empaled us. Nothing but Robert's admirable driving saved us from accident . . ."

"The running at Epsom, where we safely arrived, was beautiful. . . . A murmur arose from the gleaming crowd, like that of the sea as the tides of feeling rose and fell. The stakes were very heavy and bets incalculably disastrous because the favorite, 'Coronation,' won, contrary to expectation."

Mary continued to look thin and pretty but lacked her old zest for life. Tom, Fanny and Robert Mackintosh combined to persuade her to see a famous London surgeon. He told her that "her bones will soon recover from the horrid wrench they underwent" when Ronnie was born. This made her feel more comfortable about herself but still a prey to fits of nervous excitement followed by depression. She wanted to "get fairly away from the sound of carriage wheels and the town-feeling" but hated to leave the house where Ronnie had been born and which was her first home in England.

Part of Fanny's mission in going to visit Mary had been to find out for her father what Robert's future plans might be. At present, Robert was unemployed, a shocking state of affairs in the opinion of Nathan Appleton who had rarely missed a day's work since he was old enough to bring in the cows on his father's farm.

Fanny tried to explain tactfully. Robert was "so averse to talking much of his plans" that she could not report "how distinct they are in his own mind." Fanny had to conclude that "diplomacy was what he liked and would cling to, if Mary had not such a repugnance to its necessary evils, wandering in outlandish places. Farming, he fancies but whatever he does, it is with the feeling of an Englishman, that it is his duty to keep under Little Vic's administration, as much for Ronald as for himself. It is a loyal obligation we, in our self-governed independence, can hardly understand or sympathize with but it is evidently too strong a feeling to be up-rooted from his mind." Fanny understood both her father and her brother-in-law very well.

Tom gave much the same report and Nathan Appleton realized that it was not going to be possible for him to help Robert very much. At the same time, he could not give up trying. If the Mackintoshes would just come to Boston for a visit, he could see to it that Robert got established in a good, well-paying American job, right away! Although Harriet was expecting her second child, she wrote cordially to Mary and Robert telling them exactly where and how they could live in the house at 39 Beacon Street and what rooms the baby's nurse and other servants they might bring, could have. Poor Mary was appalled at Harriet's efficiency. She wrote that she feared a prolonged stay might "take Robert from a chance of finding some post to his mind" in Great Britain.

Mary finally realized that she must give up the house on St. Catherine's Court but it was almost impossible for her to decide what to put in boxes for storage and what to take to Woolwich Common, where Robert's sister, Mrs. Rich, had found a cottage. Finally, Tom and Fanny "steamed it" down the Thames to Woolwich while Mary, Robert, the baby and the nursemaid drove down in the phaeton. At Woolwich Common, Fanny enjoyed herself. There were "machine-like manoeuvers of the troops in parade" from the Royal Military Academy to watch. From the cottage windows there were views of "fine trees and the lordly

Thames . . . St. Paul's looming in the distance." Mrs. Rich, with her tales of life in India, proved a delightful companion.

Tom lit out for Paris. He wrote of "devouring Vaudrilles and Turbot à la crème." The American tourists had all left Paris so now the vaudevilles were more uninhibited and more fun. His old friend, the Baron de Poilly, was off taking a water cure somewhere but Tom went out to Polambray to see his dog, Brag. The dog had been re-named Boston and was "the prop of the kennel where he reigns supreme," the Baron's servant told Tom.

In August, Robert drove his wife, baby, nursemaid and sister-in-law to Tunbridge Wells — a thirty-four-mile journey requiring two days! Robert had sold his phaeton, found a new job for his young coachman, bought a second horse and harnessed them both to a landau. Then he mounted the box, himself. Tom came over from Paris to join the party and said that Robert was "an excellent whip and indeed would be perfect but for his near-sightedness which makes it possible that some day we shall quietly drive over a pig or a sheep mistaking it for a puddle."

Fanny thought that Tunbridge Wells was an old-fashioned watering place and certainly not very lively, but they took the waters because that was what everybody else was doing. When Robert left to go back to London, Tom spent his time giving his nephew Ronald donkey-rides and teaching the boys on the village green how to fly kites. Robert had gone back in the public conveyance, leaving the landau, and Tom took Robert's place as "Whip," to drive the girls over the countryside. Then they all went on to St. Leonard's. Robert came down from London again and he and Mary sat on the cliffs over-looking the English Channel — "sentimentalizing," Fanny said.

Fanny and Tom walked to Hastings, a mile away, where Fanny sketched the ancient castle and Tom wrote what he hoped was poetry. Dutifully, Fanny tried to imagine "an Apulton, or d'Apelton" sailing in William the Conqueror's fleet and fighting in the Battle of Hastings. But she had to confess that her sympathies were all with Harold and his Anglo-Saxons.

Once more Tom departed — this time for a salmon-fishing excursion into Scotland. Alone with Mary, by the middle of September, Fanny had to admit that, in spite of sea baths, which Mary had consented to try and which seemed an indication of returning health, nothing had really changed. "I am saddened by my poor sister's peculiarly distressing state . . . so pulled down from her former self — these vile nerves triumphing with the malice of Furies," Fanny wrote. It seems possible that Mary's state of mind might have been induced by medicine given her for the relief of pain. At this period, when William Appleton, for example, casually took laudanum to "regulate his stomach," the side-effects of opiates were unrecognized. Perhaps Mary's London surgeon had prescribed an opiate.

Almost at the end of Fanny and Tom's stay, "Mary was encouraged to try Homeopathy." This new theory of medicine was introduced by the German Doctor Wesselhoeft and was already in vogue in Boston. It had one great virtue — drugs were given in small quantities, as a rule. "Of course the effect is very gradual," Fanny wrote, but Mary began to "walk farther every day and she looked better than she had for months." Mary decided that she felt well enough to go to Boston with Tom and Fanny.[4] The good news reached Beacon Street and then, too late for letters to be sent, Mary changed her mind.

Tom and Fanny arrived home alone and a short time later, Mary, Robert, the baby and assorted servants arrived unannounced! No wonder the decisive Harriet found her oldest step-daughter difficult! On November 16, 1841, Harriet's daughter Harriot was born.

It was December 21, when Fanny wrote to her friend Emmeline, who was in New York, to tell her how things were going at 39 Beacon Street. "Our atmosphere trembles with the wails of '*parvoli innocenti*' — as the Infernal does with the plaints of lost souls." Listening to the "vocalizing of little innocents," Tom had declared that "he might as well be a mother himself!"

After what could never be called a quiet winter, the Mackintosh family sailed for England on the *Rosamond* out of Boston, May 8, 1842. Fanny said that they came to this "sudden decision to leave us, mainly, I believe, because the means were so comfortingly near at hand — the quiet of a ship with few passengers, to get on board of which required the fatigue of driving only through a few streets." Robert had "missed the humorous friends with whom he is entirely at his ease and who have equal leisure." Bronson Alcott was on board the same sailing vessel but no one mentioned how Robert enjoyed his "orphic sayings."

By this time, Nathan Appleton had once more become a member of the House of Representatives. His mission, as always, was to protect American manufactures by means of tariff restrictions, if he could. His deep concern was also for national fiscal policies. General William Henry Harrison had been elected President with Tyler for his running-mate and, according to the *Philadelphia Ledger*, "for two years past, ordinary operations of business had been neglected and President-making has become every citizen's chief concern. The result has been uncertainty; some have been afraid to engage in new enterprises . . . others have not dared to prosecute their business with the old vigor." [5] On Inauguration Day, President Harrison rode into Washington "mounted on a white charger."

One month later, General Harrison, the Whig knight errant, chosen to right all wrongs, was dead! Tyler immediately vetoed the Whig bill to establish a national bank. Sound currency went out the window along with what people had hoped would be a working coalition among Western, Southern and Northern partisans.

Appleton explained how it happened that he went back to Washington.[6] "In 1842, Robert C. Winthrop was the member of the House of Representatives from the district of Suffolk. In May, he resigned in consequence of the illness and impending death of his wife." This situation was similar to that of Nathan Appleton in 1833. "A successor must be appointed instantly. The public looked either to Mr. Abbott Lawrence or myself to fill the vacancy." Mr. Lawrence was already Massachusetts Commissioner appointed to settle the Maine boundary question with Lord Ashburton. Mr. Appleton "very reluctantly" took his seat in the Twenty-seventh Congress on the ninth of July, 1842.

Tom was expected to take Charley's place and send his father reports on the textile business. There were people in his father's employ who were better qualified to do this, Tom quite rightly decided. Fanny went to Brookline to visit Emmeline at the Austin's summer place. Very shortly, Tom found himself elected to escort his step-mother and the two babies to Nahant, and Fanny was summoned to help with the children. By the nineteenth of June, Tom found that he needed a change of air.

Having missed the family trip to Canada, Tom set out for Niagara Falls and points north. Realizing that his father wanted business news, Tom said that Rochester was a miracle of New York State enterprise. Charles Lee of Boston took him "around the mills and public buildings." They were all strong for the tariff. In Buffalo, Tom met his cousin, Charles Gold, a lawyer, who "seems to be one of their first young men and being rather out of pocket only makes him resemble the rest." [7] Cousin Charles sent word by Tom that he couldn't pay his debt to Mr. Appleton just now but would like a "five hundred dollar bill" to purchase houses now selling daily at chancellor's sales for taxes. Nathan Appleton did not extend his loan to his late wife's nephew. He hoped, however, that Tom would join him in Washington and listen to some tariff debates. Tom found it "positively too hot to venture upon Washington."

Tom went back to Nahant where "Mothers abound on the cliffs and broken shins and the croup keep poor Dr. Mifflin on the run from side to side of the peninsular." He "got Fanny a horse, a good one, from town and we go over the beaches nightly, to her great satisfaction, apparently," Tom wrote his father. Fanny loved the mare and named her Victoria.

Tom went back to Boston which struck him as "gloomy-genteel." He started to work with the sketches of Indians he had made in Rochester and Buffalo, composing a large painting for the fall Athenaeum show. Once more, he was in his painting-room at 39 Beacon, or "in what I believe was called your Sanctum last year," he told his father. "Your speech came on us suddenly in the *Intelligencer*," Tom went on to say. "It seemed well reported and reads extremely well." But Tom hoped his father was by now going to "give up the imbecile Tyler" and leave Washington for a summer vacation. Tyler had just vetoed the tariff bill. "Are you going to be stuffy and sit out Tyler's patience at vetoing?" Tom wanted to know.

Nathan Appleton was going to be as "stuffy" as he knew how. "Matters were in a very complicated state, in consequence of the quarrels between President Tyler and his own party, the Whigs," Mr. Appleton wrote. "Again, I felt bound to make a speech on the tariff; so that, in the three sessions in which I was a member of Congress, I was called upon to make three different speeches on the tariff on three different bills." A tremendous amount of work had been involved every time. Statistics were gathered not only from the mills Appleton was interested in but from all sorts of Massachusetts factories. This important information, when worked up into a written manuscript full of facts and figures, could not possibly be delivered in the rabble-rousing shout that passed for oratory in Congress. Nathan Appleton dreaded the ordeal of trying to hold the attention of men, many of whom were incapable of understanding the points he made. "Finally, with extreme difficulty, the tariff of 1842 was carried. After the close of the session, I resigned my seat in conformity with my own wishes and to make room for Mr. Winthrop," Appleton wrote. In a letter to Tom, his father agreed that "Captain Tyler is certainly a nincompoop." He turned his attention to railroads, banking and manufacturing — anything but politics. In 1843, "The Merrimack

Henry Wadsworth Longfellow as a Harvard professor. (Daguerreotype, picture collection of the late Harold Bowditch, M.D.)

Company will divide 6 percent — which produces some sensation," he was able to report. Cousin William Appleton, in his forecast for the year, had been only mildly optimistic. He had thanked God for a good harvest; did not look for sudden changes and had hoped only for modest gains.

Tom spent the winter writing a tragedy in blank verse. He dined out a great deal and was already famous as "T. G. Appleton, the Boston wit." When he announced that he was writing a tragedy people must have thought it was one of his jokes but Fanny, at least, took it very seriously. No one had considered it for the stage when he left Boston in May, bound for England.

The purpose of Tom's journey was ostensibly to look after Mary. The Mackintoshes had a second child, a little girl they called Eva. But there were indications that Tom planned a long stay in Paris after visiting Mary — and that he had further reasons for making Paris his home. Either he had noticed it himself, or it had been brought to his attention, that his sister Fanny stood a better chance of getting married if he were not around. She depended on him too much. They had such a good time that she needed no one else.

Tom's father wrote him a letter, dated May 15, 1843. "I have not yet found time to read your tragedy — which I hear a good deal of. The Professor has been reading it with Fanny with so much sympathy for your loss, that I am almost prepared for a termination anything but tragic." Mr. Appleton went on to say that there was not much news but that, if these readings of Tom's opus, now going on at 39 Beacon, should have romantic results for Henry Longfellow and Fanny Appleton — that would be news indeed!

Sam Ward had urged Longfellow to forget Fanny, come to New York and meet some new girls — his own sisters for example. Julia Ward, the most brilliant and gifted, had just married Dr. Samuel Gridley Howe, hero of the Greek liberation and famous teacher of the blind.[8] This happy couple were now in Europe with Horace Mann, the educator and his bride, Mary Peabody. Tom had sailed on the same ship with them and planned to call on them at their hotel in London.

Louisa, second of the "Three Graces of Bond Street," was the most beautiful and she had been urged upon Longfellow — at least by her brother Sam. Henry liked her but she was by no means as intellectual as Fanny and no one would ever call her a bluestocking. "Little Annie" Ward was sweet and pretty but Longfellow regarded her as just a dear child. Still trying to convince himself that he no longer loved Fanny

Appleton, Longfellow could not imagine why he was so out of health. Sam Ward advanced him money to go to Germany in 1841, to take the waters at a spa.

When Tom left home, Fanny said his departure was a grievous loss. He wrote her some "lines of farewell" and she cried. But before he left, she had gone to a party at the Charles Eliot Nortons' in Cambridge. Longfellow was there and they had a little talk. Fanny told him how lonely she was going to be with her brother away and asked him to call.

On April 17, Fanny wrote to Henry Longfellow.[9] "I have just received your note and I cannot forbear telling you that it comforted me greatly." Fanny admitted that there were passages that were disturbing, however. She would never have asked him to call if she had not felt sure that the past was forgotten and that they could meet now "to give each other only happy thoughts."

Fanny had a special place in her father's heart because she was so like her mother. He understood her better than she realized, but when, on May 15, he told her brother Tom that there was romance in the air, he had not quite guessed all of the secret. Fanny Appleton and Henry Longfellow had been engaged for all of five days!

Fanny accepted Henry's proposal in writing on May 10. When he read the note he set out for Beacon Street on foot, "with the speed of an arrow, being too restless to sit in a carriage — too fearful of encountering anyone." The air was full of "blossoms and sunshine and the song of birds." His heart was full of gladness and his eyes full of tears.

Tom's ship had sailed. Fanny could only write him the good news and hope no one else would tell him before he got her letter. But she too cherished the first beautiful days of secret love and did not sit down at her desk until May 24. Fanny said that she thought Tom must have seen "symptoms" of her romance before he left for Europe but his letter to his father did not bear this out.

"I have written to Fanny and the little I have to say is said but I cannot skip a post without talking to you of this marriage," Tom wrote. "I am both glad and sorry when I think how it has occurred. Sorry that it should come so soon after I left her and glad, if, as you say, my going brought the matter to a denoument. . . . I congratulate you from my heart at the event, aware as I am that you are satisfied the marriage will increase Fanny's happiness.

"Considering Fanny's peculiar need of sympathy, and it may be said without impropriety, the differences between you and Harriet and herself — we have cause for gratitude that she has found one to whom she can speak out. . . . This marriage of Fanny's leaves us, too, in our true positions. I can feel I am not false to her in leaving her — and Harriet, I believe, will be happier in seeing her snugly wedded and leaving the house free for her own wishes. It is fortunate for us all, though it gives me pain to have Fanny married and I not there . . .

"How sweet she will look, sweet and good; it is impossible to imagine happiness greater than she deserves . . ."

Tom's letter to Fanny was full of his understanding of her with just a tinge of jealousy that he tried to hide.[10] "I confess I was surprised a little — though very much that I saw in Boston looked like more than a renewal of old friendship. . . . May affection and joy be poured upon you, to recompensate the long maidenhood of so warm and noble a heart. And so you have found not all men distasteful. Pretty specimens you have had, too, in some of them. Your decidedly unpleasant experience in my sad sex will be all the more useful in starting in so sober a race as matrimony — and now that you are caught, you can look back and laugh. . . . I feel as if the lover you love ought to be a great deal better than the rest of us and of a very high flight to keep even wing with you. Longfellow I believe to be that man, capable of understanding you and loving you for the very things which would be stumbling blocks to others.

"To me, it seems as if your arm were taken from my shoulder — but these are old sorrows all loving fathers and brothers have submitted to since Eve's time. . . . Yet I am deeply grateful to that new shoulder Providence has sent you. . . . I look to see you a new creature, stepping into the Heaven Element of Love . . ."

EIGHTEEN

CASTLE CRAIGIE

FANNY APPLETON gave Henry Longfellow her sketch book with its scenes from Interlaken. He would remember how they sat together as she drew a river, then a bridge, cottages, and a castle wall. She signed the book "Mary Ashburton." Not only had she forgiven him for writing *Hyperion* but she had promised to be his heroine henceforth.

Once their secret had been told to the family, Fanny and Henry set about writing to their friends. Each wrote what amounted to an ardent love letter about the other. "I deeply feel the sacredness of my new trust — a poet's heart is the holiest of gifts and its light shall never faint in my keeping. God grant that I may aid and never dim its aspiring flame," Fanny told Matilda Lieber,[1] sending with the letter a gift dear to the hearts of young Victorians — a ring made from a strand of her hair.

For his letter to Henry Cleveland, Longfellow chose a paper with red stripes on it "as on a triumphant banner" with the joyful tidings that he had won "not Fanny Appleton's hand only, but truly and entirely her heart."[2]

Replies were almost as ecstatic as the letters to friends — with one exception. Isaac Appleton Jewett's caustic remarks concerning *Hyperion* had certainly not helped Longfellow's courtship but fortunately Longfellow did not know this. "The professor 'dears' me three times and you 'dear' me twice and all this, too, in the presence of the fact that he never wrote me before and you have been a year or more quite silent," Jewett told his cousin Fanny. "The fact is, that when folks are happy, over boils their sweet feelings just like those big kettles they make sugar in, in

New England — and I think there are no greater bores than you extremely happy people . . ."

Longfellow was anxious lest his family in Portland should fail to write to Fanny promptly and cordially. As a matter of fact, although they would have been the last to admit it, they were distinctly in awe of Miss Frances Elizabeth Appleton of Beacon Hill. Henry's younger sister, Annie Longfellow Pierce, wrote in behalf of her parents and herself. When the Appletons invited the Longfellows to come as their guests to Boston to attend the wedding "ill health," that convenient but all too often true excuse caused them to decline. Fanny wrote affectionately to Zilpah Wadsworth Longfellow, Henry's mother, and to Annie, calling them "Mother" and "Sister" — explaining her loneliness for her own mother and that her own sister was also almost lost to her, being so far away.

The wedding date was set for July 13, 1843. But tragedy had struck the William Appleton family, all over again. Beginning in January, the story of their son William was being repeated. This time, as his father wrote, "Our dear Amory left us in the *Ariosto* for Cuba . . . having a slight cough." On the following May 27, the boy's father and his brother Frank met him in Charleston and brought him home "to those he most loved." On June 29, Amory Appleton died of tuberculosis.

In view of this loss among the Appletons, there would be no array of bridesmaids and groomsmen at the Channing church for Fanny and Henry Longfellow. Dr. Gannett, Channing's successor, would perform the ceremony at 39 Beacon Street. Fanny and Henry much preferred a quiet wedding anyway. It would be in the evening by candlelight.

Longfellow's sister Annie, after having refused to come to Boston, changed her mind at the last minute. "Mother told me on Sunday, it was prudent for her to stay at home. She did not dare run the risk of getting sick again. . . . I did not like the idea that not one of us should go from the family," Annie wrote to a Portland friend.[3] "It was my darling brother Harry. My heart was brim full of joy, in sympathy with his happiness. I wanted to be a witness to it, so yielding to these feelings, on Monday I resolved to go and packed my trunk and was off on Tuesday A.M. before my courage had time to gainsay my determination."

Annie, although thirty-three and a married woman, was grateful for the escort of a family friend "direct to Cambridge to little Mary at Mr. Greenleaf's." Mary Greenleaf was Henry's sister also, now twenty-seven. "I found myself in the parlor where I felt quite at home," Annie went on. "As luck would have it, Harry came out from Boston to make his last visit of inspection at Craigie House and accidentally dropped in to ask Mary if she had heard from Portland. To his astonishment, I stood before him."

Fanny and Henry Longfellow were going to live at Craigie House, at least for a while, they had decided. In 1840, Henry had expanded his quarters there, hiring a third room and a kitchen. In 1841, old Mrs.

"Castle Craigie" or Longfellow House.
(Courtesy of the Longfellow House Trustees.)

Craigie had died, other lodgers had departed with the exception of "the Worcester family" who had leased several rooms. The house was for sale subject to their lease. Fanny had been buying furniture for her future home and Aunt Sam had invited Henry to visit her while his Craigie House rooms were made ready for the bride.

Two cartloads of furniture went out to Cambridge from Lawson and Harrington, Upholsterers, of 232 Washington Street, plus other items from other stores. Lawson and Harrington extolled their own merchandise on their bill,[4] dated June, as follows: "To a superb Black Walnut Chair" covered with "super-fine plush" — forty dollars. Then there was a "French tête-à-tête sofa of rosewood, richly carved," covered with the bride's own material and ornamented with "70 buttons," and "best elastic-stuffed." This cost seventy-five dollars and must have reminded Fanny of the apartment in Paris which they had all admired so much. There were four other chairs and also kitchen furnishings including a "French Bed," two other beds, mattresses and eight pillows along with the indispensable marble-topped commodes. From another store came a refrigerator. Lawson and Harrington sent out a seventy-five-dollar "Green Fancy Chamber set" costing twenty dollars. Fanny's most expensive wedding present was her "Rosewood piano with patented action and Square legs" supplied by Chickering at $450.

It was Tuesday, July 11, when Longfellow came out to Cambridge and found that his sister Annie had arrived. "Nothing would do but I must put on my bonnet and go with him to the house," she wrote. "It was a fine chance to see the arrangements and all the pretty things. I regaled my eyes while he gave directions to the servant."

That afternoon, Henry came back to Cambridge to take his sister Annie to Boston to meet Fanny. Annie admitted that she was "impatient to behold her. Harry and I had a nice ride," she wrote. "My first impression of the lady was most agreeable, there was something so quiet and gentle in her ways, so perfectly unaffected in her manners, so much of soul and heart about her in all she did and said. Such earnestness and love beamed from her peculiarly beautiful eyes that she won my heart at once."

Annie stayed at the Appletons' until nine that night and fell asleep in the carriage as it rolled smoothly along toward Cambridge. In her dreams, she said she saw the "sweet vision of Fanny's eyes."

Longfellow's sister Annie told of her arrival at 39 Beacon Street on the evening of July 13. "At half past eight, we assembled with the wedding guests. Taking hold of Professor Felton's arm, I followed Professor Greenleaf and wife into Mrs. Appleton's drawing room." Annie found this "an appalling moment . . ." The quiet family wedding "proved to be a roomful of some fifty bridal-dressed individuals. It was too late for me to retreat . . .

"Mrs. Appleton met me graciously, kindly whispered in my ear that she should take me under her special care for the evening and led me to her mother, an old school-mate and intimate friend of my mother's with whom I was acquainted. In the corner with her and her old husband, I took breath and put myself upon my good behavior, determined to make the best of it and look as little strange as possible.

"At this moment of self-recovery, Mrs. Appleton came up to ask me to go with her into the room where Fanny was and see her before the ceremony — taking me upon one arm and Mary [Greenleaf] upon the other. I went again through the length of the room and that array of people. It was delightful to get into the chamber where were Henry and Fanny alone, no bridesmaids, no groomsmen. Fanny looked more lovely than ever in her simple white muslin dress, her bridal veil, and the adornments of natural blossoms.

"Soon the arrival of the minister was announced . . ." Longfellow's two sisters went back into the drawing room just in time to see Fanny and Henry enter the other door. "Oh, it was a beautiful scene!" Annie decided that it was useless to try to describe it but would only say that her "darling brother never looked one half so handsome in all his life and Fanny was in all respects the perfection of brides. The soul which shone so expressively in their faces brightened and beautified the scene. . . . Dr. Gannett's ceremony was impressive and solemn, his prayers fervent and delightful. The whole as beautiful as could be . . ."

Mary Longfellow Greenleaf, more clothes-conscious than her sister, observed that the bride's muslin dress was trimmed with "splendid thread lace" and that her tunic was looped up with natural orange blossoms, "a bunch on each side the skirt." The bride's veil reached to her feet and "partly enveloped her person in a most becoming and graceful manner." Fanny looked "queenly" as she presided over the wedding collation, a cake, fruit, flowers and ices. Both Longfellow sisters observed that the bride's "magnificent presents" covered two tables in the adjoining room where the wedding supper was served. After the wedding, Fanny and Henry drove out to Craigie House by moonlight.

Family and close friends went out to see the Longfellows almost immediately but by July 20 they were glad to say that they were "as yet unmolested by mere acquaintances." However, as Fanny later wrote, "My husband's dear band of friends have a free entrée at all hours." Felton, Hillard and Charles Sumner began to dine with the Longfellows almost immediately and with great regularity. This continued, especially in Sumner's case, until, one by one, the bachelors among them were married. Fanny's cook, Margaret, was excellent.

In July, the Longfellows began to plan the sort of wedding journey all their friends seemed to enjoy. Everyone they could persuade to join them was invited to come along! To Charles Sumner, Fanny wrote, "Niagara has been magnetising us like a potent Magician but . . . we have resisted his spell and content ourselves with the Catskills. . . . We both earnestly hope that you will be able and willing to accompany us. I have written to Emmeline to urge her to join us likewise . . ." Hillard was to find out if any or all of the Nortons would like to come.

By the time Mr. and Mrs. Longfellow reached the Catskill Mountain House, they had with them Sumner, Emmeline Austin and her brother Edward, and Franz Lieber who always seemed free to leave Matilda and children whenever opportunity offered.⁵ They "sketched," they "scrambled" during the day, and in the evening Sumner read Plato's *Dialogues* aloud. Fanny said that all her delight in spending days out of doors came back to her "with renewed freshness, spite of the waning" of her "honeymoon and the soberness of matrimony."

A visit to Portland, Maine, was also accomplished during July. "A flood of strange thoughts flowed over me," Fanny wrote. She had "a great desire to appear well — worthy of such a husband" and she had "a greater fear" that she would not know what to do and say. Longfellow's mother set down her own impressions of the new daughter-in-law.⁶

"The visit seemed short to us, we had not time to become very much acquainted with Fanny but the impression we received of her was very agreeable. She seemed very lovely and affectionate, which of course would suit us better than a more fashionable display of dress and manner which we see in some town-bred ladies. Everyone to whom she was introduced seemed delighted with her, such a quiet and gentle manner, so perfectly ladylike. She is not handsome, I believe, but still she appears so, her eyes are so beautiful and brilliant when she is engaged on conversation." This adverse opinion of Fanny's looks was certainly not widespread! Fanny's mother-in-law went on. "But there was one thing which made her seem not to belong to us. She is very tall, which made her appear like a maypole among the ladies of the family."

By the end of August, Fanny and Henry were back at Craigie House again with a house guest to entertain. This was George Washington Greene, to whom Longfellow had confided the story of his once-hopeless love for Miss Appleton. As Consul in Rome, Greene had gotten into difficulties with an ill-natured tourist, but his cousin, Sam Ward of New York, was straightening out the trouble. Writing to Tom on August 30, 1843, Fanny said, "We have decided to let Father purchase this grand old mansion, if he will. Our interest in it has been quickened by our present guest, Mr. Greene of Rome. . . . He has excited our historical appreciation, or rather, reminded us how noble an inheritance this is — where Washington dwelt in every room."

Very shortly, Jared Sparks, already at work upon the publication of the writings of George Washington, fanned the flame of the Longfellows' enthusiasm. He was now a Harvard professor, married to Mary Crown-inshield Silsbee, and living in Cambridge. He gave the Longfellows "very exact information" concerning the house. His stories delighted Fanny as he walked about the house, telling of Martha Washington's arrival there in the family four-horse coach, with black coachman and postillions in scarlet and white livery. The Longfellows could almost see the Twelfth Night party given in honor of Washington's wedding anniversary on January 6, 1776, in the rooms they wanted to call their own.

"We have duly considered and discussed the question of remaining here and think that, all things considered, we could not do better else-where," Fanny told "dear Papa. . . . The house is large enough to intro-duce any modern conveniences we should desire and there is no position in Cambridge that can compare with it, for views and air . . ."

Considerably to Fanny and Henry's surprise, Nathan Appleton took a dim view of the whole idea. He wanted them to buy or build something much more modern and up-to-date. The price for the house, barn, and at least part of the farm land was ten thousand dollars which he felt was too high. But he had promised Fanny a house. "I have closed the bargain for the Craigie place," he finally wrote her.

Longfellow's mother commented in October. "In her last letter, Fanny hopes we will congratulate them on possessing the Craigie House. Their father has purchased it for them, also the lot in front, that their view of the River Charles may not be intercepted. It is a fine thing to have a noble heart with a noble fortune, is it not?"

Henry's eyes had begun to trouble him so that he could not read without pain. Before the deeds to Craigie House were signed, the Long-fellows had gone to New York to consult the famous oculist, Dr. Samuel Elliott.[7] Emmeline Austin had taken his treatments, so had Louisa Ward and various Sedgwicks. Fanny and Henry had "the gentle experience of Purgatory and Inferno in rail cars and steamer," the train to Providence being so full it took two engines to pull it and the steamer to New York equally crowded. The Astor House was full but "Henry's name seemed to have an electrical effect" on the manager so that, al-though thirty people had been turned away, the Henry Wadsworth Longfellows were given a room and a parlor overlooking "the green and still churchyard" where the "noisy, never-ebbing tide" of New York life could only be heard — not seen. This was Fanny's first experience of the effect of a well-known name other than Appleton — but now her own new name. She was surprised and proud to find her poet famous in New York.

After a look at their first week's hotel bill however, the Longfellows began to question the value of their prestige. Although negotiations had been begun by mail in plenty of time, Henry was not given a consultation with the oculist. He was told that he had arrived on the wrong day. Later, the Longfellows learned that it was the wrong day for some patients but the right day for others. Fanny went with Henry and at last they saw the stout doctor, "with shirt à la Byron," standing in the door of his inner office as if he were posing for the portrait over his head. After the consultation, although the oculist said that Henry's case was "not bad" and that he had "strained a nerve" while trying to read in a bad light, the Longfellows were told that they must stay in New York at least a month. Something had to be done about expenses. Dr. Elliott suggested Staten Island, where he himself lived, as a place where lodgings could be found at a reasonable rate. He relented concerning his rule of seeing patients three times a week only and until three o'clock only and agreed to give Mr. Longfellow more time. But the trip by the Staten Island Ferry seemed difficult. After considerable anxious hunting around among lodging houses, the Longfellows negotiated with the Astor House for a room without a parlor where their meals were being served. The big table in the Astor House dining-room was more fun, anyway.

Next to the Longfellows at the table d'hôte sat the Nathaniel Parker Willises. "Don Juan Willis," as Sam Ward irreverently called him, was already well acquainted with Longfellow. Tall, his hair waved in luxurious abundance, his clothes flamboyant, Willis had been famous since his college days. Now thirty-four, he had edited several short-lived magazines, written popular poetry and contributed travel notes to the *New York Mirror* about foreign personalities. One of the best-paid American writers at this time, his good opinion of himself sometimes even exceeded his contemporary fame. Fanny Appleton Longfellow did not bother to describe him but wrote about his wife. She was the daughter of a British general, "very pretty with her abundant curls and bright happy smile." But Fanny thought her tender looks at Don Juan were like "sunshine wasted on a dial without hands." Willis, as an editor, had free tickets to the theaters which he gave to the Longfellows and he took them into his box at the Olympic where they laughed over a farce "more like French vaudeville" then anything in Boston. They read the *Mirror* enjoying Willis' column, "having heard the gossip at first hand."

Fanny Kemble Butler was at the Astor House. She and Fanny Long-fellow renewed their old affectionate friendship and the Longfellows were invited to Mrs. Butler's table from time to time. One night they met McCready, the actor, there, and another night the William Cullen Bryants. Fanny did not say what the two poets talked about but of course they too were old friends. She found Bryant "very gentlemanly and agreeable." Mrs. Butler gave the Longfellows tickets to see Mc-Cready in *Macbeth* and in *Hamlet*. Fanny said that "McCready lacks genius but has great art and finish."

Of course Fanny wrote to her father and her friends about Dr. Elliott's treatments and the condition of Henry's eyes. She decided that Dr. Elliott was not, after all, a charlatan, as she at first suspected. The oculist had her watch him while he instructed her in the treatments she could carry on at home. "With what a business-like way he operates!" Fanny ex-claimed. "I shuddered in every nerve judging the effect from the expres-sion on Henry's face and I fear I should administer the torture rather fumblingly. . . . As he walked home with me," from Dr. Elliott's office to the Astor House, "I thought people would suppose I had been mak-ing him miserable and that he had been crying his eyes out in conse-quence."

Theater-going had to be given up but the Longfellows continued to enjoy New York especially after Henry's eyes began to improve. They went shopping, and Fanny said that they "passed all evening at that fascinating shop, Tiffany's." Among other things, they bought a pair of white antique bottles, a sewing chair and a Chinese lacquered table. About twenty items were sent on to Cambridge from Tiffany's, the bill, for Fanny's father to pay, being seventy-seven dollars.

Their most important purchase was for carpets for Craigie House. The bill came to $350 and included a little over fifty-four yards of "imperial carpeting," a hundred and ten yards of Brussels carpet, plus one Imperial rug and one Wilton rug.[8] The Longfellows felt perfectly safe in making these purchases. Fanny had money of her own.

Among Beacon Hill Appletons, the marriage of a daughter involved a dowry, and before Fanny was married, Nathan Appleton gave Henry Longfellow a statement of Fanny's assets in a formal letter. In 1838, he had invested twenty-five thousand dollars in the Massachusetts Life In-surance Company for the benefit of Frances Elizabeth Appleton. She was to receive interest in half-yearly payments on "the first day of January and July in each and every year, during her natural life, unless the inter-est was added to the principle, as provided." This was to be "for her separate use, free from the debts, control or interference of any husband she now has or may hereafter have . . ." This contract was made just before Nathan Appleton's second marriage and he settled a like sum of money upon Mary and upon Tom. As time went by, he reinvested Fanny's interest and otherwise added to her annuity so that, by 1842, the money in Fanny's trust fund was $32,520.

On July 8, 1843, Nathan Appleton had sent a letter to his future son-in-law, enclosing a copy of Fanny's annuity account, which he had "directed to accumulate until the first of August next, when the principle will amount to $34,308.78," he said, "dividends in July being $857.71 and in January $1029.26." Cautiously he added that "these dividends may, I think, be calculated upon without any variation for several years at least."

But this was not all. "It is my intention to add the further sum of $15,691.39 in order to make up the sum of $50,000 as her actual dowry; out of the money, appropriating whatever is requisite in the way of furniture for housekeeping and the balance in the purchase of a home or building one, whatever you shall decide to do."

And in addition, "I have in my hands a fund in various stocks, amounting to thirty thousand dollars, placed with me by Mr. Samuel Appleton for the benefit of my three children and which I hold subject to his disposition. I have also a fourth fund belonging wholly to Fanny which amounts to upwards of six thousand dollars. You will perceive that, with your own salary, there will be ample means for sustaining, with a reasonable economy, a comfortable establishment — whilst it will be the dictate of prudence to keep your expenditures somewhat within your income." Mr. N. Appleton signed himself "with best wishes for your future happiness, affectionately yours." He enclosed a check for a thousand dollars to cover living expenses until the July, 1844, annuity payment and promised a like sum in January.

Fanny and Henry had been surprised when Fanny's father showed so little enthusiasm for Craigie House — but he had bought it for them. The cost of Henry's treatments and of living in New York had been high but they thought they had been doing pretty well. Fanny's efforts at keeping household accounts for her step-mother had not been a success however — she forgot items. Eventually it would be her poet who had the practical streak and handled her funds carefully and successfully.

But as to the buying of Brussels carpets — Fanny should have remembered what a crusader for American-made manufactures her father was. She had read his speeches on the tariff. Moreover, his specialty was cotton — not woolen. Fanny was astonished and totally unprepared for the letter her father now wrote her.

". . . As to your arrangements for carpets, I think you are premature. I cannot think it wise to get any carpets made up in New York on account of the difficulty of making them fit. It would take a very nice and scientific plan of the rooms . . ." Fanny was to remember the near-disaster at 39 Beacon Street when her father had a carpet made in Calcutta. In spite of "Capt. Storer's very accurate plan" there were "horrid discrepancies which could only be remedied by our bungling interpolations . . ." And in the second place it would not be worthwhile for Fanny to do anything about "that part of the house" still occupied by the Craigie lodger "of which you will not get possession till next spring." Straw matting would be used all summer, as Fanny well knew, and she would have no "occasion for woolen carpeting until the autumn of next year.

"But in the third place there is a very unfortunate consideration to be made in reference to the mode of furnishing the house. The sum disposable for the house and furniture is $15,000 of which $10,000 goes for the purchase of the house and land, $3000 more at least will be necessary to put it in order, leaving but $2500 for the furniture which is less than the sum already expended." This last statement must have startled the newly wed Longfellows.

Fanny's father said that "this makes one of two things necessary. Either I must reserve a part of the land (west of the house) which might be offered [for sale] at $3000 or I must touch upon your Insurance stock — the goose which has laid too many golden eggs to be killed unnecessarily — or perhaps both. At any rate, the fact that so much money is laid out in an expensive house makes it absolutely necessary that a corresponding economy should be practised in furnishing it — and which will in fact be most in conformity with the style of living which your income will warrant, which, although perhaps larger than any of the professors (with the exception of Mr. Norton), will require a very considerable economy and restraint of many indulgences which, perhaps unfortunately, you have not hitherto experienced."

Fanny got her Brussels carpet anyway! And later, when the Craigie tenants had left, she wrote her father in one of her teasing moods. On May 5, 1844, the "Worcester family left us in complete possession, with rooms nicely cleaned, and uncarpeted stairs and entries. I enjoy like a child, my new suite. . . . I hope to get into my new bedroom this week, the carpet woman being engaged and the carpet made. Both economy and patriotism decided me to patronize the Lowell manufacture, largely. Do I not properly practice the precepts you inculcate? If anybody grumbles about the tariff, you can tell them that a very fastidious young woman of your acquaintance assures you that she infinitely prefers home carpeting for beauty, excellence and cheapness . . ."

In October, 1843, Fanny and Henry were back in Cambridge, the "home look of the Craigie" being "most refreshing to body and spirit." The great elms in front of the house had died because old Mrs. Craigie had refused to allow her lodger, Longfellow, to try to control the canker worm, saying that "our fellow worms have as much right to live as we." [9] The great trees were now cut down and sawed into firewood and Henry "ventured to transplant four very sizable young elms which took root and prospered." The Longfellows rarely went out at night because of Henry's eyes. Beside an open fire of elm wood, Fanny read aloud to her husband who had loved the sound of her voice ever since they first knew each other.

To her brother, Tom, Fanny told how it was, this first winter of her married life. Tom was to imagine Henry playing a nocturne on their piano while Fanny relaxed in a chair by the fire. The little French clock, which she had brought home from Paris long ago, now rested upon a Gothic stand between the two windows to the east. Now it ticked "merrily" where once it told the time "wearily" when it spoke from her bedroom on Beacon Street. [10]

It would never have occurred to Fanny and Henry Longfellow to call their much-loved home anything but "Craigie House" or "Craigie Castle" but already it was no longer the Major Vassal House, nor Washington's Headquarters nor the house belonging to Andrew Craigie, Apothecary. It was Longfellow House.

NINETEEN

TOM AND THE SPIRIT RAPPINGS

FANNY AND HENRY LONGFELLOW had Thanksgiving dinner at 39 Beacon Street. They had "got to the evening" when Nathan Appleton wrote to Tom. "On the whole, we feel we have abundant cause for thanksgiving on the return of this anniversary, which finds us all in health and prosperity. Certainly we miss your presence — but I prefer you should be happy abroad rather than pining at home . . ." Fanny put in a postscript. She felt like a country cousin "suddenly thus whirled into the glare of city life" but she had no regrets. "Even Boston looks large after the quiet of Cambridge but the latter is getting much nearer my heart!"

Tom was in Paris. On Thanksgiving Day he had dined at home with William Wadsworth from Geneseo, New York. "Not many, were our words, not many our toasts, for W. W. does not shine at such things," Tom told his father. But he "thought about the warm fireside" at Beacon Street with "happy Fanny's sunny mouth smiling sweet things to him; dear Em's roguishly accusative glances across the table and Henry, too, with his clear crystal let into the family circle." Within three years, Emmeline Austin would be married to Tom's present companion, the silent William Wadsworth.

Tom imagined that he could smell the Thanksgiving turkey and that he was there, saying "a second crisp sausage, I think I will take, if you please." This was not to be considered as a symptom of homesickness, however. Nothing could be snugger than Tom's Paris apartment, compared to his "teeth-chattering room" at home. He had a clean, sunny room, a capital servant and he was doing some heads in pastel crayons which he said himself were charming. He had books, society and the theater of which he was as passionately fond as ever. "Pretty taste for a man, you will say," Tom told his father defensively. What he did not say was that he helped out poor but deserving artists every chance he got — and they gave him plenty of chances.

Tom had also discovered human drama, not on stage as yet. There was a book called *Les Mystères de Paris* which he thought his father must have heard about. The story, by Eugene Sue, former French army surgeon, first appeared as a magazine serial. Tom set out to discover if its fearful pictures of crime in Paris were true to life. With Lady Elgin's son, Bruce, and a prison reformer by the name of Leduc, and taking along "two valiant guides," Tom visited "all the worst haunts of robbers. . . . We were armed and in one huge, hot cabaret, where three hundred of the worst villains in Paris were drinking and halooing-it, we were insulted and but for much coolness might have been roughly used. Our guides said these people would make nothing of falling on us and stabbing us. The police, every quarter of an hour, descend on this place and carry off a victim. We were thought to be policemen in disguise until two robbers recognized Leduc who is called 'le petit Mirabeau.' "

Tom next visited a daytime haunt of thieves. This was nearly empty, he found, evidently to his disappointment. "We went to all the vile places our friends knew of and I had the satisfaction of drinking with some vagabonds and passing off as one of them." Tom realized that his father might wonder why this oldest son of his preferred spinning yarns to vagabonds to prove himself one of them, rather than entering the cotton spinning and weaving business. Maybe some sort of explanation might be in order. "All that you read in *Les Mystères de Paris,* if you venture upon so painful a task, I can vouch for as truth. This spectacle, which I daresay you will wonder I cared to see, is the most moral lesson I have ever read," Tom declared.

Horace Mann was in Paris at this time, visiting jails. Tom Appleton seems not to have looked for moral lessons in jails with him but took him to a ball in the Champs Élysées. Writing to Longfellow, rather than to his father this time, "You may conceive the length of face with which the leader of Normal instructors contemplated the Can-Can," Tom said. "It was at *his* urgent request that I took him, moreover."

Before long, however, Tom had seen all the Paris underworld he cared for and took up a new enthusiasm — called magnetism.[1] Lady Elgin, whom Tom described as "a strong-minded, eccentric woman given wildly to mathematics," was wintering in Paris. She took Mr. T. G.

Appleton riding in her carriage and got him to "preach soul as taught by Magnetism." Tom had the time of his life. "I never enjoyed so much unlocking as then. I talked for two hours, finding full sympathy, the strong Lady Elgin weeping when I told her the spectres of lost friends could only be forerunners of re-embracing . . ." Tom wrote to Fanny to tell her to get books on mesmerism, magnetism, and spiritism and he wanted Mary Peabody Mann to be sure to buy some of these books in Paris for her sister's reading-room in Boston. In Boston, there were lectures on mesmerism which Tom's father mentioned but certainly did not attend.

Fanny was not going to bother with mesmerism either. She was her husband's collaborator in every sense of the word. "Our book flourishes famously," she told Tom. "We are now among the Danish poets, having dispatched the Anglo-Saxon and Icelandic. I write in it every morning — the red-haired [printer's] devil summoning me to deliver up 'copy' daily. It is a great undertaking which Henry half repents, but will be a valuable gathering of stray poems and literature almost unknown to any but scholars . . ." Fanny read aloud to save Henry's eyes, copied to his dictation, discussed and helped amend his text. It was "our book" indeed with all that Fanny had learned during her studious girlhood proving valuable in married life.

On May 5, 1844, Fanny wrote to her father who was in Washington. "Yesterday pm (Sunday) Tom arrived. He was looking much stouter and browner than usual and full of chat of course. . . . He met Uncle William at the wharf who took him home to tea and then furnished him with a gig in which he came direct to us and passed the night. . . . It seems very strange to see Tom domesticated here and it made me very happy last night to think he was sleeping under my roof."

"I am half in your house in Boston and half in Longfellow's in Cambridge," Tom told his father. In Cambridge he had learned that he was again to be an uncle, but for the first time an uncle to a Longfellow. He went right to Boston to buy baby clothes. On June 9, Charles Appleton Longfellow was born.

Tom did not stay long in Cambridge nor in Boston. Leaving that room downstairs at 39 Beacon "all littered up with the heedless confusion" of his arrival, he went to Nahant. Then he went to Newport but did not go to Berkshire where his father and "Mrs. A." were staying. He saw his father however — perhaps in Lowell.

At this particular juncture, much was going on in Lowell which was not as yet publicized. The directors of the Locks and Canals Company declared handsome dividends upon liquidating that company and forming a new one to regulate and sell water power for the Lowell mills. A small group of men were planning to incorporate the Lowell Machine Shops to build and sell the latest cotton-fabricating machines which would modernize the whole factory process. Confident that the Lowell mills could always produce the best quality fabrics, they would sell machines to other factories, most of them as yet unbuilt, and fear no competition. It was a "Cotton Whig" dream that textile mills could be built in the South, slaves gradually emancipated, with jobs provided for these free men in mills as well as fields. The Lowell Machine Shop charter was not granted until January 29, 1845; the first investors not known till then. But among the directors would be Nathan Appleton and Ebenezer Chadwick. Chadwick was active in promoting the building of textile mills in Maine.

There had been many preliminary meetings. Nathan Appleton was heart and soul in the project, full of enthusiasm for the new machines. He could never quite give up hope that a day would come when his oldest son would see the adventure, the excitement, in manufacturing. Perhaps he applied too much pressure. Perhaps, in the pious hope that Tom would stop trying to be an artist and a poet, William Appleton may have made some sharp remarks. Certainly Tom encountered the all too successful young Ebenezer Chadwick on some disastrous occasion. On the twelfth of July, 1844, Tom headed a letter "Boston," and wrote his father. Always over-sensitive, Tom was in a mood of self-condemnation and despair.

". . . You know as well as I do, that my life, the life of an artist (and how alone am I, ashamed of the name) counts for nothing in this country. You know that the kind of society I love, is not yet formed. . . . Do you suppose that, before Mr. Chadwick, I am fool enough to call myself a painter or a poet? The short and long of it is, that I have not any of the kind of talent needful to success here. It is a melancholy confession but true. I feel now, humbled and despicable before men who can build towns, pour whole villages into factories and undermine the everlasting hills. And I am too proud to be the scorn of my equals . . ."

If Tom had been only on a long visit so that Fanny would marry — he was now going away for good. "In other countries, I do not feel this inferiority. . . . Europe is my Boston where I am truly at home. I cannot see that a man improving his character and mind and living modestly on a moderate income is wholly despicable . . .

"I beg you not to judge me by your own standards for yourself. . . . I do not pretend to be a leader of opinion. I am but too happy when I enjoy my own, in peace. I respect all mens' opinions and do not even ask them to respect mine — only that they will not insult them to my face . . .

"My ambition is my own and it is as strong as any man's but it has no triumphs which the world can appreciate or behold. Do not be cast down that I have for once talked from within outward, and love ever your affectionate son . . ." Tom had spoken out like a man and his father understood him far better than many a parent who had hoped to have a son created in his own mold. But when Tom got to England, he was remorseful. His tender heart got the better of him as it often did and he fell back on the old excuse — ill health. "My opinion is that I shall return the instant I am all right — and live with you . . ."

This letter was written two months later while Tom was in Derbyshire, visiting the Nightingales at their summer home of fifteen bedrooms for guests. "We are quite a party of Americans in the romantic wolds of Derbyshire. . . . The Howes [Julia and Dr. Samuel Gridley], the Brookses [Boston bankers] all are here." Then there was Hallam, the historian, Lady Sitwell, plus sundry Nightingale relatives. "We breakfast at nine on some Derbyshire cakes, tough and gritty . . . lunch at two in a very modest way and dine at half past six." Tom knew what to order as a gift for his English hostesses — some Vermont maple sugar and some stone-ground corn meal to be sent from America. He told Fanny that he planned to marry an English girl and Fanny asked him if he meant to bring home an English Nightingale.

"Miss Florence and Mrs. Brooks are my excellent companions," Tom told Fanny. They were "chattering like sparrows together while Parthy and Lady Sitwell are dabbling over their water-colors." It was understood that Miss Florence would be the one to claim Tom's attention. The fact that she, like Joan of Arc, had already heard the voices of unseen visitants might have provided a mutual interest since Tom was still more hopeful of catching a glimpse of the spirit world. But Florence knew that her voices foretold a high destiny. She was also a mathematical genius but, unlike the "eccentric" Lady Elgin, she studied mathematics in secret, the subject being considered unsuitable for females. After a while, "I do not feel so sure of marrying an English woman," Tom wrote.

Lady Sitwell drove Tom in her carriage to call on Sir George Beaumont, nephew of the famous art patron and recent heir to a great art collection and a fortune. There was a painting by Washington Allston in the collection that Tom wanted to see.² On the way, Lady Sitwell explained that Sir George was "an odd person, having taken to gin to console himself after his wife's death."

And so Tom found him. "He received us at his house . . . and was in great spirits to see us — which spirits turned out to be Hollands." They saw the Allston in a small, gray, stone church near the house. It was "ill-placed and ill-lit but wonderfully fine even if the angel was a trifle robust for air," Tom thought. He began to wonder if he could negotiate a sale so that this Allston could go to America, and eventually, Dr. R. W. Hooper bought *The Angel Releasing Saint Peter from Prison* by Allston, on T. G. Appleton's recommendation. It was exhibited at the Boston Athenaeum and later presented to the State Hospital at Worcester.

Tom and Lady Sitwell spent hours wandering around Sir George Beaumont's grounds and Tom pulled Sir George out of "a pond of goldfish" when he "tipsily fell in."

By Christmas, Tom was in Rome, which "is wonderfully to my mind," he wrote. "I am here an artist, surrounded by artists and art, living and breathing amid sculpture and painting. . . . I have a studio, sky-high, near my lodgings, where I work every morning as a rule. I have a large landscape, a small picture with figures and a portrait of the celebrated Grazia on hand at once, besides a series of routine illustrations. Besides this, I attend nightly the English academy where I have made several drawings and twice a week take lessons in anatomy . . .

"No one can feel, more than I, in Boston, the ridiculous triviality of painting. In a new country, with fresh and stirring inducements to active occupation, the arts have a very pitiable look. . . . Here I see nothing to put me out all day. I could not exhaust the studios of the artists I could visit, were I to visit them for a year . . ." Although Tom tried to do too much at once and was inclined to haste, he really worked hard and eventually sent home some pictures which were pretty good.

Those visits to the studios of other artists benefited his friends more than himself. Tom felt guilty about it because his father had warned him that over-generosity was a form of selfishness — or so he told Fanny. But there was a sculptor, a Mr. Brown, a protégé of Uncle William's. It was news that William Appleton ever had an artist protégé but right now Mr. Brown was in a position where some cash would be very important to him or, better still, a sale for cash so that he could go on with confidence. Brown had just finished "a group of a boy holding back a dog" which Tom thought Uncle William ought to buy. Uncle William did not buy it — so Tom bought Brown's "beautiful bust of Grazia," the lovely model he, himself, had been trying to paint. He paid Brown $250 and had the marble bust shipped to Boston.

T. G. Appleton had a thoroughly Roman Christmas Eve with the Boston Sarah Perkins Cleveland [3] and her brothers, Edward and Charles, and friends. Like Tom, these Perkinses were escaping the mold their family had prepared for them — in their case that of merchant prince rather than of manufacturing pioneer. "Everybody at home in Massachusetts was remembered and the praises of dear old Boston were sung," Tom reported. "When the ladies withdrew, we crowned ourselves with roses in the manner of the ancients. Ned and Charley looked like some fair Greek boys with the nodding buds setting off their ringlets."

After they joined the ladies, the men presumably still crowned with roses, Tom "magnetized" George Washington Greene "till his eyes would not open." This magnetism, or hypnotism, was supposed to cure Greene's weak eyes, and Tom was pleased with his success. Nobody seemed to notice whether Greene was already half asleep from the wine or not.

By spring, Tom was "off for Greece, a rather rapid visit," he explained. He had invited Brown to go with him but because Tom had been promoting Brown's efforts among American visitors in Rome, the sculptor had too many orders to fill and could not leave. Then Tom struck up a friendship with William Morris Hunt of Brattleboro, Vermont — now twenty-one and in Rome with his widowed mother and assorted sisters. Hunt had been rusticated from Harvard, had been studying at the Düsseldorf Academy of Art — which had suited him no better than Harvard — and he was in Rome painting landscapes. It was not surprising that he and Tom took to each other at sight. Tom said he was off for Athens and Constantinople — how about coming along?

There was not a great deal of money among the Hunts but it was a well-kept secret, like many similar ones, that Tom helped with the traveling expenses for the whole Hunt family. In April, 1845, Tom merely mentioned to his sister that she was getting a letter dated Athens and that the Hunt party had decided to go too. Mrs. Hunt herself was an artist.

Tom was at last grateful to Bancroft for inflicting Greek upon him at Round Hill School. It thrilled him to hear the names of Theseus and Phidias. He saw "from every point, the Parthenon, flaming like a vast altar over our heads. One gets up early here and the pure, elastic air is something to intoxicate one — if the Parthenon were not enough alone."

They all sketched, Tom "in the lovely little temple of Victory without wings, a figure of a Victory binding its sandals."

The Hunts lingered in Athens but Tom was soon on his way to Constantinople. "Our good captain halted his boat through the night, before we arrived, that we might have a sunrise impression for the first," he wrote. Tom's talent for bringing out genius in others was at work when he declared that the ship's captain was "an artist and sympathizes with those who love the beautiful. We were all up early . . . and shining afar off in the wavering light . . . slowly rose Istanbul. . . . Like candlesticks of some heavenly Jerusalem, burned the minarets in the early air . . ."

Tom's health, so often precarious in Boston, was invulnerable in Istanbul, where he drank lemonade made with well water from some courtyard and "tried all the sweetmeats" sold in the streets. He wrote to his father about observing the "wives of various Pashas with bare breasts and faces hid" but when Miss Susan Hale of Boston came to quote this passage, years later, in *The Life and Letters of Thomas Gold Appleton*, she left out the part about the bare breasts.

Although Tom often told his father how careful he was about keeping down expenses, he could not be expected to resist the Turkish bazaars. He sent home silk to be made by Boston dressmakers into dresses for all the ladies in his family. There were scimitars, daggers, Persian boxes, amulets and beads among the parcels sent to Boston. Then Tom headed for home. He could never become a complete expatriate, no matter how hard he tried.

Nathan, Harriet and the children — Willie, five years old, Hattie, four, and Natey, two — were spending the summer in Pittsfield. Tom made them a brief visit, then found that he needed a water cure. He chose the Brattleboro Hydropathic Establishment, which had just been opened.[4] Robert Wesselhoeft, that German political refugee who had been winning over Bostonians with his homeopathic theory, had been credited with many remarkable cures. John H. Gray, a friend of the Appletons and a grateful patient, had supplied the financial aid for the Brattleboro sanitarium which had opened on May 29, 1845, with fifteen patients. When Tom Appleton got there in August there were about fifty, most of them from Boston. Carpenters were hard at work remodeling old residences so that forty-five rooms could be opened "exclusively for Gentlemen." Another building, promptly nicknamed "Paradise Row," was for ladies and there was a building between the two sections for music and dancing.

The Longfellows were already at the Brattleboro Hydropathic Establishment when Tom arrived! They had found pleasant lodgings across the street from Wesselhoeft's house. "Henry's eyes could not possibly gain much," Fanny thought, but he was "sure to benefit because he enjoys the perpetual bathing so much. . . . He is summoned every morning at three o'clock . . ." Fanny could see, half in her dreams, "a wavering of light and hear mysterious whispers in German. Steps would descend the stair and cross the road." Not surprisingly, Henry had objected to being carried across the public road, wrapped in wet sheets — which had been the doctor's idea of proper procedure. So German attendants woke him and allowed him to walk over to the doctor's headquarters where the wrapping in wet sheets took place. Blankets were put over the sheets "until perspiration starts," Fanny said. Then the attendants plunged him in the bath of ice-cold spring water.

Tom found "water in a thousand ways. It really seems as if the High German Doctor, who is the presiding genius of this town just now, is in great luck. His springs flow during this deadly warm weather and are unfailing and full enough to drench into papier-mâché a thousand stomachs . . ." Tom observed his fellow-patients. Some, "like wild Miss Caroline Sturgis, romantic in flopping straw hats, carry their dinners into the woods . . . and feed alone. Others make gay the yard in front of us by rope-skipping . . ."

The Longfellows had brought their little son Charley with them to Brattleboro. "The little fellow has not quite got used to me, yet," Tom said. "Still, I can make him laugh furiously and that is nigh attachment. He will soon find he can make use of me and then he is sure to like me."

Fanny Longfellow was not allowed to take the baths and she longed to try them. She was expecting another child and Dr. Wesselhoeft would not let her stand under waterfalls, completely clad of course, or sit in fast-flowing ice-water the way her friends did. On November 23, 1845, Fanny and Henry's second child was born. Ernest Wadsworth Longfellow was dark-eyed and thoughtful, opposite in temperament to the venturesome Charley. Eventually, he was to study art under his Uncle Tom's friend, William Morris Hunt.

Since Fanny's first labor had been long and difficult, Longfellow consented to the use of the newly perfected ether to diminish her pain. The experiment was completely successful and Fanny herself said that she was quite a heroine to try this strange new gas — and she was right. There was still much to be learned about it. Tom referred to Ernest as Fanny's "etherial child." A little over a year later Tom wrote that in Paris, "nobody talks of anything but the Boston discovery of ether."

Nathan Appleton was resigned to having Tom spend most of his time abroad but he still could not quite face the idea of having a son who was either a painter or a poet. It was all right for ladies to paint in watercolor. This was far more difficult than painting in other media but no one noticed that — the girls weren't supposed to be very good. Fanny had anxiously asked Tom to assure her father that she had not written anything — only sketched. There were no writers within the Appleton circle — Longfellow was at this point a professor, not a poet. So Nathan hoped that Tom might yet find something respectable to do. In 1848, Henry Hilliard, a North Carolina Whig but opposed to secession, hoped for an appointment as ambassador to Berlin. He told Tom's stepmother that Tom could be his secretary of legation. This would be perfect for Tom, his whole family agreed. But it was a bad year for Whigs. Hilliard did not get the post and Tom was not exactly inconsolable. He used his real gift for diplomacy to explain to his father that his health required British, French and German water cures and a Paris apartment.

Tom arrived in Paris just after the fall of Louis Philippe. It was now a different city from the Paris Tom had loved so long, where his sisters had been presented at court and where he had so many friends. He took rooms on the Rue de la Paix. "There were some 35,000 troops who escorted the provisional government to their new Chamber. . . . Everyone marched under our windows, the Garde Mobile, the new troops, composed of the 'Blouses' . . . were in new uniforms, for the most part. . . . They marched well although, a month before, most of them had never held a musket. There was not, however, great enthusiasm among the people. Things are too bad for many cheers. The faces in the streets wore an expression of lassitude — calm and patient." Tom found it "heart-breaking." At the theater, he heard "the great Rachel, with tricolor in hand, chanting, (not singing) the Marseillaise."

At Lady Elgin's Paris apartment, there was "no talk but of the state of things. . . . All told stories of the wreck of their friends' fortunes." George Washington Greene turned up in Paris and said that there was no use in counting the financial houses that "went down" — only those that were left. The servant announced "Mr. Rochefoucauld" and the young man "came in laughing and saying that two months ago he was a duke."

T. G. Appleton got a pass, on May 16, 1848, from a member of the French Assembly and went to watch proceedings. For more than two hours he saw France without a government as a wave of anarchy swept over her. The questions of Italy and Poland were to come up but the corridors were filled with groups of men carrying placards — "The Wounded of February," the "Jacobin Club" and many others. There had been a brilliant collection of fashionable ladies to hear the debates, but as these crowds began to invade the assembly room, "like frightened doves, they took flight," Tom said.

"The row began at one o'clock" and Tom left at twenty minutes past four. "Never shall I see again such a scene," he declared. "The worst heads, the most diabolical expressions, were mixed with honest but ignorant workmen. . . . The 'Blouses' insulted and struggled with the members in the body of the house, but not a weapon was drawn. At times, from without, I thought I heard the boom of cannon and guns were repeatedly fired. . . . The heat became insupportable and dust . . . obscured the sight. . . . A fever was in the air which was akin to madness. The bell of the president ceased to ring for order. . . . Friends of Poland tried to read a petition . . . the crowd being ungovernable, would not retire or do anything but bellow and wave their banners."

Tom "fraternized with the invaders and found them pleasant fellows enough. . . . One fellow said, 'You see what work we make of aristocrats.' And then he said, 'I beg your pardon, I did not, till I spoke, see you are one.' "

"My friend," said Tom, "I belong to a Republic where, to be well-dressed is a sign of the people." Tom felt that he had seen enough, however. He managed to work his way through the crowd to a door which led into a courtyard. A man helped him over the wall and he saw "a wall of bayonets wheeling into the space he had just dropped into. Government troops were coming to quell the riot in the Chamber of Deputies." Tom helped some French and some English people over another parapet. "As the soldiers wheeled in, we were obliged to cross a bridge and there a beautiful sight was to be seen. Along both Quais, along the Rue de Rivoli and the Rue Royale, the compact, respectable, quiet files of the National Guard were winding."

In June, there was fighting in the streets of Paris. The Archbishop of Paris was shot, there were six days of violence before a military dictator restored order and it was not until December that Louis Napoleon became Citizen President. Tom Appleton was no revolutionary — he remembered that he was a citizen of a more peaceful republic.

Journeys back and forth across the Atlantic continued until Tom himself lost track of them. In August, 1850, he was in Cambridge with the Longfellows. "The Craigie is grand with my antique additions," he boasted. "The Library is ennobled with my superb clock which we were hours hanging." He had brought Fanny a ball-gown and looked forward to parties among "the Beacon Street nobility" where she would wear it and he would "enjoy her good looks."

For once, about this time, Tom brought something home for himself. He had sent word from his new Paris apartment. "I am in the midst of packing a couple of bits of furniture to complete my sleeping-room. I have a chest of drawers and a glass, with a commode for clothes which will make perfect my old oak room, and I send too, some dark green paper to match the bed-hanging, which will set off famously the dark wood." Tom asked his father to "give the cases stable room," until he reached Beacon Street — or, if there wasn't room in the stable behind the house, just to leave the cases at the Customs House and he would claim them. Tom thought his belongings "worthy of a larger room than my old room and will show better with a green paper. . . . The whole furniture of my room I got at a figure far below what one would think, and, after all, carved oak better than anything, resists our climate. One of these days, I shall establish myself and then I shall have an exceedingly pretty bedroom."

Sad news had to be broken to Tom. There was storage room enough for his packing cases in the stable but there was no room for him at 39 Beacon Street, either in his old room behind the stairs or in a larger one above. Harriet had ordered his carved French bed taken down and carried to the stable already. Tom could live at the Tremont House — or he could receive funds from his father for a house of his own, just as Fanny had upon her marriage.

Tom should have seen that this was coming. He did not. He had supposed that 39 Beacon Street would always be his home as it was the home of his half-brothers and sisters. Natey was now ten, Hatty nine and Willie seven. He loved them and in some ways he was no older than they. Tom took a handsome room at the Tremont House, where they gave him plenty of service and he gave dinners to his friends. He started house-hunting, combining it with a renewed interest in psychic manifestations! "Tom is absorbed in the rapping phenomena and talks of taking your old house on Beacon Street where he would certainly want to hold séances," Fanny told her former neighbor, Emmeline Austin, now Mrs. William Wadsworth of Geneseo, New York.[5]

Corroborating this news, "Tom Appleton has got hold of a new belief now," Julia Ward Howe wrote to her sister Annie, during the autumn of 1852. "He has found a man who can magnetize tables and make them stand on end and walk about by pure magnetism." Tom went to dinner with the Howes at Perkins Institute and afterwards attempted "table-tipping" himself. Everyone sat around in a darkened room, hands resting lightly on a table — which refused to move. At last Tom gave up, laughing, and declaring that the table must be "very poor mahogany."

Mrs. Nathan Appleton's state of mind is understandable. Harriet was a woman who loved orderly procedures and a conventional sort of life. Table-tipping at 39 Beacon Street would not have pleased her at all and séances next door would have seemed almost as undesirable. Fanny thought Tom had better go back to Paris — and this he did.[6]

In a letter dated May 4, 1853, Tom told about a séance he organized at the home of Samuel Griswold Goodrich, at that time United States consul. Goodrich had written immensely popular moral tales for children under the name of "Peter Parley." Tom invited his friends, Lady Elgin and her daughter, many savants, as he called some French intellectuals, and Mr. Coste, a government agent. Tom had very much wanted Dominic Arago to be there. Arago was a celebrated French astronomer, discoverer of the magnetic properties of iron, and his work led to the production of magnetism by electricity. But Arago was now "too infirm to come," Tom said. He sent his two nephews in his place. In all there were about fifty guests.

"Not a person witnessing the séance but found it genuine," Tom announced.[7] Alice Goodrich, daughter of United States Consul Goodrich, "besides being a very sweet girl, is a very strong medium. Magnetic fluids come through her by an unconscious projection of a second personality accompanied with clairvoyance . . ." Alice often produced "automatic writing" for her father and his friends who were earnestly trying to study psychic phenomena but on this occasion "physical manifestations alone were called for."

"We made Coste make the table move by his unspoken will and Arago's nephews were seen hugging a little table in a corner which moved under their hands . . ." Tom was elated. "I was avowedly the introducer here," he said. "Peter Parley wrote yesterday a sketch of our séance."

Tom was still happier a month later when he wrote, "You must not be surprised to hear any day of my attempting a bit of selfishness in the marriage way. But not with Miss Tiffany. Perhaps you have heard that I am her intended, as all my friends insist. *Non, jamais!* It would be a very good match . . ." but not for Tom. "She is a dark, impulsive temperament like my own and I could not live with her a week. . . . If I have yet the luck to live with a young woman neither smart nor nervous,

Children of Nathan and Harriet Appleton: Hattie, Willie and Natey, and their dog Bruno. (Daguerreotype, courtesy of The Society for the Preservation of New England Antiquities.)

the long *enfer* of my American life, unblessed by wife or mistress, may be somewhat forgotten in a little happiness." Tom was writing to his father. "There! I do not remember ever writing you on anything so tender before."

There was no mention of the name of the girl Tom wanted to marry. But without pause or paragraph he continued. "You ask about the rappings. We have them here at my door in perfection. My friend Alice Goodrich [8] is as good a medium as any I saw in America. At Lamartine's the other night, the poet was in ecstasy. . . . The great Hungarian Magnetist I took to see Alice. He was enchanted too but holds that spirits do not exist. It is a new extension of the Magnetic condition . . . out of the dreamland of the spirit's abode — as if we had a dream while awake. I think he is right but it is an open question . . ."

Tom already knew Elizabeth Barrett Browning. He described her. "She is a little concentrated nightingale, living in a bower of curls, her heart throbbing against the bars of the world. . . . She looked at me wistfully, as she believes in the Spirits and had heard of me." In 1853, Mrs. Browning had heard *from* Tom about Alice Goodrich. Again, he had described her as "a very sweet girl" and told about taking her "by Lamartine's desire" to the poet's house where "all the phenomena were reproduced and everybody present convinced. . . . Among other spirits came Henry Clay who said, '*J'aime Lamartine*.' " Tom left this out of his letter to his father and it was probably just as well that he did.

If Alice Goodrich was really Tom's "dream while awake" nothing came of his 1853 romance. In 1853 he made a short visit to the United States without a bride and without doing any house-hunting. He was in his room at the Longfellows' house when he wrote, "Fanny is downstairs — as lovely as ever and in the pauses of the wild winter blast comes the baby's cry, spirit-like, above." The Longfellows had had their first, much-wanted daughter in 1847. But their little Fanny had died in 1848 — nearly breaking their hearts. Now the children were Charles, Ernest, Alice Mary, born in 1850, and the baby, Edith, crying "spiritlike" upstairs, born on October 22, 1853.

In 1857, Tom's interest in having a home of his own revived while his passion for holding séances remained as strong as ever. This time he was looking at Cambridge real estate — and writing to his friend Charles Norton, aged thirty, about strange events taking place, he did not say where. Norton was abroad, having gone, as Tom put it, "to sow his tame oats."

"The other night, Story, Eldridge and I had experiences almost beyond what you read anywhere," Tom told Norton. "I confess I never felt so near that great gate through which Dante seems to have passed." [9] Tom, his two friends and others had several mediums, whom he did not name, with them. "After the most cheerful and hilarious doings with one strength, who almost shared a supper with us and gave us his toast, 'May the scythe that would cut thee down strike against a stone,' and after taking, as it were in his teeth, a big table and reducing it to splinters, we went into a large, dark bed-room — quite dark there. We touched hands all around (mediums included) and waited; all at once, amid a *feu de joie* of wood-raps, the table rose breast high and repeatedly. Great currents of cold air were felt and *whiz*, something struck me on the left side of the head, a little hurting the left eye. This turned out to be a curtain, left several feet from us on a sofa. This was repeated. A cigar holder was tossed from the mantel and put behind us and a blackened end of a cigar thrust against Story's cheek so that afterwards we saw the mark. I asked to see a hand and on my left a large, luminous, dim yet brilliant one appeared. Suddenly we were all in terror and turned on the gas for a big white thing pressed against us which turned out to be the bed, a very heavy double one which left its corner and came down on us with great swings . . .

"I cannot say that all this is quite pleasant but I am delighted to be justified in all my faith and to find that I and not old Goosey Common Sense was right in trusting to my instincts in this direction. Story and I both agree that there can be no further discussions of the cause of these things. It is as settled as your own existence. But why are they permitted? Can it be for evil? . . .

"Longfellow has been to two of our previous séances and saw and believed. I do not wish him to see too much," Tom said. "As a beautiful angel hovers above his voice, steeping it in the lustre and promise of the hereafter, he comes into this belief as to his own and must not have a string to his nerves that shall get into his lyre."

Longfellow was more of a mystic than Tom, needing no medium-induced "phenomena." He "saw and believed" a vision of Mary, his first wife, while writing a poem for the memorial service for Bayard Taylor, years later, in 1878. Tom Appleton was a mystic, perhaps through his inheritance from the poetry-loving Maria Gold. But he was also an Appleton, demanding practical demonstrations. He was giving another séance, he told Charles Norton, serving supper and bringing along a guitar. He was also going to bring matches to light a scene where he thought he might discover deception.

Meanwhile, Tom had seen a very real Greek-Revival house on a country road in Cambridge, almost directly behind Longfellow House. He bought it on October 1, 1857.[10] Fanny described Tom's house. "It looks very pretty, with all his pictures on the wall. He has a small crimson-papered study, opening into a drawing-room which is only separated from his dining room by curtained draperies. . . . Although snug, it is very pleasing. He has a quiet, good sort of woman for a cook, a very nice looking girl for a maid, and his coachman, James." Very shortly, Tom also had "one large white Newfoundland dog, male, with mouse-colored head," according to Cambridge town records.

By March, 1858, Tom told Charley Norton that his first cook had been only tolerable but that now he had an excellent one who could make omelettes equal to the French. He gave dinners and Sunday suppers, serving grouse and lobster. A sister is not always easy to please, but Fanny said that Tom's dinner for Fanny Kemble, Charles Sumner, Longfellow and herself went off better than she expected — "although the bouquet did not arrive in time."

Speaking for himself, "I am in the midst of some pictures which interest me much," Tom wrote. He worked in his *atelier* every day — he planted rhododendrons in his garden on Phillips Place, Cambridge. There were no mentions of spirit rappings in this first home of his. After all, Tom Appleton appreciated good manners and it seems probable that he did not invite guests, seen or unseen, who might make free with his own tables and his carved oak bed.

TWENTY

YEARS OF OPTIMISM

ALTHOUGH THEY ALL LIVED on the same street in winter, the Appletons scattered during the summer months. Samuel had bought a large farm in Cambridge. By 1838, William had bought a place in Muddy River — not that he ever called Brookline by its early name! Nathan, Harriet and the children went regularly to Pittsfield, then to Nahant, to Lenox and finally to Lynn.

"What a pity you did not remain a day longer," Fanny wrote to her father from Cambridge in 1844. Nathan Appleton had gone to Pittsfield but Fanny would have liked to have seen him in cap and gown, receiving his Honorary Master of Arts degree from Harvard, "viva voce," as she put it, "in all the dignity of their Latinity." At the president's crowded reception afterwards, she saw Mr. Abbott Lawrence who expressed himself entirely pleased and considered the giving of this degree to Mr. Appleton as "the best thing ever done in Cambridge and what should have been done long ago." Harvard honored Nathan Appleton again with a Doctor of Laws in 1855 but again he did not appear — his close friend Abbott Lawrence having just died.

Nathan's absence in 1844 was explained by the state of Harriet's health. He had taken her to Saratoga Springs and Harriet described the scene for Fanny in a postscript to one of her father's letters. "We have seen the great and small, the high and low of this place! Mrs. Harry Otis in full force, concerts, water-drinking, promenading, eating, talking — everything but sleeping." [1] Nathan said that they were glad to get to their cool domicile in Pittsfield.

During Pittsfield vacations, Nathan Appleton worked on articles on some phase of current problems, manufacturing, banking, or religion, and these articles were printed in the local papers. Custom required that such contributions should be signed with a pseudonym, the author's identity being an easily guessed secret at the time. Nathan amused himself by thinking up names for himself; "Bullionite" for his articles on banking and currency, "A Layman of Boston" for his discussion of "The doctrine of Original Sin and the Trinity." In 1844, he was writing on "Labor; its Relations in Europe and the United States Compared." Later, he would take up "Slavery and the Union."

Nathan, Samuel and their cousin William all believed that slavery in the United States could be ended by gradual means, without bringing economic ruin to the South. In the light of history, it seems incredible that such intelligent men could have been so wrong. Meanwhile, however, they enjoyed some years of optimism.

The American Colonization Society had been organized as early as 1820, with Henry Clay as president of the group.[2] The theory was that freedmen, with their own consent, would want to go to a country of their own where they would set up a democracy patterned after that of the United States. Approximately 43,000 square miles of land were bought on the west coast of Africa and named Liberia. Men of Boston were willing to invest in this idealistic dream. William Appleton, astute businessman that he was, gave $2,400 for "half the expenses of sending 80 Negroes to Liberia." But the Abolitionists denounced colonization, claiming that Southern plantation owners were only using it to get rid of trouble-makers. William Lloyd Garrison came out against "the enormous expense of the Colonization plan."

Recently, there seemed to be another solution. With the Lowell Machine Shops ready to equip Southern factories and with the help of government to indemnify slave-owners, it seemed as if a whole new economy could be worked out to employ a wage-earning labor force in field or factory. "Cotton Whigs" were hopeful and not unduly perturbed by the eloquent name-calling of the "Conscience Whigs" in the press.

Charles Sumner was the Abolitionist with perhaps the greatest gift for coining an unforgettable phrase. Nathan Appleton tried to be friends with him; he was distantly related to Harriet and was one of Longfellow's dearest friends, constantly enjoying Fanny's hospitable board. In 1845, Mr. Appleton praised Sumner's Fourth of July oration on the horrors of war — taking exception only to Sumner's view that total United States disarmament would bring peace with Europe. Remembering the cannonading once heard off Boston Harbor, Nathan wrote that he thought it "unwise to have our harbors unprotected and to rely for safety on the character of non-combatism."

Nathan Appleton's patience with Sumner was severely tried however, in 1848. In a speech delivered in Worcester, Sumner used his most powerful phrase, referring to slave-holders as "Lords of the Lash" and cotton manufacturers as "Lords of the Loom." "Lords of the Lash" were slave-holders, of course, and no one claimed that Lowell mill girls were beaten during Nathan Appleton's lifetime. But in articles for the *Boston Whig*, Sumner made it clear that one "Lord of the Loom" was Mr. Nathan Appleton, pioneer cotton manufacturer, that he was the "living embodiment of the cotton industry" — contributing to the slave-holding interests by buying cotton from the South — and that he had "entered into a conspiracy" with the South to elect General Taylor to the Presidency.

Nathan spent a part of his 1848 summer in Pittsfield writing pleasantly but firmly to Sumner. The charge of "conspiracy" was "utterly untrue, without a shadow of truth to rest upon," he said. Whigs had hoped that General Taylor could effect a compromise between conflicting interests. Judge Winchester of Louisiana, whom Mr. Appleton had met in Saratoga, had said that Taylor was "high-minded, direct, intelligent and honest."

"Have we not as good a right to our opinion as you have to yours?" Nathan Appleton asked. Charles Sumner replied that he found in Mr. Appleton's letters "a lordly tone and bravado."

Fortunately for his own peace of mind, William Appleton did not engage in debate with Charles Sumner. As the owner of 54 Beacon Street, he rejoiced that his part of town became not only more "delectable" but also more fashionable every year so that his property increased in value. But he heartily detested the social activities of his children, and called his younger children "drones."[3] He disapproved of the Otis balls, Aunt Sam's dancing parties and his wife's efforts at entertaining their own children. Mary Ann gave a party: "about 60 persons; called pleasant; a band of musick, but there was very little pleasure for me," William wrote.

Thirteen-year-old Hattie got an equally poor press from her father. "Hattie gave a party for Ladies and Lads [her own age] of about 60. I do not like them." If a pianist and a "scraper," or violinist were hired, William liked the party even less. When his wife made him go to a concert, he put cotton in his ears.

William Appleton, at fifty-four, still suffered from his dyspepsia. He had been dieting, of course — eating only "a small quantity of meat and crackers after going through a course of physick" and taking, before each meal, "a preparation of Creosote." When this made him feel no better, the answer must be a journey for health, and William asked Dr. Warren to break it to Mary Ann. The doctor did his best but Mary Ann was "much excited at my leaving; she thought I might avoid it," William wrote. He sailed for England with his third son, Warren, and his man servant, Ira Giddings. As to Mary Ann — "She will soon get over it," William thought.

After some weeks in England, calling on bankers and ordering clothes from London tailors, Mr. William Appleton reached his official destination, Leamington — then a famous watering-place, the water being both saline and sulphurous. "Dr. Jephson called," William wrote, "and on seeing me he asked if I was usually so thin and said that my liver wanted looking into but concluded that, unless I was going to remain some weeks it would not be well for him or me to proceed further."

William remained. His treatments began very properly with "some Physick" which he drank at the Apothecary's. Leamington was within convenient reach of sightseeing so William set down in his diary that Kenilworth Castle was "very beautiful" but that there was "no pleasure in looking at fallen greatness." He observed, at Stratford on Avon, that "Shakespeare was born in a very small dwelling about fifteen feet front, two stories high."

On the last day of September, Dr. Jephson made his final call. "I think well of him," William wrote. "He told me my complaints were within controul [sic] but that . . . if I ate and drank like a person in health I should very soon be in my grave." William sailed on the *Great Western* arriving in Boston on the seventeenth of October and bringing some of the passengers to his house to pass the evening and meet some of his friends. There was a party of fifty in all. William complained that Mary Ann was sometimes upset over trifles, and fifty unexpected guests might have been one of these occasions.

In the course of his travels, William and his son Warren were "much pleased to see A. Lawrence — son of Amos Lawrence" who had just come from Ireland. Young Mr. Lawrence joined forces for some sightseeing, much to Warren Appleton's satisfaction. Returning home to Boston, young Mr. A. Lawrence was often to be found in the 54 Beacon Street parlors. By April, the engagement between Sarah Elizabeth Appleton and Amos A. Lawrence was announced.

"I have not been very willing that she should accept him at present," William wrote, "feeling that she was very young, had seen little of the world, with much to attract in her person and manners." Sarah Elizabeth was nineteen. Her father wanted her "to take her time to deliberate, but she thinks she knows her own mind."

As to young Lawrence, "He is a young man of good common sense, with business habits, a very safe man to entrust a daughter with." It was just as well that William Appleton did not know that Amos Adams Lawrence, upon graduating from college, thought that he would like to be "a literary man in some measure" and wanted to live in "a happy rustic cottage somewhere in the suburbs." [4] This would have sounded altogether too much like Tom Appleton of whom Uncle William so heartily disapproved.

Fortunately, Amos, according to his son, William Lawrence, believed that a man should be "willing and glad to be rich and willing to endure the labor of taking care of his property for the sake of others whom he can so much benefit by it." These sentiments would have suited Mr. William Appleton. Young Amos Lawrence's father was among those who encouraged the building of cotton mills in the South as part of an economic solution to the slavery problem.

On the last day of March, 1842, William Appleton, father of the bride, went to prayers at the chapel in the morning and then "attended to the preparation for the marriage of our dear Sarah to Mr. Lawrence." He found his feelings "various and conflicting; the giving up of an affectionate, kind, lovely daughter causes sensations not easily described," he wrote. The evening ceremony was "performed by Mr. Vinton [rector of St. Paul's] in a very agreeable manner." Afterwards the double parlors at 54 Beacon were filled with friends but they "generally left at half past ten" and then "the wedding party of about 60 supped informally.

"Thus ended the day and I surrendered my dear second daughter to another's care." Surrender of any kind troubled William Appleton. Intensely religious and well acquainted with Scripture, he suspected that he ought to surrender more of his wealth to the church than he really enjoyed doing. He worried about his soul and he worried the Rev. Mr. Alexander H. Vinton about it. Mr. Vinton had a suggestion that appealed to William at this time.

In his diary record for April 30, 1842, "Went to Cambridge with Mr. Vinton; called on Mr. Greenleaf, much talk as to Theological Seminary," William wrote. Professor Simon Greenleaf of the Harvard Law School and some of his friends had been trying in vain to raise money to establish an Episcopal Seminary. "Now is the time to begin," Mr. Appleton told Professor Greenleaf. "If you gentlemen will put things as they should be" — or in other words make a clear plan and get it down on paper — "I will purchase the House opposite the Craigie place, if it is to be had for ten thousand dollars."

Since there were hay fields and an uninterrupted view of the Charles River in front of Craigie House when Nathan Appleton bought it for his daughter, William must have referred to a house behind Craigie stables and barns. In any case, it was not for sale for ten thousand dollars at this time. Three years went by and nothing happened. Then, in 1845, William Appleton pledged $25,000 toward the founding of the "Protestant Episcopal Divinity School of Massachusetts" on condition that another $25,000 be subscribed "within two years." His proposition was "well received," he said but he "doubted that anything would come of it." Land was finally acquired behind Longfellow House and also beyond it on Brattle Street in the direction of Harvard Square. But, like so many of William Appleton's prophecies, this one was correct. Nothing came of his efforts and it was not until 1867, after William Appleton's death, that Benjamin Tyler Reed contributed nearly $100,000 and the theological school got under way. A chapel and other buildings were constructed out of Roxbury puddingstone, a kind of sandstone with pebbles imbedded in it. A dormitory was built in William Appleton's name, and William Lawrence, a son of Sarah Elizabeth Appleton and Amos A. Lawrence, graduated from the school. William Lawrence became Bishop of Massachusetts and Dean of the Theological School in 1889. Next door to Longfellow House is the beautiful white house with its semicircular entrance and Greek-Revival columns which became the home of a second William Lawrence, Bishop and Dean.

William Appleton might believe he had surrendered his daughter Sarah Elizabeth but he had by no means given up looking after her interests. In November, 1843, he had a conversation with his daughter's father-in-law, the elder Amos Lawrence, "as to his son's going into the house of A. A. Lawrence." William "feared there was trouble in the business" and used his uncanny gift for making the right move at the right time. Young Amos was not going to have time to be a literary man, even in some measure. He was going into business full time and he proved exceptionally successful.

With his brother William Lawrence, young Amos bought some ninety acres of land, two and a half miles west of Boston — in Longwood. He took his father-in-law out to look at the property. "A poor sort of business, I think," William Appleton recorded in his diary. "So I told him . . ." But for once, William was wrong.

Amos and William bought the land which soon increased greatly in value. For his rustic cottage, Amos Lawrence built an American version of an English country mansion, out of Roxbury puddingstone. It had "large open fireplaces and a great hall, really unique in its time," according to William Appleton's grandson, William. He said his mother never liked the country but was persuaded that it would be better for the children.

Some understanding of Sarah Lawrence's feeling may be gathered from her son William's description of the journey from Beacon Street to Longwood.[5] "Some years before we moved out to Longwood, a causeway had been constructed, running west from the dump at Arlington Street, through the water to the marshland where Beacon Street and Commonwealth now intersect . . ." This was the Mill Dam. "On the south side was the Back Bay and on the north the Charles River. A plank walk ran along the south side and a line of poplar trees.

"Driving out from Boston on a winter day was a cold trip. . . . Through holes in the ice, men were spearing eels. . . . Half-way across the Dam was the tollgate where every team and carriage stopped to pay toll: and just beyond, where at flood tide the Charles rushed in under a cut in the road to fill Back Bay, and at ebb tide rushed out again, were the mill and mill-wheel which ground the corn hauled in from Brookline and Newton by the farmers. At the fork, the Brighton Road ran out where Commonwealth Avenue now is. . . . Straight out Beacon Street we drove, over the marshes, crossing the Boston and Worcester . . . railroad tracks. Over the road was a great sign, 'Railroad Crossing, Look out for the Engine while the bell rings.' On reaching solid land, we turned up to the right to 'Cottage Farm' where my father built our house . . ."

Amos Lawrence rode his horse into town every day. Sarah Elizabeth "drove in when necessary," but she was not expected to order out the carriage just for pleasure. The Lawrence carriage was "a large English coach with C springs, a great brocaded coachman's box, massive lamps heavily mounted with silver and a brocaded platform and straps at the back for the footman . . ." Eventually there were seven Lawrence children. When they drove out from Boston on a Christmas evening after spending the day at the Appletons' they rode "nine inside the carriage" their father "riding as footman behind." The ninth passenger was perhaps a nursemaid.

William Appleton had been afraid that his son Amory had inherited his own "infirmities." Amory had been married, in 1840, to Mary Lyman. "I think well of his choice," William had written. The Lymans were in the textile business. In 1843, Amory died of tuberculosis. "God has taken him," William wrote. "I feel that I can truly say, 'Thy will be done.' I pray I may continue to feel so." As time went by, William Appleton, the father of ten children, would be considered fortunate because he lost only six of them during his lifetime.

Resignation was harder for Mary Ann. She had suffered in giving birth to the children, watched over them alone during her husband's absences in search of health. It was by no means easy for her to see their loss as the will of God and to say "Amen." William worried over her soul too, along with his own.

Feeling both satisfaction and anxiety, William Appleton recorded the marriages of his remaining children. Marianne, named for her mother but spelling her name differently, married the Rev. Mr. Copley Greene. Her father was pleased and gave her what Fanny Appleton Longfellow described as "a beautiful villa in Waltham." Warren, the third son, changed his name to William and married Emily Warren, the doctor's daughter. Later, William Appleton wrote that Dr. Warren never sent him a bill — not even for recommending Creosote for dyspepsia, nor for the leeches and bleedings as treatment of tuberculosis. In return, Mr. Appleton took care of Dr. Warren's investments. These prospered so that, in 1856, when Dr. John Collins Warren died, William was able to write, with pride, "He leaves his family more than Four Hundred Thousand dollars and not a bad piece of Property amongst it."

On Emily Warren's wedding day, October 9, 1845, William said he was "fully satisfied" with his son's choice. Emily was "a fine woman with excellent principles and a good disposition." When Frank married Georgianna Silsbee the following year, William Appleton was again "quite satisfied" and seemed to think it was a good thing that Georgianna "had a fair share of understanding." There were bluestocking girls around whom Mr. Appleton might have considered altogether too bright.

Harriet and Mehitable, those teen-agers called Hattie and Hetty, whose parties had irked their father, were finally married, Hattie in 1851 to Franklin Gordon Dexter and Hetty, in 1852, to Thomas Jefferson Coolidge. The bride's father said that he thought F. Gordon Dexter would make Hattie "a kind husband" but William did not "think highly of his business qualifications."

In works of reference, T. Jefferson Coolidge was to be described as "merchant, financier, diplomat." But on November 4, 1852, all William Appleton had to say of Mr. Coolidge was that, again, he was "quite satisfied with the connection."

But Thomas Jefferson Coolidge, great-grandson on his mother's side of Thomas Jefferson, was the author of an autobiography in which he made certain pertinent remarks about his father-in-law.[6] "In 1852, I married the daughter of William Appleton. My father-in-law was a singular man, devoted Episcopalian, a man of highest integrity and greatest ability for affairs. He had a large family whom he treated kindly but despotically. He was most benevolent. I think I never knew him to do an unkind thing and never heard him say a kind word.

"He was nervous and made himself uncomfortable to his sons-in-law, Amos A. Lawrence, F. G. Dexter and myself." This would have surprised Mr. Appleton. Of course he kept a sharp eye on his sons, and when Amory and later, Frank, died, he saw to it that their widows were taken care of. If he bedeviled his sons-in-law, demanding business success — it was only for their own good!

William Appleton said he was "much surprised" when he was "pressed" to have his name "used as a Candidate for Congress" in 1850. He agreed to stand for election but had "strong doubts as to the wisdom of the decision." He thought he was "not suited for the situation." But next day, when "many congratulations and complimentary remarks were made," William was pleased.

William cast back over the year now coming to an end. He had been "less engaged in business than for the last thirty years" but had not "suffered from want of occupation." Income from investments allowed him to "disburse freely" while his property increased. He thought that too many railroads were being built and that such roads as the Massachusetts, Vermont and Rutland and the Vermont Central were "bad property." But business for the coming years was going to be good. There had been very little mention of dyspepsia on William's part but he was not a completely changed man. "To increase my fortune I can hardly desire yet I am as much displeased by a bad speculation as when I had very limited means," he confessed.

In this comparatively optimistic state of mind, William Appleton contemplated going to Washington, and on November 11, 1850, he was elected. "I have many doubts as to the propriety of accepting the trust, I fear I shall disappoint my friends," he wrote. On the thirteenth of November he gave "a party at dinner, consisting of twenty," the first of a series, all the guests being men, with no ladies present except Mary

Ann and his daughter Hattie. On each occasion, William set down the names of his distinguished guests; "Sir H. L. Bulwer, Mr. Webster, Mr. Winthrop, Mr. Everett" — and at another, "Charles Perkins, Edward Perkins, A. Otis, John Lowell, T. G. Appleton . . ."

The menu for just one of these dinners "consisted first of cold Oysters, then Sherry wine offered; brown and white soup, followed by Oyster Pâtés, Hock wine offered; boiled and baked fish, pass the wine; next boiled Turkey, roast Mutton, Veal with Peas and Ham; Sweet Breads & Croquettes; then Wine and Roman Punch. After Course, two pair Canvas-Back Ducks, two pair Grouse, Wood Cocks & Quails with Salad; Blanc Mange, Jelly, Baked & Frozen Pudding etc., etc., with Ice Cream, Grapes, Pears, Apples, Oranges & Ornamental Sweets from the Confectioners; a Bouquet for Centre costing twenty-five Dollars." As usual, William's capital letters expressed the importance to him of the words he used. All the different dinners went well — William made no mention of dyspepsia!

After sending off the horses to Washington the first week in November, the William Appletons set out by rail and by steamer. William made his "first appearance in the Hall as a Representative from Suffolk" on December 1, feeling "doubtful of the result." He was delighted to find himself on the Ways and Means Committee. The rooms at the Willard Hotel were "in good order and comfortable."

On New Year's Day, 1851, William wrote in what was for him a mellow mood. There was a fine bright sky over Washington and the whole city seemed "in motion; every person out making calls of congratulation. . . . We had some fifty persons calling on us." But not for the first time William was a trifle anxious over Mary Ann's reactions. "Mrs. A. I trust will continue to like this place; she is freed from the responsibility of Housekeeping which is always irksome to her; unwilling to relinquish what she thought a duty, she has been often perplexed in doing what she was not, from habit well qualified for; with the kindest feelings often mortified by feeling she lost her self-command when in contact with those in her employment." It had required four servants, two hired from outside, just to wait at table during those dinners at 54 Beacon Street. Perhaps Mary Ann had good reason to lose her temper, not during the "well served" dinner, necessarily, but during the hours of supervised preparation that went before it.

Congressman William Appleton now gave dinners, one right after the other, but the Willard Hotel was in charge of all the details that might

Samuel Appleton, by George Peter Alexander Healy.
(Courtesy of the Boston Athenaeum.)

have made poor Mary Ann feel unqualified. Daniel Webster was a constant dinner guest, among others chosen from both North and South. Socially, Washington was "very pleasant," William thought. Politically it was a different matter and by April, political compromise between North and South was getting nowhere. "Caucus at evening not looking well for Whigs," William wrote and then in exasperation he added, "but the true course is to cut all Abolitionists." On June 21, he wrote, "We have this morning the nomination of General Scott for President; not agreeable to me." And on the 24th, "I am rather tired of Washington." He was nominated for another term in Congress and accepted, planning to decline another year. He had no sense of achievement and his dyspepsia had returned.

The night of July 12, 1853, was a sad one for all the Appletons on Beacon Street. William was at home and told about it. "At an early hour, I was apprised by a note from Mr. N. Appleton of the decease of my early and constant friend and cousin, the Honorable Samuel Appleton." As was his custom, William wrote his appraisal of those who died. "Samuel Appleton possessed a strong intellect, a kind and benevolent disposition; strikingly the artificer of his own fortune and he laid open the way for his brothers and others to fortune. We had been very intimate for many years; there was much mutual confidence; I have not known the man more studiously intent on doing right."

William remembered that long ago his cousin had a high temper and was at times "irritable and overbearing" but all that had changed with the years. It did not occur to William that cousins sometimes resemble each other. However, it was also "in early life" that Samuel Appleton had been "of great benefit" to William "in credit, loaning his stocks etc." He was "more than a brother" and William felt "his departure much."

Fanny Appleton Longfellow told her sister Mary of the death of "dear Uncle Sam which has overwhelmed us all; it was so sudden and unlooked-for." [7] Uncle Sam had "seemed lately so well and more than likely to survive many of us. He had been 87 on the 22 of June, just passed. . . . Aunt Sam was actually lying on the outside of the bed beside him and heard his last breath without knowing it."

Fanny went into Uncle Sam's house, "forever changed for us," on the day of the funeral. Shapleigh, the butler, "graver than ever but serene as usual, met me at the door," she said. "Uncle William took me up to see Aunt Sam who was seated in the front drawing room next the one so familiar to us." Aunt Sam had been almost hysterical with grief but was calm now and liked "to dwell on the great sweetness and goodness" of her husband's character.

The hardest thing for Fanny was going into the next room where she saw "the green Morroco chair vacant and the table with the bell and books, just as Uncle Sam had left them. I did not look upon his dead face," she told Mary, "for I could not destroy my happy memory of him in his beautiful old age, and so I shall always think of him with the same freshness of color and glory of silver locks crowning him like a halo. Of late years his house has seemed to me more like a home than ever and it is hard to think of any different picture but his serene image will hallow it always."

In Boston Harbor, "the shipping was at half mast and bells tolling" in honor of the man who first came to town with two chickens to sell. The funeral was at Stone Chapel and children from the Warren Street Settlement were there.[8] Samuel Appleton had built their church, Sunday school, recreation rooms and library. On the previous Fourth of July, they had come to serenade him in front of his house. Aunt Sam had asked them in; Shapleigh had gravely handed them cakes and cookies. Now they had come to sing for Mr. Appleton for the last time.

According to William Appleton's inventory, Samuel Appleton's estate came to "one million, one hundred sixty-five thousand, two hundred eighty-nine dollars and sixty-three cents." But during the last years of his life he had taken great pleasure in giving away money so that later records show only part of the picture. Back in 1848, he had given his New Ipswich brothers and sisters or their descendants a total of $204,786, including $7,190 for "repairing house and barn," and there was that $20,000 given to the descendants of Charles Barrett, the man who advised Samuel Appleton to leave New Ipswich.

The New Ipswich Academy, now Appleton Academy, had received substantial sums of money from time to time as well as Akers' remarkably unflattering bust of Mr. Appleton. Dartmouth, the college Sam would have liked to attend, received $25,000 and Mr. Appleton was pleased with his honorary M.A. degree.

It troubled Nathan Appleton to learn that Aunt Sam's bequest, including the house and contents, horses and carriages, would be only $200,000. But it was all right with Aunt Sam. She sold this most impressive of the Appleton houses on Beacon Street; it was razed to the ground, the only one of them to disappear completely. Some particularly ugly brownstone apartment houses took its place.

In 1855, just up the hill from number 54 Beacon, Aunt Sam built her-

Appleton Chapel, 1858–1931. (Courtesy of the Boston Public Library. Photograph by George W. Cushing.)

self what Fanny called "a little birdcage of a house." It curved outward toward the street, all bow-window in shape but only two narrow windows wide. The front door had a grille with the initials S. A. in it. The ground floor was of granite, the upper floors of brownstone. It rose higher than William's delicately balustraded roof next door — and there it still stands.

At some point, the famous Appleton ancestral helmet that Sam had refused to give to Nathan came into the Nathan Appleton family. Aunt Sam must have given it to Nathan's son, William Sumner Appleton. It was certainly hers to give away as part of her house furnishings. William Sumner Appleton left it to his son William.

As soon as it was learned that Samuel Appleton had left money to be given away by his executors, all sorts of requests came in, some causes being worthy, others false.[9] All had to be investigated but the large grants under consideration had to be attended to by Nathaniel Ingersoll Bowditch and Nathan and William Appleton, personally.

After much questioning and deliberating, Amherst College got $10,150 in Merrimack Mills, Appleton, Hamilton, Amoskeag and other stocks. Edward Everett, former president of Harvard, had a great deal to say about a donation for Harvard.

Everett pointed out that it would take at least fifty thousand dollars to finance "a worthy monument to the noble-hearted munificence" of Mr. Samuel Appleton. Everett got the money which eventually amounted to $68,000. He was given his choice of a library or a chapel for Harvard, Nathan Appleton and Longfellow and their friends favoring a library. Everett chose otherwise and in 1858, Appleton Chapel was built, handsomely to dignify and dominate Harvard Yard.[10]

Around 1858, the *New York Evening Post* published two letters about the new chapel at Cambridge. It was then nearly completed "in a species of Byzantine architecture of drab-colored freestone and the style was one of the ugliest specimens which the genius of man had yet devised." There was a reply to the effect that no building built in the vicinity of Boston during the last dozen years had given more general satisfaction. In 1931, Appleton Chapel was torn down.

Samuel Appleton lived to be eighty-seven years old but his memorial chapel was in existence only seventy-three years. The present church in Harvard Yard has, on the outside of the apse, a bronze plaque with a bas-relief of the original Appleton Chapel — to preserve the name, the inscription says.

TWENTY-ONE

BEACON STREET BALCONIES

MARY AND ROBERT MACKINTOSH left London for the British West Indies on May 16, 1847.[1] Much to Nathan Appleton's satisfaction, his son-in-law had found a well-paid post in keeping with his dignity and that of his proud but not wealthy Scottish family. Robert had been appointed governor of Saint Christopher. Lord Morpeth was his patron, and just before Mary and Robert sailed, he stood godfather to their infant son, James.

The governor and his wife arrived safely after a pleasant six weeks without a storm. They found the climate of St. Kitts delightful, tempered by a sea breeze and not as hot as Boston in summer. Their garden was full of orange trees.

Tom, who later visited them, had a word to say to his father about the new governor. "Robert pitches himself at a dignified tone in his speeches and I hope will keep up to his mark. He has plenty of talent and I make no doubt he will enjoy his island much. The chief matter will be his irritability and whether he can retain his suavity always, enough to be liked."

Mary was herself again, having recovered from the severe backaches and the lassitude suffered after her first child was born. She loved her new experience in the West Indies, writing of views of high mountains from all the windows of the governor's palace, of an excellent staff and of the native guard resplendent in a red uniform who paced back and forth before her door. She was addressed as "Your Excellency" just as her husband was.

In August, their Excellencies, Mary and Robert, made a tour of their island by carriage and pair, driving all twenty-three miles down the length of St. Kitts and across its five-mile width. Mary thought that Mt. Misery, at the end of a chain of "brimstone hills," lived up to its name as the "Gibraltar of the West Indies," and she wrote Fanny about lunching at the fort there, "800 feet in air." But Fanny was not to suppose the experience was quite like Quebec. There was no band music.

On returning to Government House, Mary set up a school for her children and sent to England for a governess. There were refreshing showers of rain "which saved the next year's crop of sugarcane." They had thunder and a good deal of wind but considered themselves safe from hurricanes — at least for August. Two slight shocks of earthquake did not frighten Mary Mackintosh but only reminded her "of a great power and mystery." She seemed again like the girl who delighted in climbing the roaring brooks in Berkshire where she first met Robert James Mackintosh.

There was a Philadelphia brig in port and Robert "very kindly proposed my setting off with the two youngest babies" for a visit to Fanny and her father. But Mary decided against it. "The little babies have been very unwell, so as to make me uneasy for the last week," she told Fanny. The "babies" were Angus, about two, and six-months-old Jamie. From the first, there had been only one seemingly small drawback to life at St. Kitts. The "supply of ice, paid for by subscription," failed — but vessels loaded with ice "came constantly from New Haven." The baby had been premature and Mary had to wean him earlier than she had hoped. She found that there was almost no milk on the island, there being so little pasturage. "Nothing keeps either, a day in this climate," she wrote. The ice supply, now coming from Boston, had been irregular. Little Angus had suffered most but the baby also had attacks of food poisoning. "Baby, however, is vastly better and is going out tomorrow for a drive and I trust has really weathered this attack," Mary told her family in Boston. After that, "letters went astray."

Fanny's next news from her sister was brought her by a stranger. Three months had gone by when "a young man, a native of St. Kitts who has been studying medicine at one of our colleges," called on Nathan Appleton to offer to "carry anything to Mary as he was to sail for her island in a few days." He said "his mother wrote him of the death of Mrs. Mackintosh's baby." [2]

That was all anybody knew. Which of the two younger, "for they are both babies," Fanny had no idea, but thought it was most probably

Angus, because he was teething. At that time "teething" was regarded almost more as a disease than as a natural process, knowledge of food contamination being still so far in the future. It was the baby, James, who had died.

In 1848, Mary sailed for New York with her remaining three children. Her father went to New York to meet her and help her with babies and baggage, since Robert had remained at his post and Tom was in Paris. The steamer arrived, but no Mackintosh family. Again, letters had miscarried. But after a few anxious days a sailing vessel came in with Mary "and the chicks," as Fanny called them, on board.

"My joy at seeing her at Father's house, after such a separation, was sadly damped by her appearance," Fanny wrote to Tom. "A year in that tropical climate and all the anxieties she has suffered have miserably thinned her. I was so disappointed, thinking to see her" as Tom had described her when she left London, "and when she appeared and spoke in a different voice and an English accent, I hardly knew her." But after the first shock, Fanny found her sister "less nervous and excitable," and "much stronger" in spite of the loss of her child, "her first *own* sorrow."

Mary's children were charming, Fanny told her brother. "Ronnie has the same merry look as when a baby." He also seemed "very gentle and well-behaved" in contrast to her half-brother whom she described as "ungoverned Willie who would not suffer from a little English discipline." Her father and Harriet's oldest son, William Sumner Appleton, had been eight years old in 1848. Master Ronald Mackintosh would be eight in October.

Mary's second child, "Eva, with her golden curls and pensive, sentimental air, is very like, all say, Mary at her age" — which was not quite five. Eva had not yet recovered from her sunburn, acquired on shipboard, Fanny explained, "but is very pretty in spite of it and looked picturesque with her tartan ribbons and muslin dress. . . . Little Angus is very rogueish and is much the worse in flesh for the climate and, though the same age as Erny," Fanny thought her own son, who would be three in November, was "quite the man beside him."

Longfellow House, with its fields and gardens, was an ideal place for children to play. Mary's children were "happy upon the spacious verandas where the boys rode Charley's velocipede poney" with "gig behind it," recently "reduced in price low enough for a prudent papa to purchase." Fanny watched Eva who "sat singing to herself" while the boys played with the toy horse and gig, "weaving buttercups together — a new flower for her and therefore admired," though Eva was fresh from tropical splendor. On June third, Eva's fifth birthday, her aunt, Fanny Longfellow, gave a party for her which "went off charmingly, the day was so warm and so many pretty children enjoyed the hay "in the field in front of the house" and then danced and had supper in the library.

After a short visit to Nahant, Mary, Fanny and their children went to Pittsfield to stay at "the Melville House out on the Lenox Road which Father had very kindly" engaged for them. They occupied "the whole house which takes in boarders," Fanny said. It had been "newly furnished with carpets, ottomans etc" — those items of luxury everyone admired so much. The house belonged to a cousin of Herman Melville and Fanny sometimes referred to its location as "Typee Valley."

Renewing Stockbridge and Lenox friendships, Mary and Fanny took tea with the Sedgwicks. Fanny Kemble Butler was there, "as picturesque as ever" but Fanny Longfellow was shocked to hear people speak casually of Pierce Butler's "engagement" to marry his children's governess. Mrs. Butler would have been willing to put an end to her unhappy marriage except that her husband demanded total custody of the children. They were now in a seminary near Philadelphia where he had given orders that they were not to see their mother or any of her friends. "One of her friends who had given her news of the children is now cut off from sending the mother even this consolation," Fanny Longfellow was told. "What useless cruelty is this."

Fanny Kemble's eyes "kindled with the fire of a tigress" as she said, "I will not be *branded* as a woman who would desert her children."

Fanny Longfellow and Mary "felt rather sad in returning together" to scenes and people they loved and finding such a difference. In Pittsfield there was one more sad difference. The Gold mansion, where their mother was married, had now been sold. The clock on the stairs had another home — at Longfellow House. It was moved to Longfellow's study because, in 1877, Longfellow bought another which he called his "newest plaything," the Dutch clock now on the stairs. New owners of the Gold house remodeled it with a mansard roof and fake battlements of wood in one of the most extraordinary examples of American Gothic ever perpetrated. Even this monstrosity, when old enough to rate as an interesting antique, was razed to give way to a brick schoolhouse. Lawns and gardens were covered with asphalt to make the sort of playground favored over grass.

On the last day of August, 1848, Fanny was back in Cambridge, writing to her father. "My poor baby is very ill with her teeth." Little Fan had been singing and dancing with glee at Nahant, in Berkshire and in her own sunny garden. The doctor said that the sudden return of hot weather had brought on dysentery in September but that, since little Fan was teething, "he did not venture to check the disease too suddenly." He gave the baby "a little mercury." Four days later, Fanny and Henry Longfellow watched their child "sinking, sinking away from us." Fanny held the baby's hand and heard the breathing "shorten and then cease without a flutter."

Now it was Fanny, who, like Mary, had suffered her first own sorrow. She had not really understood before what it was like to lose a child. She was, however, firm in her religious faith. "I fancy a cry in the nursery and listen, thinking she must be there. But I thank God all tears are wiped from her eyes and she can never know such grief as mine." Her remaining children were dearer to her than ever but she could not shake off the fear that she might lose another.

On November 16, Mary and the children sailed on the steamer *Bermuda* for St. Kitts, her brother Tom going along as escort. Her husband was rather disappointed that Mary had not gained more weight, but Fanny said that she looked so differently when she left that it was "a consolation for the shock her appearance gave us." In a day when matrons were supposed to look matronly, it was only Tom, with his artist's eye, who approved of Mary's slim figure and said that she was very pretty. Mary gave a ball for the governor general, who was visiting St. Kitts, and it went very well. The children again astonished the tropics with their pink cheeks.

It was decided, however, that Mary was not to spend summers in the West Indies. She usually sailed for England with one or more children, nursemaids and governesses, with Brother Tom at the dock in Liverpool to meet her more often than not. Tom was gratified when the British government provided Mary with "a mounted manservant with a cockade," which impressed the street gamins in front of her house in London. In December, 1849, Robert James Mackintosh was "promoted to be governor general of the Leeward Islands."

Mary and Robert enjoyed a furlough together in London before the governor general took up his new duties. "They see much of the Lawrences who are very kind," was the news Fanny relayed at home. Abbott Lawrence, friend and business associate of both William and Nathan Appleton, had become minister to Great Britain. Fanny hoped that these Lawrences would keep their "grandiloquence of style within bounds!" Mrs. Lawrence was the daughter of a Medford lawyer and congressman but apparently the Appleton ladies did not approve of her taste. Mary reported a breach of etiquette. Mrs. Abbott Lawrence had "caressed the royal children!" The children liked it, however, and Mrs. Lawrence continued *persona grata*. Then there was the matter of the dress she would wear to be presented at Court. Mary was going to Paris with Tom and "at Mrs. Lawrence's request" they selected something beautiful, expensive but not "grandiloquent" for her to wear. Mrs. Lawrence didn't wear it!

Robert's new Government House was in Antigua. He wrote to Mary to send him "harness and more plate" because he took only a minimum but found his house "a much grander place." It was evidence of Mary's regained health that she selected harness and family silver and sent packing boxes on their way without delay. She dined with Lord Carlisle, she said, and was glad to see him chancellor of the Duchy of Lancaster, which was rather an honor "and will be a little variety, at any rate, from sewers. . . . When I see appointments given away here, I do so wish Robert could be here in almost any respectable capacity," she confessed.

And in another letter, Mary said that "whenever it shall be consistent with his public duty," she thought Robert would "be glad to retire — perhaps that may be possible next spring. Then we shall be too happy if he returns in health and strength. I never know how he is, for he never complains . . ."

In Mary's opinion, Robert Mackintosh "had better qualities of head and heart" than the whole British cabinet put together, "although he can't talk quite so glibly as some. I daresay you won't believe it," Mary told her sister Fanny, "and certainly nobody else will. But 'them's my sentiments.' "

Robert himself wrote to Fanny Longfellow in February, 1850. He was going up to Antigua in about a month, being then at St. Kitts. "Antigua, you know, is in a red tape point of view a considerable place," he said.

"I have been leading, as you may suppose, a very solitary life. There are, however, a good many pleasant, companionable people for so small a spot. Among them, I am keeping a wife for your brother — a very charming character — and a superb beauty." But Robert admitted that when he asked Tom Appleton if he thought this girl was handsome, Tom said, "not *immoderately.*"

Robert told Fanny that she should put herself and her children on board one of the packet vessels that came to St. Thomas, "which is just around the corner from us." He was equally cordial about Nathan Appleton's coming to visit — Fanny was to persuade her father to spend the winter in Antigua.

Nathan Appleton and Harriet "lingered still in Baltimore," in 1850, because a physician, renowned for curing bronchial trouble, had Nathan under his care. This doctor, they hoped, had effectively cured Mr. Appleton's cough by cutting "the elongated uvula" which kept up the irritation in his throat. It was "rather a painful operation," the uvula being "shortened by caustic," Harriet said, putting it mildly. Not only was the operation painful but the caustic burn failed to heal. It seemed a good idea to accept Robert Mackintosh's invitation and in April, 1851, Nathan wrote his impressions.

"The house is pleasantly situated, just out of the town of St. Johns which rises gradually from the water. . . . It is very spacious, mostly of one story with windows and green blinds and lattice-work so contrived that the air breathes through it as through the human lungs."

Life was organized as follows: "At seven a cup of coffee — at nine the governor reads prayers to all the household. . . . The servants are all black except a nursery woman. A footman, coachman, groom and boy and two women. At nine, breakfast — at one, lunch — at nine, dinner at which one is expected to be dressed. At lunch we meet the children and grownups." This included Robert's young secretary, Mr. Laughton, a distant relation only lately arrived, an intelligent young man of the army. At four in the afternoon "we usually ride out in the governor's barouche and return some of the numerous calls," Nathan said. The roads were excellent, "all macadam and entirely free from dust. The planters' houses are, many of them, beautifully situated and well furnished with English comforts."

Mary said that they had "a villa on the sea into which they dip at sunrise." This was while Fanny was writing of deep snow in Cambridge — but sea bathing was nothing their father cared for. In May, he sailed for London to see the exposition at the Crystal Palace. Harriet, who had stayed in Boston with the children, joined him there, with Hatty. The best part of the exposition was the American display of recently invented machines of all sorts, as far as Nathan Appleton was concerned. He was immensely proud of his nation's achievements.

There were what Fanny called "exciting times" in Boston which her father was probably glad to have missed. The Fugitive Slave Act had gone into operation and a man named Shadrack was caught but escaped in April with the help of Abolitionists. Very shortly afterwards a waiter, Thomas Sims, was caught and could not get away. Fanny sent her father the newspapers. "The seizure of a supposed slave and his summary trial without judge or jury and return to slavery was a great indignity in

Massachusetts and the courthouse was chained against an imaginary mob." Sims was "marched off with 300 policemen as guards." Not only Massachusetts, but Boston especially, felt this to be an indignity. "It rather helped Sumner's election," Fanny said, "which I fear will not give you much pleasure."

Fanny never understood her father's attitude toward Sumner — his fear that Sumner's oratory would make a peaceful abolition impossible. But Nathan explained to her. "Cotton Whigs" though they were, Appletons were never pro-slavery, whatever their antagonists might claim.

Fanny and Henry Longfellow, however, were equally dedicated to peace. They hated war so much that Fanny was shocked when she found her friend Emmeline's children reciting Tennyson's "Charge of the Light Brigade" and playing soldier, one lying on the floor and another dragging a cart over him, pretending it was a cannon. But somehow, in 1856, Charley Longfellow talked his father into letting him buy a gun with money he had saved. Twelve-year-old Charley promised to fire only percussion caps but one day he and another boy took the gun out to Fresh Pond and loaded it with black powder from a flask. When Charley pulled the trigger the gun exploded. The boys wrapped Charley's hand in a handkerchief, tied it tightly with the cord from the powder flask and walked over a mile, back to Brattle Street. The older boy said Charley never cried once.

The doctor gave Charley a whiff of ether before dressing the horribly mangled left hand that had supported the gun. Charley remarked that ether was better than gunpowder. He lost his thumb, his father blaming himself but marveling at Charley's bravery. The adventurous Charley was to have other narrow escapes — from drowning at Nahant and from wounds when, eventually, he ran away from home to join the Union army.

However carefully they might be shielded from war-like influences, the Longfellow children were allowed to watch parades from their grandfather's balcony on 39 Beacon Street. Fanny, the children and Longfellow were there to see the Franklin celebration on September 21, 1856. Longfellow was no longer a professor. He had resigned his chair at Harvard to devote his entire time to writing — his father-in-law having doubts that such a move would pay.

Nathan Appleton was not on the balcony. He had gone to the park in front of City Hall where Richard Saltonstall Greenough's heroic statue of Franklin was unveiled. The oration was by the Honorable Robert Charles Winthrop. The point brought out was that Franklin had founded and was first president of the Society for the Abolition of Slavery in 1789. Mr. Winthrop had opposed the Fugitive Slave Act — to no avail. He now wanted General Scott to go to Kansas to defend Free Soil but he was having no luck with that idea either.

Meanwhile, everybody "roasted in the sun on the blazing hot balcony" at 39 Beacon while "the endless pageant was passing." There were floats and "vast vans, more for the glory of the trades than in honor of Franklin," Fanny thought. But "the day was splendid and all went off triumphantly" except of course that horses and vans, riders and marchers were stalled from time to time. When they stopped in front of 39, "buckets of cold water were sent out to the exhausted school children." They looked up at the balcony.

No congressman was there, and no famous manufacturer, but they saw someone they recognized. A cheer went up for Henry Wadsworth Longfellow, the poet! It was a period when school children memorized verses and recited poems at exhibitions. They all knew "The Village Blacksmith." He was a real person, people said. The *Song of Hiawatha* had come out the year before — panned by critics, loved and memorized by "enthusiastic youths" such as these who cheered and clapped.[3] This was a different sort of fame for Beacon Street, and Fanny Appleton Longfellow loved it.

"Harriet feasted her balcony-full of hungry guests and no sooner was our appetite appeased than in rushed Willie with six starved freshmen just loose from the Porcellian," Fanny said. Her half-brother now "insists on being called William and is immensely important" as a Harvard man, "and not over-reverent to those at home. He gave us all the jokes and slang he had picked up" at his boarding house.

By this time the food was gone and "poor Papa, who followed later, found hardly a morsel to eat."

There was another balcony scene, three months later, this time at 54 Beacon. Uncle William was again a candidate for Congress. He explained in his diary that several Whig leaders, "among them my long-tried friend Nathan Appleton," desired and advised him "to stand." On the evening of election day, newspapers announced that Mr. William Appleton had won, and a crowd, with a brass band, appeared. Mr. Appleton came out on his balcony to say a few appropriate words. Suddenly, newsboys came tearing across the Common, yelling "Extra! Extra! Read all about it!" William Appleton had lost the election by seventy votes out of twelve thousand. The crowd melted away and the band marched off to serenade his victorious opponent, Anson Burlingame.

"I can truly say that I was never more satisfied that I had escaped a most unpleasant duty," William Appleton wrote. Uncle William's friends cheered him by telling him that Burlingame would probably be shot as soon as he got to Washington.

They were not too far wrong. Burlingame made a speech castigating Preston Brooks for his attack on Charles Sumner. Brooks challenged him to a duel. Burlingame accepted but named a place on the Canadian side of Niagara — dueling being by then unlawful in the United States. Brooks refused on the ground that he could not get there safely, and the Appletons and their friends had something to talk about for weeks to come.

Life on Beacon Street proceeded much as usual. Fanny watched her half-sister Hatty grow up and with a twinge of envy saw her re-enact some of the scenes long gone. In February, 1860, Fanny wrote to her sister Mary about Hatty's debut.

"Harriot received in the old green room on nearly the same spot where I so well remember you, blushing in your blue crepe by Mother's side at your coming-out ball. It seemed like a dream to me all the evening . . .

"The whole house was open and the display of flowers most beautiful, festooned over the mirrors, hanging in baskets from the door-tops and showing in every available space, with endless camellias and other exotics. Hatty looked very pretty in a simple French dress of white tulle, caught up with white clematis . . . and with a wreathe of the same in her hair. It was most suitable for a young girl and as she has a bright color it became her well. Harriet was in black velvet and I in pearl-colored silk with many flounces, trimmed with lace and cherry velvet — with white feathers and a band of cherry velvet in my hair. . . . Charley [Long-fellow] was honored with an invitation and it was quite an event for him to remember . . .

"I do not think there is much beauty in Hatty's set," Fanny said, though she saw "pleasing damsels. Hatty is as nice looking as any, having a pretty figure and a very intelligent, good face with fine eyes . . .

"Father bore the fatigues of the ball very well, as he could retire into the card room when tired. . . . I suppose he now looks forward to Hatty's marriage as the next event he would like to see well over" but Fanny looked around and did not "discover any desirable young men about her."

In October, 1860, there was a third balcony scene on Beacon Street. Edward Albert, Prince of Wales and future Edward VII of England, made a three-day visit to Boston. He was traveling under one of his minor titles, "Lord Renfrew," and people called it "incognito," as though there were anyone who didn't know who he was. The Appletons saw him as he rode from the State House down Beacon Street, along the Common, his black horse and red coat, and the golden autumn trees, as bright as the gold on his saddle, making so gay a picture with his glittering staff. He bowed to the ladies on the balcony and they saw his charming, bashful face. Alice Longfellow, just turned ten, was "quite captivated."

But the Grand Ball at the Boston Theater was the climax of the prince's visit. A dancing floor, made in sections so it could be stored, was bolted together and laid over the tops of the theater seats in the circular auditorium on Washington Street. It was ninety feet in diameter. On the stage a red velvet tent was set up for the prince, which impressed the newspapers. Fanny said it was "garish."

Hatty Appleton, Fanny's half-sister, was invited to dance with the prince. She couldn't think of a thing to say to him except to ask if he were not much bored by all he had seen here. "No, indeed," he told her. "It was all very interesting," and that was all she could get out of him, she told Fanny Longfellow. Hatty had the fifteenth dance.

The mayor's wife got the first dance and the governor's wife was furious. A governor outranked a mayor, surely! Other dances went to the daughters of politicians and a few debutantes. Hatty Appleton was lucky to come in fifteenth. But in the end she outranked them all. She lived to be "for many years the only surviving partner of the Prince." [4]

The prince had been expected at Harvard during the morning and breakfast was prepared. "Henry received many compliments from the Royal party," Fanny said. She thought that President Felton was rather nervous but got through it very well. His Highness asked to see a student's room and Fanny said later that he saw a pretty damsel there whom he admired. Time went by and the royal breakfast turned out to be a luncheon. Lord Renfrew asked for wine and there wasn't any. President Felton sent in haste to his house for some, explaining that the college did not give wine to students. The president's wife, the former Molly Cary of Temple Place, Boston, thought the whole thing was a plot to steal some of their fine table wine — and didn't send any.

No wonder President Felton seemed nervous. But the prince had expressed a desire to see Craigie House and Fanny was not nervous at all. There wasn't time for the royal call but she would have had some choice vintage, selected and given her by her brother, to offer to Prince Edward.

The Longfellows would have liked to live abroad part of the time, now that teaching and lecturing were no longer a part of the poet's life. Fanny had been reading an advance copy of Hawthorne's *Marble Faun* which made her "homesick for Rome," it being "a novel of the present day," she said. The Nortons urged them to take a slow steamer to Spain. "But for the children I would not hesitate, for I think Henry needs a change," Fanny said. "This country is too dry and juiceless for a poet — he needs to have the fountains within refreshed by the dews of a different sky now and then, or it stagnates in our emotionless life — emotionless except with great joys and sorrows . . ." But they could not leave the children.

Longfellow's study, at the top of the stairs, which he had occupied since 1837, was his no longer. It had been first invaded in 1845 when Fanny moved Charley's nursery across the hall so she could "hear his little voice, so near." It took Longfellow three months to get his new study in order — in the downstairs room to the right of the front door.

Besides Charley and Ernest, there was Alice, born in 1850, two years after the death of little Fan. Edith was born in 1853 and there was a discussion as to her name. Nathan Appleton favored Rose, "romantic as it is," Fanny said. Longfellow said Rose was "bar-maidy" and liked "Edith" because it was Anglo-Saxon. In 1855, Annie Allegra was born, named Annie for Longfellow's sister, Annie Pierce — and Allegra because that was how her parents felt about her.

At work on lectures, research or poetry, Longfellow heard his children playing overhead. This was the inspiration for one of his best-loved poems, "The Children's Hour." When it was published, countless Americans knew by name, "Grave Alice and laughing Allegra and Edith with golden hair."

Fate disposed of the dream of going to Europe, anyway. The "horse railroad" from Boston to Cambridge had just been built, double tracks laid on Brattle Street in front of Longfellow House. Longfellow was boarding the car for Boston one morning when the driver started up too soon and the poet was thrown against the steps, his knee injured painfully.[5] Nahant was not out of the question, however. At the end of the season, Henry Longfellow and Tom Appleton bought a Nahant cottage jointly. There was anchorage for Charley's boat and a room in which Tom could paint.

Nathan Appleton, after the Gold property was sold, bought what Fanny described as a "villa" in Lynn, with a fine view of the ocean. He enjoyed riding in his carriage across the causeway to Nahant — accomplished at low tide — to see Fanny and the children. With a touch of amusement, Fanny said that her father was engaged in a correspondence with a British clergyman on the concept of original sin. Nathan refused to believe that children were born sinful because of the fall of Adam. "Twelve long letters" signed "A Layman" appeared, one by one, in the papers. They were later published in a pamphlet under the title: *The Doctrine of Original Sin and the Trinity*.[6] Fanny may not have attempted to read this treatise.

TWENTY-TWO

FULL CIRCLE

"OLD AGE COMES VERY KINDLY ON ME," William Appleton wrote on November 16, 1859.[1] It was his birthday. "I am as able to attend to business or pleasure as when half as old — now seventy-three. I have a large property and the kind wishes of my neighbors, I do not know a person whom I should not take by the hand with pleasure."

Then Christmas came and there was a serious flaw in William's happiness. "Mrs. Appleton much distressed that she could not be with us at church," he wrote. "I am not a little troubled by her present illness; I fear it will give her much pain."

Mary Ann had Christmas plans she was determined to carry out, however. She gave a dinner next day for all the children and most of the grandchildren. Surrounded by so many people she loved, Mary Ann forgot about missing a chance to go to church — she was feeling joyful and free from care. Then she had a terrifying pain in her chest and had to leave the table!

After a consultation on the last day of the old year, "Drs. Jackson and Warren" told William that Mary Ann's disease was "on the heart."

"I have almost from the commencement of our married life contemplated, from my Age and broken Constitution, that when we separated, I should be the first called," William wrote, almost indignantly. Mary Ann was eight years younger than he. She did not have his permission to die.

"From the time I was making my first will, in 1816, she was my first consideration. I then gave her half the property I might have, and in all

*William Appleton. (Photo-
graph kindness of the Rt.
Rev. Frederic C. Lawrence.)*

*Mary Ann Cutler Appleton.
(Photograph kindness of the
Rt. Rev. Frederic C.
Lawrence.)*

the changes since, I have ever thought of her comfort and independence when I was gone and provided accordingly." But William tried to reassure himself. "This is the first serious illness she has had during our marriage of forty-five years, within a few days." He had evidently forgotten that Mary Ann once fell downstairs and had to keep her bed for some time. She had had ten children with never a miscarriage which was certainly proof of a strong constitution, however.

"We have lived happily (I think) as the World goes, but I would not be understood to say we always thought alike and that difference of opinion was always expressed in as mild and considerate terms as it should have been. There was never a want of love, confidence, or respect. She always leaned on me, I always loved her dearly and never doubted her affection for a moment . . ."

William had not forgotten about those parties Mary Ann was always wanting to give the children, however. And that music which bothered him so much. Mary Ann had never liked to see him go off without her on those journeys for health and she had made rather a fuss about it. Someone might read his diary someday. "Were I to say there was never a Word passed that was not in harmony, my children, should this come to their eyes, would not give me that credit for sincerity that I wish from them. I am writing under a cloud, a depression of spirits; we may yet live happily together in health."

The doctors were encouraging to a certain extent. Mary Ann would probably get up and move about thinking she was well. She might even ride out in the carriage again. This Mary Ann did with courage and determination, knowing perhaps better than William did how he would hate to have to live without her.

William went on about his business, assessing his income for the previous year at one hundred thousand dollars, only half of which he either spent or gave away. He had never approved of Samuel Appleton's plan of spending a whole year's income at a time. There was a vestry meeting about selling St. Paul's Church on Tremont Street. William did not like the idea but he let the majority agree to sell without putting up an argument. He planned to sell his Brookline summer place and build in Longwood where the Lawrences had bought acreage. William had disapproved of the location but now he had changed his mind. A house all on one floor might be good for Mary Ann. He looked over a site and Mary Ann rode out in the carriage to Longwood with him.

A few days later, William sent for three doctors for Mary Ann. They all found her desperately ill. When they left, she asked William what they had said. He told her that she was "on the right road," would soon be able to walk around the house and drive with him again. She asked him not to leave her, so he sat down beside her bed. That evening, March 29, 1860, Mary Ann Appleton died.

William's daughter Hetty and her husband, T. Jefferson Coolidge, came to live with him at 54 Beacon Street. "Mr. Coolidge says, and he wrote me, he was disposed to come, yet it must be a great sacrifice to him to give up their establishment; I shall do all I can to make it pleasant," William promised himself.

Hetty and her husband had been "living economically in a house on Beacon Street lent us by my father-in-law," T. Jefferson Coolidge wrote.[2] He had been a commission merchant in partnership with his friend and Harvard college classmate, Joseph Peabody Gardner, at 45 Commercial Wharf. Together, they owned three merchant vessels, the last of them being the *Fire Fly*, bought in 1856.[3] The autumn of 1857 "saw a great commercial crash" and the young partners had a hard time because money due them was not paid. "Still, we got through," Coolidge wrote, "partly by our own merit but partly because our connections with wealthy men helped out our credit. Mr. Appleton was, however, so much frightened that he insisted on my giving up business and taking the treasuryship of the Boott Mills with a salary. I shall say nothing more of my business as it would interest nobody." This salaried job was evidently of no interest to Mr. Coolidge, himself. In his autobiography, he went on to tell how he "began to succeed" in the commodity market in 1861.

In 1860, William Appleton was again nominated for Congress. He was sure that his opponent, Burlingame, would defeat him and gave a day-by-day report beginning with November 5. "Very exciting day. At evening was Complimented by a Torch Light Procession, very well arranged; I made a short speech. The feeling of my friends is that I shall be elected to Congress. The other side is equally confident. I do not think I shall be elected nor do I in my heart wish it.

"6th. At three o'clock I went to Vote, I found the report of chances in favor of Mr. Burlingame. Mr. Coolidge reported at four o'clock that, as advices were from Cambridge, Mr. B. must be elected. Went with Hetty to Longwood, told them what we supposed was the result of the Election; I said I was pleased; the dear daughters, Mrs. Lawrence and Coolidge said, 'If you, Father, are satisfied, we are delighted, we never wished you to go again to Washington.' On our return, we found the report was that I was elected; and before nine o'clock our street was crowded with those who favored my Election, with Musick, Torch Light Processions, etc., etc. . . ." William was "addressed from the crowd," he made a speech — speeches continued. "At twelve, Gentlemen came and serenaded us. Mr. Coolidge gave them some wine."

The next day, there was "much excitement in the City. The whole Lincoln Ticket in the state" had been elected except in William Appleton's district. A recount was demanded. Appleton was still elected, Burlingame defeated. The Honorable William Appleton admitted that after all the excitement, he was "rather tired." His son-in-law, T. Jefferson Coolidge was "done up."

William's next birthday caused him to set down some further reflections. "Seventy-four years Old. My health as good as most persons of my age; I walk upstairs as quick as when much younger, my weight is about the same as for twenty-five years, not varying more than one or two pounds from one hundred; my memory in most things is not to be depended upon. My opinion on business subjects is considered as good as formerly . . .

"I have had my severe trials, but the death of my dear wife changes all my plans for this existence; I loved her much more than I could have supposed and all my recollections of her are pleasing . . ."

There were political meetings and the usual big dinners to be given to backers. Hetty was her father's hostess and she seems to have had no trouble in coping with those endless menus. On December 12, William started for Washington with William Amory and a servant, George. In New York, financial affairs were in better shape than he had expected but the political situation was worse than in Boston. When he got to Washington, William was pleased to receive many callers at Willard's Hotel but everyone was "talking of Secession; there is great doubt and gloom," he wrote.

"The President sent his Secretary to ask me to dine; I went." It was a very private party "with only the President, Secretary, Miss Lane and myself. The President was cheerful and talked freely of the State of Affairs. I fancy he has more hope than most . . ." The subject of the state of the forts at Charleston came up, and Mr. Appleton learned that the only available reinforcements for them would have to come from Norfolk, or Old Point Comfort, the School for Exercises and the Men of War. Congressman Appleton from Massachusetts knew that he was not being told all the plans for the defense of Charleston but he was impressed with the new President, Mr. Abraham Lincoln. "I feel more comfort than from talking with anyone else," William said.

Coming home for Christmas was sad. Only a year ago, Mary Ann had been with him and the children. He was taken ill with something very like pneumonia — his strength did not return, so he decided to go south, leaving early in April and taking with him William Amory and George. He expected to leave New York on the steamer *Nashville* for Charleston but departure was delayed — no one knew why. The *Nashville* left three days later, the news being that "vessels had departed a few days since, bound for Charleston to reinforce Fort Sumter. We doubted the fact," William said.

After a rough voyage, "we arrived off Charleston Bar on Thursday evening; the steamers *Atlantic*, *Harriet Lane* and two armed vessels" were near where the *Nashville* was, all moving slowly during the night, waiting for the tide to rise so they could get over the bar. "About four o'clock, Friday morning, we were apprised by the sound of Cannon that an Attack was made on Fort Sumter; after some time the fire was returned with vigor, firing at Fort Moultrie and again at the Batteries on Morris Island and other Works. . . . Every flash we could see; then the smoke; then followed the report; the bomb shells we saw ascend and would anxiously watch whether they fell in Fort Sumter, from which place no shells were sent, having no mortars.

"The firing was continued during Friday without any cessation from either party; at one time we thought most of the men in the fort must be destroyed by fire, but again they shew they were alive by commencing again their works. The firing stopped in the afternoon of Saturday; we were compelled to remain outside the Bar until Sunday morning. On arriving in the city, finding no one killed, produced emotions of gratitude in my breast that I seldom or never felt. I went to Church; pleased with the discourses and services . . ."

With the permission of General Beauregard, Congressman Appleton, with the mayor of Charleston and a party "not to exceed twelve," visited Fort Sumter. "It was a most awful wreck," William said. "One cannot realize that no one should have been killed."

Back in Boston, Fanny Longfellow had been keeping her sister Mary in touch with the news. The Republicans, a party name she used for the first time in November, 1860, had been organizing torch-light parades in all the small towns of Massachusetts and parading every night. They turned the streets into rivers of fire, not only with torches but with rockets and colored lanterns. The parades had been notable for order and discipline as they wound "like firey serpents" through Cambridge. Beacon Street had been brilliantly illuminated for Uncle William. Far from understanding Uncle William's stubborn hopes that slavery could be eliminated, state by state, Fanny hoped he would be defeated and thought he was "indifferent to the sorrows of slavery." She marveled that "a man of such piety, such tender heart," could differ from Abolitionists like Charles Sumner who constantly preached instant emancipation.

In December there was "a beautiful ball at Papanti's" and Fanny wore the new Paris gown Tom had just sent her. It was "moiré antique" in a new color called "Ashes of Roses." Tom was promising her more dresses while Longfellow remonstrated because it embarrassed him to see his wife look so regal in strictly intellectual Cambridge. Tom disarmingly explained that Fanny's letters of thanks meant so much to him that he could not give them up. He spent very little money on himself but he loved to give his family presents, he said.

"You ask after Hatty's hat . . ." Fanny wrote her sister on January 7, 1861. It was a present from Tom. "She wears it proudly whenever she skates, to the admiration and envy of Jamaica Pond. . . . The shape is novel here and two plumes very rich and fine and most becoming."

Fanny just happened to mention to her brother Tom (in Paris as usual) the secession of South Carolina.[4] "The departure of the Palmetto Kingdom made very little stir; but the splendid act of Major Anderson in leaving Fort Moultrie, which the President refused to strengthen, and saving his devoted band by removing to Fort Sumter, which is impregnable, sent a thrill through all the country and he is the hero of the hour. Such an act of patriotism was so refreshing amidst the treachery of the Cabinet and the President! This has so aroused the people that the latter tries now to be a little firmer and truer to his duty — but hardly Arnold has been thought of with such indignation!" This President to whom Fanny referred was Buchanan, but Fanny's opinion of Lincoln was little better. "The poor Negroes, from their Masters' talk, think Lincoln is to free them all and will be sadly disappointed," she said. But she was afraid that "Lincoln may be attacked at some unguarded moment . . ."

Fanny would like to go to Italy. She saw a sketch of Story, the sculptor, his wife and children, sitting in a garden with the Brownings and their only child. A friend was reading aloud, the ladies had their needlework and in the background "the little Browning boy with his long curls was driving the two little Story boys as his ponies. Think of a summer palace in Sienna for a hundred dollars a year!" Fanny exclaimed. "They retreat there from the heat of Rome," and the Longfellows could easily afford such a vacation.

Nathan Appleton was ill, however and Fanny had no intention of retreating anywhere too far away from her father. "He still retains all his mental vigor and all his senses perfectly," she said, "but his oppressive cough seems at times more than his enfeebled frame can bear. . . . He is naturally depressed by the state of the country."

"Do not fear any Civil War," Fanny assured Mary, urging her to cross the ocean to see her father once more at least. This letter was dated March 27, 1861. On April 19, 1861, Fanny was obliged to write, this time to Emmeline Austin Wadsworth, who was in Europe, "You will be pained to hear that war is upon us.

"My Uncle William, having had delicate lungs this winter, sailed for Charleston and arrived the day after Sumter fell so he is now in the enemy's camp with Mr. William Amory and we know not how they will be treated . . ."

Ten days later, Fanny told how she felt about the coming of the Civil War. "Now the North is aroused with a glorious heart-beat of Liberty such as has never been before in our time. The South cannot understand the intense love of country and not of state only, all classes here display. I am pleased to live at such a time — and sublime as was the spectacle this summer of such a prosperous people working for an ideal of right — it is even more thrilling to see it aroused like one man and making every sacrifice to sustain the flag. . . . It is not against the South that we wage war but against the rebels and traitors who have silenced their loyalty and tried to overthrow ours. Our young men that remain are all drilling and many have gone to defend the forts in the harbor which are quite unprotected . . .

"Many ladies are offering themselves for nurses and some are studying in the hospitals — all the rest of the sex are working in some way for the soldiers but Mrs. Agassiz's girls had the mortification of having their work returned as not done well enough, i.e., not strong enough."

Louis Agassiz, often a guest at Longfellow House, had married Elizabeth Cary of Boston whom Fanny had known all her life. When Tom heard about it he declared that he had always been fond of Lizzie and did not want her married "to that *fish*," the famous ichthyologist. Mrs. Agassiz was now running a school for girls in her home, teaching them French, Latin and mathematics — but not "strong sewing."

"Sewing machines are going like a factory in many homes," Fanny said, and she knew what a factory was like. Papanti gave the Boston girls the use of his hall for a week — winding up with a ball for them.

William Appleton had telegraphed home that he was not a prisoner in Charleston. He had proceeded to Savannah, convinced, like everyone else at the moment, that there would be no war. He got back to Washington where he went to work in behalf of merchant shipping. During his career he had owned, wholly or in part, more than thirty vessels, had worried over their voyages, rejoiced over their safe return, only to grow

Bark, **Emerald,** *William Appleton owner. (Photograph of painting, courtesy of the Peabody Museum, Salem, Massachusetts.)*

anxious all over again as they once more set out. There was the bark *Emerald.* She was armed and in 1827 she sailed, Augustin Heard of Ipswich in command. She carried $140,000 in specie, making the city of Calcutta in a hundred and five days. But in 1828 a pirate ordered her to surrender. Captain Heard told his crew to keep out of sight, had his guns loaded, then rammed the pirate ship and sank her. Luckily for William's state of mind, he only learned the story upon the *Emerald's* safe return. The *Nabob,* the *Huntress,* and eventually the *Union* were all of them lucky ships.

"The situation in Washington was at first exhilerating," he wrote. He went to see the Massachusetts troops arrive and to join in the cheers for the boys, some of whom he knew. Then, only four days later came "sad accounts of our army — total defeat, as appears by report." Report was right. It was the first battle of Bull Run.

After dining with members of the Ways and Means Committee on July 21, William, on leaving his bed the next morning, was taken seriously ill. The "Physician called three or four times" and the Honorable William Appleton was advised to go home as soon as he could. Next day, although "quite feeble," he met with the committee and asked if there was anything more he could do. They complimented him on his usefulness and told him his work was well done. "They all took me by the hand and said they hoped I would return in September," William wrote. He set out that evening by way of Baltimore and arrived safely in Newport, "glad to be with those I love."

William's old enemy was upon him. The Newport doctors exasperated him by giving him nothing much in the way of strong medicine and saying that he only needed rest — so after a few weeks he went home to Boston. Aunt Sam tried to cheer him by taking him to ride in her carriage. Her sister, Maria Goodwin, read to him out of the Bible. There was no escaping a profound loneliness, however. William Appleton had returned to find himself the last of the Beacon Street Appletons.

On Saturday, July 7, 1861, intense heat had enveloped Boston. Fanny had been putting off going to Nahant because she wanted to be only a carriage-ride away from her father. He was so feeble that he could not move across the room without help. Tom, on hearing of his father's increasing illness, had taken the next steamer home and was there "bright and cheerful" before the end of April, but Fanny had sent him off to Nahant with the Longfellow boys. Now Fanny had decided that she and the rest of the family must go during the coming week. Wearing one of her prettiest light muslin dresses, Fanny went to see her father, once more — to say goodbye.

Maria Goodwin was there. Fanny "was never in better health," she said, "and we all remarked on her great beauty."

Ernest took the Nahant ferry for the mainland and went up to Cambridge to lunch on July 9. As he was "stepping on the horse-car to go into town to take the boat" back to Nahant, his mother drove by. She waved her hand.

Many and varied are the accounts of what happened at Longfellow House after Ernest had gone. President Cornelius Felton, long the close friend of both Henry and Fanny, gave the earliest and what seems to be the most accurate account, written next day.[5]

"Yesterday afternoon," Fanny Longfellow "was sealing a small paper package containing a lock of one of her children's hair." She sat at a little desk beside an open window, wearing the same muslin dress she had worn when she went to see her father. A lighted candle for melting sealing-wax stood on the desk.

"The light sleeve took fire; in an instant she was wrapped in flame, flying from the library to the front room where Longfellow was sitting. He sprang up, threw a rug around her but it was not large enough. She broke away, flew towards the entry; then turned and rushed towards him. He received her in his arms; so protected her face and part of her person but she was dreadfully burned, her dress entirely consumed. It was all light and gauzy; no woolen on any part of her person. She was carried to her room: physician sent for. . . . The first efforts were to quiet her suffering by ether . . ."

Fanny's hoop-skirt made it all the more impossible to put out the fire. People from the kitchen came running with pails of water — too late and to no avail. Later, T. Jefferson Coolidge saw marks on the lower stair-steps made by the red hot hoops from Fanny's skirt.

Fanny "sank into quiet" as the ether took effect. She was "conscious through the night; asked for coffee in the morning, breathing until ten minutes past ten — died." Her face "was pale and calm and sweet as ever in life."

Longfellow was "dreadfully burned. His hands and face suffered most severely . . ." When Ernest came home and saw him, he raised his bandaged hands and said, "I couldn't save her!"

Fanny Appleton's funeral was "on the eighteenth anniversary of her wedding day. The day was the loveliest of the summer; the sky soft and blue with a few silver clouds here and there moving in the warm breeze," Felton wrote. Friends gathered together in the library, "the scene of so many pleasures and one awful tragedy . . ."

Friends had stripped "their greenhouses of their choicest exotics" so that there were flowers all through the house but it was the scent of roses that filled the room. There was a wreath of orange blossoms in Fanny's hair. Her face, "in its magnificent and tender beauty," was unharmed by fire. "A cross of white roses lay upon her breast."

Longfellow was not there. He was "too ill to attend" and Felton thought "perhaps this was fortunate."

"After a time, the procession started for Mt. Auburn [Cemetery].

Arrived there, we surrounded the tomb and listened to a short and fervent prayer from Dr. Gannett." It was "impossible to express the beauty of the hour and the place. The tomb is surrounded by tall trees, now in full leaf. The sun stole through the over-arching foliage and fell in bright spots upon the green earth where still lay the open coffin and we still looked upon the placid countenance, more lovely at the very last moment, than ever . . ."

Nathan Appleton died on July 14, the day after Fanny's funeral which he also was too ill to attend. To Maria Goodwin went the task of writing to New Ipswich to tell of the death of the last of those sons of Isaac Appleton who went to Boston to seek their fortune.

"It was thought best to tell Mr. Nathan Appleton of the dreadful calamity which had befallen Mrs. Longfellow and its results. He was very weak and had felt for some time that his end was near and it is not thought that his death was hastened by the intelligence. He wanted to hear all the particulars of the accident and he saw all the family after their return from Cambridge and was told of the funeral. He was rather restless and could not sleep that night and at four o'clock on Sunday morning he quietly passed away."

William Appleton was still in Washington when it all happened. He did not attempt his usual summing up of character in his diary but said of his "long-loved friend," Mr. Nathan Appleton, "Great purity of heart he possessed."

TWENTY-THREE

BOSTON IN WARTIME

THE ALOES would soon be "reaching for their buds," Tom wrote from Paris in 1861. Along the streets and in the gardens he saw pictures only his friends could paint and he wrote poetry only in letters to friends, now and then, when he assumed he was writing prose because his lines did not rhyme. "I have the temperament of genius without the genius," he decided.

One morning there was a letter from home, and Tom was on shipboard before midnight that same day. His father was ill — not expected to live. Tom spent a part of every day at 39 Beacon but lived in his own home on Phillips Place, Cambridge. Although it was April there was no sign of spring. "It would seem as if the season held back as time does for me now," he told Charles Norton who was still in Italy. "The snow almost puts an embargo at my door now, especially in Cambridge" which was like " 'Windy Troy.' Perhaps we might be able to bear better being told in classic tongue that we are muddy." [1]

New England's brief springtime came and went. When a heat wave closed in over Boston and Cambridge, Tom took pity on the Longfellow boys and himself. Fanny's accidental death while Tom was in Nahant was a dreadful blow to him for he had always loved her dearly. His father's death, following so closely, broke his heart all over again but it was expected, and came as a release from a painful illness at the end of a reasonably long life. It was typical of Tom that he tried to think what he could do for Fanny's children. [2]

"Longfellow makes good progress," Tom wrote, toward the end of

July.[3] "The scars on his face have wholly disappeared" although Long-fellow's face was so swollen, the skin so tender, that it was impossible to shave. He had just begun to dress himself, his right hand being "nearly well" and the left "almost painless." Those heavy doses of laudanum which had made Longfellow afraid he was losing his mind were no longer needed. His sister and his children were always in his room or nearby and they were all trying their best to bear "the terrible change" in a home that had been so happy.

Tom took the little girls on daily drives in his carriage. He had a beautiful pair of dappled-grays and a phaeton. The children seemed "cheerful and happy" especially when riding with their uncle. He would try to get them all down to the Nahant cottage as soon as Longfellow was able to travel but on the island they would feel the terrible change all over again because they had been happy there as well as at home.

In the autumn of 1861, William Appleton, as one of three executors, attended to Nathan Appleton's will.[4] A month later, William "made return of inventory" of Mr. N. Appleton's estate. Each of his and Maria's children had been given a hundred thousand dollars at the time of his second marriage. Nathan Appleton's will provided the same amount to each of his and Harriet's children. Cousin William found Nathan's estate "worth about eighteen Hundred Thousand dollars."

William met with his own lawyers and had his own will drawn up. He requested that no inventory be required because he knew altogether too well what a nuisance it could be to his executors. A case in point was William's experience while attending to the inventory, in 1856, of his friend Dr. Warren's estate. While personally checking up on horses and carriages, "I was bit by a dog at the stable of the late Dr. Warren," he wrote. "I was bit after turning from the dog, which was tied with a long rope. His bite was through my coat, pants and drawers." William did not say what valuation he put on the dog.

In 1856, when he declared he would "withdraw from commerce," he had assessed his wealth at "a moderate valuation" of "fifteen hundred thousand dollars," but now, in 1861, he confessed that he was interested in making money again. "I am thinking what I shall do with the profits on the Salt Peter and Pepper I have bought and sold. I shall give part to the public and the balance to my distant relatives." He went to work on the very considerable trust fund he was setting up for his children and grandchildren.

Hetty and T. Jefferson Coolidge no longer lived with Hetty's father. Charles Hook Appleton, William's youngest son, and his wife, Isabella

Mason, took over. But before long, William decided to go to Longwood and live in that house designed with no stairs, which he had been building for Mary Ann. Building proceeded slowly and William wanted to keep an eye on things so he arranged to stay with his sister, Mrs. Burnham, on Mountfort Street, Longwood. He found "excellent rooms and all kindness," he wrote, and perhaps he paid for the rooms, since he inspected them carefully beforehand. Wheeler, his coachman, drove the Honorable William Appleton to Longwood every night and back to Boston every morning, taking him to 54 Beacon from time to time.

On January 1, 1862, "We are going rapidly into paper currency," William Appleton wrote. "Prices of all kinds of stocks will advance materially. I cannot avoid taking an interest in the prices and speculations; I am endeavoring to show the younger part of the Merchants that an old man of seventy-five has energy left."

Some articles in the papers made the Honorable William angry. "I have been particularly noticed through the newspapers for my giving aid to the rebels by sending Wine etc. to the prisoners at Fort Warren. Mr. Faulkner, who was for four years in Congress with me, and Mr. Eustace, son of my old friend Judge Eustace, were those to whom I gave comfort, which I was willing to defend on the basis of Christianity. . . . Those who wrote that I had better send my money to aid the poor invalid soldiers, had not paid a dollar for the aid of the War, while I paid thousands."

During the autumn of 1861, William called on Dr. Jackson who said he had had a consultation with young Dr. Warren. They thought Mr. Appleton should go to a milder climate for the winter and favored Madeira. But William was through with journeys for health. He told the doctor, "I should rather have the comforts of home to those of a better climate to live in and much prefer to die with those I most love."

January storms did not keep William from driving into Boston from Longwood. On the 20th, "Storm continues," he wrote in his diary. "Went to City but did not get out at our house." Three days later, "sold the sugar and most of the Salt Peter." On January 23, the completed papers for the family trust were handed to him, he said. This was the last entry in the seventh and last volume of his diary.

On February 15, 1862, William Appleton died in Longwood at the home of his sister. His funeral would have pleased him. His "remains were carried from his late residence in Beacon Street . . ." The Reverend Doctor Vinton, Bishop Potter of Pennsylvania, the Reverend Doctor

Stone of Brookline and the Rector of St. Paul's — all four of them offici-
ated at his funeral. Family, friends and members of the city government
were present, and when the cortège set out along the snowy roads to
Mt. Auburn, it was a long procession of "a very large company in
carriages."

The first generation of Appletons had exchanged Beacon Street for
Mt. Auburn Cemetery, and the second generation was engaged in the
Civil War. Charley Longfellow presented the greatest problem. He
wanted to join the Union army but his father, ardent abolitionist though
he was, refused to let Charley enlist. In March, 1863, nineteen-year-old
Charles Appleton Longfellow ran away from home and joined up.[5] He
had been refused by recruiting officers for the regular army because of
his mutilated left hand. It was said that he concealed this by wearing a
glove with the left thumb filled out in some way when the cavalry took
him. He wrote to his father from Portland, Maine, saying he had tried in
vain to resist the temptation to enlist without permission.

Longfellow's reply was severe. This "mad-cap expedition" had not
surprised him but Charley had "done wrong."

Charley joined the First Massachusetts Battery, light artillery, as a
private. On March 27, 1863, he was commissioned second lieutenant,
company G, first regiment, Massachusetts Volunteer Cavalry, and mus-
tered in for three years. Ernest, not yet eighteen, admitted enviously that
he had never been able to stay on a horse, much less ride one the way
Charley could.

Tom Appleton was no longer happy in his Cambridge house. He had
hoped that the Longfellows would need him but he soon saw that they
could do without him since Henry had a clergyman brother and two
sisters ready to help. Portland Longfellows were of a serious turn of
mind and it may be that Henry's sisters found Tom too gay an uncle.
Now Tom began to realize what a lot of trouble he had been to Fanny
when he casually went off to Europe, leaving her to find places for his
servants, sublet his house and put away the personal belongings he left
lying around. On March 1, 1864, Tom Appleton sold his house on Phillips Place, Cambridge. Including his improvements, he got seven thousand dollars for it, having paid $7,600. But anyway — the roof leaked.

From his rooms at the Tremont House in Boston, Tom kept in touch
with Charles Longfellow and his own half-brother Nathan Appleton,
Jr., who was only a year older than Charley. "It is very noble of you,
dear Natey, going down there to fight your country's battles, with all

the hardships, when you might be in comfort at home. . . . Can I do anything for you? Shall I send you anything?"

On the day after her seventeenth birthday, November 17, 1863, Tom's half-sister, Hatty, was married to Major Greeley Stevenson Curtis of the First Massachusetts Cavalry. He was thirty-three years old.[6] Because of trouble with his eyes he had left the Lawrence Scientific School to ship as a sailor before the mast. He had subsequently worked in the mines in California, and Hatty's wedding ring was made from gold he had brought home as a forty-niner.

Greeley Curtis had been an engineer in Canada, Nova Scotia and Boston, then an architect in Boston before he joined a group of friends who daily drilled on Boston Common in 1860. He was the first man to sign up in Gordon's second regiment, Massachusetts Volunteer Infantry, according to his friend Henry Higginson. After training at Brook Farm, he marched south as a captain to take part in the first attack on Charleston. Disgusted with the infantry, he and Henry Higginson were delighted with a chance to transfer to cavalry where they were given the rank of major.

Major Curtis was unwounded but invalided home with malaria in the summer of 1863. He was still at home on December 2 when Tom Appleton wrote, "Curtis and party returned last evening and I had to dash their happiness with the news." Charley Longfellow had been seriously wounded. "As it was cavalry on both sides, we may hope it is a saber wound." Partly because of infection, bullet wounds were much more generally fatal.

Major Curtis returned to duty but came home for good when he could no longer sit in the saddle because of recurring malaria. During the summer of 1863, Charley Longfellow had been invalided home with camp fever but he had returned to duty and was wounded in the Mine River campaign.

Charley had dismounted in order to penetrate heavy undergrowth to find men in a picket line which had been broken. He found two Confederate pickets instead. One of them took aim. Charley had raised his gun when the second Confederate picket, whom he had not seen, shot him across the back just under the shoulder blades. The men shouted that they had got him.

Charley plunged into the undergrowth with the rebels after him. He dodged sidewise to a road, where he fell, but some of his own men saw him and carried him into the church at the town of Mt. Hope Church in the Wilderness. A newspaper man saw him there, covered with blood, and telegraphed Longfellow that his son was badly wounded in the face.

Longfellow and his family got the telegram while they were eating lunch. "Father and I immediately started for Washington by the Fall River boat," Ernest said. In Washington there was no news. People at the Sanitary Commission tried to help but at the War Office a "supercilious clerk" said there had been no battle. The clerk admitted that a train with wounded might come in at Alexandria next day so they "journeyed down the river" and waited two days. Then they were told that a train was expected in the evening "at the station on the Washington side of the Long Bridge."

"So we went there and waited at a little tumble-down station with the telegraph key clicking away," Ernest wrote, and he thought how easy it would be for a spy who could read the code to be sitting around among the "loafers." Two hours went by and then "a train of freight cars came in, crammed with wounded, lying or sitting on the straw-covered floors. . . . As the poor wrecks were lifted out, we finally came upon my brother." Charley's wound had not been dressed for three days, and before reaching the railroad he had been "bumped and banged over bad roads for two days in an ambulance, with hardly anything to eat or drink." A second lieutenant, nineteen years old, the officers over him had been killed and Charley had been in "charge of his company." He had been worrying about his men. But at the hotel in Washington, after a doctor had dressed his wound and he got into bed, "he became quite cheerful."

Charley's face was tanned by the Virginia sun, Tom Appleton noticed. At Longfellow House Charley "sat magnificently in his velvet coat with much courage and faithfulness in his heart. He is a fine fellow and we love him much."

Natey had actually seen Charley at Mt. Hope Church, Virginia. His appearance had scared Natey, not knowing how lightly he was hit. According to Tom, the "ball went in at one shoulder, glanced across the spine and came out at the other side. It touched the bone and that may make him stiff." Tom was writing to Natey and added, "I hope now this bad game is nearly over and that soon you will return to us . . .

"I find by a letter today, that I am a conscript, but unluckily the draft don't touch me. You lucky dog to be so young. I should go with the heavy Dragoons, if I went." Tom Appleton was now fifty-one and rather stout.

Lieutenant Nathan Appleton, Fifth Massachusetts Battery and aide-de-camp, Army of the Potomac, gave his address as "Head and Hind-quarters in the Saddle" near Spotsylvania Courthouse, on May 9, 1864. He signed himself "Natey" and said that this was the "fifth day of fight." [7]

"The fighting has been perfectly terrific and our losses tremendous," he told his mother. "I write to let you know thus far I have not been hit. We fired some on the 3rd day's fighting at Wilderness but lost nothing. The Infantry has suffered tremendously. Almost all Massachusetts field officers are killed or wounded. It ain't fun."

Natey sent home another bulletin on May 24. "You see we have been pushing on towards Richmond." He was "South of the N. Anna River and about six miles from Hanover Junction." Natey was now aide to Colonel Wainwright and found "the position much better than always being with the battery. . . . Yesterday afternoon we had quite a pretty little fight, in fact the first one I have been in where bullets whistled pretty lively. . . . We have been now four weeks constantly on the go." Again Natey was all right "up to now." The country was more open than the wilderness, "so the artillery comes considerably into play but the shells, although they frighten you terribly, don't do much damage. . . . Keep a good heart in the North and send down all the spare men you have."

"Buffalo robes" were a much sought-after trophy from the West which Boston young people loved to pile over them in their sleighs on moonlit nights. Although always called robes, they were flat like steamer rugs. "My buffalo robe is a great comfort," Natey wrote from Virginia. "Splendid to sleep on when the ground is damp." The battle of Spotsylvania Courthouse was ending with that "pretty little fight" that Natey wrote about. Lee had just been forced from his position, south of the North Anna River. In June, Natey was wounded.

Harriet Appleton wrote to her step-son Tom on the 28th. "Nathan is doing well. The arm does not heal yet, it is still supperating" but she "rejoiced in having him home."

Experience in Virginia had taught the well-off Massachusetts men a costly but valuable lesson. The Virginia Cavalry were magnificent. Natey's crowd were nothing but a bunch of fox-hunting squires or riders in city parks. But they had good horses and as soon as Natey was able to ride again he helped to organize a better cavalry.

In Boston everyone was working hard to raise money "for the Sanitary," that forerunner of the Red Cross which saved many lives in Washington. Tom painted several pictures, he said, "one of a little girl working for the Sanitary . . . and her sister at her feet reading a letter from the Army." Natey must have written that people from the West were beating the East all hollow with their contributions for the hospital. "We will beat the Western people, you will see," Tom told him.

Natey returned to his post as a brevetted captain and by April, 1865, he took part in the battle of Five Forks.[8] At the crossroads, near Din-widdie Courthouse, southwest of Petersburg, Virginia, Sheridan attacked Lee's extreme right under General Pickett. There was a day-long battle, a night vigil, and in the morning an assault which broke the Confederate line. This hard-won victory led to the evacuation of Petersburg and Richmond. Two weeks later came the surrender at Appomattox but Nathan Appleton, Jr., was not there. He was badly wounded at Five Forks. Captain Nathan got home to Beacon Street in pretty good condition but spent the summer at Sharon and Saratoga, recovering from his wound. Whether taking the waters did him any good or not, these elegant spas were splendid vantage points where a wounded young man could look over the ladies. There was also time to think. This fifth son of Nathan Appleton must have been told all about the value of hard work, just as his half-brother Tom had been. But Nathan Appleton's life was over. He could point to great achievement in the manufacturing world, but as far as Tom and Natey could tell, their father never had any fun. Natey had heard the bullets whistling around his ears, had stopped two of them and had been cited for "gallant and meritorious conduct at the battle on the Virginia Central Railroad." But that was that. Now he was going to see what he could do to enjoy life while he had it.

At Saratoga Natey met "Billy Howe," he said, who put him up for the Somerset Club with Ogden Codman for second. This was the old Somerset Club on the corner of Somerset and Beacon streets, as Natey made it clear.[9] "Well do I remember the cosiness of those rooms, the pleasant and free sociability of the members. . . . Never again shall I taste such good chops as those brought into the little dining room and mysteriously served by the elegant David and the aged and ceremonious Michael! No such lobster salad will disturb my midnight digestion and no such games of billiards and poker parties can I hope to enjoy again. . . . Even the old cat that used to come purring about the rooms, inspired affection . . ." Natey wrote it all down, ten years later.

On Sundays it wasn't proper to use the lower rooms at the club house. "On week days, the members would generally drop in between two and three o'clock. Billy Otis would pose himself at the great corner window, criticize the passersby and make comic remarks about everything and everybody, at which we would roar with laughter."

As soon as he became a member, Natey and Billy Fay gave a breakfast for the "Marquis of Lorne who afterwards married the Princess Louise of England." Afterwards Billy Fay took the Marquis and his traveling companion, each in turn, "for a drive behind his trotters at which they opened their eyes."

Of all the "big Jamborees" at the Somerset Club, "the most lively was a two day and two night's reception for General Phil Sheridan who was there with all his staff and made everybody like him for his simple, unaffected gaiety . . ."

Natey enjoyed seeing his "own phaeton or coupé" or his "handsome Tandem with the immaculate groom standing before the door" of the Somerset Club "and receiving the econiums of all. Never, probably, shall I have finer horses than my three chestnuts, 'Trumps,' 'Revoke' and 'Besique,' " Natey said.

"Does he tool a drag down Beacon Street?" an elderly friend of Natey's mother wrote to inquire. He did indeed. Harriet remonstrated in vain and even his half-brother Tom suggested that Natey might "get his fingers burned" playing Besique at Newport.

"You can't do nothing in such a place as Boston and vicinity for any length of time," Natey discovered. His mother proposed that he do something serious, like "studying medicine." Natey went in for steeplechasing instead and endeavored to "get up a flirtation with a fair creature 'of excelent family, you know,' " as he confided to a former comrade-in-arms.

Among post-war changes in Boston was an emboldened press. "What a stunning thing the Income Tax list is, as published in the papers for all the designing Mamas of marriageable daughters to read!" Natey exclaimed. Since his father's large fortune would have to be divided among five living children and Fanny's children and his mother, Nathan's fortune could not have attracted the more designing of the mamas at Nahant, Newport or Boston. Natey was afraid his flirtation would not succeed and he was right.

"Nahant is gayer than ever and Bostonians are beginning to be swell in a mild way," Natey decided. He had his portrait painted by Richard Staig as a present for his mother. Standing tall and handsome in his uniform, Natey posed holding the bridle of his favorite horse and it was said that he insisted on bringing the horse to the studio so that the artist could get a good likeness. Unfortunately, Staig couldn't draw a horse even when he saw one.

Natey convinced his mother that what he needed next was a trip to Europe. He was angry with Staig and refused to pay for such an improbable horse, so Staig billed his mother who handed over a thousand dollars. "Don't dash about and make yourself conspicuous as you did in Newport," Harriet wrote anxiously. Natey would soon meet Tom in Paris, but Harriet had no great opinion of Tom as an exponent of discreet behavior.

Tom had been enjoying the Nahant cottage which he and Longfellow owned.[10] He invited his friends to visit him, among them John Frederick Kensett whom he had met abroad, financed and befriended. With his soft chestnut hair curled outward over his ears and cut at collar-top, his dreamy eyes, and delicate droopy moustache, Kensett looked like the nineteenth century ideal of a young artist. He could also paint — giving a landscape mystery, subtlety and at the same time, human interest. At Nahant, he and Tom painted little landscapes on pebbles picked up along the shore! These were best-sellers at Sanitary fairs. Tom sold twenty at the Newport fair, and admirers of his and Kensett's efforts took them home for paper weights or door-stops.

In 1866, Tom Appleton had the "sloop yacht *Alice*" built in a Portsmouth, New Hampshire, shipyard.[11] The fifty-four-foot, twenty-seven-ton yacht was a present to himself and to his nephew, Charles Longfellow. On July 11 of that same year, at nine-thirty in the morning, at Nahant, the *Alice* weighed anchor and set sail across the Atlantic, bound for Cowes, Isle of Wight, headquarters of the Royal Yacht Club. People crowded house-tops and hotel piazzas cheering and waving. The *Alice* replied with "a booming gun and a dipping of colors."

On board were Arthur H. Clark, captain, three seamen, the Chinese steward, "a jewel in his department," and as passengers, Charles Appleton Longfellow with his friend Harry Stanfield. T. G. Appleton, owner, was not there. Tom had always loved to sail, had rejoiced in strong winds and high seas just as his sister Fanny did so many years ago. But he had grown lame from varicose veins supposedly cured in Paris. He crossed in the Cunarder *China*, joining the *Alice* at Cowes. Charley promised to write an account of the voyage of the *Alice* for him.

Captain Clark also kept a log of the *Alice* which he afterwards presented to the Nahant Yacht Club. "I am more than pleased with the boat's performance, more in love with her than with any inanimate thing on earth," the captain said. He scarcely slept more than two hours at a time during the whole voyage, "passenger" Charley being willing and competent to take a trick at the wheel. As they reached their goal, "This is probably the only yacht that has ever crossed the Atlantic with her racing sails bent the whole passage," the captain wrote. From Nahant "to the Needles," he considered the run up to this time to be 19 days, 8 hours and 20 minutes.

At four A.M. July 31, they "filled away for Cowes" and at six-thirty "came booming along through the fleet of yachts (about forty in number) and receiving their salutes . . ." The *Alice* had broken all records.

Tom shared all the glory. He included Charley Longfellow's account of the voyage in his book, *A Sheaf of Papers*, published by Roberts Brothers, in 1872. He also wrote a poem to his yacht.

In October, Charley and Ernest Longfellow and Nathan Appleton, Jr., all met in Paris. Tom had gone home to Boston — Natey and Charley were planning a trip to Russia.

Ernest had come to Paris to study art.[12] He said he had become interested in painting one summer when he was ten or twelve years old and stayed with his uncle in Newport. Tom Appleton and John Frederick Kensett were "in the same house," expenses undoubtedly underwritten by T. G. Appleton. Ernest watched Kensett paint, "and when he lent me some of his paints and brushes, I painted my first picture in oils. It was a sailor in a rough sea, painted on a piece of tobacco-box." Ernest was certain that his uncle Tom might have been a real artist instead of "an amateur of some talent" if he had been willing "to devote himself to art and had not been too indolent to take lessons and work hard."

Young Ernest was not going to be "indolent." Moreover, his uncle the Reverend Samuel Longfellow had come along as tutor, "to keep me out of mischief," Ernest said. The reverend uncle took Ernest to all the galleries and discoursed learnedly on art but he had no idea how to go about getting painting lessons for his charge. Finally an American tourist turned up, who knew an American artist who recommended the "atelier Hébert" near the Place Pigalle on Montmartre. Ernest found the atelier more like a club than a school but he was very anxious to get to work and set up his easel. The other students began shouting at him. Evidently his French lessons at home had done him very little good because he thought he was about to be hazed until a boy who spoke English haltingly explained that, as a new student, he would have to stand treat. Ernest told the boy to go out and buy whatever he liked — he would be glad to pay for it. "I became popular at once at the expense of a few francs," he said.

Ernest went to work with paper and charcoal but his first sight of a naked woman model horrified him. He had "a Puritan's mind," he said, "and reverenced woman," so that it seemed a "dreadful desecration to put this poor naked girl up for those ribald youths to stare at."

Ernest saw "no wild doings in the Latin Quarter," although, in retrospect, he admitted he "might have been surrounded with sirens without knowing it." He went only once to the Jardin Mabille, then in its glory. It was a beautiful place just off the Champs-Élysées, but the rather plain, hired ladies, who kicked off gentlemen's hats and displayed as much lingerie as possible, soon palled upon him. Ernest Longfellow painted very well and eventually became a professional artist with much in his work to commend it. At present, however, he really didn't like Paris.

"All good Americans go to Paris when they die," Ernest's uncle, Tom Appleton, had told him. Although Ernest declared that some of the famous witticisms attributed to his uncle should have been credited to others — this one he vouched for.

If Ernest Longfellow was not tempted to go to Russia with Charley and Natey, Natey's older brother William would have been even less inclined. William had graduated from Harvard in 1860, in "the top half of his class." Unlike Tom, he was never "admonished for absence from prayers." He studied law but, in the family tradition, never practiced it. In 1863, he went abroad as all young gentlemen should but met no French barons nor visited the haunts of thieves in Paris. He probably never even went to a cabaret. Willie spent a good deal of his time in England, looking up the ancestors of the first American John Winslow, of whom he was the descendant in the seventh generation, through his mother.

All this, William reported to the New England Historic Genealogical Society of which he had been a member since 1858.[13] If he had a gainful occupation, it was rarely if ever mentioned. In 1864, he gave the New England Historical and Genealogical Library a "Hebrew manuscript of the Book of Esther, written on a parchment roll and enclosed in a gilt case," and likewise "an elegant Arabic Koran in beautiful handwriting with introduction and illuminated letters," both items purchased at Damascus.

Willie also gave the Society a great deal of advice. Hardly a number of the *Register* appeared, beginning in 1860, without a correction in someone else's work, "such a blunder as ought to diminish confidence," and then would come a "communication," signed "William S. Appleton, A.M.

of Boston," concerning a "hitherto unknown first name" of some early settler's first wife drawn from land deeds written in 1650, and representing hours of research.

During the summer of 1866, Willie was in London, sending home an extract from the journal of a Persian prince, "H.R.H. Najaf of Koolee Meerza, without date," to the effect that "America is known in the Turkish language by the name of Yankee Dvoniah, or the New World." William, or "W.S.A.," suggested that here was the origin of "Yankee Doodle"! Languages, the more obscure the better, were William's delight. He collected ancient coins and medals, working hard and successfully at deciphering inscriptions and relating them to history. He also, eventually, grew a long wispy beard in the style of a Chinese mandarin.

The Massachusetts Historical Society, the Boston Museum of Fine Arts, the Athenaeum and the Bostonian Society could hardly have gotten along without William Sumner Appleton, as he might have been the first to admit. In 1869 he became editor of the *Heraldic Journal*. But when asked what his older brother was doing, Natey replied, "Oh, crawling around among gravestones, I suppose." This was literally true. Willie felt a tremendous sense of triumph when he discovered, in a Concord, Massachusetts, cemetery, the name "Showually — 1717." No notice had ever been taken in the *Register* of this strange name. It wasn't in *Savage's Dictionary* either. This would make an exciting communication for the *Register*. He continued collecting antique objects and items.

William Sumner Appleton had not yet collected a wife but in 1871, the thirty-one-year-old Willie was married in Berne, Switzerland, and the bride did not have to change her name. She was Edith Stuart Appleton, daughter of William Stuart Appleton of Baltimore. It goes without saying that the best and most accurate Appleton genealogy is by William Sumner Appleton.

Willie never caused his mother any anxiety but she worried over Natey — sent him letters with news from Boston and with admonitions. "Willy has actually purchased his pair and expects his carriage from N. York this week," Harriet wrote on November 25, 1866. "It rather astounds people, his breaking out like this." But in January, 1867, when the bills came in, Natey's florist bill was "huge" and the cost of keeping Natey's horses was $1,280. Natey countered, disarming his mother as always. "Don't you want me to bring you home a nice little French 'Victoria'?" He thought she had ridden long enough in "the old family ark" imported by Uncle Sam and, after his death in 1853, given to Natey's father.

*Nathan Appleton, Jr., (Natey) standing, with his nephew
Charles Appleton Longfellow, seated. Photo taken in Russia.
(Courtesy of the Longfellow House Trustees.)*

Of course Harriet would consent to no such extravagance but she sent Natey a thousand dollars to buy her some Russian sables, "a cape or pelisse, a muff and a pair of cuffs." Natey was not to "dash around" and make himself "conspicuous" in Russia either, the way he had in Paris and Newport.

At Christmas, 1866, Natey wrote to his mother on letter paper ornamented with a picture of the Kremlin in color. He was with Charles Longfellow. "We are now in Moscow, a truly Russian City and as different from St. Petersburg as Boston is from Paris," he said. He and Charley had bought Russian great coats and fur hats and had their picture taken. Natey was shopping for the finest sables money could buy to bring to his mother.

Harriet had a cousin, Eliza Coffin, whose father established himself in business in Moscow. Eliza married a German, named Carnatz, lived in Moscow and frequented high society. She was charmed with the Boston boys, had them presented at Court where they had an extremely formal time of it, dancing with archduchesses. Natey took a good deal more interest in horses, horse-and-carriage fashions and in acquiring a turn-out of his own.

"The 'swell' groom here has a *chic* quite his own, and totally different from the London 'tiger,' which has spread over the rest of the continent and America. My 'Tom' with his neat tights and top boots, carefully trimmed whiskers and square shoulders, is very different from your bearded Russian coachman, the stouter the better, with lozenge-shaped, pincushion-like velvet hat, long tunic with gorgeous colored sash and big boots. They drive with both arms stretched out at full length, and have four reins for a single pair of horses."

When Natey got home, "I had a pretty sleigh," he said, "with the appearance of a Russian one, as I had what looked like a 'Duga' over the saddle of the horse, with the waving plume. I once drove down State Street in it with my colored groom, the same old 'Joe' who was with me in the army, sitting behind in the rumble, and from its striking appearance, with the white fox fur robes . . ." Natey made quite a sensation.

Charles Longfellow, having acquired a taste for travel, made a trip to the Orient in the early eighteen seventies. He, too, had an anxious parent at home who worried when Charley, having fallen in love with Chinese and Japanese art, sent home some choice treasures. "How much I lament that you have not limited yourself to your income, which was ample for your needs," Longfellow wrote to his son. He had been obliged to sell some stocks and bonds to cover Charley's letter of credit. Now Charley's fortune was half gone and consequently half his income. Charley replied from Hong Kong. He was ashamed, he said, and would come right home, giving up Burma, Siam, Java and some other places.

The Beacon Street Appletons had cared little for Fanny's choice of a professor and poet for a husband, but Longfellow took good care of the funds in trust for his children and of his own considerable earnings as his work found more and more public favor. His books were carefully kept. At the time of his death his estate was valued at $356,320, including an allowance of $75,000 for Craigie House and land. This last was an investment frowned upon by Nathan Appleton.

Nathan, Jr., was glad that he had returned to 39 Beacon Street early in 1867 — his last letter from Russia was dated February 3. It was a leisurely return of course. In March, his mother was still sending him news — Ernest Longfellow was "engaged to Miss Hattie Spellman." Brother Tom had just dropped in "talking very fast and pleasantly — he says he has his passage engaged in *two* ships." Harriet was surprised by this. Tom had "sent for his yacht," a British crew bringing it home. The *Alice* was damaged in a hurricane but arrived safely. Everybody supposed Tom would settle down at Nahant to enjoy the summer.

Harriet said the Boston girls looked thin and lanky now that they no longer wore hoop-skirts. They looked silly with "little wreathes of flowers a-top their heads instead of hats or bonnets."

Natey arrived at 39 Beacon Street in time to see his mother again but she may never have worn the Russian sables he brought her. She told him she got tired easily these days but it was nothing to worry about. On October 10, 1867, Harriet Sumner Appleton died of a heart attack. Her son Willie did not set down the date of her birth in his genealogy but she was sixty-three. Harrison Gray Otis had been right about her at the time of her marriage. She was a very nice woman.

Harriet left her house on Beacon Street to her two sons. In 1871, Natey sold his share to his brother Willie and by 1884, William Sumner sold out so that there was no longer an Appleton at 39. A new and still more delectable spot had been discovered — at least in the opinion of Tom.

Thomas Gold Appleton bought a lot on Commonwealth Avenue where he built a house for himself in 1863.[14] "I suppose T.G.A. is in his house by now," Natey had written, in 1865. "I shall expect a swell dinner there when I get home."

TWENTY-FOUR

T. G. APPLETON, BOSTON WIT

TOM APPLETON'S WITTICISMS were quoted, misquoted and plagiarized wherever Bostonians got together. In his day, conversation was an art, puns were applauded and a so-called *bon mot* continually repeated. Those endless dinner parties always needed enlivening and if Tom were not there to think of something new to say, some friend would remember what he had said previously.

There was competition. Maud Howe Elliott remembered that, as a young girl, she had been allowed to arrange a dinner for her cousin, F. Marion Crawford, at her mother's house.[1] She had invited both Oliver Wendell Holmes and Thomas Gold Appleton. The dinner was a disaster. Maud's mother, Julia Ward Howe, told her why. "It is like asking two prima donnas to sing at the same entertainment."

Mrs. James T. Fields, in her diary, rather favored Holmes over Appleton, but Richard Henry Dana, in *his* diary, said, "Tom is the prince of rattlers. He is quick to astonishment and has humor and thought and shrewd sense behind a brilliant fence of words."[2]

Ernest Longfellow gave his uncle's wit perhaps the most valid endorsement. "I have known him to be more amusing at breakfast with only some children as audience than when he had more important listeners. He simply couldn't help being original and funny."[3]

Tom loved everything that was new during the last half of the nineteenth century. A new and exciting invention called a steam excavator was loading gravel into freight cars at Needham, eight miles from Boston. Gentlemen wearing top hats had their picture taken standing in front of the steam shovel which worked "with rapidity and ease" to fill Back Bay. On March 25, 1863, Tom bought of Erastus B. Bigelow a house lot on newly created Commonwealth Avenue. His lot was close to the Public Garden, his house to be numbered 10 Commonwealth Avenue. Tom Appleton made 10 Commonwealth Avenue as well known in his time as 39 Beacon. The south side of Commonwealth had been filled only as far as Clarendon Street as late as 1861. It took ten years more to complete the filling of Back Bay as far as Exeter Street. People called it "the new West End."

There was no reason for Tom to describe his new house. He just invited all his friends to see it and told friends from abroad to come by whenever they were in Boston. Susan Hale wrote about 10 Commonwealth Avenue.

By this time, Tom had left Nahant which everybody knew he had called "Cold Roast Boston." Ladies of good family but uncertain age were forever calling on him, either for a donation to charity or in the hope of improving his mind. Nahant, Tom said, "had the quiet of the grave but none of its peace." He built a Newport cottage, three stories high, with a French chateau roof equipped with a little wrought-iron fence for birds to perch on. Walls here and there were half-timbered or had geometric patterns in tile. Newport was fashionable, much more fun than Nahant, but not without its guardians of morality, as Tom found out when he took Miss Hale there.

"Is it true that Miss Hale is living *alone* with you at your cottage?" Miss Bruen, a clergyman's daughter, asked him.

"Yes," Tom told her. "Did you expect me to bring *all* my harem from Boston?" [4]

Julia Ward Howe and her family were at their Newport home when this story went the rounds. Miss Hale, although handsome, was forty years old at the time, and Tom had known her all his life. Her father had been editor of the *Boston Daily Advertiser*. Her older sister, Lucretia, went to Miss Peabody's School in Boston and to George Barrell Emerson's, just as Fanny Appleton had done. Edward Everett, minister and author of *The Man Without a Country*, was Susan's older brother. Lucretia wrote the *Peterkin Papers* to the delight of a whole generation of children.

Susan was the youngest of eight. When her parents died and the family money disappeared, she "took rooms" and, having studied art abroad, gave painting lessons, much to the Reverend Mr. Hale's dismay.

*Thomas Gold Appleton at
10 Commonwealth Avenue.
(Courtesy of the Longfellow
House Trustees.)*

*Thomas Gold Appleton
house, 10 Commonwealth
Avenue. (Courtesy of the
Boston Athenaeum.)*

She defied her brother, insisted on her personal independence, refusing to live as the maiden aunt and unpaid servant in some relative's family.

When called upon to write an introduction to *The Letters of Susan Hale*, a nephew, Edward E. Hale, could not bring himself to admit that Aunt Susan had ever been Tom Appleton's paid secretary. "She used also to go in the evening to read to Mr. T. G. Appleton and these regular

Thomas Gold Appleton's Newport cottage.
(Courtesy of the Longfellow House Trustees.)

engagements, together with her morning classes, made for a number of years, the background of her winter occupation. . . . She used often to go over to Mr. Appleton's for dinner and as one was a wit and the other a humorist, it is not likely that they spent all their time in reading even so interesting a book as Gibbon's *Decline and Fall* . . ." It was perfectly all right for a lady to teach school, but in his efforts to conceal Susan's occupation as secretary, her nephew managed to sound as if Miss Bruen had been right in her suspicions!

Tom's house was big enough to hold a whole harem, although, unfortunately, there seems to be no record that it ever did. Susan Hale said he built 10 Commonwealth "under the advice of an experienced architect" but she didn't tell his name. The house was built "around a long, large room in the middle of the lower floor," she said. It was lighted by a big skylight. This was the library, lined with books in carved oak cases with glass doors.

Instead of reaching from floor to ceiling, as in older houses, Tom's bookshelves ended at about eye-level, with room on top for the display of all sorts of curios — or what his friends would have called "art objects." The advantage of a skylighted room was that Tom had space on all four walls for pictures, with no windows to cut down his space. Tom's pictures were hung not only side by side, but one over another, large and small, wide or long — like the pieces of a jig-saw puzzle, assembled but not quite locked together. They overflowed into the drawing room which occupied the front part of the house, and into the sunny dining room behind; they climbed the stairs, ornamenting the halls and invading the large bedrooms, penetrating to the very top where the billiard room occupied the front of the upper story.

On a partial list of two hundred and twenty items,[5] there were two landscapes and a portrait of Alice, by her brother, Ernest Longfellow. Tom Appleton himself was well represented by twenty-six landscapes, one seascape, seven sketches, his portrait of his sister Fanny, a picture called *Girls and Flowers* and one called *Sancho Panza*. There was a landscape by Susan Hale, which she did not mention but said Mr. Appleton "never bought a picture unless he liked it."

During the eighteen sixties, Tom bought the most admired of his pictures, a Troyon. In 1872, he bought a second Constant Troyon, whose animals and landscapes were still tremendously popular. He promised to lend Annie Fields his second Troyon, and she was so pleased that she wrote it down in her diary.

Ernest Longfellow wrote that his uncle had given an order to Jean François Millet for a painting to cost two hundred dollars. Millet set to work but was so long finishing the picture that Tom countermanded the order. The picture was "the celebrated *Angelus* which afterwards sold for a hundred thousand dollars," Ernest commented in 1922. The *Angelus* went to the Louvre, but Tom was unaware of having missed this treasure. He was very much aware, however, that Boston had no museum of art.

On November 6, 1870, Mrs. Fields made a long entry in her diary:[6]

"Appleton (Tom, as the world calls him) came in soon after breakfast on Sunday morning. He talked very wisely and brilliantly upon art, its value and purpose to the state, the necessity for a museum. He said our people are far more literary than artistic. The sensuous side of their nature was undeveloped. The richness of color, the glory of form was less to them than something which could set the sharp edge of their intellect in motion.

The first Boston Museum of Fine Arts. Tom Appleton said that, if architecture were "a kind of frozen music," he would call the museum "frozen Yankee Doodle."

" 'Besides, what is Boston going to do when these fellows die who give it honor now; Longfellow, Holmes and the rest? They can't live forever and with them its glory will depart.' " Boston must have a " 'foundation for art in another direction. . . . Unless a distinct effort be made now, Boston will lose its place and go behind . . .' " Tom Appleton was crusading for a Boston Museum of Fine Arts, contributing and raising money for it, and eventually he wrote the first catalogue.

When in 1872 the first museum was built at the corner of Huntington Avenue and Dartmouth Street on newly filled Copley Square, it was the pride of local citizens. The style was neo-Gothic. Arches of Vermont marble and courses of other light-colored stone with brick gave it a striped effect while walls had squares of imported terra cotta in two colors. There was "much elaboration of decorative detail," said an article in *The Memorial History of Boston*. This was an understatement. No mention was made of the architect and to judge by the heliotype of this masterpiece, it seems just as well. "I have heard that architecture is a kind of frozen music," Tom Appleton said. "If so, I should call the Art Museum frozen Yankee Doodle."

Tom gave pictures to the Boston Museum of Art but kept during his lifetime the statue, *Love Disguised as a Shepherd*, by John Gibson.[7] The son of an English market gardener, Gibson had managed to get to Rome where Thorwaldsen took him on as a student. A wax statue of *Time* brought the young man his first success; eventually his *Queen Victoria* was commissioned for the Houses of Parliament. Perhaps because excavations revealed that the Greeks painted their statues, Gibson began to experiment with color. The results shocked the admirers of pure white marble goddesses inhabiting Boston parlors, but Tom was just the man to applaud an innovator of humble origin.

Tom kept all his marble busts in his house at 10 Commonwealth. There was one of himself, one of Shelley, one of Emerson and one of Edith Longfellow, to look down on him from shelves and mantels. The family were to take their pick when he was gone.

Tom seems not to have given patronage to contemporary women sculptors. Aunt Sam ordered an ideal bust of *Daphne* from Harriet Hosmer, the American girl with a studio in Rome. *Daphne* pleased Aunt Sam so much that she ordered the companion piece, *Medusa*, with carefully waved marble hair changing to snakes at the top and back of her head. Tom could not resist an opportunity for a pun when Emma Stebbins of Boston completed Horace Mann's statue for the front of the State House. "It ought to be called 'Mann by Woman,' " Tom said.

In 1868 Tom went abroad with Longfellow, Ernest and his wife, the three girls, two of Longfellow's sisters and a brother. The director of the museum in Naples "gave us an excavation," Tom said. They hired some workmen and sallied forth to a burial mound. Their men dug in with pick and shovel, paying little attention to what they might break or toss away. "We did not find much," Tom remarked. "The ancient inhabitants must have come back for their things. Still, the excitement was pleasant and we did find a skeleton and sundry amphorae and bits of bronze."

Tom had an even better time at Castellani's, a dealer, where he bought "a very choice and rare collection of Etruscan pottery. . . . This is very high art indeed and these are really old masters. Two of the vases are exquisite and of the best Greek time. In all, I have seven periods represented, which tell the whole story of this art . . ." Tom wrote to Natey who was in Paris. He said that his Etruscan pottery was to go to the Boston Athenaeum and while he and the Longfellows were in Rome, he bought "the second most important print collection" to give to the Boston Public Library. "I shall draw heavily for this and for the pottery soon," he warned Natey. "If I over-run my account with your house, I wish at once to know it. But it is not likely as I have sent for more money to be dispatched which will reach you before I draw. I have not received the yearly balance sheet." Barings had always sent theirs promptly. Tom hoped that Natey would have good success in his association with Bowles and Company but warned him not to "get made a full partner."

Nathan Appleton, Jr., had discovered that it was going to take more money than he had inherited to have the kind of a good time he craved in Paris.[8] He was going to make a big fortune, fast, he declared and his friend Bowles, an American, encouraged him with heavy doses of flattery, getting him to invest in wildcat schemes besides putting up money for a Paris banking house.

Natey paid no attention to Tom's warnings. Before long an American tourist decided to cash his letter of credit at Bowles and Company all in one lump sum. Bowles had to suspend payment; Nathan Appleton, Jr., was sued and obliged to file for bankruptcy. Tom was back home by this time, his transactions with Bowles completed, so he lost nothing, and with the help of his lawyers, Natey managed to salvage some of his inheritance. But before long, he became involved with Count de Lesseps in the abortive French effort to build a Panama canal.

Nathan Appleton had regarded his oldest son Tom as hopelessly impractical, but Tom was not. He handled his property well and gave Natey a home at 10 Commonwealth whenever he needed it. Tom was not the sort to lecture Natey but it was significant that when he left this half-brother $200,000 in his will, the money was to be held in trust with only the income paid.

While abroad on this and subsequent trips, Tom always got in touch with his sister, Mary Mackintosh. After her father and Fanny died, Mary never came home again. Tom and Longfellow saw to it that her inheritance from her father was safeguarded so that she was able to use the income. British law made it difficult for a woman to control her own money.[9] The happy years of retirement she looked forward to with Robert never came. Robert James Mackintosh died of a fever in 1864, while still governor general of the Leeward Islands. Mary was in London attending to the children's education. She was fond of her husband's family and they of her, but she had a rather lonely life most of the time.

Alice Longfellow spent a Christmas in London with her Aunt Mary. Natey came by and urged her to send Eva to visit Boston. Eva wasn't having any fun, Natey said. Tom's Commonwealth Avenue house was often enlivened by nephews and nieces, but Mary's children never came.

In response to an inquiry concerning Willie, who was in Europe when both Tom and Natey were there, "Willie of course we have no news of," Tom replied. "He is a whale who is under a long time before he spouts."

Willie did spout; Tom later said that "it wasn't that he bit off more than he could chaw, but that he chawed more than he bit off."

Mrs. Henry Adams repeated this remark, applying it to Henry James. But she did not plagiarize; she gave Tom Appleton the credit.

When Tom Appleton got home to Commonwealth, his packing cases from Rome and Naples had arrived. Bridget, his cook, helped him to unpack them and he told her that some of those queer-looking objects were cooking utensils, three thousand years old.

"Lor, Sir!" she exclaimed. "What improvements we have made!"

Bridget worked for Mr. Appleton for ten years. She could make French bread and omelets because Tom Appleton never had a cook who didn't. She must have made a variety of sauces because Tom could never eat a meal without them — and she made codfish cakes because Tom loved them. But Susan Hale described Bridget's masterpieces as being somewhat hearty. "Marvelous were the huge turkeys, fat capons and generous sirloins that appeared on the table!" Miss Hale said. There was no limit to Tom's hospitality. He never hesitated to invite extra, unexpected guests, so that a dinner for four could expand to a dinner for eight, but Bridget's only anxiety seemed to be that the soup might not go round. She had plenty of everything else — and fortunately plenty of help, for Tom employed considerable staff. The round dining table would be "bright with fine damask and tasteful appointments. . . . The host [was] always genial, never more entertaining than when he saw a circle of merry faces around the board."

If Bridget could have read some of Mr. Appleton's discussions of food in his books of essays and travels, she would have said, "Lor, Sir," all over again. In *Nile Journey*, T. G. Appleton described the prowess of his cook aboard the dahabeah. It was not surprising that Antonio's dates stuffed with almonds would transport a person "to Badoura or Bagdad." What was remarkable was that Antonio, a man from Malta, could make a sauce to accent the flavor of a dish of chicken "as a clever girl will wear a ribbon to bring out the violet in her eyes." He could also make fish balls that reminded Tom "of a past, starry with fish balls."

In *Windfalls*, a collection of essays, Tom spoke out against the Puritan principle of hard work and the idea that pleasure is sinful. "Here we only retire from business when the strength to continue retires from *us*; business is our life and in our rush, we stumble over our grave. . . . Nature invites us to a table magnificently spread, if the proper artist were there to intelligently profit by its bounty. Heaven has sent us its food and the Puritan has sent us his cook. . . . The Puritan doctrine is fading away. Alas! their kitchen remains . . ."

"The quality of a plover or a snipe cannot be trifled with; it is perfect or it is nothing." Game birds must be cooked over a flame, and in *Windfalls* Tom gave Mr. Taft of Taft's Hotel great praise as "caterer and cook," who "presides at the cooking, watch in hand." Then he almost broke the poor man's heart by complaining that at Taft's the bread was poor, the pickles "virulent" and the butter — "Oh breathe not its name in Philadelphia." Mr. Taft apologized in the newspapers and said he would use "gilt-edged butter henceforth."

Tom's favorite game bird was canvasback duck. "Canvasback ducks eat the wild celery," he said, "and the common black ducks, if they ate the wild celery, would be just as good, only damn 'em, they won't eat it!"

Tom Appleton reported on life in Boston in 1871. On December 9, "We go into fits over the young Bear, the Duke Alexis," he said. "America chucks her whole head at anything that comes along, Japs, Chinese, Chimpanzees or crowned heirs. It is our way and I should be unmannerly if I did not go into my private fit too. So I shall go to the Revere House and look at the young gentlemen and hear their speeches." Willie Appleton's wife was running a fair for the benefit of stray dogs. "As it is good and humane, I shall take a hundred dollar bill and spend it," Tom said. "It may well be called 'throwing money to the dogs.' "

Dictating to his amanuensis, as Susan Hale liked to call herself, Tom held forth in the press on what he called "the outrageous practice of covering objects of national beauty with advertisements." When the Tweed gang scandal broke in New York, Tom said that "the combined false estimate of riches as the chief end of man, without any knightly ideal of government" had produced the modern alderman. He was shocked that Tweed had sunk into such a "morass of capable selfishness and dirty pillage" with its "tone of vulgarity and absence of high aim." Tom looked back upon his father's day when Appletons were office holders. "There was a time, with us, when, as an office was filled, there was a modest reluctance in the incumbent, who felt his deficiency and aimed to do justly and well."

To such an ardent New Englander as T. G. Appleton, it was comforting to discover evil in New York, but Boston was not going to get off without blame. There was a "policy of premeditated shabbiness in high places" in Massachusetts and in Boston.

In 1874, Tom went on his rather lonely way again in Europe, trying to find traveling companions enough to fill a dahabeah on the Nile. In Venice, he watched an artist copying in a gallery and struck up a conversation. "You must be Tom Appleton," the painter said. Tom was properly astonished and was told that his old friend John Frederick Kensett had described him so accurately that the stranger knew him.

The painter was thirty-five-year-old Eugene Benson who had managed to make a living writing for the New York papers, signing the name "Proteus." He had studied at the National Academy of Design, then lived in New Haven, Connecticut, and the previous year had arrived to study in France and Italy. Benson was married to Mrs. Henriette Fletcher of Geneva, Switzerland, and had with him in Venice her daughter, referred to by Susan Hale as Miss Fletcher. Her name was Julia Constance and Tom called her "Dudu."

It didn't take Tom long to discover that the Bensons would like to go up the Nile with him, all expenses paid. Tom wrote in his Nile journal for a while but soon discovered that Dudu could write while he dictated, just the way Susan could. He was delighted when Benson's *Bazar in Cairo* and *Slave Tower* were exhibited at the National Academy, press notices good and both paintings sold. Julia Constance Fletcher became a novelist and wrote the tremendously popular book, *Kismet*. Considerably to his surprise, T. G. Appleton's *Nile Journal* had good reviews.

He went to visit Syria and *Syrian Sunshine* was full of amusing digressions and shrewd observations. "We soon began to know what a road in Judea can be. No horse in any New England stable but would laugh at the idea of his trying it. But to our clever Syrian nags it was the correct thing. They rather liked it. They did not care much for little stones in the way, but when the road became like the bed of the stoniest brook, when boulders of the size and with the edge of ice houses filled the way, they were quite at home. Like dancing masters they would measure their steps to such music . . ."

*Thomas Gold Appleton's study, 10 Commonwealth Avenue.
Tom Appleton's portrait has been placed in his chair, probably
to symbolize the fact that his death had occurred before the
picture was taken. (Courtesy of the Longfellow House Trustees.)*

Tom visited Mary on his way home and took his niece Eva and one of her Scottish cousins to Scotland with him. He described "Highland soldiers in kilt and sporran, the pipers playing at their head," a Scottish wedding, "the bride handsome, her dress perfection" and himself as "an oldish gentleman" with two young girls. He was sixty-three, with almost ten good years ahead of him. Tom took no more trips abroad, however, and his sister Mary and his niece Eva he was not to see again. Mary died, still a resident of London but in Pau, France, where she had gone in 1889 to escape the winter weather.

Susan Hale described Tom's routine on Commonwealth Avenue. "Mr. Appleton was an early riser. Even in winter, he was up and out for a little walk before breakfast, often without overcoat, greeting the letter-carrier, the newsboy and his early neighbors as they went downtown." Tom had always hated hot weather in Boston but when he was a home-sick schoolboy at Round Hill in Northampton, he longed to race his sled down Beacon Street, beating out the other boys. Now, too many gourmet meals had changed the once thin Tom into the portly Mr. Appleton. Some time earlier, Holmes had met Tom who was driving "Miss G." (perhaps Grace Norton) in his phaeton. Tom got out. "We embraced — or rather he embraced me and I partially spanned his goodly circumference," Holmes said.

In her letters, but not in her *Life and Letters of Thomas Gold Appleton*, Susan Hale described meeting Mr. Appleton at the corner of Clarendon Street and Commonwealth Avenue. He had a new dog with him "whose tail curled up very tight behind and whose name is Pop," she said. This sounds like a fashionable pug dog but Tom had several dogs along with some birds in cages. Aunt Sam, that dearest of Appleton in-laws, had died May 19, 1870, age eighty-two, at her "little bird cage of a house" on Beacon Street. She always kept caged birds. Perhaps Tom gave them a home.

After breakfast and after reading his paper, Tom usually went upstairs to the studio that his architect had designed for him at 10 Commonwealth. The smell of oil paints and turpentine never failed to give him a lift. He had sketches which he had made on the deck of the dahabeah, sketches from his tent in Syria and from a window in Paris. The hope of turning one of these into a really good picture never deserted him. Descriptions in his travel books showed an artist's eye for lively detail, even though scenes in his mind's eye refused to go down on canvas. After a couple of hours of work he would go for another walk — this time to check up on the art dealers, poke around in antique stores or shop for new carpets. In his study, he had so many oriental rugs that they were laid one upon another. Doll and Richards the picture dealers "pricked up their ears" when they heard the tap of his light cane on their stairs, Susan Hale said. Sometimes Tom found it a good idea to stop in at a favorite confectioner's for a cream cake on the way home.

One of Tom Appleton's greatest pleasures, next to seeing old friends, was hearing from them. In 1877, a letter came, headed Lisbon and dated January 18. The stationery was engraved with a capital E, drawn as though it were a flowering branch and having a crown perched on it, rather like a hat on a rack. The letter was eight pages long, the last page cross-hatched, and it was from Elise Hensler, who was once a young singer and Tom's protégée and who was now almost a queen.[10]

Back in 1857, Tom had told his father about it. Elise was singing at the Newport Casino that year, and Tom thought her voice was wonderful. Although billed as an American, Elise lived with her elderly German father in New York, helping to support the younger children. Her father had been a musician, her mother was no longer living. After her engagement at the Newport Casino, she got a part in opera, but only at the end of the season. Tom went to New York, got hold of Sam Ward and his cousins the "Chanlers and Winthrop" who "agreed to take a box and hit her with bouquets." They didn't know Elise as yet but Tom said they would "gladly lend themselves to a pretty girl's debut." Next, he went around to the newspapers and offered the reporters a champagne supper party. Tom told his father that "the papers were disposed to speak well of Elise." He realized that the town was thinning out, but he thought they would have something of a house.

They had a house, all right, but the leading tenor was jealous of all the attention paid to Elise and refused to come out on the opera house balcony and sing her a serenade. A crowd had gathered in the street to hear this and there was "something of a riot," Tom said. "Miss H was vexed but took it very well." The supper party had to be given up because of the street disturbance but Tom distributed bottles of champagne to the gentlemen of the press. The tenor was mollified and Elise got her serenade next day.

Later, Elise went to Paris where she sang in opera. She reminded Tom of the time she had spent with him in his Paris apartment, "in the days of Nathalie." Tom was beginning a portrait, she said.

In 1869, she married Ferdinand, former king of Portugal who, in that same year, accepted the crown of Spain. He made Elise countess of Edlar, hence the crown on her letter-head.

In 1877 the Countess Elise had just been reading Tom Appleton's *Nile Journey* and wrote to tell him how much she liked it. The book made her laugh and she remembered the old days in Paris. She envied him his freedom to travel where he pleased and do as he liked.

"All you Americans are so different to the Europeans. You are such dear, good-hearted people, a thing which is not known generally here," Elise said. But she was happy with the king — he was very good to her.

Tom Appleton's most intimate friend for many years, now, was his brother-in-law, Henry Longfellow. During the autumn of 1881, Longfellow had what they called a violent attack of vertigo, followed by nervous prostration. At first he could not leave his room but gradually recovered. Tom's phaeton was often at his door. The finest wines that Tom could lay his hands on were shared. In March, 1882, Longfellow walked up and down his deep piazzas which had been such a satisfaction to Fanny when the mud of springtime in New England kept her from the garden. Although carefully wrapped, Henry caught cold. Among Tom Appleton's papers was a card, evidently a note to someone he never sent. "Our dear poet died today at 3:10," the note said. A pencil addition read, "Longfellow died Friday afternoon, 24 March, 1882." To Oliver Wendell Holmes, Tom wrote, "There will be a private service tomorrow at Mr. Longfellow's house, at 3 P.M. Private but a few friends are invited. Please come to that. Also later there will be at Appleton Chapel a memorial service for the general world of admirers and friends." [11]

Found among Longfellow's papers, but never published until after his death, was a sonnet concerning Fanny Appleton Longfellow.[12] It was written July 10, 1879, after Longfellow had seen a book of Western scenes containing a photograph of a glacier, high on a cliff — the snow forming a cross. Longfellow's poem was:

THE CROSS OF SNOW

In the long, sleepless watches of the night,
*   A gentle face — the face of one long dead —*
*   Looks at me from the wall, where round its head*
*   The night-lamp casts a halo of pure light.*
Here in this room she died; and soul more white
*   Never through martyrdom of fire was led*
*   To its repose; nor can in books be read*
*   The legend of a life more benedight.*

There is a mountain in the distant West,
That, sun-defying, in its deep ravines
Displays a cross of snow upon its side.
Such is the cross I wear upon my breast
These eighteen years, through all the changing scenes
And seasons, changeless since the day she died.

The poem was put away in Longfellow's desk. Perhaps Tom Appleton never saw it. But, as he had done when he lost his sister, he tried to look after the children. Alice went to study at Newnham College, Cambridge, England. She must be sure to give his love to Aunt Mary and tell her how good the bloaters were that she had sent him. Tom would be anxious about Charley, who was a daring sailor. One summer, Charley sailed as far out as St. Kitts in the *Alice* when a storm struck. He made Bermuda however where he was all battened down for several days. The married Longfellows, Ernest and Edith, were less on Tom's mind although he loved them all. Edith had married Richard Henry Dana, III, and lived at Longfellow House, her children being the only grandchildren Longfellow knew before his death.

Tom liked to go to Washington in the spring — coming home by way of New York. One of his young friends noted that he was growing deaf, although he still enjoyed the theater. She asked sympathetically if ear treatment might help — was it wax in his ears? "Not wax, my dear, but wane," he told her.

Tom was in New York, on his way home, in April, 1884, when a cold settled in his chest. It rapidly developed into pneumonia. "Tom Appleton alone in New York!" exclaimed Julia Ward Howe. But Tom was not alone. His friends at his favorite hotel notified the Longfellows of his dangerous illness. They came and found him cheerful although aware that he was not going to live. "How interesting all this is," he said. "It will be a new experience."

Thomas Gold Appleton died in New York on April 17, 1884. His good friend Oliver Wendell Holmes wrote about him in the *Atlantic Monthly*.[13]

"How sad it is to see his name stretched out at full length and shrouded with all its syllables! For Westminster Abbey did not better know Ben Jonson by his shortened appellation than Boston knew our dear familiar friend, Tom Appleton. . . . The city seems grayer and older since he left us, the cold spring wind coming from the bay, harsher and more unfriendly . . .

"I once heard him say that all we are and do is invisibly photographed and that Heaven keeps the negatives. If all that he said worth recollecting was set down by a recording angel, the Celestial scribe must have filled many of his great folios and found occasion to smile . . ."

ACKNOWLEDGMENTS

DURING THE PERIOD of early American industry, of stage-coach and carriage, early railroads, sailing ships and the first Cunarders, the Appletons were diarists and letter-writers to an astonishing degree. The manuscripts on which this book is based are preserved in several important collections in the Boston area.

Perhaps the largest collection is at Longfellow House, Cambridge, Massachusetts. I want to thank Thomas H. de Valcourt, curator, for his kind permission to use these papers; for information from his great store of knowledge about Cambridge friends of Longfellow and for providing space where my husband and I could work at odd hours. I am grateful to Frank Buda, Mr. de Valcourt's assistant, whose knowledge of the collection is extensive and whose helpfulness to us was superb.

At the Massachusetts Historical Society, there is another large collection of Appleton manuscripts and I am most grateful to Stephen T. Riley, director, for permission to work with letters to and from Thomas Gold Appleton and his father, those among the Appleton brothers and others.

It would have been impossible to present William Appleton as a human being without the use of his diary. I want to thank the Rt. Rev. Frederic C. Lawrence for permission not only to quote from this diary but for the loan of this rare book and use of pictures of the William Appletons. Mrs. Marian Lawrence Peabody also encouraged me in my research, her genealogical chart being of great service. I want to thank Dr. Richard W. Dwight, also an Appleton, for his help and interest in my work. I am grateful to Mrs. William Appleton Lawrence, who arranged for me to see family paintings.

At Baker Library, Harvard Business School, are letter books containing correspondence between William Appleton and Mary Ann Cutler Appleton soon after their marriage. I want to thank Robert Lovett, curator of manuscripts, and his assistant Mrs. Eleanor Bishop for their help in connection with this valuable material.

Letters from Thomas Gold Appleton to his friend Charles Eliot Norton are at Houghton Library, Harvard University, and I am grateful for Miss Carolyn Jakeman's kind assistance. I want to thank Clark A. Elliott, assistant curator, Harvard Archives, for information about the short existence of the original Appleton Chapel. Charles Norton, bursar, and Daniel Siegenthaler, librarian, of the Episcopal Theological School, were most helpful.

Edward Wagenknecht, my friend for twenty years, has engaged in extensive research at Longfellow House. Once more, he has generously shared with me his knowledge of the Longfellow family and has urged me to use material he has gathered for his own work. I am most grateful.

It would hardly be possible to write about Beacon Street without the help of Walter Muir Whitehill and David McKibbin of the Boston Athenaeum. I want to thank them both for information and suggestions as to source material.

I am particularly grateful to Mrs. Frederick Sayford Bacon for her encouragement, even before this book was begun. Her knowledge of 39 Beacon Street, as the former president of the Women's City Club of Boston, is extensive, and her original research on Fanny Appleton Longfellow's wedding was most useful. Her friend and mine, Mrs. Abigail Washburn, also provided information about the wedding. Other friends have found material for me: Mrs. Thomas Clark Howard, concerning Beacon Hill; Mrs. Charles Darrow Gowing about Elise Hensler, the singer who was almost queen. Professor and Mrs. Harold Fisher most kindly sent me excerpts from letters of Mrs. Samuel Appleton.

Other sources of information are libraries, historical societies and associations. Everywhere I have met helpful people: at the Boston Public Library, department of Rare Books and Manuscripts, James Lawton, curator of manscripts; Dartmouth College, Archives Department, Baker Memorial Library, Kenneth C. Cramer, archivist; New York Public Library, Timothy F. Beard, Mrs. Elizabeth E. Ross; Yale University, Sterling Library, Beinecke Rare Book Library, Art Library; Pittsfield Public Library, Mrs. Harold W. Edwards; the Berkshire County Historical Society, Pittsfield, Mass., Donald Smith; Forbes Library, Northampton, Mass., Stanley Greenberg, Miss Mary Blake; Ferguson Library, Stamford, Conn., Mrs. Doris Goodlett; Darien Free Library Association, Darien, Conn., Mrs. Lois Keeler; Kirkland House, Harvard University, Arthur Smithies, master; Appleton Academy, New Ipswich, N.H., Charles David Markham, headmaster; New Ipswich Historical Society, Miss Gratia Eagleson; Ipswich Historical Society, Ipswich, Mass.; New Haven Colony Historical Society, New Haven, Conn.; Darien Historical Society, Darien, Conn.; New Canaan Historical Society, New Canaan, Conn.

CHAPTER NOTES

ONE. THE DELECTABLE PART OF TOWN

1. Nathan Appleton to his brother Samuel, June 17, 1809; to his brother Eben, July 20, 1809; to his father-in-law, Thomas Gold, June 26, 1809. Massachusetts Historical Society, hereinafter referred to as Mass. Hist. Soc.
2. James Colburn built numbers 54 and 55 Beacon Street in 1806, and Asher Benjamin built his own house, number 58 Beacon, that same year. In *Beacon Street, Its Ancient Pastures and Early Mansions* (Boston, Houghton Mifflin, 1925), Allen Chamberlain ascribes the Colburn and Appleton houses to Benjamin. In *Greek Revival Architecture in America* (Toronto, Oxford Press, 1944), Talbot Hamlin ascribes these houses to Peter Banner, an English architect in Boston between 1805 and 1822, on the ground that Banner's style was attenuated in comparison with Asher Benjamin's delicacy.
3. Unless otherwise noted, all correspondence between the Appleton brothers, Samuel, Nathan and Eben, is in Mass. Hist. Soc.
4. Information concerning the architecture of 39 Beacon Street, and Alexander Parris, architect, is given in an article by Dorothy Richards Pesce, Women's City Club Historian, in the Ninth Antiques Show Catalogue of the Women's City Club of Boston. Material previously gathered by the club was kindly supplied by Mrs. Frederick Sayford Bacon, former president. See also "Alexander Parris, 1780–1852" in the *Dictionary of American Biography*, hereinafter referred to as *D.A.B.*, which says, "The David Sears house, on Beacon Street, now altered and used as the Somerset Club, is dated by a stone in the basement as 1816; Parris' name appears as architect."
5. For a map showing Boston as the Appletons first knew it, and for further information, see *Boston, a Topographical History*, by Walter Muir Whitehill (Cambridge, Mass., Harvard Univ. Press, 1959).
6. First-person comments by William Appleton are from *Selections from the Diaries of William Appleton, 1786–1862*, edited by Susan M. Loring, a grand-daughter, privately printed, 1922, hereinafter called *Diaries of William Appleton*, Loring. A copy of this invaluable book was lent me by the Rt. Rev. Frederic C. Lawrence.
7. Samuel Appleton's letter to the citizens of Peterborough (sometimes spelled Peterboro) on the occasion of their centennial jubilee, Oct. 22, 1839.

8. *Memoir of the Hon. Nathan Appleton, LL.D. Prepared Agreeably to a Resolution of the Massachusetts Historical Society by Robert C. Winthrop, 1861,* hereinafter referred to as Nathan, *Memoir.*

TWO. FIRST SAMUEL

1. Appleton genealogies are by Isaac Appleton Jewett, compiled for his uncle, Samuel Appleton, and by William Sumner Appleton, son of Nathan Appleton. William Sumner Appleton made corrections in the earlier work of his cousin, Isaac Appleton Jewett, and Frank T. Waters, who wrote genealogical notes for the New England Historical and Genealogical Register, corrected William Sumner Appleton's genealogy.
2. *The Old Bay Road from Saltonstall's Brook to Samuel Appleton's Farm and a Genealogy of the Ipswich Descendants,* by Frank T. Waters, published by the Ipswich Historical Society, Salem Press, 1907, provides maps and early Ipswich records. *The History of Ipswich, Essex and Hamilton,* by Joseph B. Felt, ed. of 1934, tells of the Appletons in military service; the Ipswich Agawam Indians; wolves and "sufficient hounds."
3. *The History of New Ipswich, 1736–1852,* compiled and edited by Charles Henry Chandler with the assistance of Sarah Fiske Lee, contains Appleton material as well as historical events.
4. *Mason Bicentennial, 1768–1968,* "In commemoration of the two hundredth anniversary of the incorporation of Mason, New Hampshire," Elizabeth Orton Jones, editor, copyright by Mason Historical Society, tells of the Mason Grant. My copy of Belknap's *History of New Hampshire,* Dover, 1784, chap. IV synopsis, ends with the words, "Mason discouraged." This account of New Hampshire grants and claims gives ample reason for the statement.
5. New Ipswich Academy, now Appleton Academy, is discussed in *Old New England Academies Founded Before 1826,* by Harriet Webster Marr (New York, Comet Press, 1959).
6. At Appleton Academy, Charles David Markham, headmaster, was most helpful. The present building is the fourth on the site, the others having burned. I felt that Samuel Appleton would be proud of his academy today. It overlooks the village green, once the parade ground. Fine Colonial houses surround the green.
7. At the New Ipswich Historical Society, Miss Gratia Eagleson gave careful directions so that my husband and I could locate the Isaac Appleton farm, on what is now Appleton Street, a dead-end country road leading off the road to Peterboro. Records say that Deacon Isaac's house was "about one hundred rods southeast of the site of his later residence." A "later residence" but an old house was in the process of restoration. At the end of the road were small fields surrounded by hills. Boys were herding some cows. On the side of a steep hill across the Peterboro Road and a good distance away, is the primary schoolhouse, now remodeled beyond recognition.
8. In *The New American Guide Series, Maine* (Boston, Houghton Mifflin, 2nd ed., 1969), the village of Appleton is described: population, 672, "residents live off blueberries, logs and poultry . . ."

THREE. THE YOUNG MERCHANTS

1. Nathan, *Memoir.*
2. A copy of *The West Indian* by Richard Cumberland and of *The Busy Body* by Mrs. Centlivre were supplied through library loan by Mrs. Lois Keeler, reference librarian, Darien Library Association. The Nathan Appleton children, in their letters, sometimes referred to an acquaintance by the name "Isabenda." Their father would know whom they meant — some girl like Isabenda, daughter of Sir

Jealous, whose parents were trying to find a rich husband for her. There must have been a copy of *The Busy Body* at 34 Beacon Street.

3. Nathan Appleton diaries for 1802 and 1804 and business letters from Nathan to his brothers, Mass. Hist. Soc.

4. The farm industry of preparing pearl ash and potash is clearly described in *Vermont Tradition*, by Dorothy Canfield Fisher (Boston, Little, Brown, 1953). The expression, "they had to rake and scrape" is my own conclusion.

FOUR. NATHAN AND MARIA THERESA

1. Letters from and to Maria Theresa Gold and her father are at the Longfellow House.

2. *America's First Hamlet*, by Grace Overmeyer (New York, New York Univ. Press, 1957). See also *D.A.B.*

3. *Alonzo and Melissa, a Tale*, by Isaac Mitchell, first appeared in installments in the *Political Barometer*, Poughkeepsie, N. Y. in 1804. It was never copyrighted by the author but, under slightly different titles and sub-titles and in shortened forms, it was published at least eleven times. See *The Sentimental Novel in America, 1789–1860*, by Herbert Brown (Durham, N.C., Duke Univ. Press, 1940).

4. The name Gold is also spelled Gould. Jay Gould of New York, railroad financier, was the third cousin, once removed, of Maria Theresa Gold.

5. Across the Cornwall, Conn., covered bridge and high on the hillsides facing west are lands once owned by the Gold family. The Rev. Hezekiah Gold was born in Stratford, Conn., January 18, 1731, and died in Cornwall May 30, 1790. He graduated from Yale in the class of 1751. Sarah Sedgwick, his first wife, was the daughter of Deacon Benjamin Sedgwick. She died at the age of twenty-seven, leaving five sons. Thomas Gold of Pittsfield was the oldest of them. *Historical Records of the Town of Cornwall*, by Theodore S. Gold and Gen. John Sedgwick (Hartford, Hartford Press, 1904).

6. Thomas Gold was graduated from Yale in 1778 and set himself up as a lawyer in Pittsfield, Mass. He married Martha Marsh, born in Dalton, Mass., in 1765. According to her obituary in the *New York Observer*, Nov., 1842, "she possessed great beauty of person and the highest accomplishments of the day . . ."

7. Maria Theresa descended the famous stairs as a bride April 13, 1806; Eliza, or Elizabeth Sedgwick Gold, January 19, 1812; Frances Jeanette, December 24, 1818; Caroline Wolcott Gold, July 15, 1818, and Sarah Williams Gold, January 29, 1820.

FIVE. MR. MADISON'S WAR

1. Baedeker's *Great Britain*, 1906 ed.

2. *The Lowells and their Seven Worlds*, by Ferris Greenslet (Boston, Houghton Mifflin, 1946).

3. Maria Theresa to her father, Longfellow House.

4. After her marriage on Jan. 10, 1812, to Charles M. Lee of Utica, Eliza and her husband went to live in Rochester, New York, where Eliza died in 1822.

5. Accounts of the building of the *Constitution* and of affairs in Boston in 1812 are from *The Memorial History of Boston*, edited by Justin Winsor, 1883, vol. III, "Boston Soldiery in War and Peace," article by General Francis W. Palfrey.

6. "Eliza Cabot . . . came breathless with haste into our house and asked my mother if she knew why the bells were ringing . . ." *Life of Josiah Quincy of Massachusetts* by his son, Edmund Quincy (Boston, Ticknor and Fields, 1867), p. 360.

7. An account of the early Cabot family mill is in the *History and Genealogy of the Cabot Family*, by Thomas Vernon Briggs (Boston, Goodspeed, 1927).

SIX. WILLIAM AND MARY ANN

1. James Cutler, letter to Jonathon Amory, 1795. Baker Library, Harvard Business School.
2. Gentlemen "seriously gay," Maria to her father, Thomas Gold, Longfellow House.
3. William's complaint of the bowels, letter, January 21, 1816, and letters following, in Baker Library.
4. Letters to and by Mary Ann Cutler are from letter books in the F. Gordon Dexter papers, Baker Library.

SEVEN. SAMUEL AND AUNT SAM

1. The identification of Mary Lekain Gore Appleton presents a genealogical puzzle, solved with the help of staff at the Genealogy and Local History Room of the New York Public Library. There were two John Gores who were first cousins who died the same year, 1817. Both had wives named Mary. John Gore, son of Samuel and Mary Pierce Gore and nephew of Governor Christopher Gore, was born in Boston June 27, 1780. He married Mary Lecain (or Lekain) of Boston in Albany, New York in 1804, and he died October 23, 1817. Mary Lekain Gore married Samuel Appleton in Boston before November 18, 1818.
2. The real-estate transactions of Uriah Cotting are from *The Memorial History of Boston*, vol. IV, p. 33 and note 5; p. 157, note 1.
3. "Long as for him who works for debt the day," Alexander Pope, *Imitations of Horace*, "Epilogue to the Satires," Epistle I, Book I.
4. Aunt Sam's May Day party, May 5, 1835, described by Fanny Appleton to Susan Benjamin, Longfellow House.
5. Horatio Greenough (Sept. 6, 1805–Dec. 18, 1852) *D.A.B.* Greenough was born in Boston, his father a wealthy merchant whom the Appletons knew well. This fourth of eleven children showed a talent for sculpture, much to his father's dismay. He was required to go to Harvard before being allowed to study art in Rome but received his diploma in 1825, after he had arrived in Europe. Within the year, however, malaria, or "Roman fever" caused him to come home. He recovered and went back to Rome in 1828, in the meantime "busting" Samuel Appleton as a bald-headed, long-faced gentleman, scowling just as Fanny said. *White Silence*, by Sylvia E. Crane (Coral Gables, Fla., Univ. of Miami Press, 1972), includes a photograph of this bust.

   In Longfellow's diary, Longfellow House, I found a comment dated December 19, 1852. "Hear that Horatio Greenough died yesterday at the Insane Hospital, Charlestown. What a gloomy end! He was a noble, gallant fellow, so full of life!"
6. In the Akers bust, Samuel Appleton is square-headed with a jaw like a cave man. I have seen three examples, two in New Ipswich and one at Longfellow House. There may be more but which is the original and which the copy seems not of record.

   Paul Benjamin Akers was born in Saccarappa, Me., in 1825. He grew up in Salmon Falls, Me., the son of a wood turner. Akers was a dreamy fellow called "St. Paul" by his schoolmates. According to *D.A.B.* Akers came to Boston in 1849 to learn plaster casting and returned to Portland, Me., where he had been a printer. The *Encyclopedia Americana* indicates that Longfellow sat to him in Portland but Fanny Appleton Longfellow makes it clear that the young man from Maine was her guest in Cambridge when she took him to see Aunt Sam. Akers would, of course, take his clay busts back to Portland to work on them in the studio he had opened there.

EIGHT BUILDING A CITY

1. The material for this chapter is from Nathan Appleton's first-person account: *The Introduction of the Power Loom and Origin of Lowell* printed for the Proprietors of the Locks and Canals on Merrimack River, *1858.*
2. In wooden two-story cottages painted white, the matron had a room and a parlor of her own on the ground floor. The smaller cottages had no dining room or kitchen. The girls ate in a big dining room in one of the brick dormitories. Almost always there was a "cottage piano" in the parlor, a luxury that astonished Mr. Dickens. *Mill and Mansion, A Study of Architecture and Society in Lowell, Massachusetts, 1820–1865,* by John Coolidge (New York, Columbia Univ. Press, 1942), shows a floor plan of a cottage, *circa* 1850.
3. No sooner was the Episcopal church built than churches of other denominations began to go up. Funds were solicited among Baptists and Congregationalists for instance — lest girls be led astray into the fold of a different creed.
4. The Merrimack Valley Museum, North Andover, Mass., contains a remarkable collection of textile machinery well worth a visit. Woolen textile machinery is featured. At Old Sturbridge Village, Sturbridge, Mass., an early fulling machine is in actual operation.
5. Dr. Samuel L. Dana, *D.A.B.*
6. This flattering description of Lowell is from Old Residents Historical Association, Lowell, Mass. See also *The Saco-Lowell Shops, Textile Machinery Building in New England, 1813–1949,* by George Sweet Gibb (Cambridge, Mass., Harvard Univ. Press, 1950), p. 744, note 15.
7. Alexander Parris: *D.A.B.* See also chap. 1, note 4.
8. Nathan Appleton to Richard Walsh, Mass. Hist. Soc.
9. Extracts from the *Autobiography of Mrs. Thomas Botts* (Isabella Batchelder) copied for William Sumner Appleton, 1914.
10. George Washington Whistler, *D.A.B.*
11. Caroline Appleton to Fanny Longfellow, Longfellow House.
12. Charles Dickens: *American Notes* (my ed., London, Chapman and Hall, n.d.).

NINE. GROWING UP ON BEACON HILL

1. *Letters and Recollections of John Murray Forbes,* edited by his daughter, Sarah Forbes Hughes (Boston, Houghton Mifflin, 1900). Vol. 1 contains an account of Croneytown and mentions Tom Appleton's prowess with bow and arrow.
2. Tom Appleton's early letters to his father, Mass. Hist. Soc. Maria Appleton and Fanny to Tom, Longfellow House.
3. George Bancroft's letters to Nathan Appleton concerning Tom are almost identical with the letters written by Bancroft to Samuel Ward, the banker, concerning young Sam. In both cases Bancroft suggested that the boys stay longer in his school and apply themselves to Greek. The two boys were lifelong friends.
4. My husband and I went to Northampton, Mass., in the hope of finding a picture of Round Hill School in the early days. At the Northampton Historical Society, Mr. Everett W. MacRae was most helpful, and we saw engravings of Round Hill School after it was greatly enlarged to become a health resort. At the Forbes Library, however, Miss Mary Blake of the Art Department found us an early print which shows buildings that are certainly more impressive than anything described by either Tom Appleton or his brother Charles. There are vegetable gardens such as the Appleton boys mentioned, while in the foreground are fruit trees which might be those Cogswell and Bancroft planted as an experiment. At first glance, the signature looks like "P. G., Jr." but the dedication certainly sounds like one that Francis Graeter might have composed to please Bancroft

and Cogswell. A magnifying glass brings out a bar on the supposed *P*, making it an *F*. While at Northampton, my husband and I drove along Round Hill Road where the Clarke School for the Deaf now stands, approximately on the site of the Round Hill School. The slope of the hill is fully as steep as is shown in the early print, the views of the Mt. Holyoke Range and the Connecticut River as fine as Round Hill students always remembered.

5. Tom's walk with Graeter is told in *Life and Letters of Thomas Gold Appleton*, prepared by Susan Hale (New York, D. Appleton, 1885), hereinafter referred to as *Life and Letters*, Hale.

6. For William Russell and Elizabeth Peabody's school, see my book, *The Peabody Sisters of Salem* (Boston, Little, Brown, 1950). Correspondence, Mary and Elizabeth Peabody to and from Mrs. Russell and others, formerly Horace Mann private collection, now at Berg Collection, New York Public Library.

7. Fanny's school exercises, letters to Charles Appleton, Longfellow House. Tom and Charles' letters to their father, Mass. Hist. Soc.

TEN. *CONGRESSMAN NATHAN APPLETON*

1. Nathan's indignation at being put on the Invalid Pensions Committee and other first-person comments, Nathan, *Memoirs*.

2. The account of McDuffie's style is from *The Age of Jackson*, by Arthur M. Schlesinger, Jr., (Boston, Little, Brown, 1950) who quotes from the *Portland Daily Advertiser*, p. 95, note 21.

3. The *Boston Daily Advertiser*, Jan. 30, 1832, Beinecke Library, Yale Univ.

4. Elias Boudinot, *D.A.B.* Fanny's letter, Longfellow House.

5. A Buccleuch was a woman's cape, apparently named for the Scottish border chieftain, Sir Walter Scott of Branxholm and Buccleuch, featured in *The Lay of the Last Minstrel*. The Appleton girls must have found this a romantic name for a garment.

6. Houston trial, see Samuel Houston, *D.A.B.*

7. Fanny and Mary's letters, Longfellow House.

8. Franz (or Francis) Lieber, 1800–1872, according to *D.A.B.*

9. Charles to his father, June 27, 1832, Mass. Hist. Soc.

10. Richard Henry Wilde, 1789–1847 is described as a poet, congressman, and Italian scholar, in *D.A.B.* He and Nathan Appleton became friends and they were to meet again in Italy.

11. The details of Dr. Warren's treatments are from Fanny Appleton's diary, Feb. 11, 1833, Longfellow House. "She kept her eyes anxiously fixed on the clock. . . . Father arrived much agitated and fatigued . . ."

ELEVEN. *FIRST JOURNEY*

1. Charles to his sisters, Feb. 26, 1833, Longfellow House.

2. Opinion of Tom's departure as "very sudden and unwelcome to us," Appleton diary, Mary's handwriting, Friday, Mar. 29, 1833, Longfellow House.

3. Nathan's advice to his son Thomas, Mass. Hist. Soc.

4. Combined diary, Fanny and Mary, Longfellow House. Where possible, I have indicated which girl wrote passages quoted.

5. Fanny said these paintings were by Mrs. Minot. Mr. David McKibbin very kindly searched the Boston Athenaeum records for me, on the chance that a Mrs. Minot had an exhibition there which Fanny and Mary might have seen. There was no such reference. The *Dictionary of Artists in America, 1564–1860*, New York Historical Society gives Minot — "painter of two views of Niagara Falls, dated 1818" Belknap Collection. The *Dictionnaire des Paintres, Sculpteurs, Dessinateurs et Graveurs* lists "Minot, Blanche, nature painter."

6. Mary and Fanny's diary is so explicit that my husband and I were able to mark maps and follow their route southward from Montpelier. We could not locate all the waterfalls, to be sure, but the "Gulph Road" was beautiful and we were rewarded for leaving the super-highway.

TWELVE. "YOU WILL HAVE BUT THREE CHILDREN"

1. *Life and Letters*, Hale.
2. Nathan Appleton and Charles' letters to Tom and his replies are from the Mass. Hist. Soc. unless otherwise noted.
3. Fanny and Mary's letters to Tom and to their friends, Longfellow House.
4. *Mrs. Longfellow, Selected Letters and Journals of Fanny Appleton Longfellow*, edited by Edward Wagenknecht (New York, Longmans, Green, 1956), are also from the Longfellow House and I am grateful to Professor Wagenknecht for his permission to quote. Wherever possible, I have chosen material not previously published. Dr. Wagenknecht's book will be referred to as *Mrs. Longfellow*, Wagenknecht.
5. William Appleton's part in the bank crisis is covered in his diary and that of Nathan in Nathan, *Memoir*. Of value also is *A Century of Banking in New York*, by Henry Wysham Lanier (New York, Gilliss, 1922), hereinafter called *A Century of Banking*, Lanier.
6. Fanny's first meeting with Fanny Kemble, *Mrs. Longfellow*, Wagenknecht.
7. *Further Records*, by Frances Ann Kemble (New York, Holt, 1891).
8. The following account, Fanny to Robert Apthorp, *Mrs. Longfellow*, Wagenknecht.

THIRTEEN. EUROPE BY SAILING SHIP

1. Fanny Appleton's journal of her first ocean voyage, unpublished journal, Longfellow House.
2. The Baron, see *Life and Letters*, Hale.
3. Mrs. Welles, see *Famous Families of Massachusetts*, by Mary Caroline Crawford (Boston, Little, Brown, 1930).
4. Fanny Appleton's sketch books, and some of Tom's, Longfellow House.
5. Richard Henry Wilde, see note 10, chap. 10.
6. A Longfellow passport gives his height as 5 feet 8 inches, eyes blue, nose large, mouth medium, complexion fair, face oval.
7. Death of William, Fanny Appleton's diary, Longfellow House and *Mrs. Longfellow*, Wagenknecht.

FOURTEEN. APPLETONS AT THE COURTS OF KINGS

1. *Longfellow: A Full-Length Portrait*, by Edward Wagenknecht (New York, Longmans, Green, 1955), is the source of information concerning not only Longfellow but his family as well. Hereinafter referred to as *Longfellow*, Wagenknecht.
2. *The Diary of Clara Crowninshield, A European Tour with Longfellow, 1835–1836*, edited by Andrew Hilen (Seattle, Univ. of Washington Press, 1956).
3. General Lewis Cass, 1782–1866, after five years in Jackson's cabinet, left because of ill health and was sent to France as minister in October, 1836. *D.A.B.*
4. Fanny to Emmeline Austin, Jan. 7, 1837, Fanny Appleton's journal, Longfellow House.
5. John Crosby flirtation, Lizzie Bryant to Fanny Appleton, Feb. 21, 1837, Longfellow House.
6. In Fanny Appleton's diaries she refers to "Attaché Ledyard." His first name was Henry.

7. Byron on foreign mistresses, *La Vie de Byron*, André Maurois (Paris, Grasset, 1930).
8. Fanny copied out the "Dramatic Ode," Longfellow House; later, she wrote that the grippe had "nullified Mary's chances of immortalization," Feb. 23, 1837, Fanny's diary, Longfellow House.
9. Comments on Longfellow by the William Appleton family, Baker Library, Harvard.
10. News from Boston about the financial situation is from Lizzie Bryant to Fanny, Boston, June 30, 1837, Longfellow House.

FIFTEEN. TWO BRIDES

1. *Diaries of William Appleton*, Loring.
2. *A Century of Banking*, Lanier, p. 204.
3. *The Presidency, A Pictorial History of the Presidential Elections from Washington to Truman*, by Stefan Lorant (New York, MacMillan, 1951), hereinafter referred to as *The Presidency*, Lorant. Bank crisis, p. 148.
4. *Diaries of William Appleton*, Loring.
5. *Cambridge Sketches*, by Frank Preston Stearns (New York, Lippincott, 1905) has it that Tom's lawyer friend was Wendell Phillips.
6. Mrs. Butler's costume, Fanny to Emmeline, Longfellow House. Also, *Records of Later Life*, Fanny Kemble.
7. Otis Collection, Mass. Hist. Soc.
8. Mary to the Liebers, on the new Mrs. Appleton, Longfellow House.
9. *Speak for Yourself, Daniel, A Life of Webster in his Own Words*, edited by Walker Lewis, (Boston, Houghton Mifflin, 1909), note p. 276 refers to Samuel Appleton Appleton and Webster's reasons for wanting an English wedding. Samuel Appleton Appleton's daughter Caroline married Newbold Edgar and after his death she married Jerome Napoleon Bonaparte in 1871. *Appleton Genealogy* by W. S. Appleton, and *The Bonapartes in America* by Clarence E. McCartney and Gordon Dorrance (Philadelphia, Dorrance, 1939).
10. Description of Mackintosh, Fanny to Emmeline Austin, July, 1839, Longfellow House.
11. Sedg'ick, Sedg'ick, from *The Happy Profession*, by Ellery Sedgwick (Boston, Atlantic, 1946).
12. Fanny to Emmeline Austin, Longfellow House.

SIXTEEN. THE COURTSHIP OF HENRY LONGFELLOW

1. The Letters of Henry Wadsworth Longfellow, Andrew Hilen, editor (Cambridge, Mass., Harvard Univ. Press, 1966), vols. I and II, contain every letter at Longfellow House as far as December 29, 1843. Hereinafter referred to as *Letters, Longfellow*, Hilen. The notes in Prof. Hilen's book are also of great value. Letters concerning Fanny Appleton begin with vol. II.
2. *Longfellow*, Wagenknecht. Also *Letters, Longfellow*, Hilen, vol. II, p. 31, note 3.
3. *Longfellow*, Wagenknecht; *Letters, Longfellow*, Hilen, vol. II.
4. *Hyperion, a Romance*, by Henry Wadsworth Longfellow, 1839.
5. Henry and Matilda Cass Ledyard's son Henry Brockholst Ledyard, was born in Paris, 1844, graduated at West Point, became an engineer and eventually president of the Michigan Central Railroad. *Who's Who in America*, 1912–13.
6. Eliza Lee Cabot Follen, 1787–1860, and Charles Follen, 1796–1840. *D.A.B.*
7. Fanny to Tom about Washington, D.C., a series of letters beginning about January 13, 1840; also Fanny to Emmeline Austin, Jan. 5, 1840, Longfellow House.
8. Fanny to Mary about "Big Daniel," Oct. 3, 1840, Longfellow House.

9. Fanny to Jewett, May 9, 1840, Longfellow House.
10. James Winthrop Andrews to Fanny Appleton, Feb. 10, 1841, Longfellow House.

SEVENTEEN. TO HIM WHO WAITS

1. Fanny to Emmeline Austin, May 2, 1844; to her father, May 2, 1844; letters "at sea," Longfellow House.
2. The location of Mary's house is described in *Baedeker's Handbook for London*, 1905 ed., p. 313.
3. Fanny headed her letters, "St. Catherine's, London." Those concerning Mary's health and Robert Mackintosh's prospects are to her father, as indicated in text. Emmeline Austin was her other correspondent. All letters, Longfellow House.
4. Aunt Sam wrote to Fanny, July 16, 1841, to say that "a few confidential remarks from Harriet led me to think it expedient to hint to you that any news I may have communicated to you may not change Mary's intentions of passing the winter in Boston . . . she begged me not to mention her situation. . . . Harriet has arranged all the rooms in her own mind . . ."
5. *The Presidency*, Lorant, quotation from the *Philadelphia Ledger*, p. 169.
6. Nathan, *Memoir*.
7. Tom to his father, Cousin C. Gold, etc., June 29, 1842. Mass. Hist. Soc.
8. Their romance is told in my book, *Three Saints and a Sinner*, (Boston, Little, Brown, 1956).
9. *Longfellow*, Wagenknecht.
10. Tom to Fanny, June 13, 1843, Longfellow House.

EIGHTEEN. CASTLE CRAIGIE

1. Fanny to Matilda Lieber, Longfellow House, June 10, 1843.
2. Longfellow to Henry Cleveland, May 22, 1843, Longfellow House. Also *Letters, Longfellow*, Hilen, vol. II, letter No. 782.
3. Annie Longfellow to Mrs. John M. Poor, Aug. 15, 1843. A copy of this delightful letter was given me by Mrs. Frederick Sayford Bacon, former president of the Women's City Club of Boston.
4. Bills on furniture are at Longfellow House.
5. Fanny to Tom, Catskill Mountain House, Aug. 13, 1843, Longfellow House.
6. Zilpah Wadsworth Longfellow, Fanny's mother-in-law, to her son Samuel, Portland, Oct. 13, 1843, Longfellow House.
7. Fanny told Emmeline Wadsworth of doings in New York, Oct. 14, 1843, Longfellow House.
8. Bills from New York and correspondence between Nathan Appleton and his daughter Fanny concerning carpets, Longfellow House.
9. Mrs. Craigie's friends, the canker worms, *Mrs. Longfellow*, Wagenknecht, p. 99, note 19.
10. Visitors to Longfellow House will recognize Fanny's little French clock in the parlor.

NINETEEN. TOM AND THE SPIRIT RAPPINGS

1. Franz Anton Mesmer, 1733–1815, gave his name to what he called animal magnetism. Tom enjoyed speaking and reading French but he probably preferred *Histoire Abrégée du Magnétisme Animal* rather than anything unabridged.
2. Tom described Allston's picture to Richard Henry Dana, Feb. 2, 1844, and tried to persuade Dana to buy it. Mass. Hist. Soc. His letter to Fanny about the Allston and Sir George "in great spirits," Longfellow House.

3. Sarah Perkins had married Henry Cleveland, one of Longfellow's group of friends called The Five of Clubs. These Perkins young people had wonderful adventures abroad, as related in the Fayerweather Papers, Berg Collection, New York Public Library.

4. At the Public Library, Brattleboro, Vt., my husband and I were given directions to the site of the health resort. A factory usurps part of the river gorge but it is easy to see where Bostonians could have found "water in a thousand ways," as Tom Appleton said.

5. Fanny to Emmeline Austin, hereinafter referred to as Emmeline Austin Wadsworth.

6. It was not only Fanny's advice. As early as Dec. 8, 1849, Longfellow wrote to Tom, "You are going to Paris. That is right, I wish we were going with you." Houghton Library, Harvard Univ.

7. *Life and Letters*, Hale, p. 285 tells of séances in Paris.

8. Alice Goodrich is probably referred to in *The Letters of Elizabeth Barrett Browning*, edited by Frederic G. Kenyon (New York, MacMillan, 1902), vol. II p. 133. Mrs. Browning to Miss Mitford, Aug. 20 and 21, 1853.

9. Tom's letter to Charles Norton, Jan. 11, 1857, Houghton Library, Harvard Univ.

10. Armed with a copy of the deed from Somerset County Courthouse records, and a compass, my husband and I set out to locate the site of Tom's house in Cambridge, "on Phillips Place, (a part of Phillips Place was formerly called Central Court) and bounded and described as follows, viz., northerly by land of Oliver Hastings 156 feet and 4 inches . . ." and so on. We found ourselves near the Episcopal Theological School dormitory which has inscribed on the wall the name of William Appleton. Helpful young men asked if they could direct us to the address we were looking for and were appropriately amused when we explained that it was a house bought in 1857. The school's recently completed library occupies the site of Tom's house and there Mr. David Siegenthaler, librarian, found photographs for us showing Tom's house at the time when construction began. It was not demolished but moved, and is now 170 Brattle Street.

TWENTY. YEARS OF OPTIMISM

1. Harriet Appleton, postscript, telling of Saratoga society, Aug. 7, 1844, Longfellow House.

2. *The Memorial History of Boston*, vol. III, p. 388, tells of the Colonization Society, making it clear that this was a sincere effort to end slavery.

3. William Appleton diaries are quoted concerning his children's parties, except that it was Fanny who called the violinist hired for parties a "scraper," and the family story of William's putting cotton in his ears is a footnote in the diaries.

4. Amos A. Lawrence's ideas upon graduation from Harvard are from *The Lords of the Loom, The Cotton Whigs and the Coming of the Civil War*, by Thomas H. O'Connor (New York, Scribner's, 1968), p. 69.

5. Sarah Appleton Lawrence's early days in Brookline are from *Memories of a Happy Life*, by William Lawrence, D.D., LL.D., Bishop of Massachusetts (Boston, Houghton Mifflin, 1926).

6. *The Autobiography of T. Jefferson Coolidge, 1831–1923* (Boston, Houghton Mifflin, 1923). Copyright Mass. Hist. Soc.

7. Fanny wrote her sister Mary of the death of Samuel Appleton, July 12, 1853, Longfellow House.

8. On May 13, 1834, Nathan Appleton wrote to his son, Tom, that a "marble mausoleum . . . for Uncle Sam, for Mt. Auburn," had arrived by the brig *Byron*. "Uncle Sam's monumental temple is put up at Mount Auburn and is very beautiful," Nathan wrote on July 13, 1854. But very shortly, "Howard Payne, in an article in the *Evening Gazette* made a most ill-natured comment on it — and

learning that it was discovered who wrote it — has made in the paper of last evening a sort of miserable evasion of any general allusions by virtue of an *if*. He is a poor creature and I shall have nothing further to do with him."

"The Will of Samuel Appleton with Remarks by one of the Executors" was printed in 1853. Under Remarks, "He was buried at Mount Auburn, in a lot which he purchased many years ago, on which he had erected a costly monument. . . . When completed it was not in accordance with the simple taste of Mr. Appleton. He even desired to be buried in his tomb under a Boston church, rather than in Mt. Auburn, but city ordinances would not permit it." Appleton papers, Mass. Hist. Soc.

9. Among others, Rufus Choate reminded the Samuel Appleton executors of Mr. Appleton's regard for Dartmouth, his endowment so "munificently begun" and asked for more money. Dartmouth received $15,000 in 1854. In 1909, the Samuel Appleton Fund came to $54,520.32. In 1853, the Boston Athenaeum received a gift, so that in 1907 the Samuel Appleton Fund came to more than $30,000.

TWENTY-ONE. BEACON STREET BALCONIES

1. Mary and Robert Mackintosh's letters from St. Christopher's tell of their life there. Nathan Appleton added his own description in letters to Fanny. And in letters to Annie Longfellow Pierce, and to Jewett, Fanny retailed news by the summer of 1847, Longfellow House.
2. The death of one of Mary's children is from a letter from Fanny to Emmeline Austin Wadsworth, Oct. 18, 1847, Longfellow House.
3. In *Longfellow*, Wagenknecht, George Washington Greene is quoted as saying that no poet was ever so fully recognized in his lifetime as Longfellow. Professor Wagenknecht comments that this was true and mentions that the *New York Ledger* paid $4,000 for *The Hanging of the Crane*.
4. Mrs. Jack Gardner was at the ball, as I told in my book, *Mrs. Jack* (Boston, Little, Brown, 1965). She did not dance with the prince and there is no mention of her in the Appleton letters. That Hatty Appleton was the last living partner of the prince is from *Famous Families of Massachusetts*, by Mary Caroline Crawford (Boston, Little, Brown, 1930).
5. Tom told Norton in 1858 that Longfellow, to amuse himself while recovering from his knee injury, "is growing a Boatswain pair of moustaches to be annexed to his paddle boxes [sideburns]. He looks in the transition stage, but very well, and I think the J. Alden submerged in Capt. Miles Standish may be for a time an improvement." Houghton Library, Harvard Univ. *The Courtship of Miles Standish* was written in 1857. *Longfellow*, Wagenknecht, p. 76.
6. *The Doctrine of Original Sin and the Trinity*, by Nathan Appleton, correspondence between N. Appleton and Rev. W. E. Hygate. Printed in 1859.

TWENTY-TWO. FULL CIRCLE

1. *Diaries of William Appleton*, Loring.
2. *The Autobiography of T. Jefferson Coolidge, 1831–1920.*
3. For the names of the ships owned by Gardner and Coolidge, see *Gardner Memorial*, compiled and arranged by Frank Augustine Gardner, M.D., 1933.
4. On Oct. 22, 1860, Fanny wrote to Tom, "We did not believe you were gone until a gentleman told me he saw you on board. I hope you will enjoy your winter." On Nov. 5, 1860, Fanny had a tenant for Tom's house in Cambridge. "I have packed up in a chest all your linen and in another all the clothes you left (the few moth-eaten ones separately). Also your boots and everything loose about and put them all into your storeroom for which I must get a key made as I cannot find one . . ." Longfellow House.

5. The account of Fanny Longfellow's death is by Cornelius C. Felton to Charles Sumner, Cambridge, July 10, 1861, Houghton Library, Harvard Univ. and from *Mrs. Longfellow*, Wagenknecht. There are quite a few other accounts with varying details. It has also been stated that Nathan Appleton was at his daughter's funeral. Maria Goodwin makes it clear that he did not go. Maria Goodwin to "My dear Friend," Boston, July 21, 1861, Longfellow House.

TWENTY-THREE. BOSTON IN WARTIME

1. Tom to Charles Norton, Tremont House, Boston, Houghton Library, Harvard Univ.
2. "We are expecting the Longfellows down here every day. Tom and he own together the old Wetmore cottage . . ." Letters of John L. Motley, vol. II, p. 176.
3. Tom to Charles Norton, Cambridge, July 27, 1861. Houghton Library, Harvard Univ.
4. See Suffolk County Probate Court records, Boston, Mass., for wills and probate records of Samuel and Nathan Appleton, and Norfolk County Probate Court, Dedham, Mass., for those of William Appleton. A printed copy of Samuel Appleton's will is in Longfellow House.
5. Charles Longfellow's enlistment and the events following are told in *Random Memories*, by Ernest Wadsworth Longfellow (Boston, Houghton Mifflin, 1922).
6. *Famous Families of Massachusetts*, by Mary Caroline Crawford, vol. II p. 171, note 1, tells of Major Curtis' early life.
7. Natey's letters to his mother, Mrs. Harriet Appleton, and hers in return are from the Appleton papers, Mass. Hist. Soc.
8. *Battles and Leaders of the Civil War*, edited by Ned Bradford (New York, Appleton-Century-Crofts, 1956), has been valuable in clarifying the action described in Natey's letters.
9. References to the Somerset Club are from an article written by Captain Nathan Appleton, called "Hermann the Prestidigitator at the Old Somerset Club, 1865–1875," Mass. Hist. Soc.
10. *Some Annals of Nahant*, by Fred A. Wilson (1928), includes a picture of the Nahant cottage Tom Appleton and Henry Longfellow owned. It burned in 1896.
11. *Yachting*, vol. LXIV, Nov., 1938, gives the story of the *Alice*.
12. Ernest Longfellow tells of his life in Paris in *Random Memories*.
13. *The New England Historical and Genealogical Register*, July, 1904, carried the biography of William Sumner Appleton, A.M., LL.B., by William Theophilus Rogers Marvin, A.M.
14. Tom bought his 10 Commonwealth Avenue house lot from Erastus B. Bigelow, March 25, 1863. Suffolk County Courthouse, vol. 825, p. 195. On June 10, 1885, T. G. Appleton's Estate sold 10 Commonwealth Avenue to Ralph M. Pomey. Suffolk County Courthouse, vol. 1680, p. 635.

TWENTY-FOUR. T. G. APPLETON, BOSTON WIT

1. *Three Generations*, by Maud Howe Elliott (Boston, Little, Brown, 1923).
2. *Early Days of the Saturday Club, 1855–1870* by Edward Waldo Emerson, (Boston, Houghton Mifflin, 1918).
3. *Random Memories*, by Ernest Longfellow.
4. In *This Was My Newport* (The Mythological Co., 1944), Maud Howe Elliott recalls this story, p. 149.
5. There is a list of Tom's pictures at Longfellow House.
6. *Memories of a Hostess, a Chronicle of Eminent Friendships drawn chiefly from the diaries of Mrs. James T. Fields*, by M. A. DeWolfe Howe (Boston, Atlantic, 1922).

7. *Yankee Stonecutters, the First American School of Sculpture, 1800–1850*, by Albert TenEyck Gardner (New York, Columbia Univ. Press, 1945), discusses John Gibson and his "tinted Venus" and also the women sculptors.
8. Natey's financial troubles are from letters at Mass. Hist. Soc.
9. After Nathan Appleton and Fanny died, there was very little correspondence between Mary Mackintosh and her family. The letter concerning her inheritance, Appleton papers, Mass. Hist. Soc. Information concerning Mary's death, Longfellow House.
10. Mrs. Charles Darrow Gowing shares my enthusiasm for Tom Appleton's protégée, the opera singer who almost became a queen. Tom's letters to his father about Elise Hensler and hers to him are at Mass. Hist. Soc.
11. *Longfellow*, Wagenknecht, tells of Longfellow's death, and of course there are many other accounts. Tom's note to Holmes, Mass. Hist. Soc.
12. "The Cross of Snow" appears in *Mrs. Longfellow* and in *Longfellow*, both by Wagenknecht.
13. The Oliver Wendell Holmes article appeared in the *Atlantic Monthly*, vol. 53, June, 1884, pp. 848–850.

INDEX